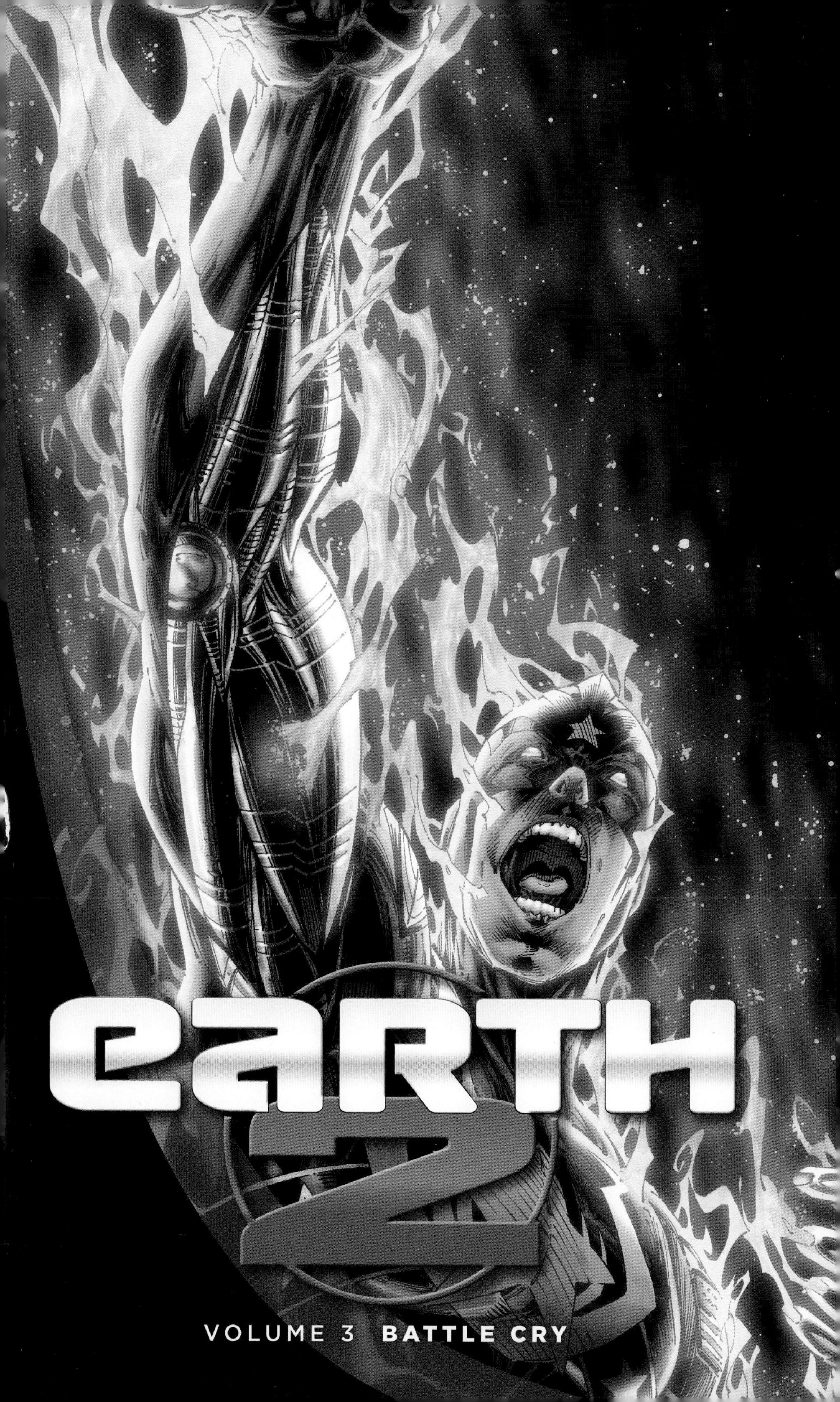
EARTH 2
VOLUME 3 BATTLE CRY

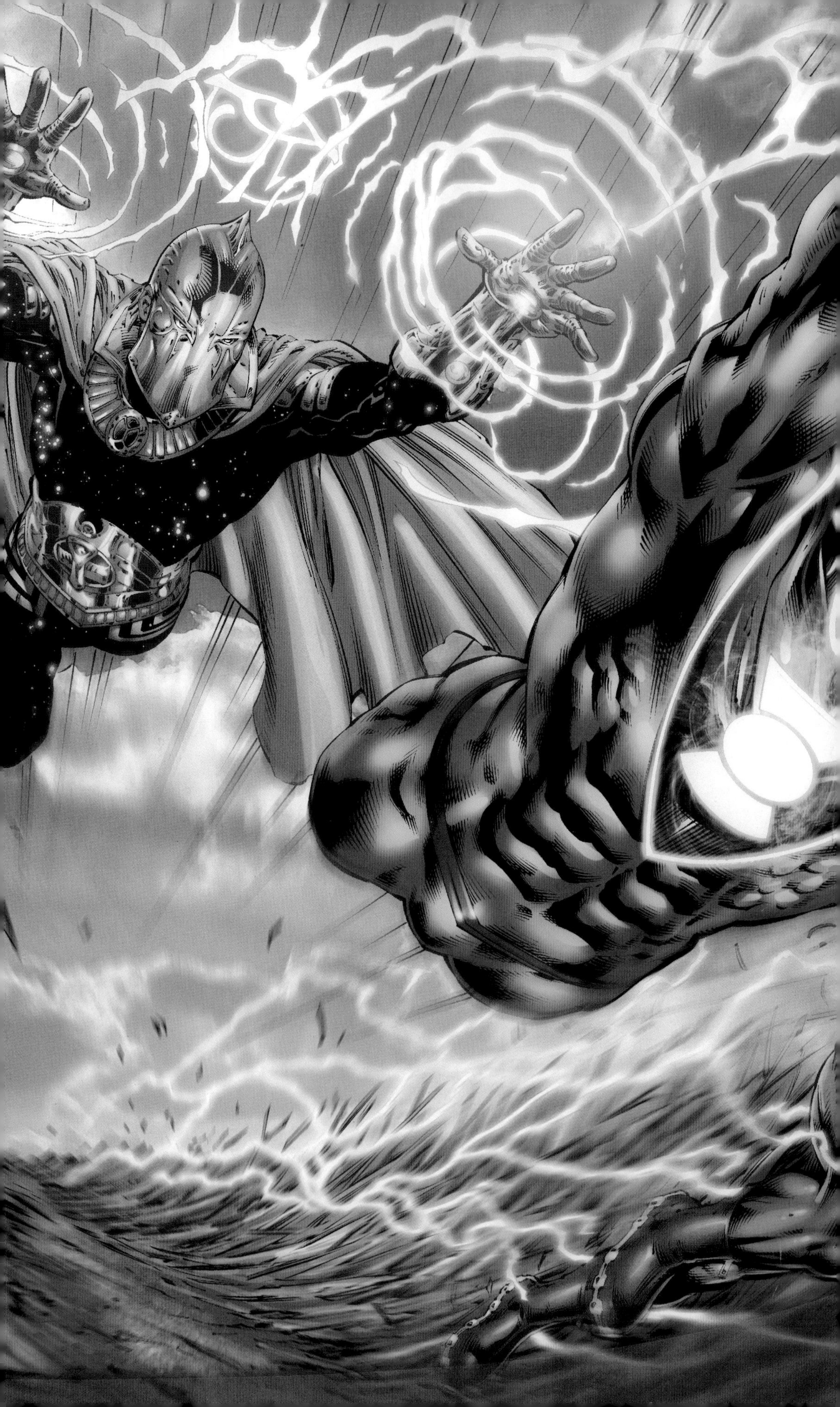

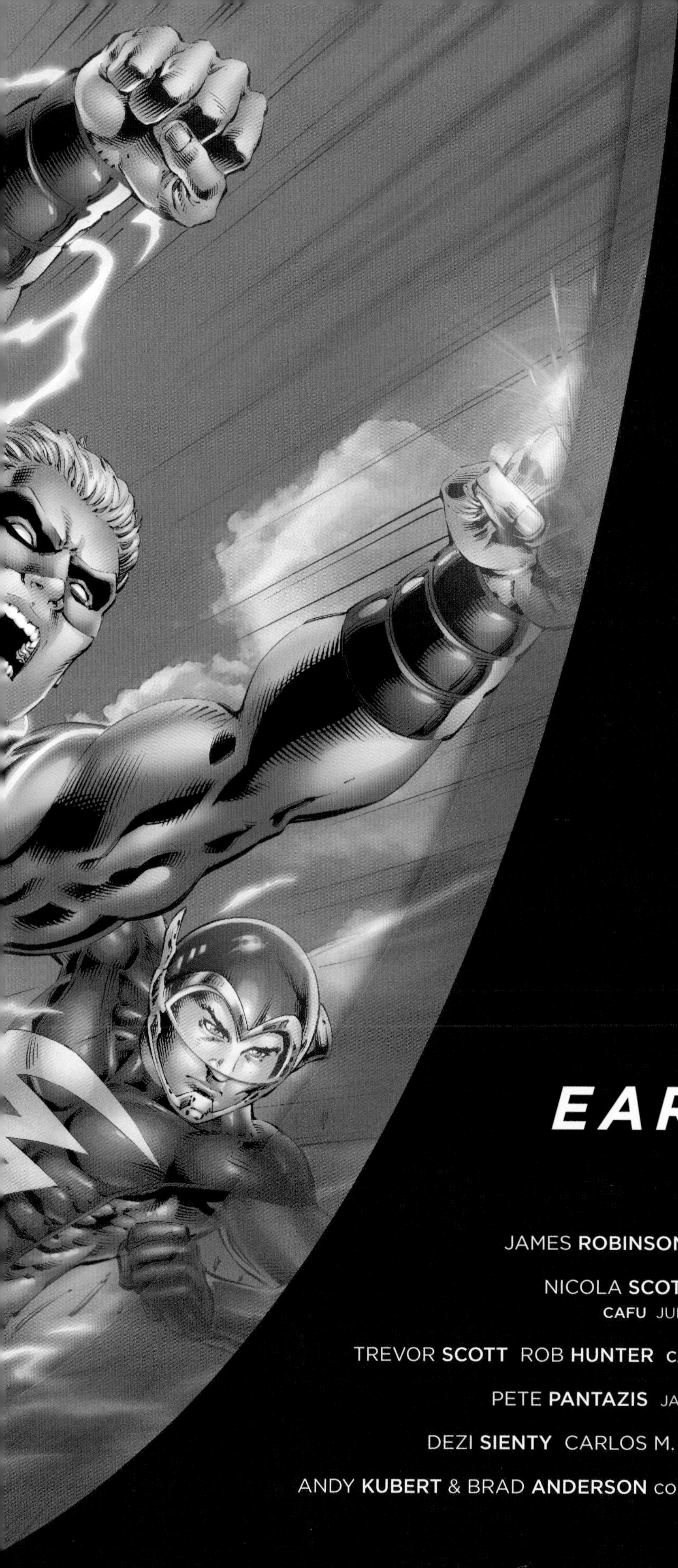

EARTH 2

VOLUME 3
BATTLE CRY

JAMES **ROBINSON** PAUL **LEVITZ** writers

NICOLA **SCOTT** YILDIRAY **CINAR**
CAFU JULIUS **GOPEZ** pencillers

TREVOR **SCOTT** ROB **HUNTER** **CAFU** CAM **SMITH** inkers

PETE **PANTAZIS** JASON **WRIGHT** colorists

DEZI **SIENTY** CARLOS M. **MANGUAL** letterers

ANDY **KUBERT** & BRAD **ANDERSON** collection cover artists

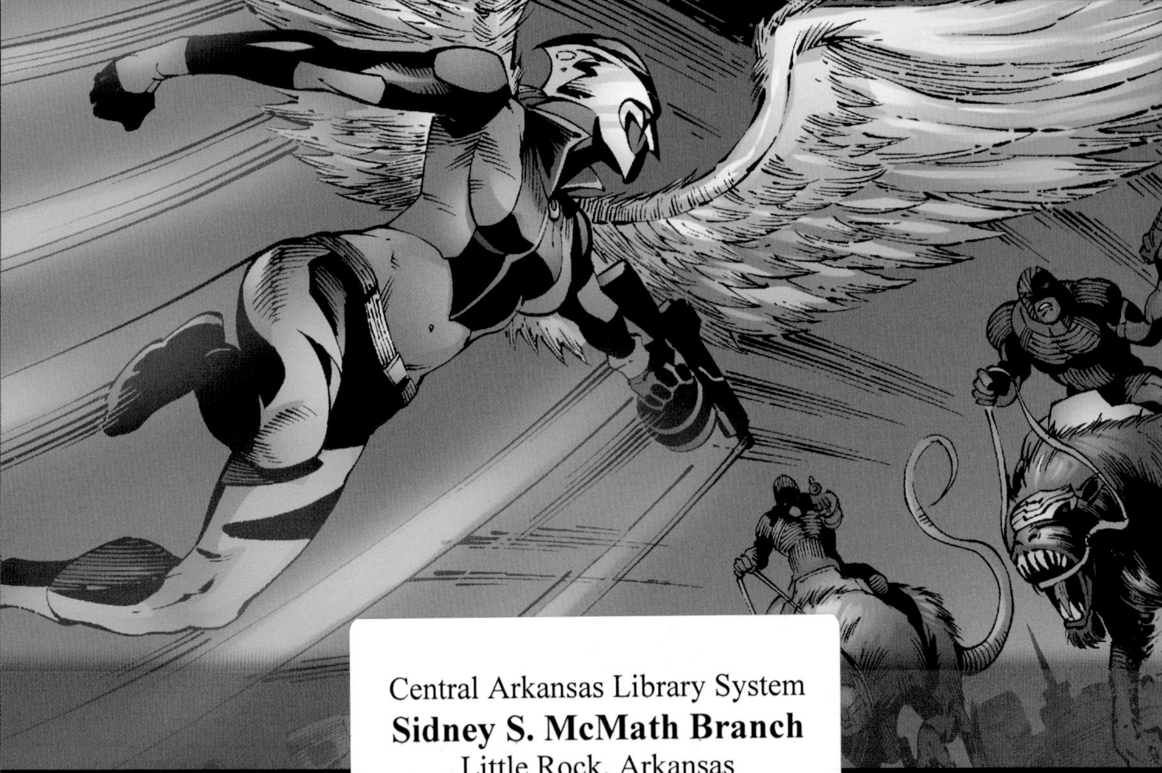

MIKE COTTON Editor - Original Series ANTHONY MARQUES Assistant Editor - Original Series
ROBIN WILDMAN Editor ROBBIN BROSTERMAN Design Director - Books ROBBIE BIEDERMAN Publication Design

BOB HARRAS Senior VP - Editor-in-Chief, DC Comics

DIANE NELSON President DAN DIDIO and JIM LEE Co-Publishers
GEOFF JOHNS Chief Creative Officer
JOHN ROOD Executive VP - Sales, Marketing and Business Development
AMY GENKINS Senior VP - Business and Legal Affairs NAIRI GARDINER Senior VP - Finance
JEFF BOISON VP - Publishing Planning MARK CHIARELLO VP - Art Direction and Design
JOHN CUNNINGHAM VP - Marketing TERRI CUNNINGHAM VP - Editorial Administration
ALISON GILL Senior VP - Manufacturing and Operations HANK KANALZ Senior VP - Vertigo and Integrated Publishing
JAY KOGAN VP - Business and Legal Affairs, Publishing JACK MAHAN VP - Business Affairs, Talent
NICK NAPOLITANO VP - Manufacturing Administration SUE POHJA VP - Book Sales
COURTNEY SIMMONS Senior VP - Publicity BOB WAYNE Senior VP - Sales

EARTH 2 VOLUME 3: BATTLE CRY

DC Comics, 1700 Broadway, New York, NY 10019
A Warner Bros. Entertainment Company.
Printed by RR Donnelley, Salem, VA, USA. 3/7/14. First Printing.

HC ISBN: 978-1-4012-4615-0
SC ISBN: 978-1-4012-4938-0

Library of Congress Cataloging-in-Publication Data

Robinson, James Dale , author.
Earth 2. Volume 3, Battle Cry / James Robinson, Nicola Scott, Yildiray Cinar.
pages cm. - (The New 52!)
ISBN 978-1-4012-4615-0 (hardback)
1. Graphic novels. I. Scott, Nicola, illustrator. II. Cinar, Yildiray, 1976- illustrator. III. Title. IV. Title: Battle Cry.
PN6727.R58E25 2014
741.5'973-dc23
2013049630

SUSTAINABLE FORESTRY INITIATIVE
Certified Chain of Custody
At Least 20% Certified Forest Content
www.sfiprogram.org
SFI-01042
APPLIES TO TEXT STOCK ONLY

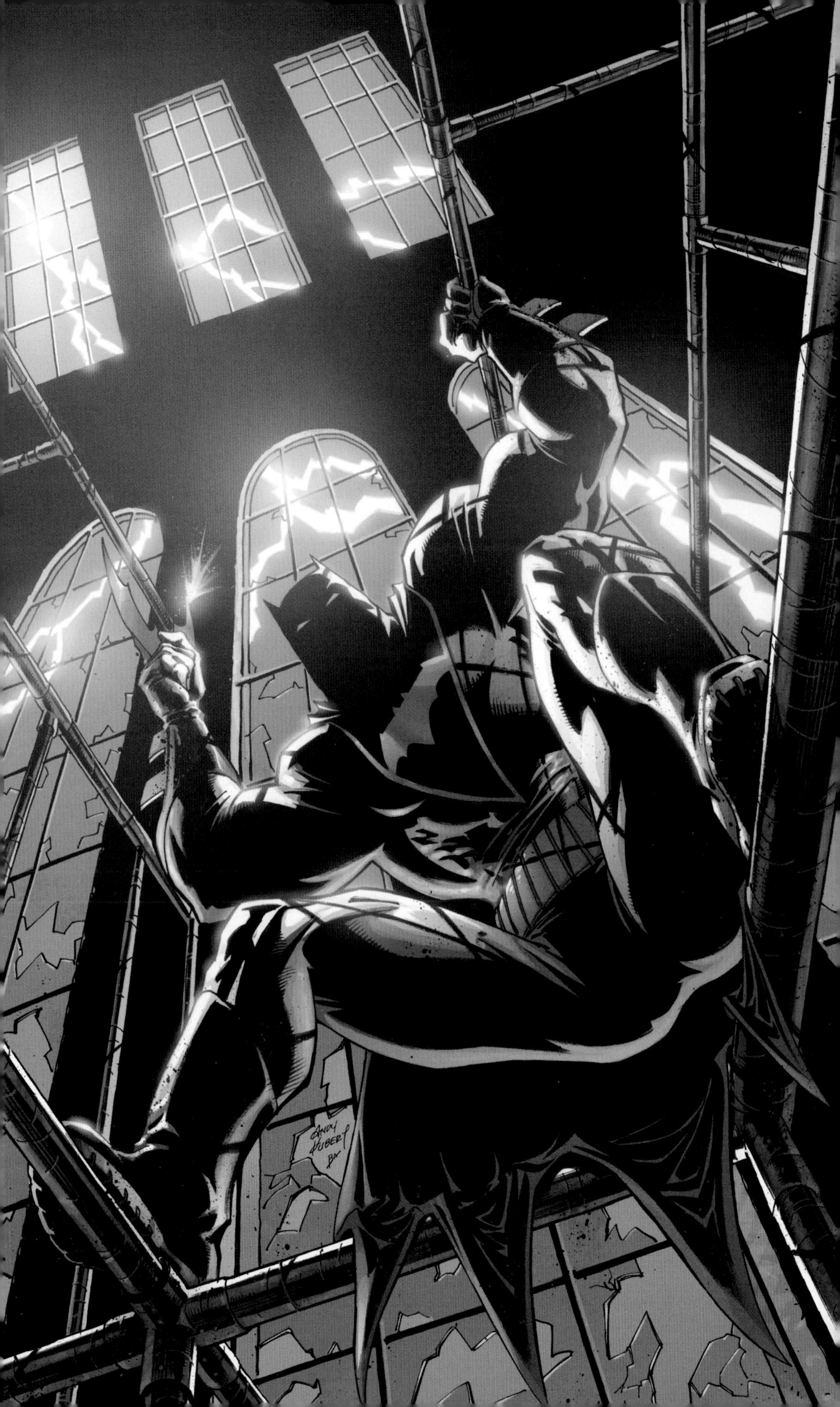

JAMES ROBINSON
writer

CAFU
JULIUS GOPEZ
pencillers

CAFU
CAM SMITH
inkers

PETE PANTAZIS
colorist

ANDY KUBERT & BRAD ANDERSON
cover artists

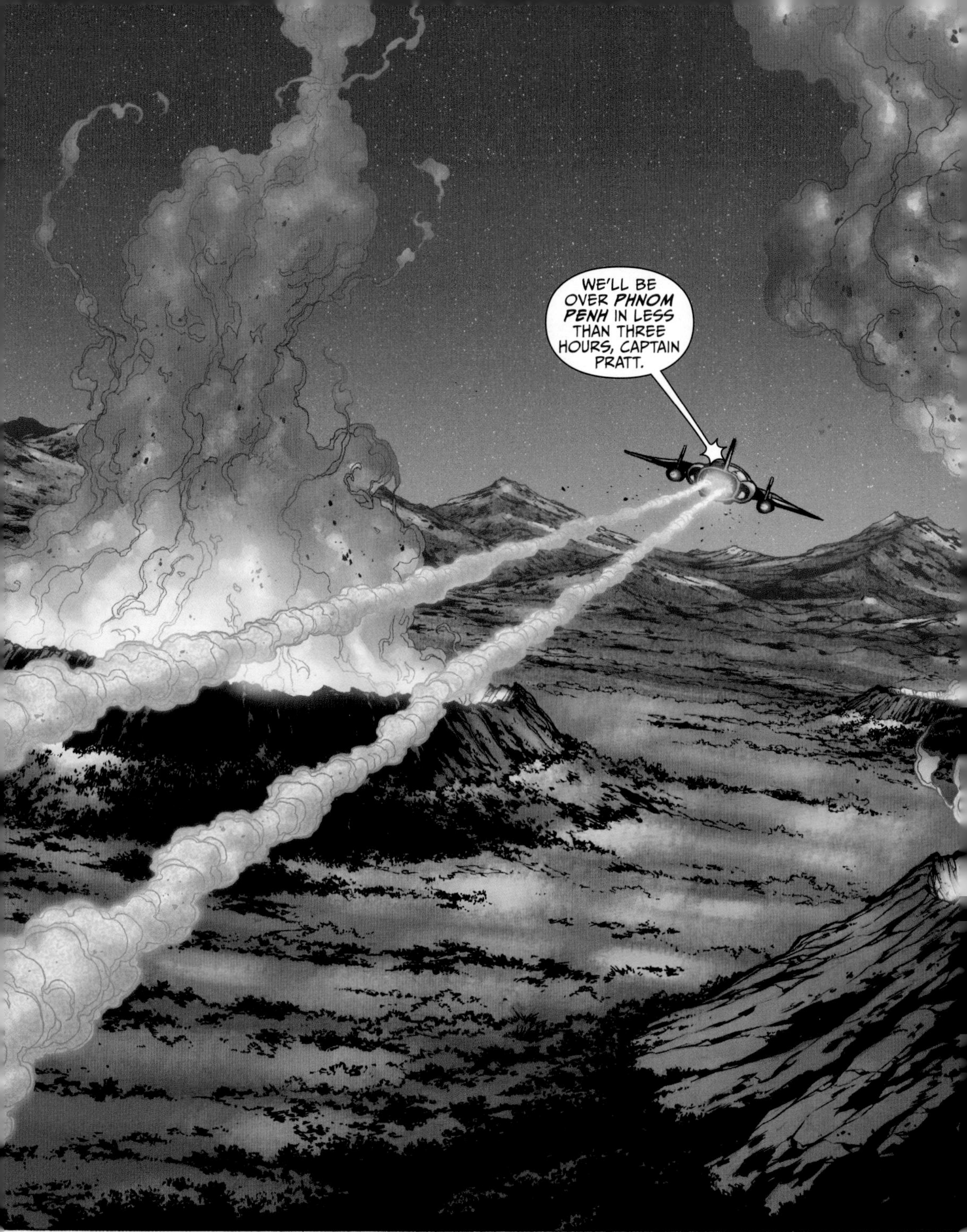
WE'LL BE OVER PHNOM PENH IN LESS THAN THREE HOURS, CAPTAIN PRATT.

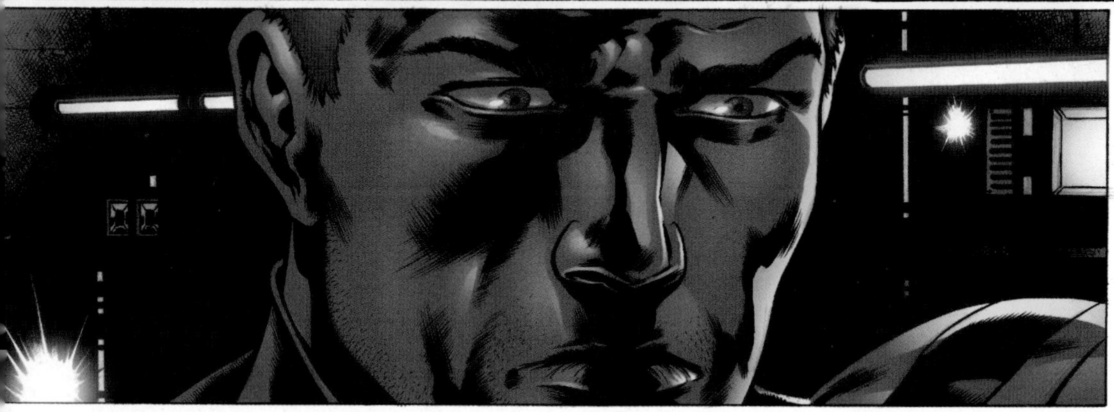

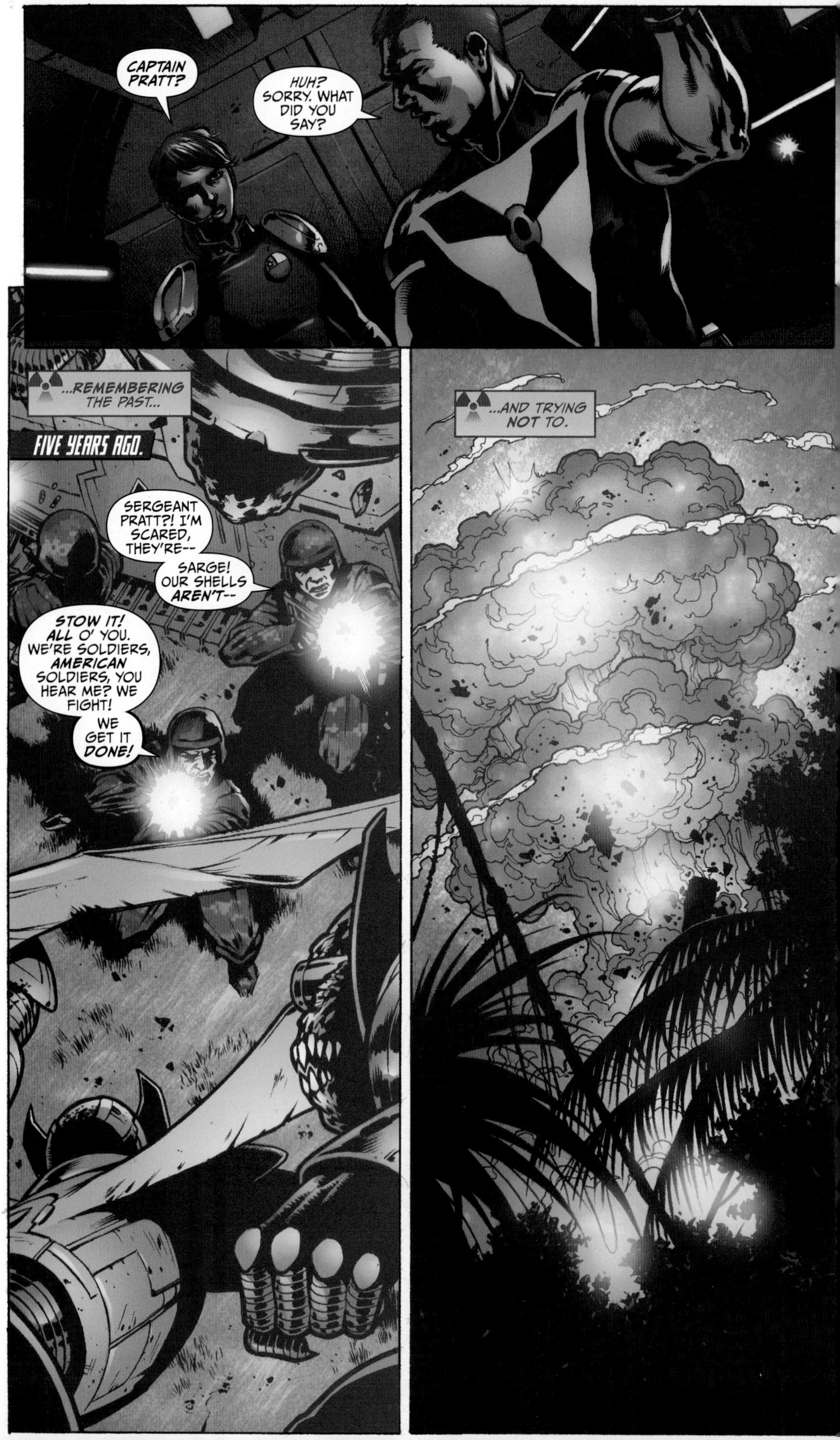
CAPTAIN PRATT?
HUH? SORRY. WHAT DID YOU SAY?
...REMEMBERING THE PAST...
FIVE YEARS AGO.
SERGEANT PRATT?! I'M SCARED, THEY'RE--
SARGE! OUR SHELLS AREN'T--
STOW IT! ALL O' YOU. WE'RE SOLDIERS, AMERICAN SOLDIERS, YOU HEAR ME? WE FIGHT!
WE GET IT DONE!
...AND TRYING NOT TO.

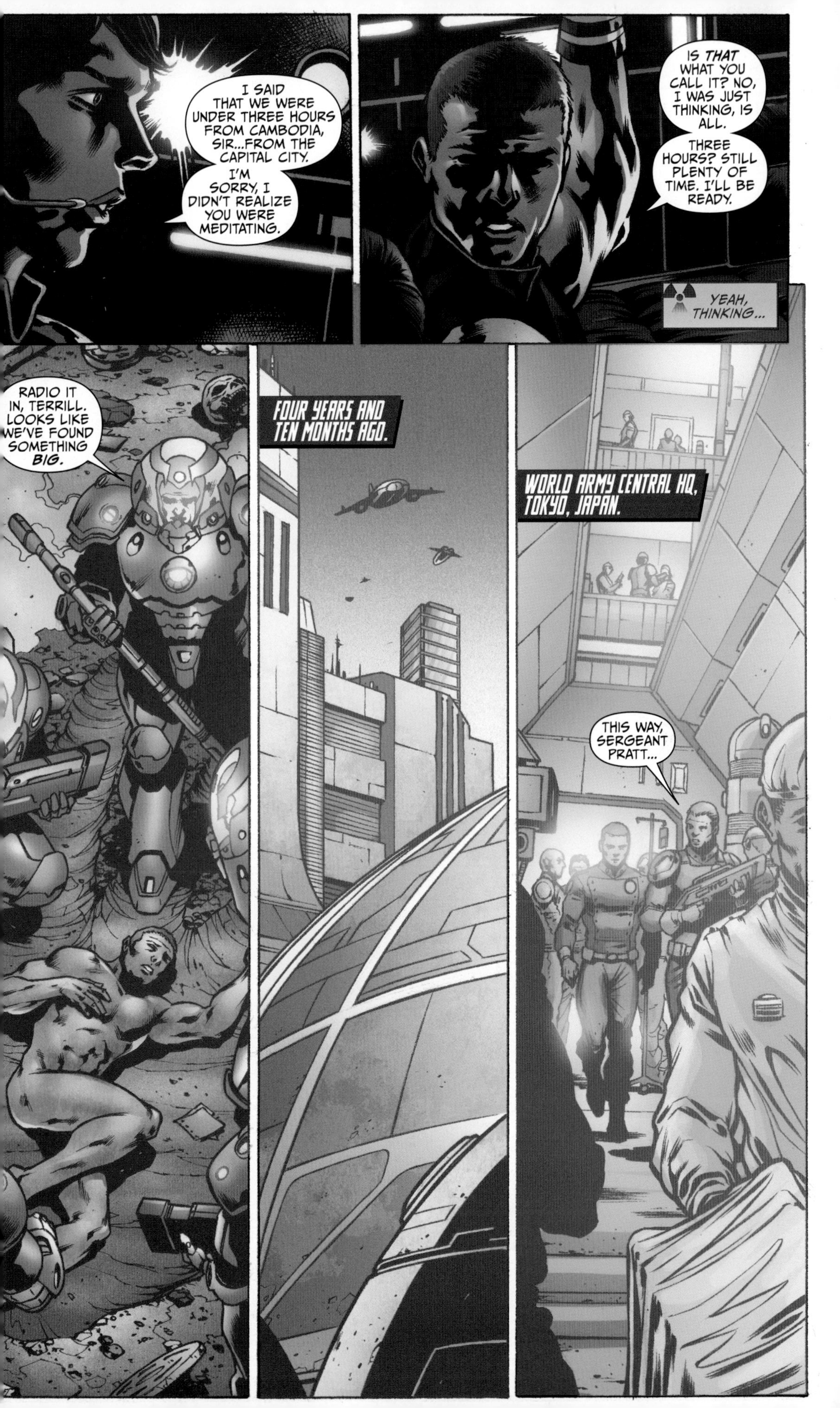
I SAID THAT WE WERE UNDER THREE HOURS FROM CAMBODIA, SIR...FROM THE CAPITAL CITY.
I'M SORRY, I DIDN'T REALIZE YOU WERE MEDITATING.
IS *THAT* WHAT YOU CALL IT? NO, I WAS JUST THINKING, IS ALL.
THREE HOURS? STILL PLENTY OF TIME. I'LL BE READY.
YEAH, THINKING...
RADIO IT IN, TERRILL. LOOKS LIKE WE'VE FOUND SOMETHING *BIG*.
FOUR YEARS AND TEN MONTHS AGO.
WORLD ARMY CENTRAL HQ, TOKYO, JAPAN.
THIS WAY, SERGEANT PRATT...

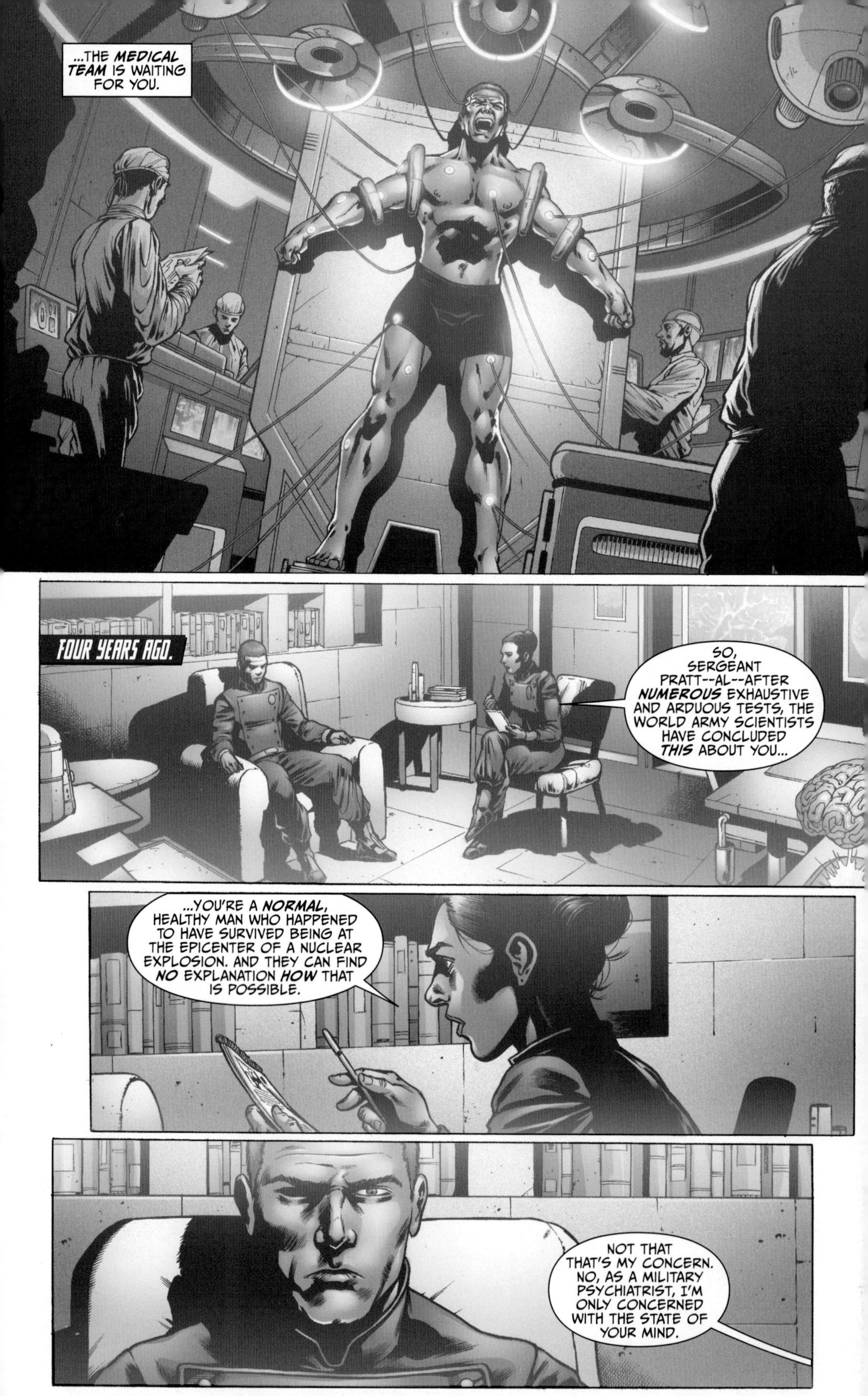
...THE MEDICAL TEAM IS WAITING FOR YOU.
FOUR YEARS AGO.
SO, SERGEANT PRATT--AL--AFTER NUMEROUS EXHAUSTIVE AND ARDUOUS TESTS, THE WORLD ARMY SCIENTISTS HAVE CONCLUDED THIS ABOUT YOU...
...YOU'RE A NORMAL, HEALTHY MAN WHO HAPPENED TO HAVE SURVIVED BEING AT THE EPICENTER OF A NUCLEAR EXPLOSION. AND THEY CAN FIND NO EXPLANATION HOW THAT IS POSSIBLE.
NOT THAT THAT'S MY CONCERN. NO, AS A MILITARY PSYCHIATRIST, I'M ONLY CONCERNED WITH THE STATE OF YOUR MIND.

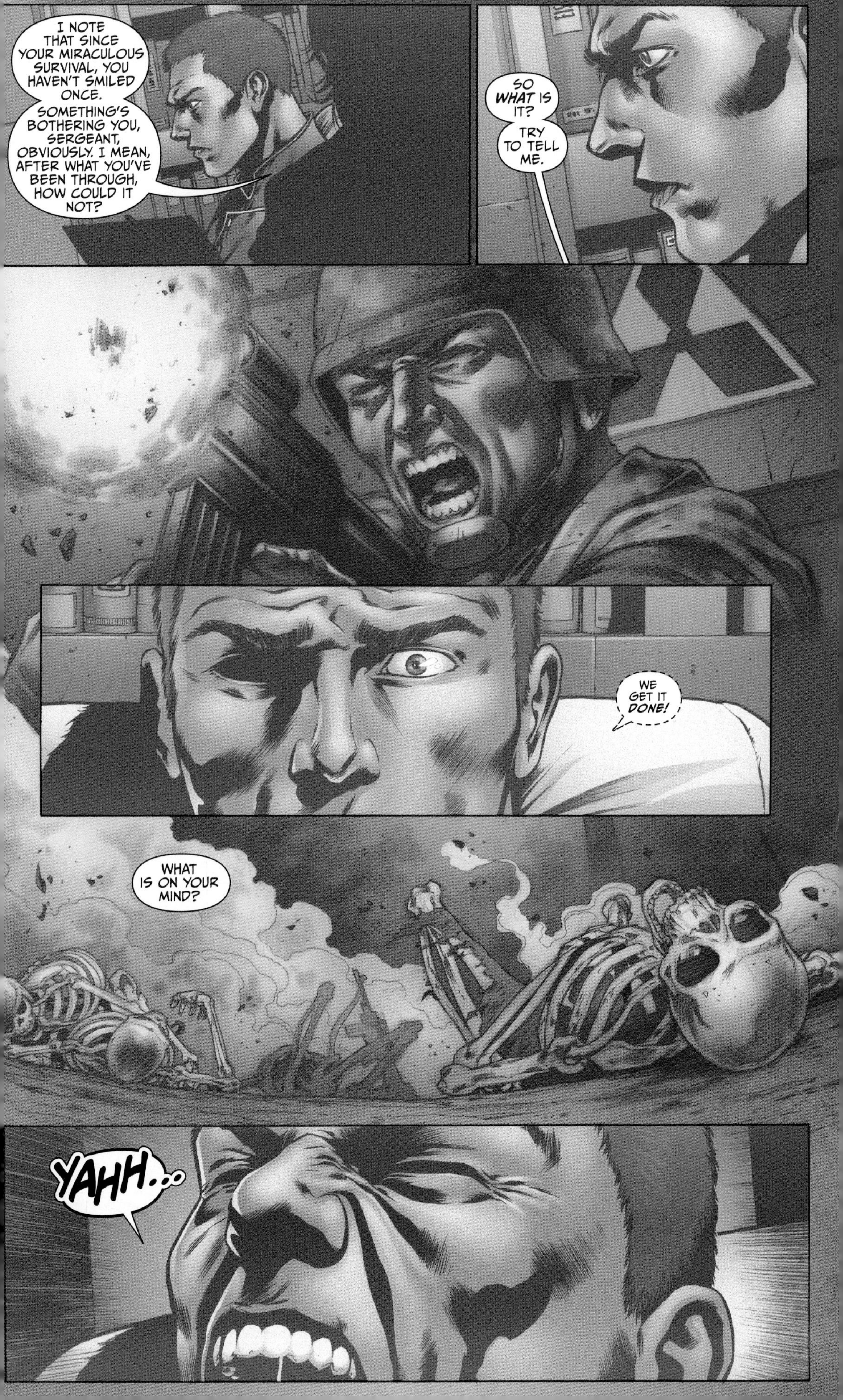

I NOTE THAT SINCE YOUR MIRACULOUS SURVIVAL, YOU HAVEN'T SMILED ONCE.
SOMETHING'S BOTHERING YOU, SERGEANT, OBVIOUSLY. I MEAN, AFTER WHAT YOU'VE BEEN THROUGH, HOW COULD IT NOT?
SO WHAT IS IT?
TRY TO TELL ME.
WE GET IT DONE!
WHAT IS ON YOUR MIND?
YAHH...

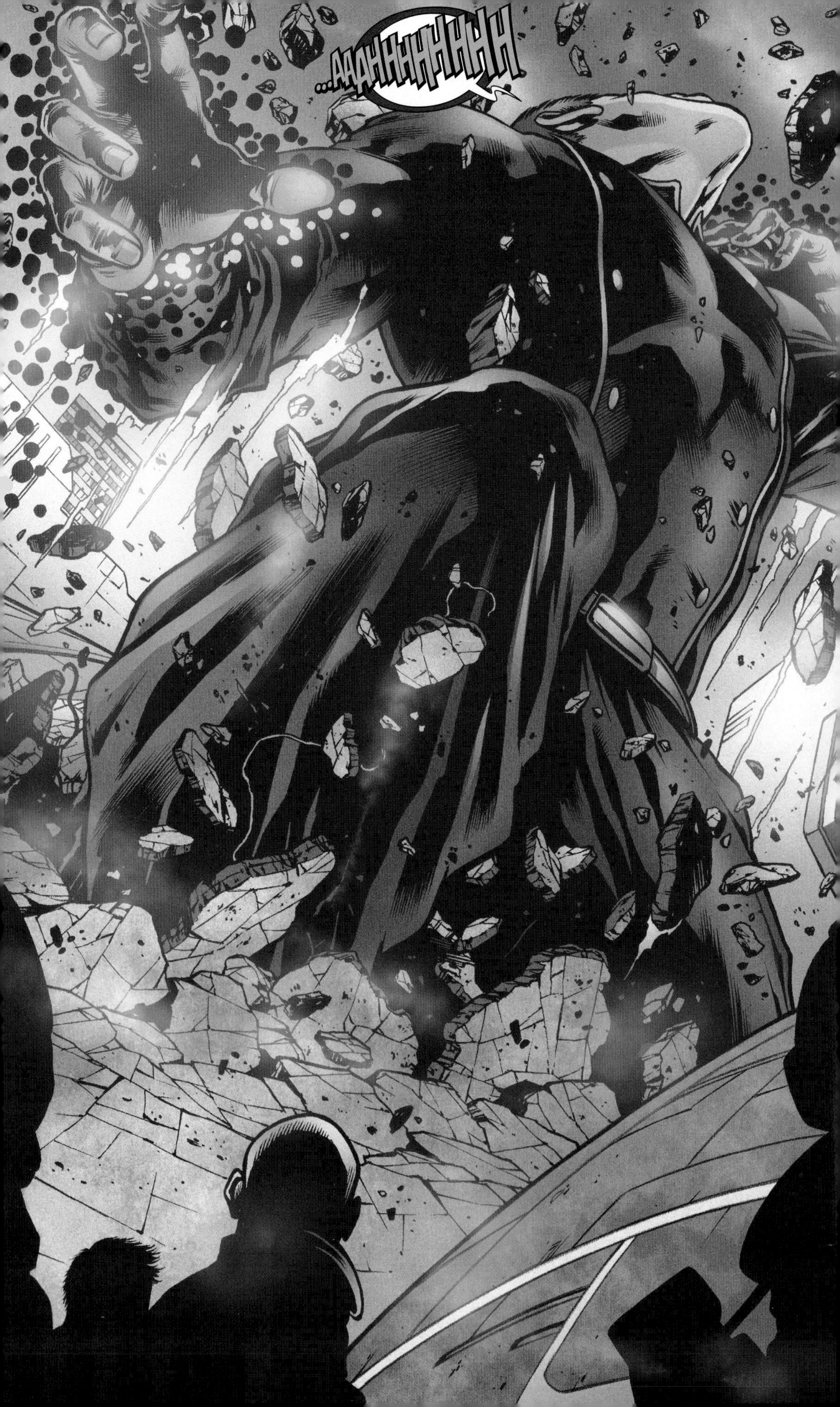
...AAAHHHHHHHH

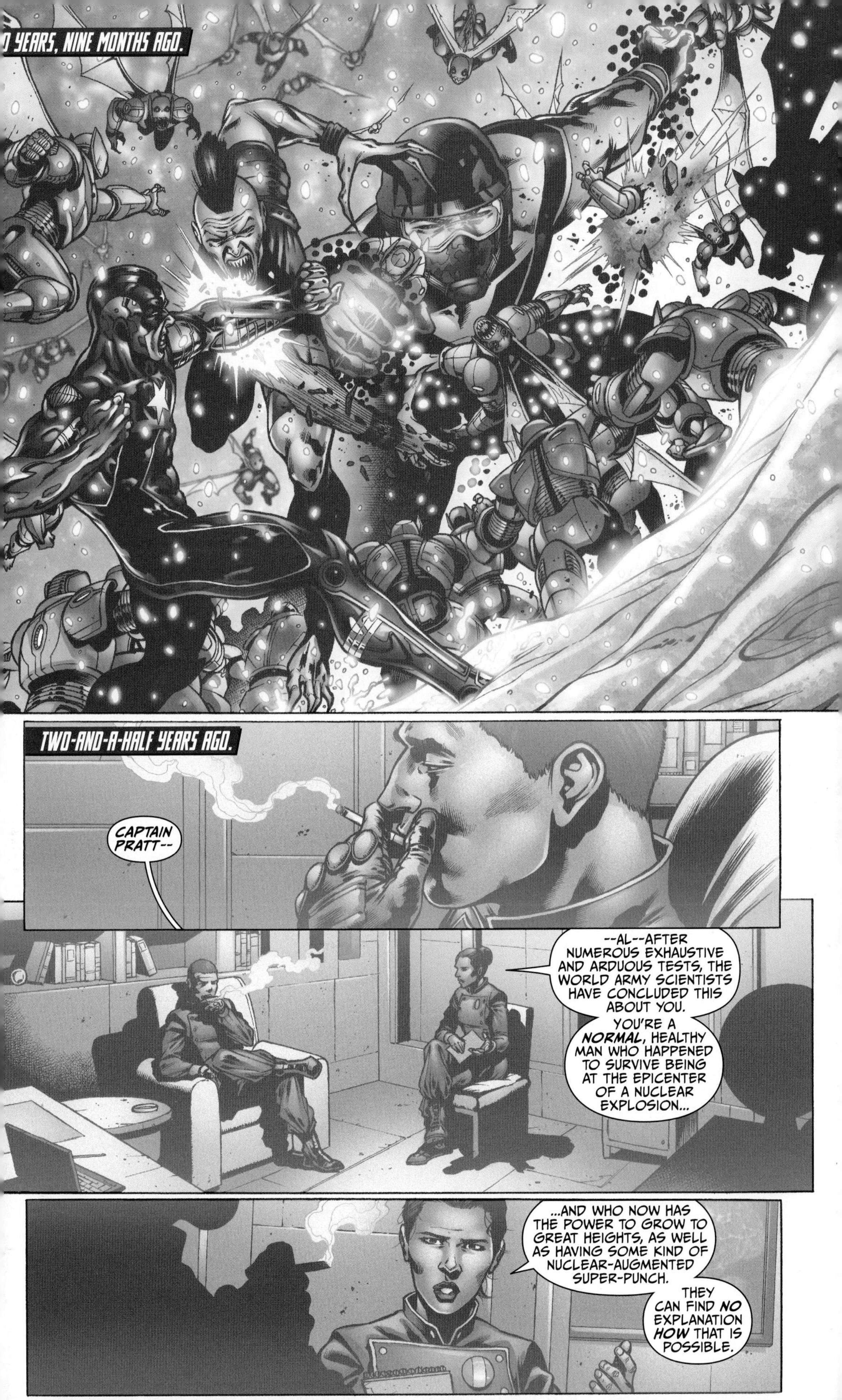

0 YEARS, NINE MONTHS AGO.
TWO-AND-A-HALF YEARS AGO.
CAPTAIN PRATT--
--AL--AFTER NUMEROUS EXHAUSTIVE AND ARDUOUS TESTS, THE WORLD ARMY SCIENTISTS HAVE CONCLUDED THIS ABOUT YOU.
YOU'RE A NORMAL, HEALTHY MAN WHO HAPPENED TO SURVIVE BEING AT THE EPICENTER OF A NUCLEAR EXPLOSION...
...AND WHO NOW HAS THE POWER TO GROW TO GREAT HEIGHTS, AS WELL AS HAVING SOME KIND OF NUCLEAR-AUGMENTED SUPER-PUNCH.
THEY CAN FIND NO EXPLANATION HOW THAT IS POSSIBLE.

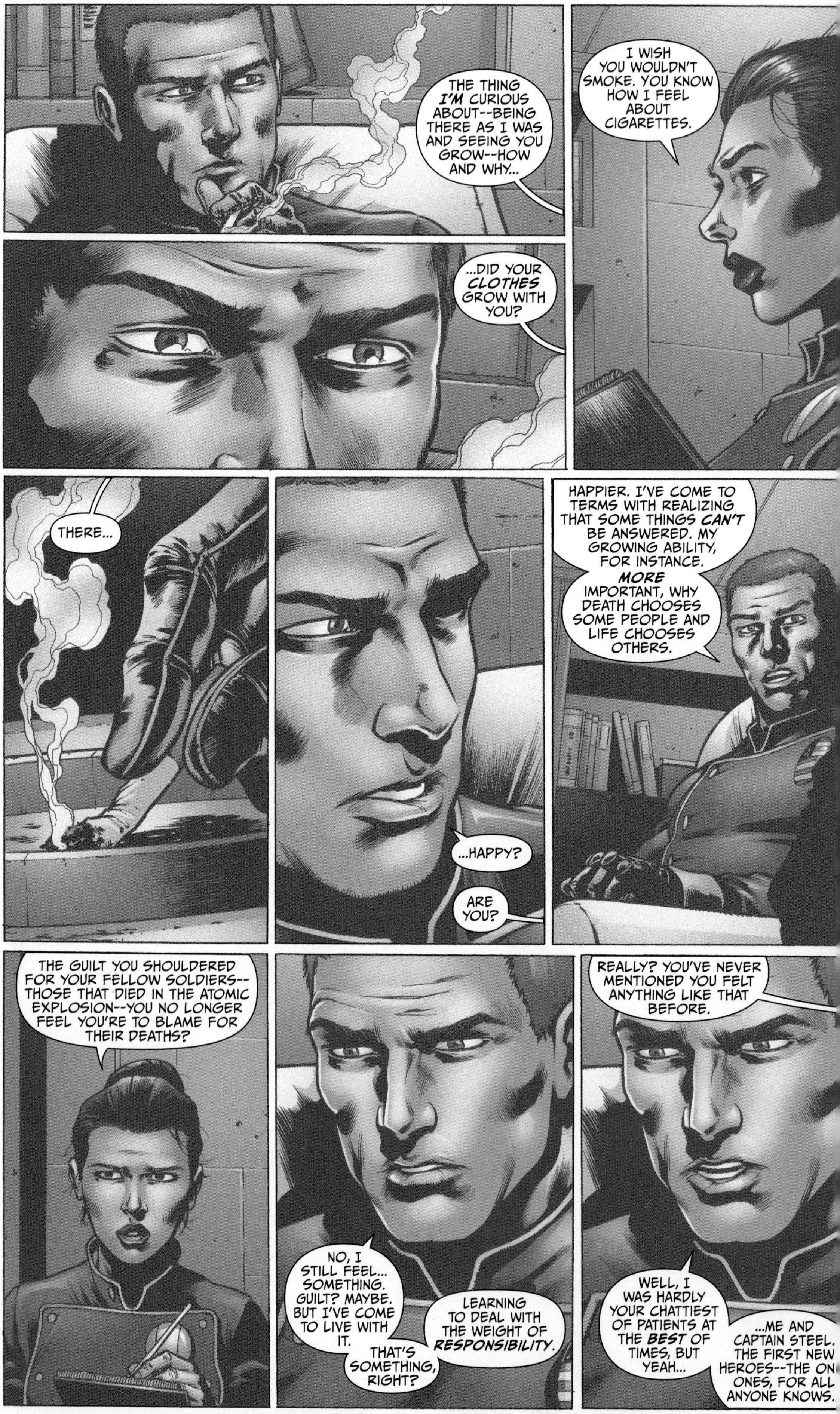

THE THING I'M CURIOUS ABOUT--BEING THERE AS I WAS AND SEEING YOU GROW--HOW AND WHY...
I WISH YOU WOULDN'T SMOKE. YOU KNOW HOW I FEEL ABOUT CIGARETTES.
...DID YOUR CLOTHES GROW WITH YOU?
THERE...
...HAPPY?
ARE YOU?
HAPPIER. I'VE COME TO TERMS WITH REALIZING THAT SOME THINGS CAN'T BE ANSWERED. MY GROWING ABILITY, FOR INSTANCE. MORE IMPORTANT, WHY DEATH CHOOSES SOME PEOPLE AND LIFE CHOOSES OTHERS.
THE GUILT YOU SHOULDERED FOR YOUR FELLOW SOLDIERS--THOSE THAT DIED IN THE ATOMIC EXPLOSION--YOU NO LONGER FEEL YOU'RE TO BLAME FOR THEIR DEATHS?
NO, I STILL FEEL... SOMETHING. GUILT? MAYBE. BUT I'VE COME TO LIVE WITH IT.
LEARNING TO DEAL WITH THE WEIGHT OF RESPONSIBILITY.
THAT'S SOMETHING, RIGHT?
REALLY? YOU'VE NEVER MENTIONED YOU FELT ANYTHING LIKE THAT BEFORE.
WELL, I WAS HARDLY YOUR CHATTIEST OF PATIENTS AT THE BEST OF TIMES, BUT YEAH...
...ME AND CAPTAIN STEEL. THE FIRST NEW HEROES--THE ON ONES, FOR ALL ANYONE KNOWS.

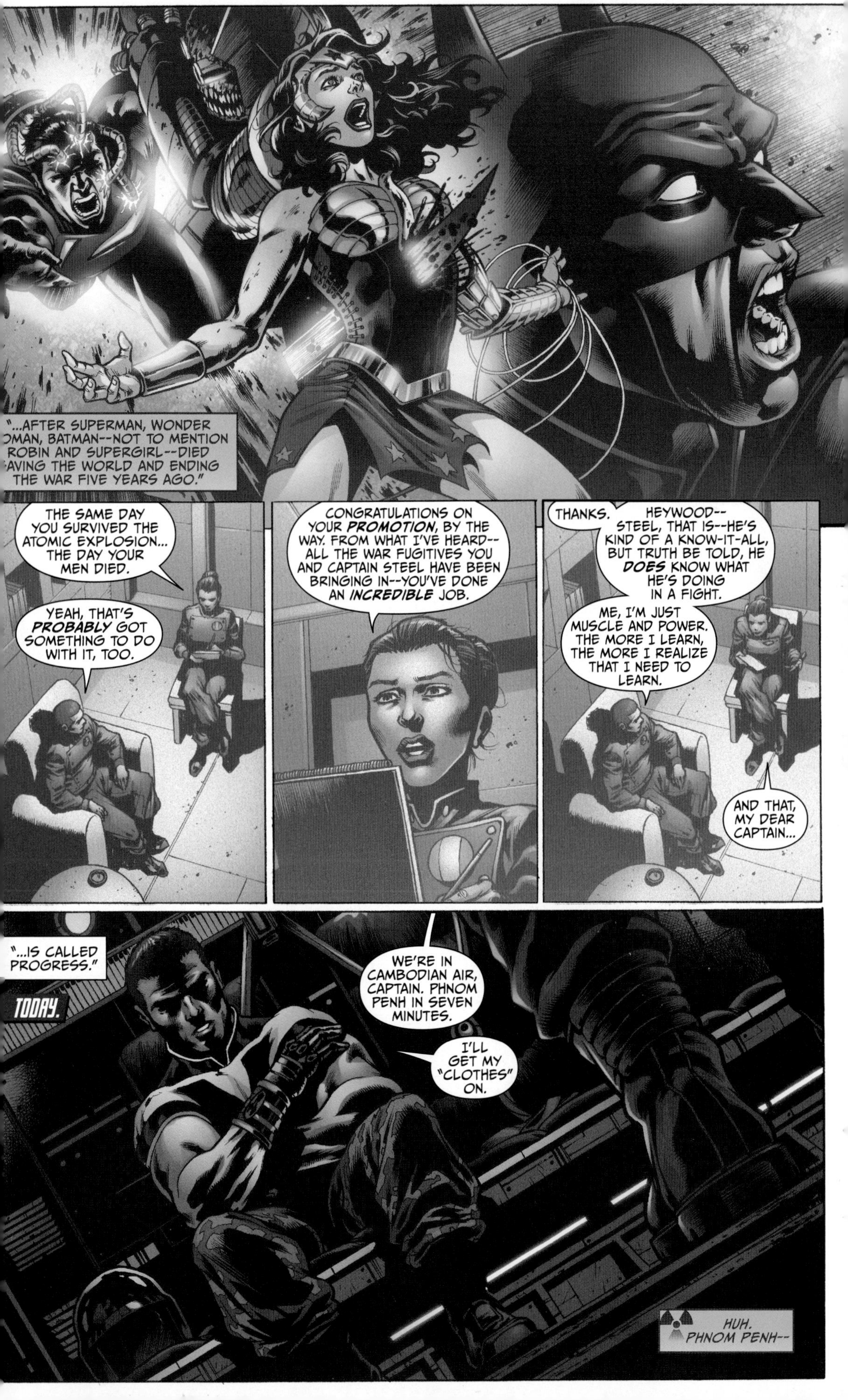

"...AFTER SUPERMAN, WONDER OMAN, BATMAN--NOT TO MENTION ROBIN AND SUPERGIRL--DIED AVING THE WORLD AND ENDING THE WAR FIVE YEARS AGO."
THE SAME DAY YOU SURVIVED THE ATOMIC EXPLOSION... THE DAY YOUR MEN DIED.
YEAH, THAT'S PROBABLY GOT SOMETHING TO DO WITH IT, TOO.
CONGRATULATIONS ON YOUR PROMOTION, BY THE WAY. FROM WHAT I'VE HEARD--ALL THE WAR FUGITIVES YOU AND CAPTAIN STEEL HAVE BEEN BRINGING IN--YOU'VE DONE AN INCREDIBLE JOB.
THANKS.
HEYWOOD--STEEL, THAT IS--HE'S KIND OF A KNOW-IT-ALL, BUT TRUTH BE TOLD, HE DOES KNOW WHAT HE'S DOING IN A FIGHT.
ME, I'M JUST MUSCLE AND POWER. THE MORE I LEARN, THE MORE I REALIZE THAT I NEED TO LEARN.
AND THAT, MY DEAR CAPTAIN...
"...IS CALLED PROGRESS."
TODAY.
WE'RE IN CAMBODIAN AIR, CAPTAIN. PHNOM PENH IN SEVEN MINUTES.
I'LL GET MY "CLOTHES" ON.
HUH. PHNOM PENH--

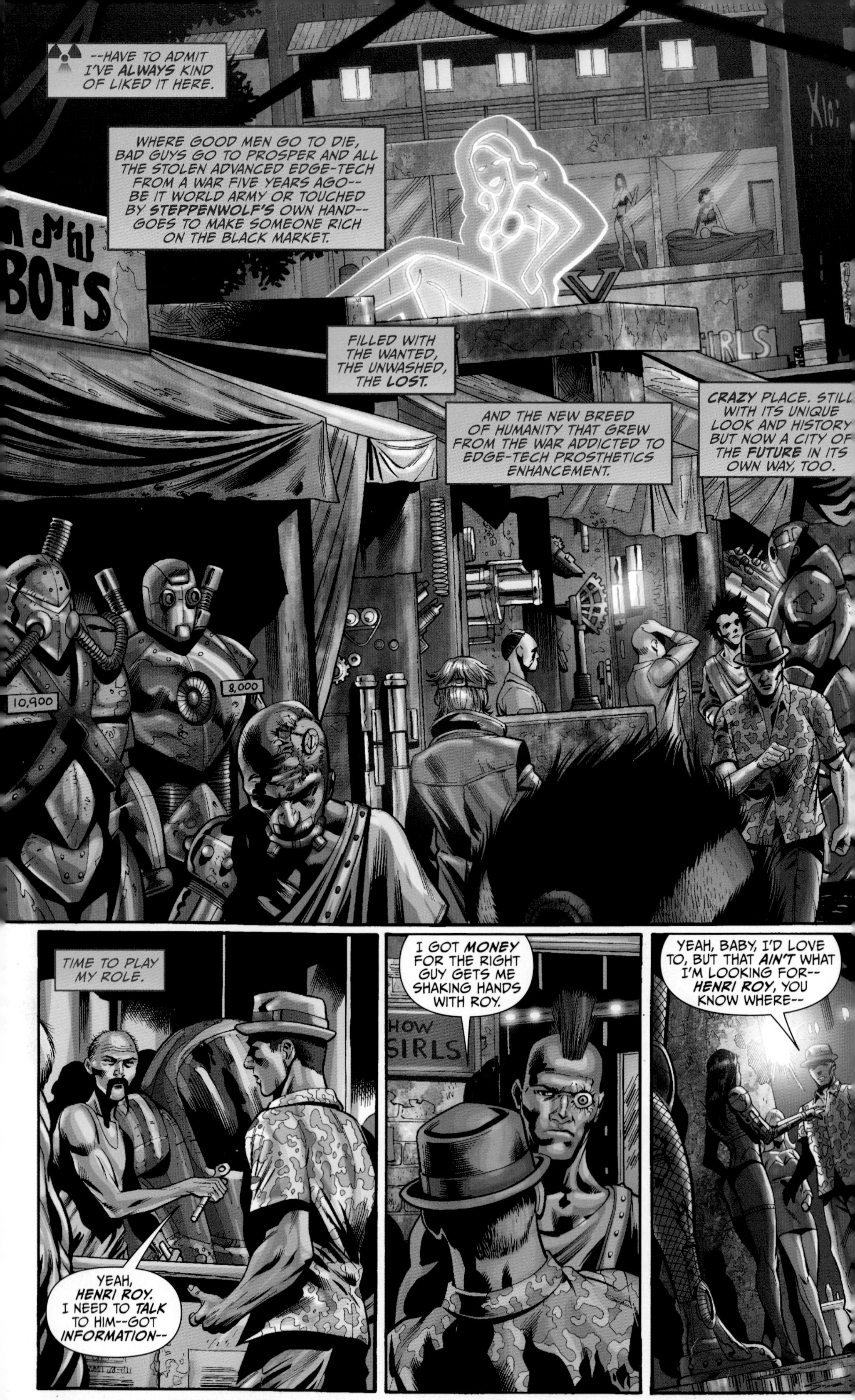
--HAVE TO ADMIT I'VE ALWAYS KIND OF LIKED IT HERE.
WHERE GOOD MEN GO TO DIE, BAD GUYS GO TO PROSPER AND ALL THE STOLEN ADVANCED EDGE-TECH FROM A WAR FIVE YEARS AGO-- BE IT WORLD ARMY OR TOUCHED BY STEPPENWOLF'S OWN HAND-- GOES TO MAKE SOMEONE RICH ON THE BLACK MARKET.
BOTS
FILLED WITH THE WANTED, THE UNWASHED, THE LOST.
AND THE NEW BREED OF HUMANITY THAT GREW FROM THE WAR ADDICTED TO EDGE-TECH PROSTHETICS ENHANCEMENT.
CRAZY PLACE. STILL WITH ITS UNIQUE LOOK AND HISTORY BUT NOW A CITY OF THE FUTURE IN ITS OWN WAY, TOO.
10,900
8,000
TIME TO PLAY MY ROLE.
YEAH, HENRI ROY. I NEED TO TALK TO HIM--GOT INFORMATION--
I GOT MONEY FOR THE RIGHT GUY GETS ME SHAKING HANDS WITH ROY.
YEAH, BABY, I'D LOVE TO, BUT THAT AIN'T WHAT I'M LOOKING FOR-- HENRI ROY, YOU KNOW WHERE--

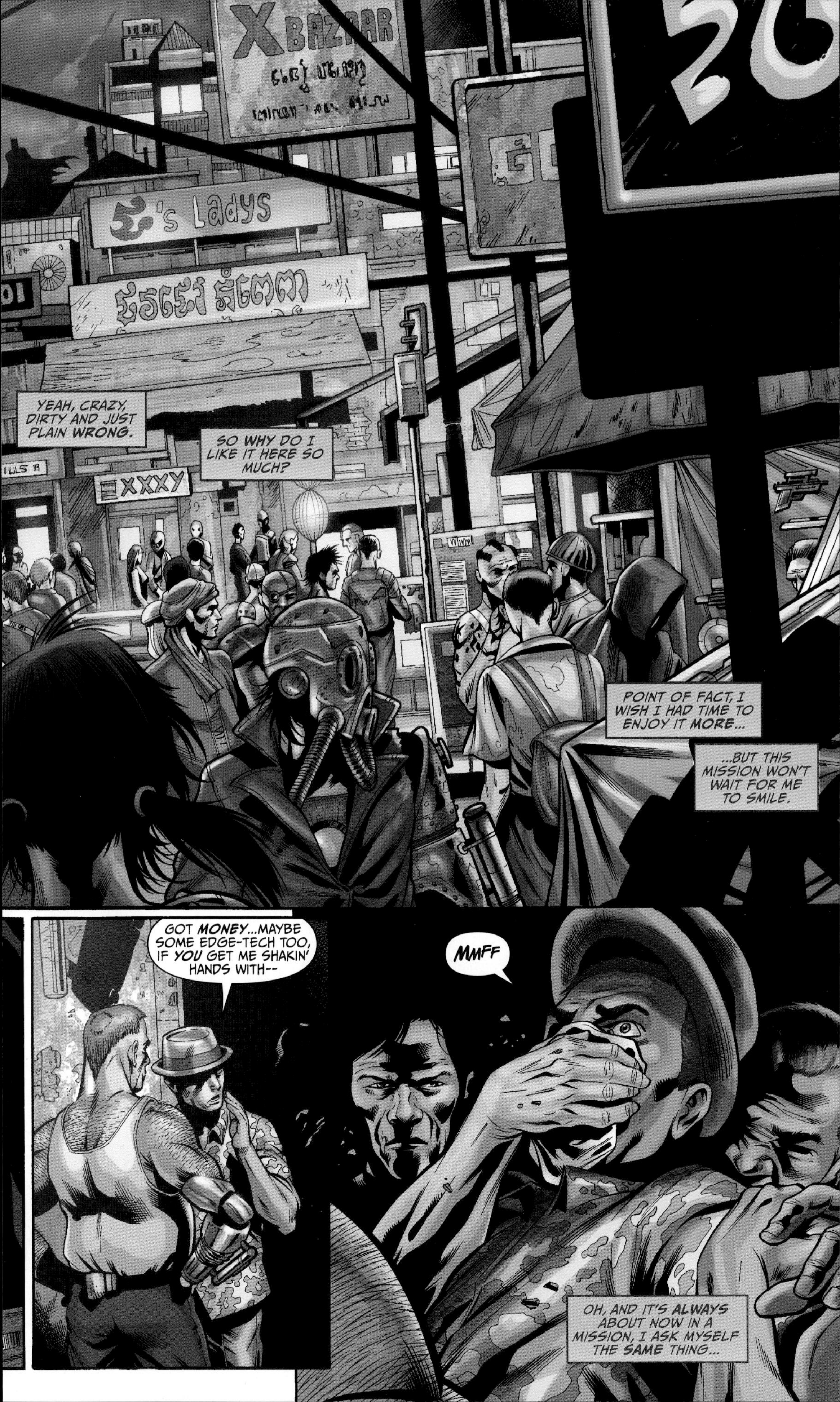
X BAZAAR
'S LADYS
XXXY
YEAH, CRAZY, DIRTY AND JUST PLAIN WRONG.
SO WHY DO I LIKE IT HERE SO MUCH?
POINT OF FACT, I WISH I HAD TIME TO ENJOY IT MORE...
...BUT THIS MISSION WON'T WAIT FOR ME TO SMILE.
GOT MONEY...MAYBE SOME EDGE-TECH TOO, IF YOU GET ME SHAKIN' HANDS WITH--
MMFF
OH, AND IT'S ALWAYS ABOUT NOW IN A MISSION, I ASK MYSELF THE SAME THING...

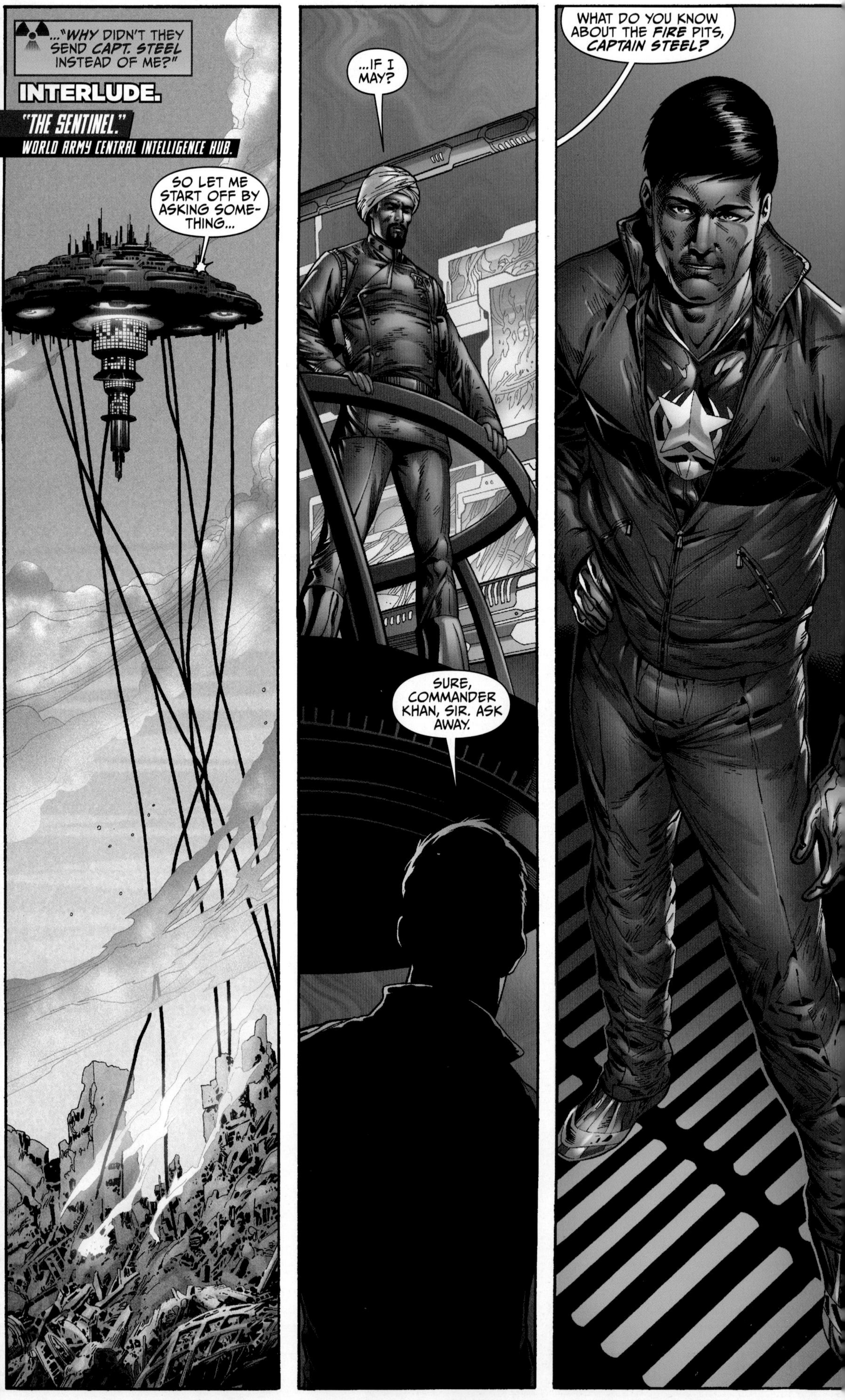
..."WHY DIDN'T THEY SEND CAPT. STEEL INSTEAD OF ME?"
INTERLUDE.
"THE SENTINEL."
WORLD ARMY CENTRAL INTELLIGENCE HUB.
SO LET ME START OFF BY ASKING SOME-THING...
...IF I MAY?
SURE, COMMANDER KHAN, SIR. ASK AWAY.
WHAT DO YOU KNOW ABOUT THE FIRE PITS, CAPTAIN STEEL?

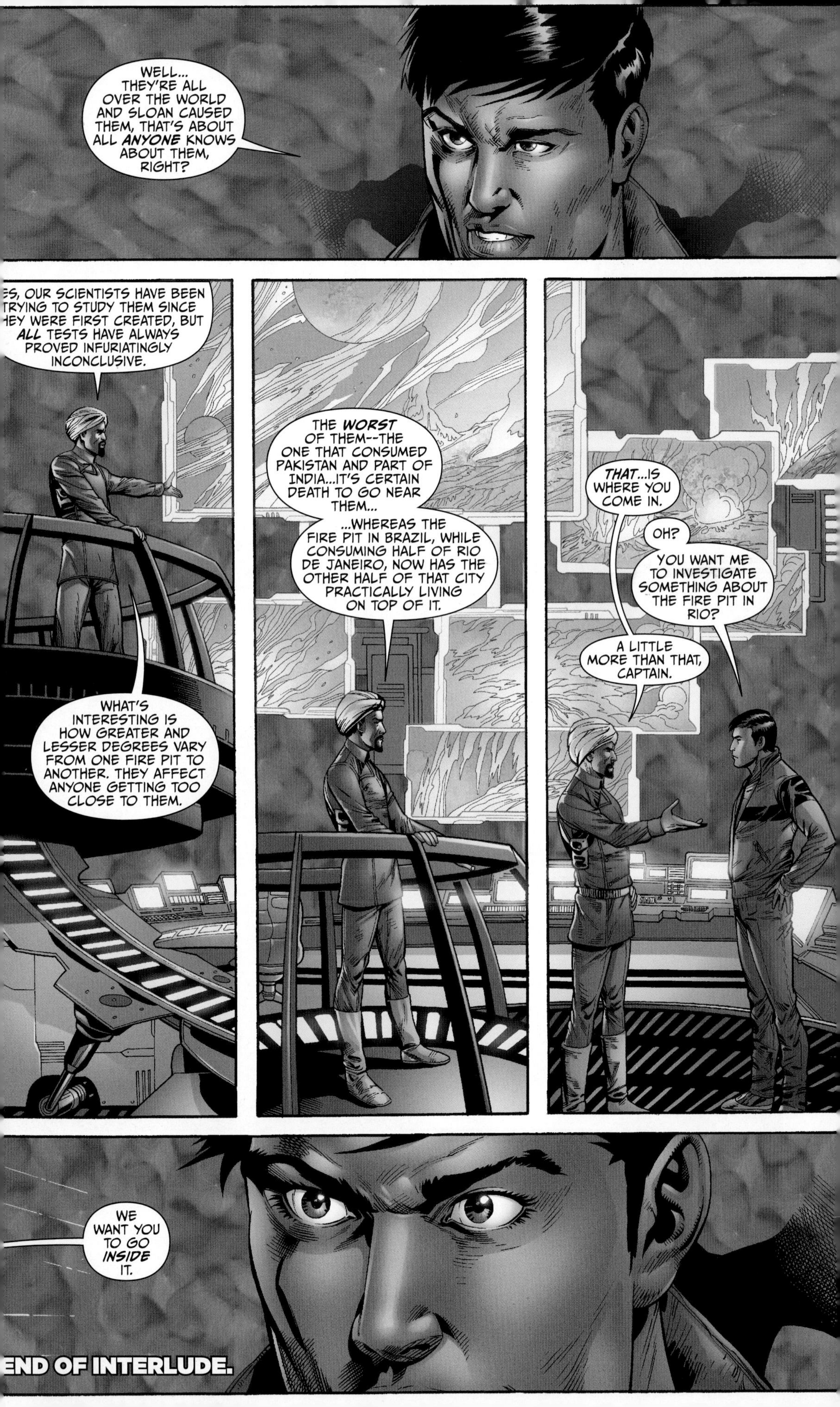

WELL... THEY'RE ALL OVER THE WORLD AND SLOAN CAUSED THEM, THAT'S ABOUT ALL *ANYONE* KNOWS ABOUT THEM, RIGHT?
ES, OUR SCIENTISTS HAVE BEEN TRYING TO STUDY THEM SINCE HEY WERE FIRST CREATED, BUT *ALL* TESTS HAVE ALWAYS PROVED INFURIATINGLY INCONCLUSIVE.
WHAT'S INTERESTING IS HOW GREATER AND LESSER DEGREES VARY FROM ONE FIRE PIT TO ANOTHER. THEY AFFECT ANYONE GETTING TOO CLOSE TO THEM.
THE *WORST* OF THEM--THE ONE THAT CONSUMED PAKISTAN AND PART OF INDIA...IT'S CERTAIN DEATH TO GO NEAR THEM...
...WHEREAS THE FIRE PIT IN BRAZIL, WHILE CONSUMING HALF OF RIO DE JANEIRO, NOW HAS THE OTHER HALF OF THAT CITY PRACTICALLY LIVING ON TOP OF IT.
THAT...IS WHERE YOU COME IN.
OH?
YOU WANT ME TO INVESTIGATE SOMETHING ABOUT THE FIRE PIT IN RIO?
A LITTLE MORE THAN THAT, CAPTAIN.
WE WANT YOU TO GO *INSIDE* IT.
END OF INTERLUDE.

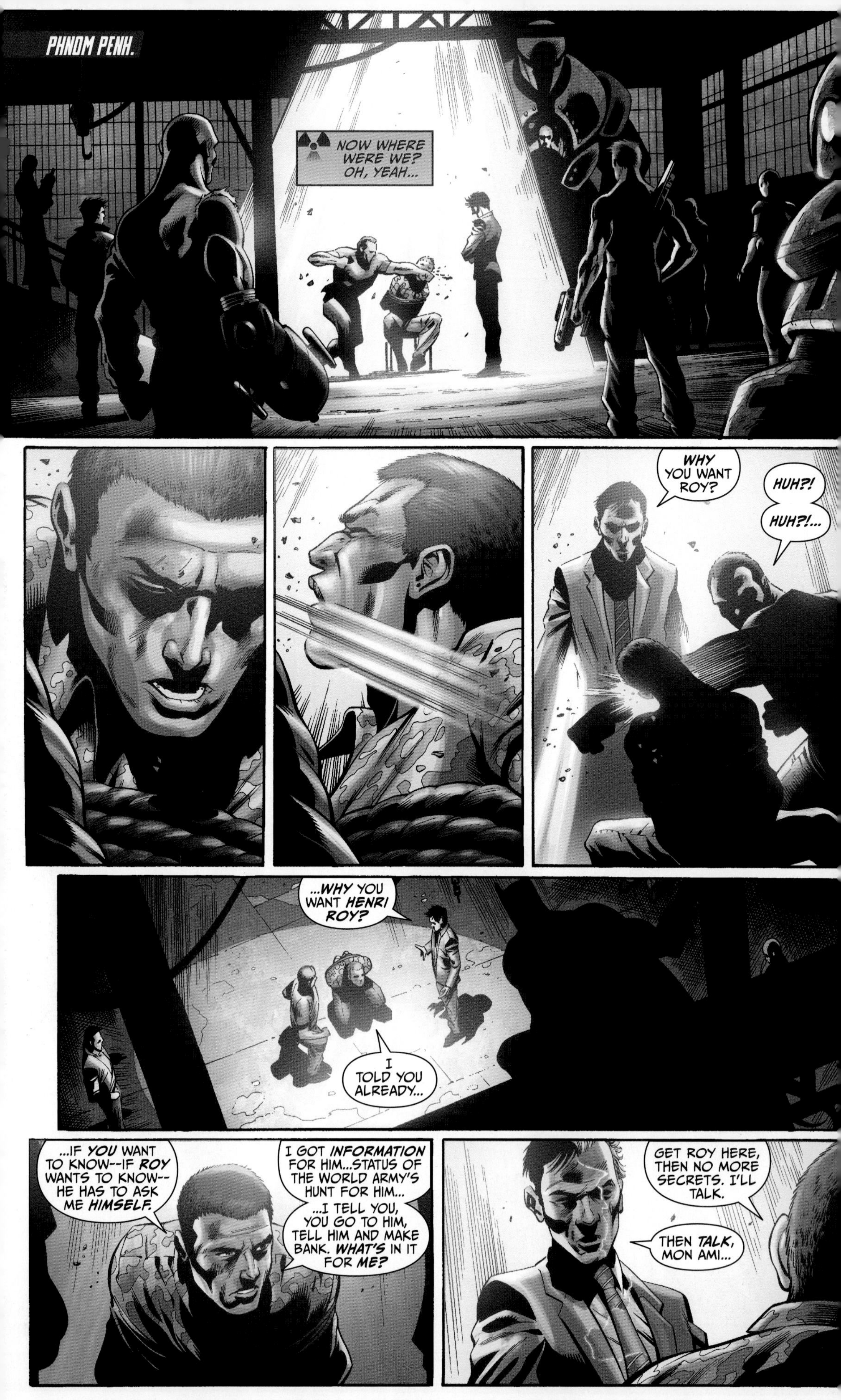
PHNOM PENH.
NOW WHERE WERE WE? OH, YEAH...
WHY YOU WANT ROY?
HUH?!
HUH?!...
...WHY YOU WANT HENRI ROY?
I TOLD YOU ALREADY...
...IF YOU WANT TO KNOW--IF ROY WANTS TO KNOW--HE HAS TO ASK ME HIMSELF.
I GOT INFORMATION FOR HIM...STATUS OF THE WORLD ARMY'S HUNT FOR HIM...
...I TELL YOU, YOU GO TO HIM, TELL HIM AND MAKE BANK. WHAT'S IN IT FOR ME?
GET ROY HERE, THEN NO MORE SECRETS. I'LL TALK.
THEN TALK, MON AMI...

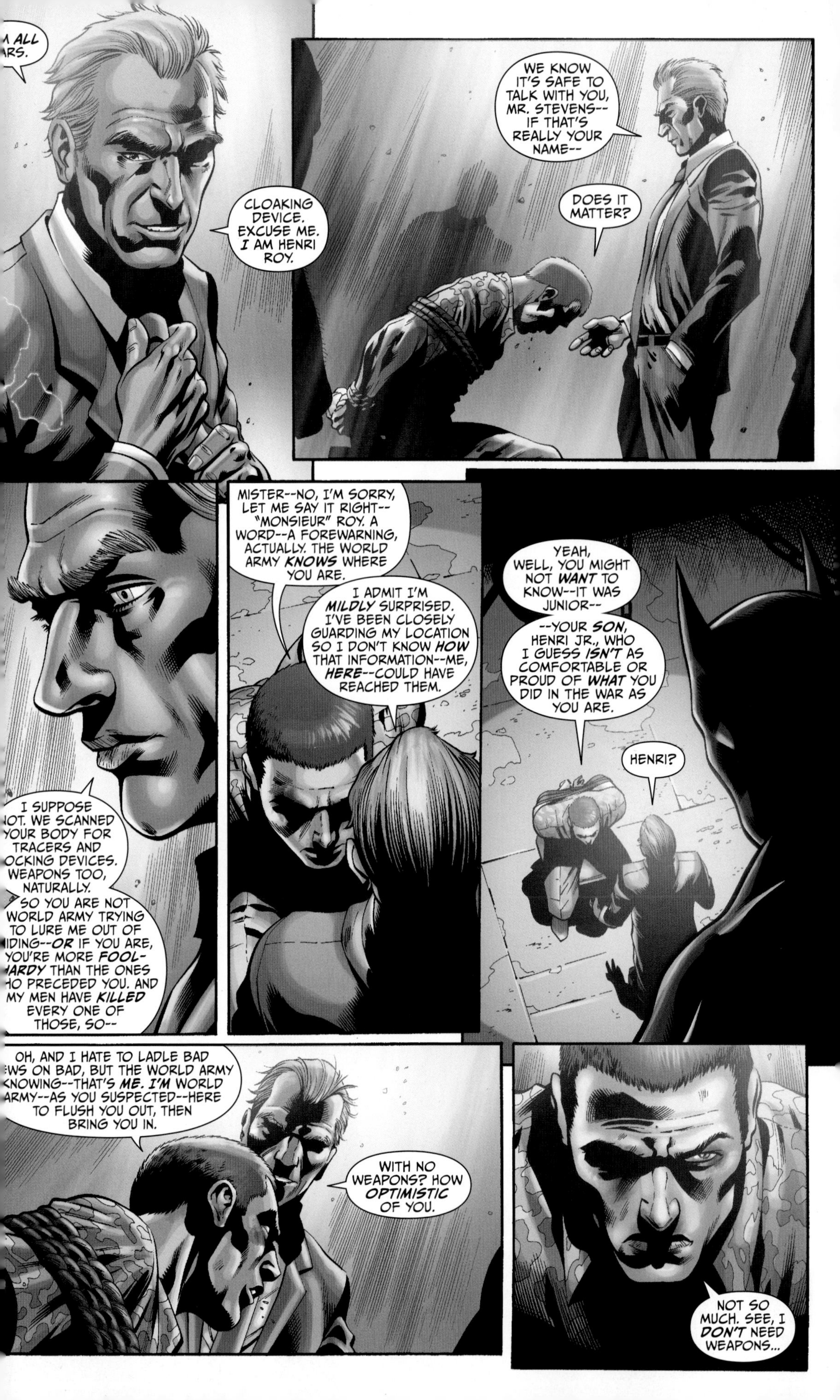

...M ALL ...ARS.
CLOAKING DEVICE. EXCUSE ME. I AM HENRI ROY.
WE KNOW IT'S SAFE TO TALK WITH YOU, MR. STEVENS-- IF THAT'S REALLY YOUR NAME--
DOES IT MATTER?
...I SUPPOSE ...OT. WE SCANNED YOUR BODY FOR TRACERS AND ...OCKING DEVICES. WEAPONS TOO, NATURALLY.
SO YOU ARE NOT WORLD ARMY TRYING TO LURE ME OUT OF ...IDING--OR IF YOU ARE, YOU'RE MORE FOOL-...ARDY THAN THE ONES ...HO PRECEDED YOU. AND MY MEN HAVE KILLED EVERY ONE OF THOSE, SO--
MISTER--NO, I'M SORRY, LET ME SAY IT RIGHT-- "MONSIEUR" ROY. A WORD--A FOREWARNING, ACTUALLY. THE WORLD ARMY KNOWS WHERE YOU ARE.
I ADMIT I'M MILDLY SURPRISED. I'VE BEEN CLOSELY GUARDING MY LOCATION SO I DON'T KNOW HOW THAT INFORMATION--ME, HERE--COULD HAVE REACHED THEM.
YEAH, WELL, YOU MIGHT NOT WANT TO KNOW--IT WAS JUNIOR--
--YOUR SON, HENRI JR., WHO I GUESS ISN'T AS COMFORTABLE OR PROUD OF WHAT YOU DID IN THE WAR AS YOU ARE.
HENRI?
OH, AND I HATE TO LADLE BAD ...EWS ON BAD, BUT THE WORLD ARMY ...NOWING--THAT'S ME. I'M WORLD ...ARMY--AS YOU SUSPECTED--HERE TO FLUSH YOU OUT, THEN BRING YOU IN.
WITH NO WEAPONS? HOW OPTIMISTIC OF YOU.
NOT SO MUCH. SEE, I DON'T NEED WEAPONS...

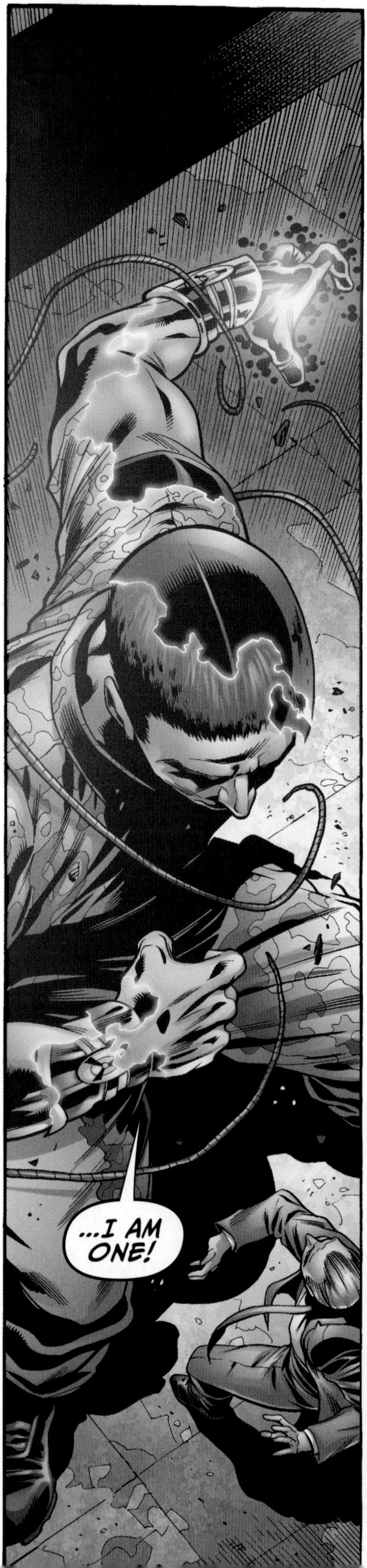
...I AM ONE!
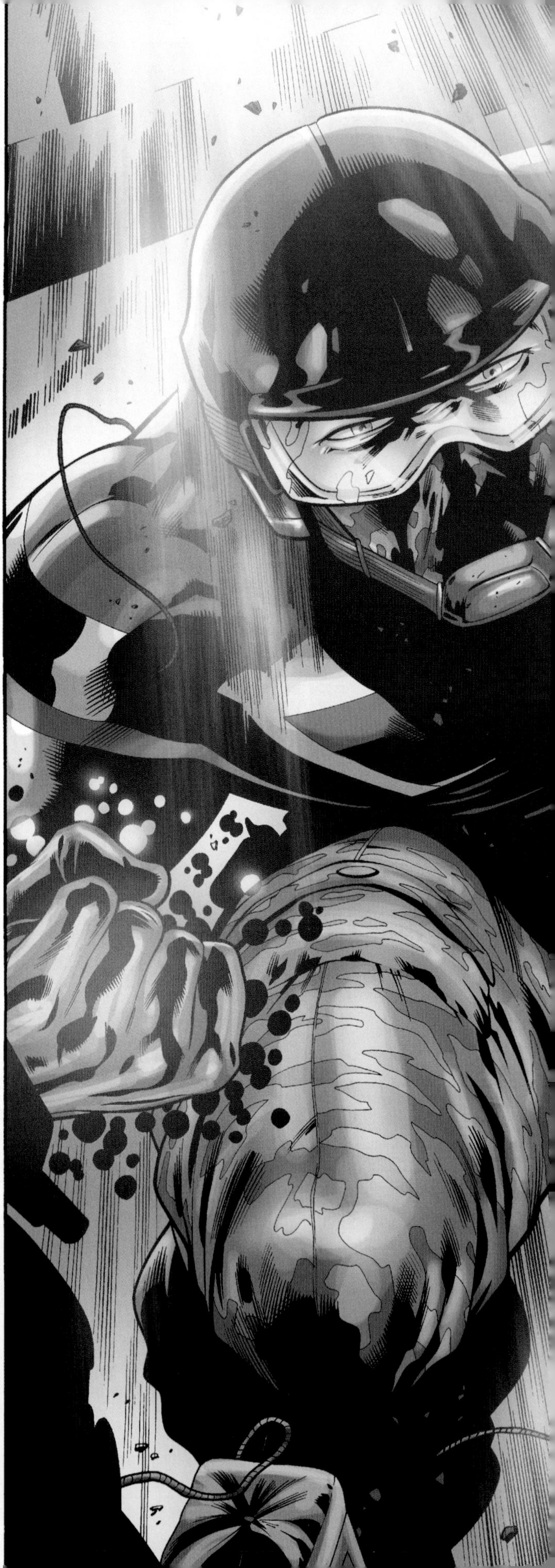

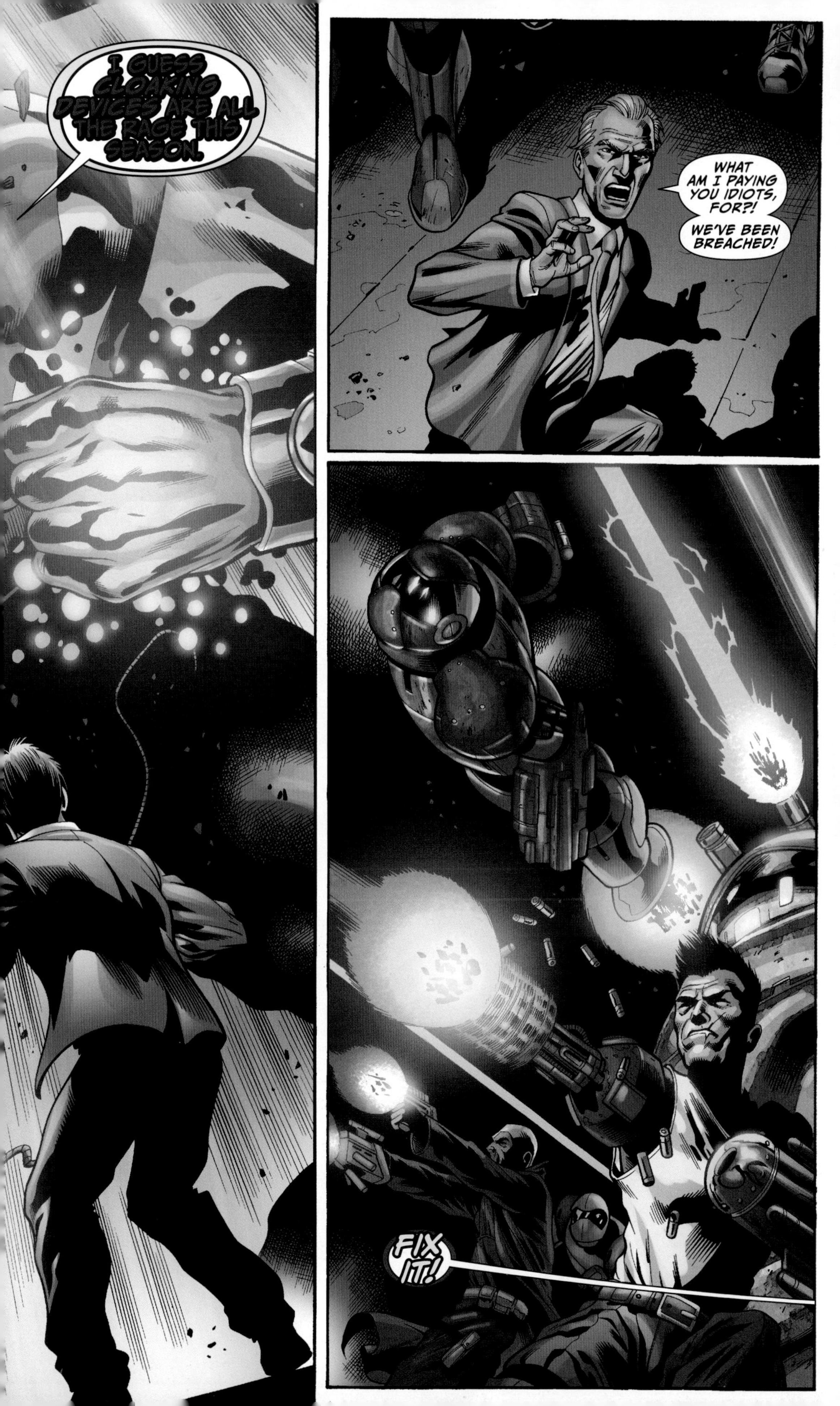

I GUESS CLOAKING DEVICES ARE ALL THE RAGE THIS SEASON.
WHAT AM I PAYING YOU IDIOTS, FOR?!
WE'VE BEEN BREACHED!
FIX IT!

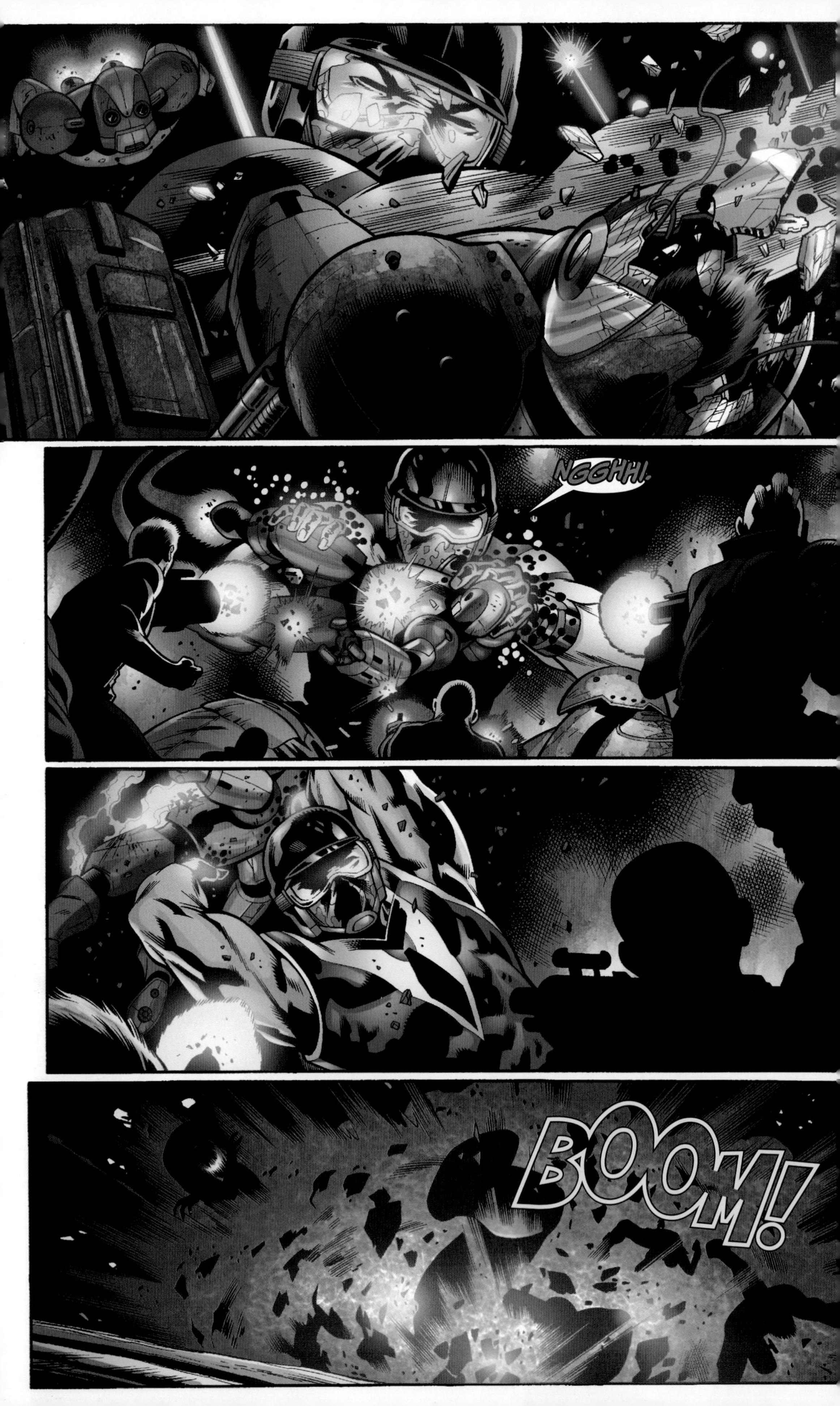
NGGHH!
BOOM!

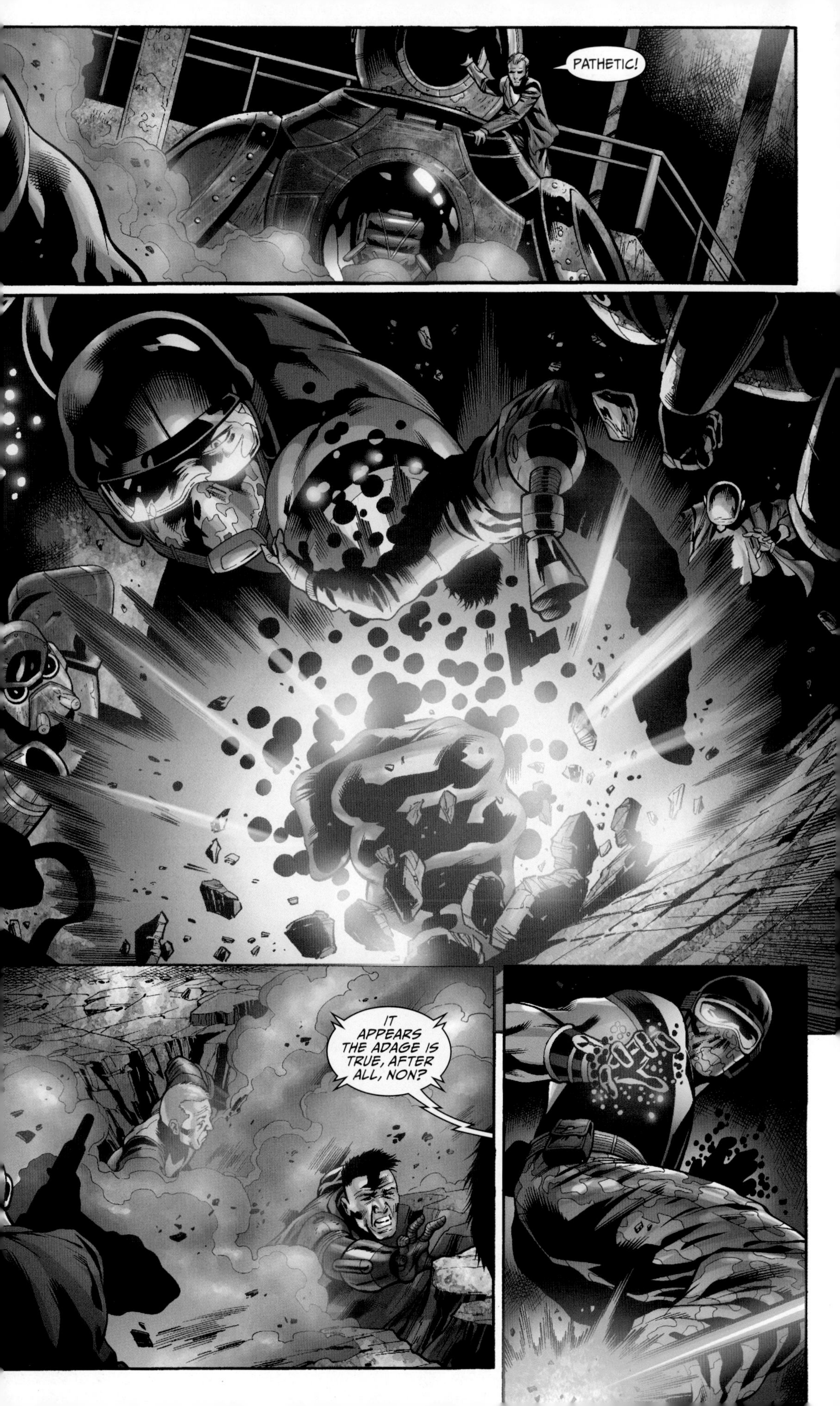
PATHETIC!
IT APPEARS THE ADAGE IS TRUE, AFTER ALL, NON?

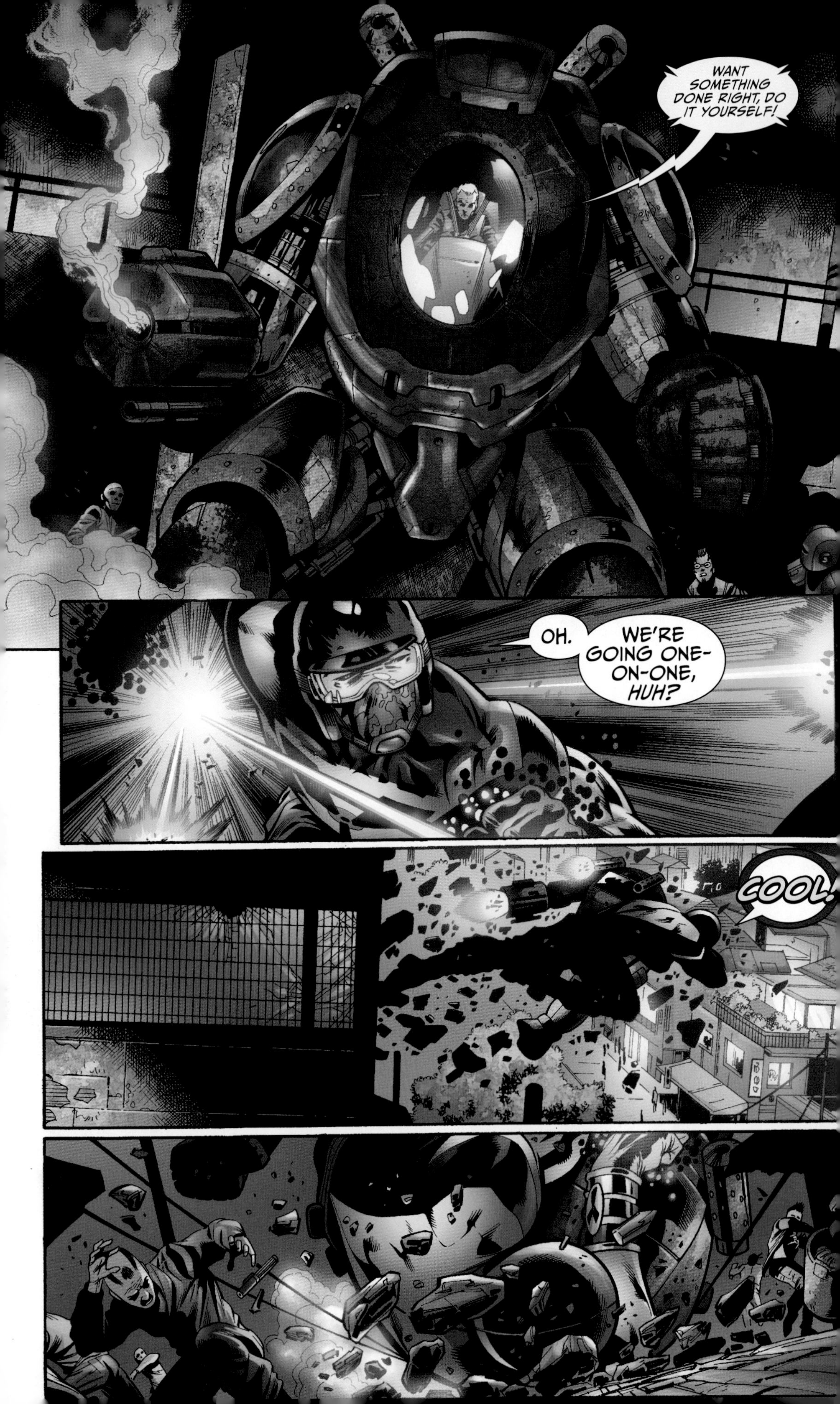
WANT SOMETHING DONE RIGHT, DO IT YOURSELF!
OH.
WE'RE GOING ONE-ON-ONE, HUH?
COOL!

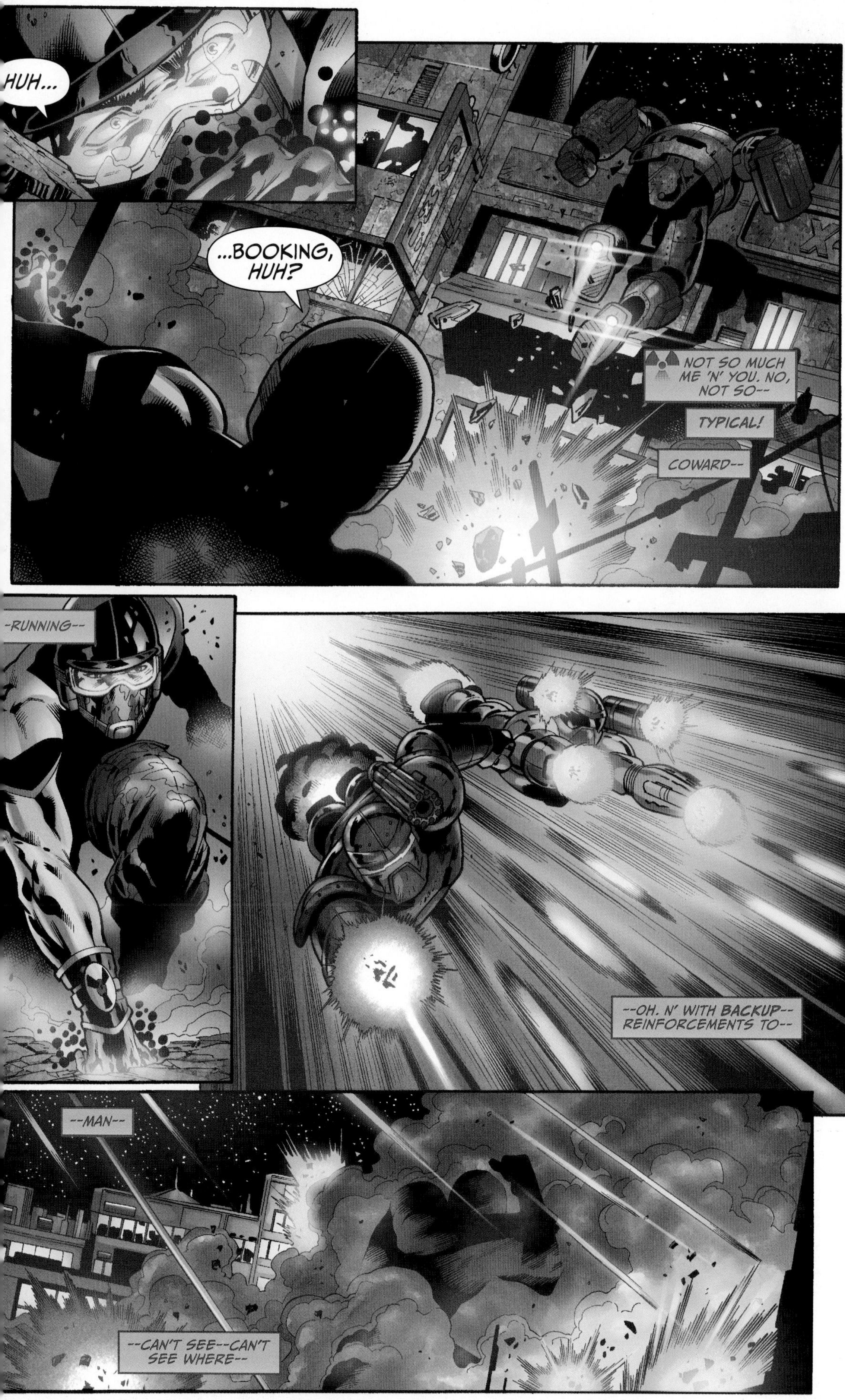
HUH...
...BOOKING, HUH?
NOT SO MUCH ME 'N' YOU. NO, NOT SO--
TYPICAL!
COWARD--
-RUNNING--
--OH. N' WITH BACKUP--REINFORCEMENTS TO--
--MAN--
--CAN'T SEE--CAN'T SEE WHERE--

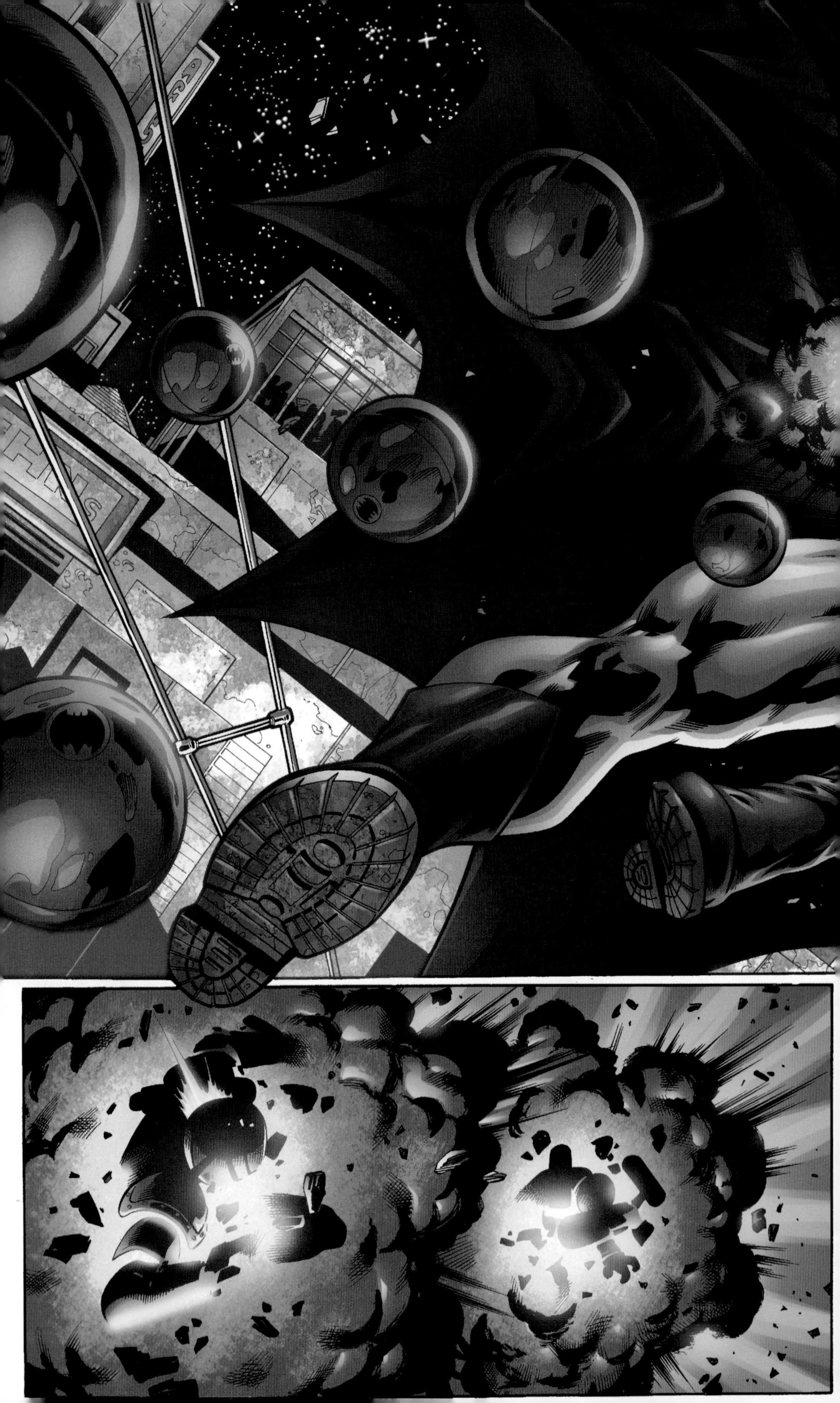

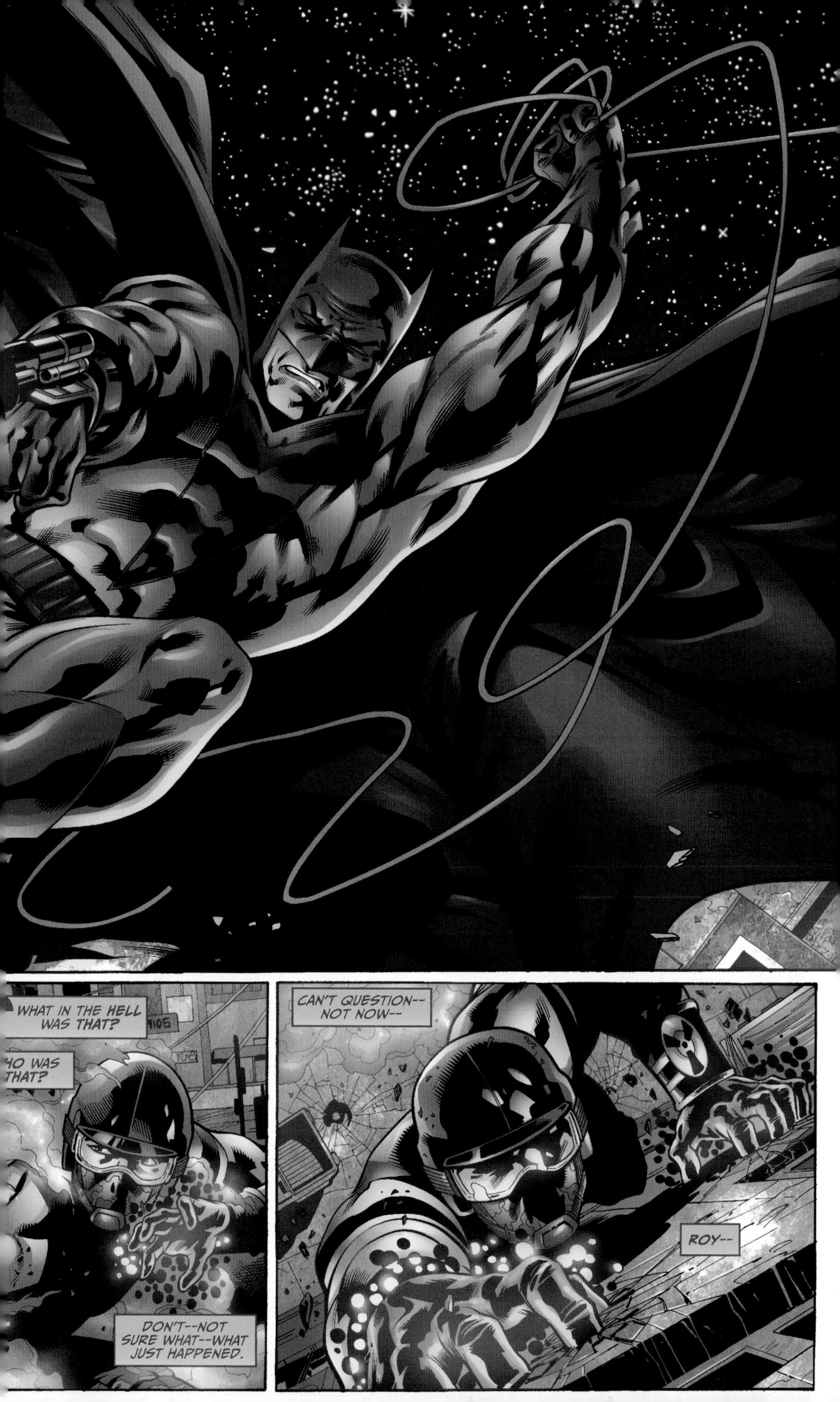

WHAT IN THE HELL WAS THAT?
HO WAS THAT?
DON'T--NOT SURE WHAT--WHAT JUST HAPPENED.
CAN'T QUESTION-- NOT NOW--
ROY--

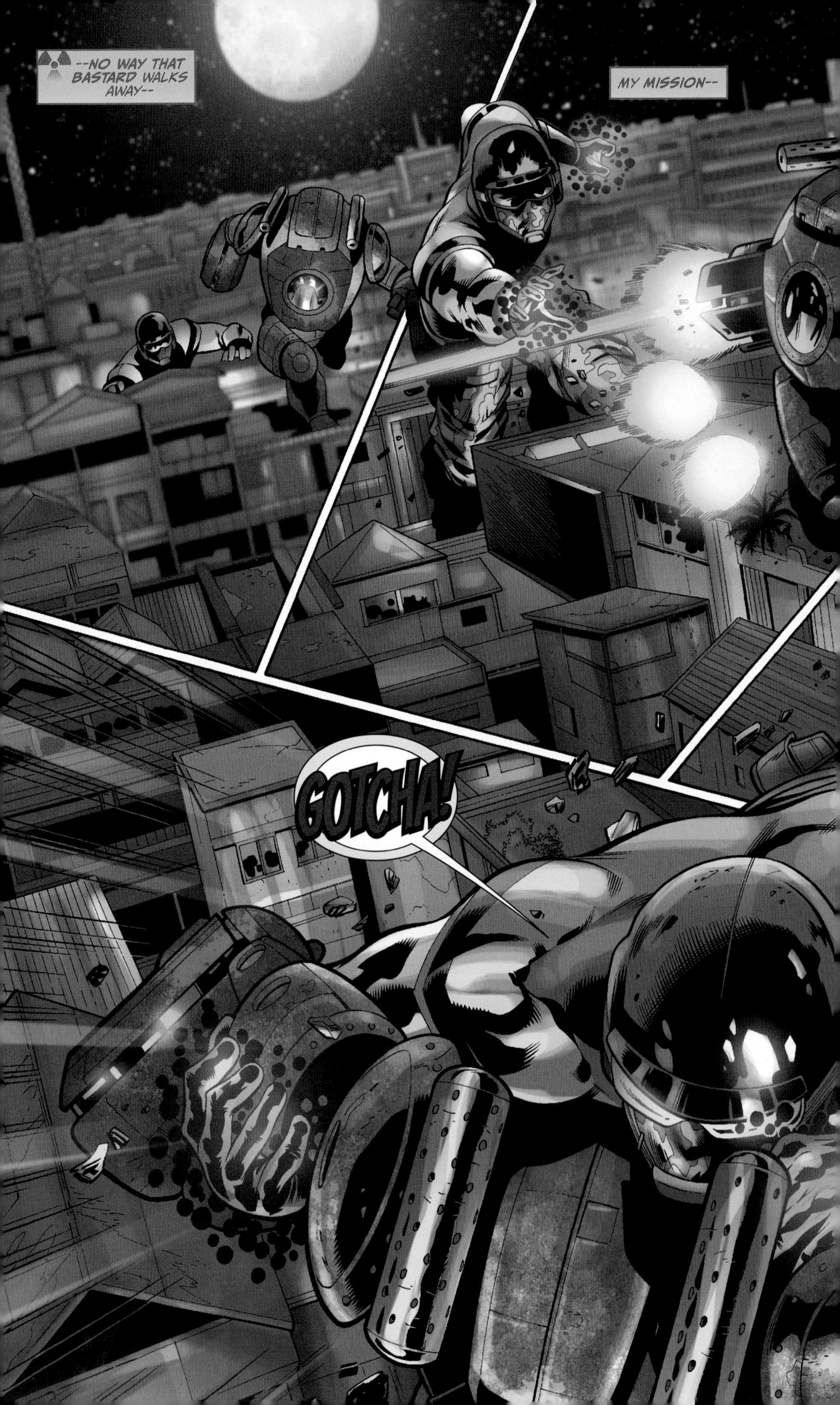
--NO WAY THAT BASTARD WALKS AWAY--
MY MISSION--
GOTCHA!

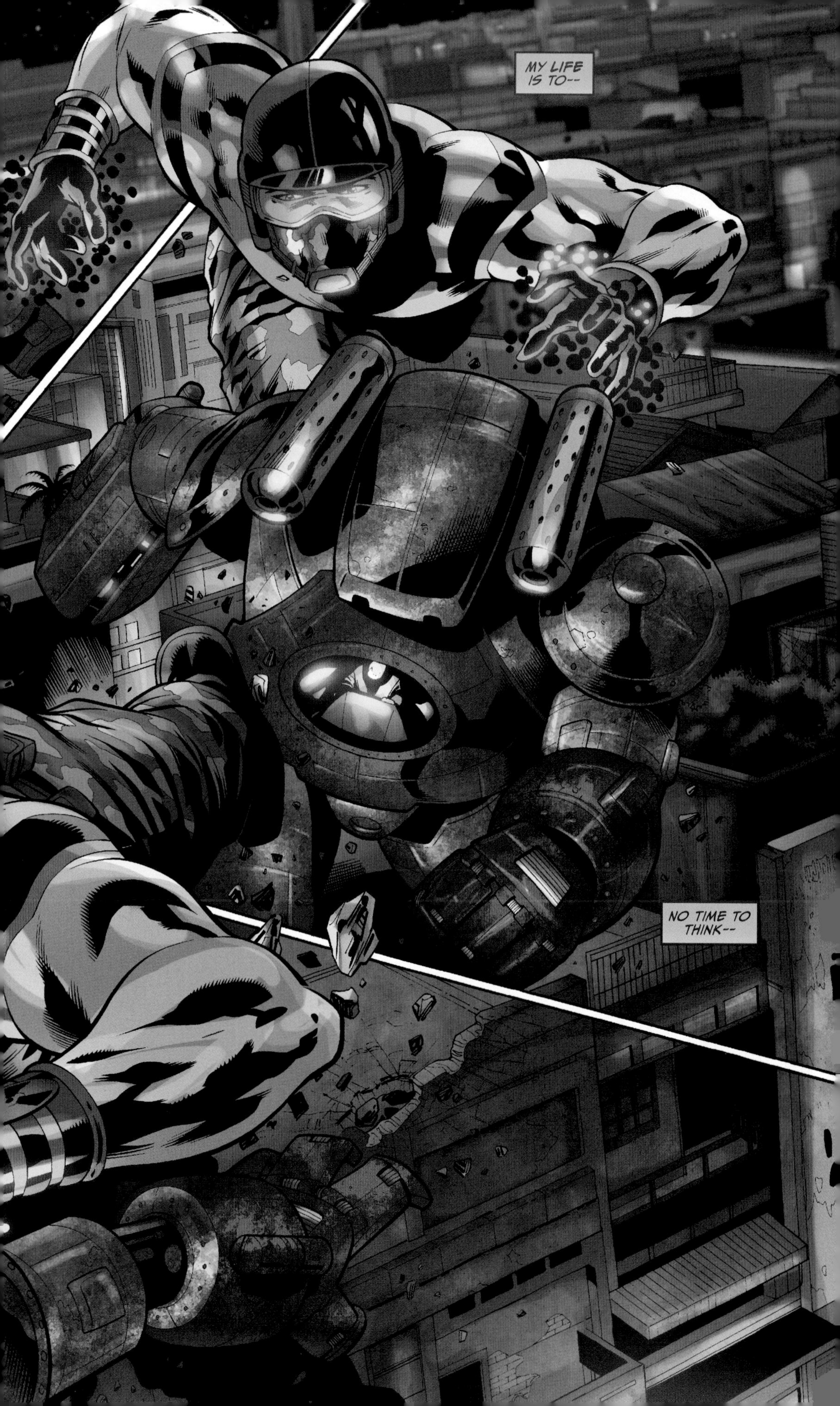
MY LIFE IS TO--
NO TIME TO THINK--

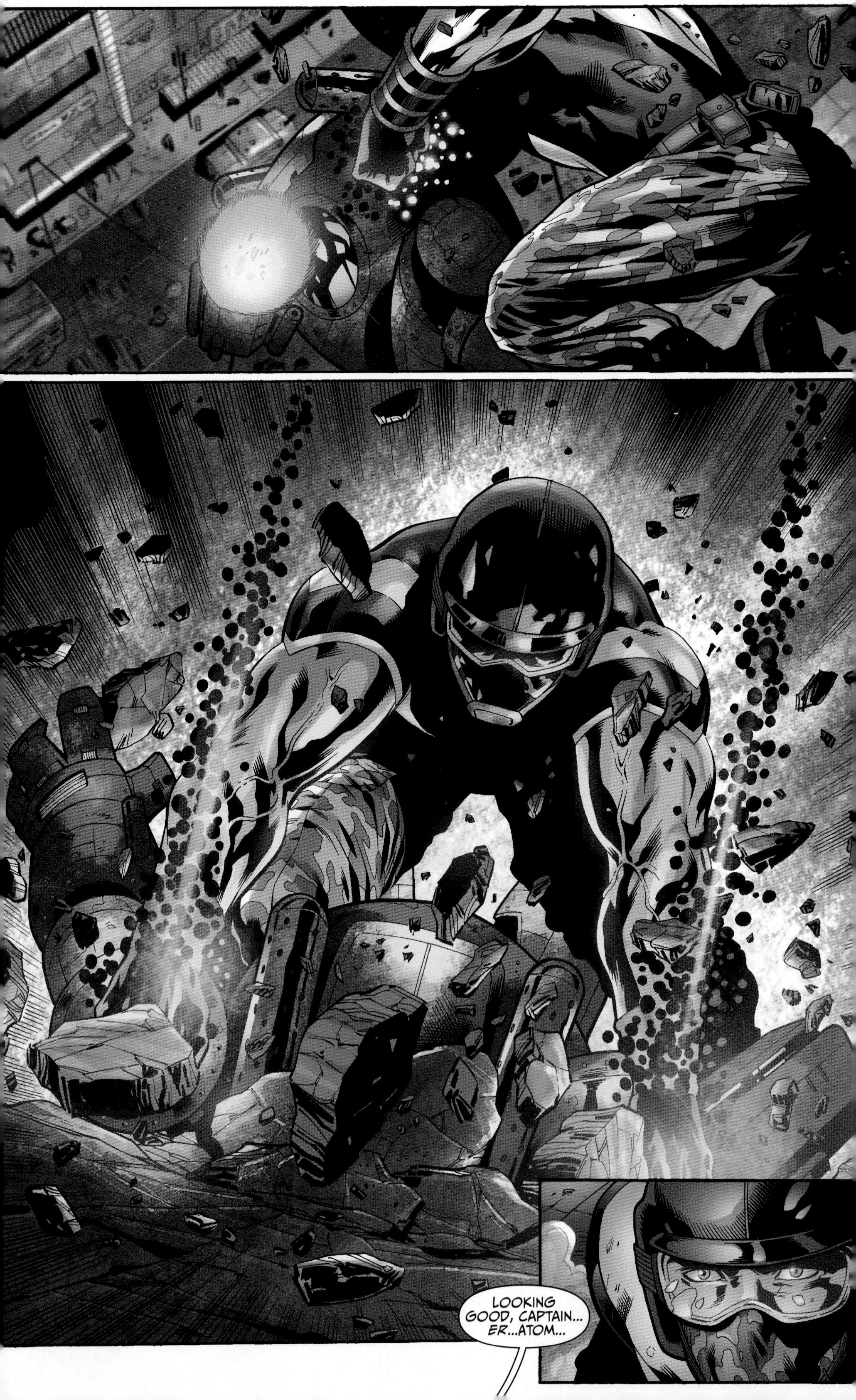
LOOKING GOOD, CAPTAIN... ER...ATOM...

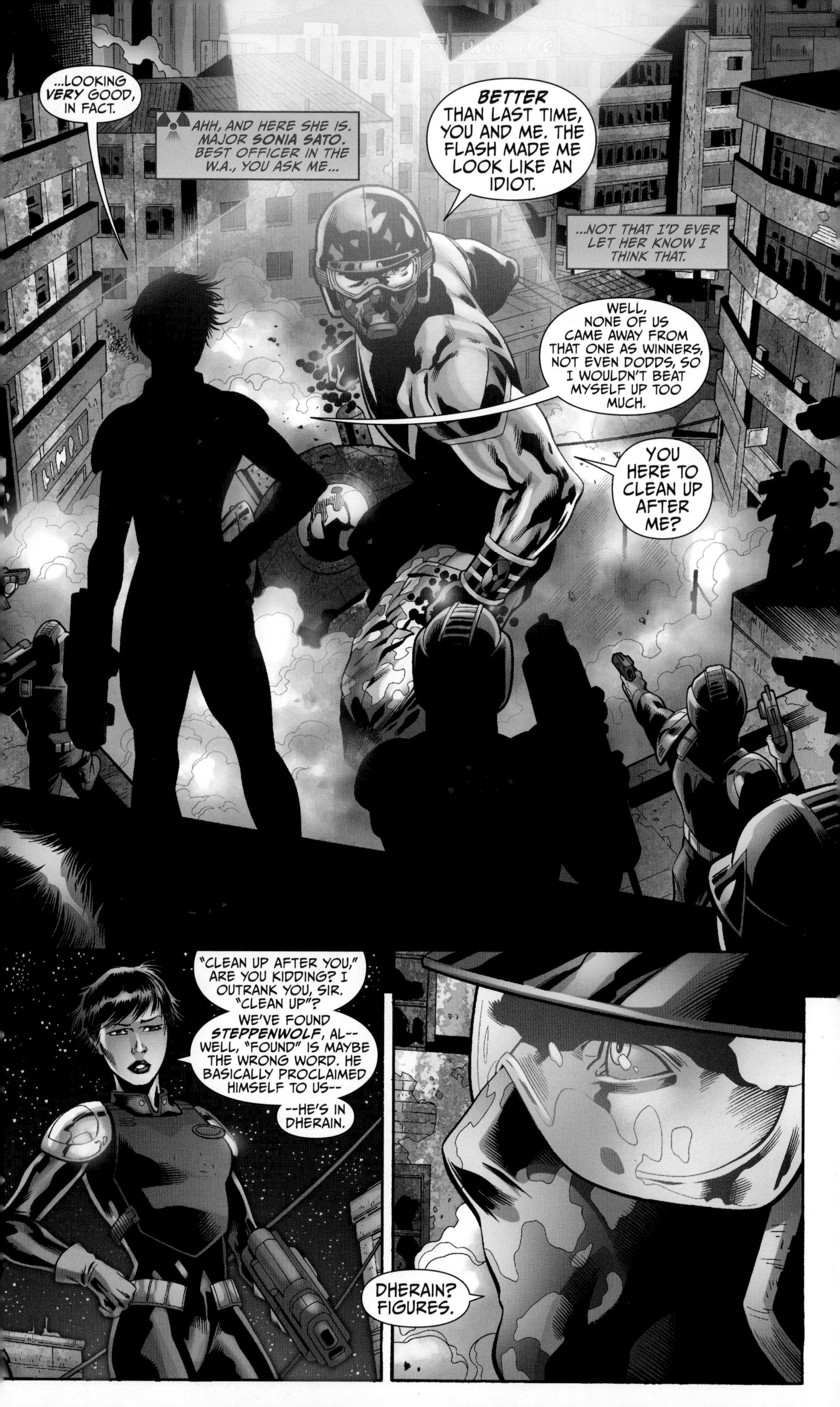

...LOOKING VERY GOOD, IN FACT.
AHH, AND HERE SHE IS. MAJOR SONIA SATO. BEST OFFICER IN THE W.A., YOU ASK ME...
BETTER THAN LAST TIME, YOU AND ME. THE FLASH MADE ME LOOK LIKE AN IDIOT.
...NOT THAT I'D EVER LET HER KNOW I THINK THAT.
WELL, NONE OF US CAME AWAY FROM THAT ONE AS WINNERS, NOT EVEN DODDS, SO I WOULDN'T BEAT MYSELF UP TOO MUCH.
YOU HERE TO CLEAN UP AFTER ME?
"CLEAN UP AFTER YOU," ARE YOU KIDDING? I OUTRANK YOU, SIR. "CLEAN UP"?
WE'VE FOUND STEPPENWOLF, AL-- WELL, "FOUND" IS MAYBE THE WRONG WORD. HE BASICALLY PROCLAIMED HIMSELF TO US--
--HE'S IN DHERAIN.
DHERAIN? FIGURES.

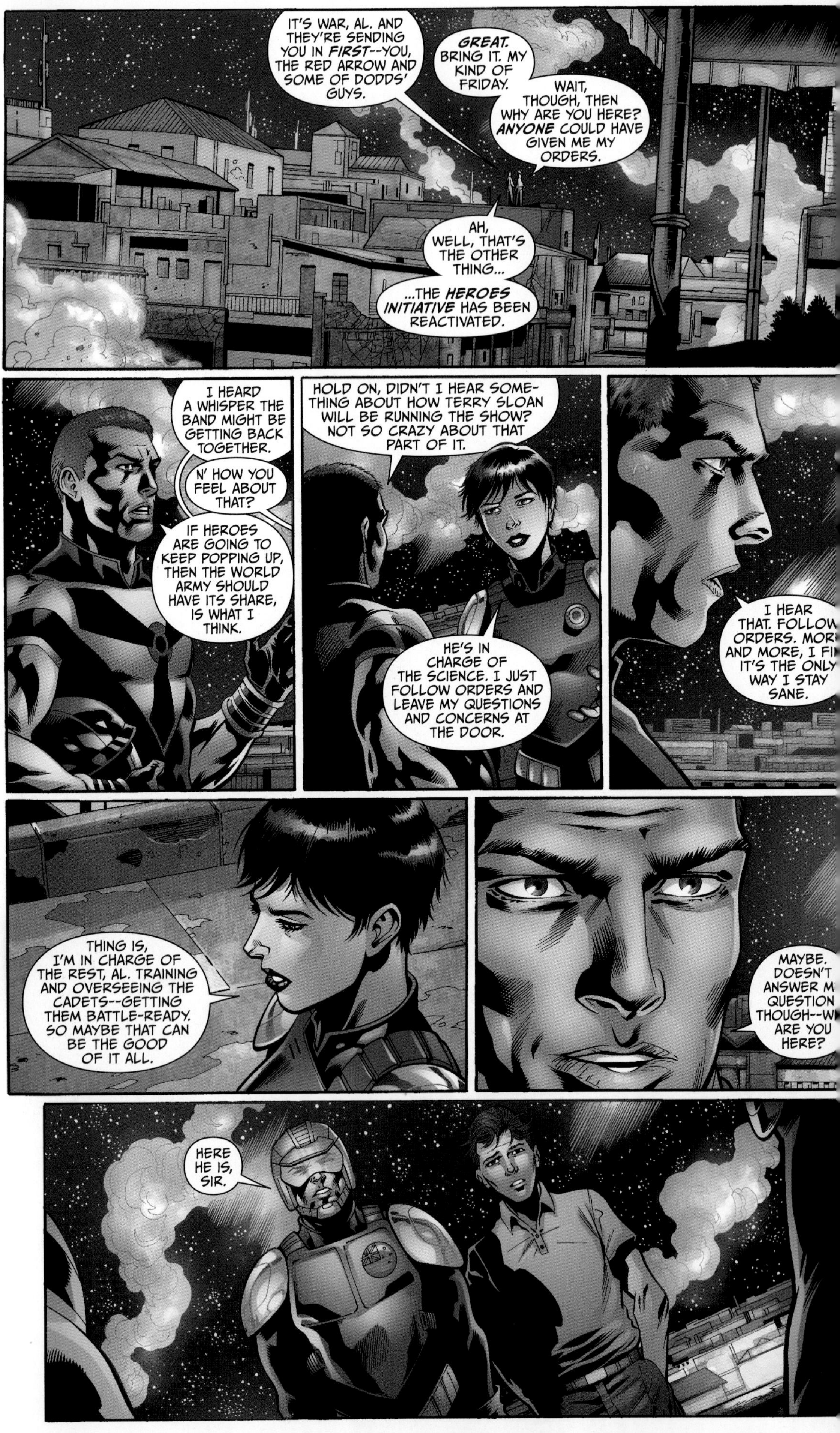
IT'S WAR, AL. AND THEY'RE SENDING YOU IN FIRST--YOU, THE RED ARROW AND SOME OF DODDS' GUYS.
GREAT. BRING IT. MY KIND OF FRIDAY.
WAIT, THOUGH, THEN WHY ARE YOU HERE? ANYONE COULD HAVE GIVEN ME MY ORDERS.
AH, WELL, THAT'S THE OTHER THING...
...THE HEROES INITIATIVE HAS BEEN REACTIVATED.
I HEARD A WHISPER THE BAND MIGHT BE GETTING BACK TOGETHER.
N' HOW YOU FEEL ABOUT THAT?
IF HEROES ARE GOING TO KEEP POPPING UP, THEN THE WORLD ARMY SHOULD HAVE ITS SHARE, IS WHAT I THINK.
HOLD ON, DIDN'T I HEAR SOME-THING ABOUT HOW TERRY SLOAN WILL BE RUNNING THE SHOW? NOT SO CRAZY ABOUT THAT PART OF IT.
HE'S IN CHARGE OF THE SCIENCE. I JUST FOLLOW ORDERS AND LEAVE MY QUESTIONS AND CONCERNS AT THE DOOR.
I HEAR THAT. FOLLOW ORDERS. MOR AND MORE, I FI IT'S THE ONLY WAY I STAY SANE.
THING IS, I'M IN CHARGE OF THE REST, AL. TRAINING AND OVERSEEING THE CADETS--GETTING THEM BATTLE-READY. SO MAYBE THAT CAN BE THE GOOD OF IT ALL.
MAYBE. DOESN'T ANSWER M QUESTION THOUGH--W ARE YOU HERE?
HERE HE IS, SIR.

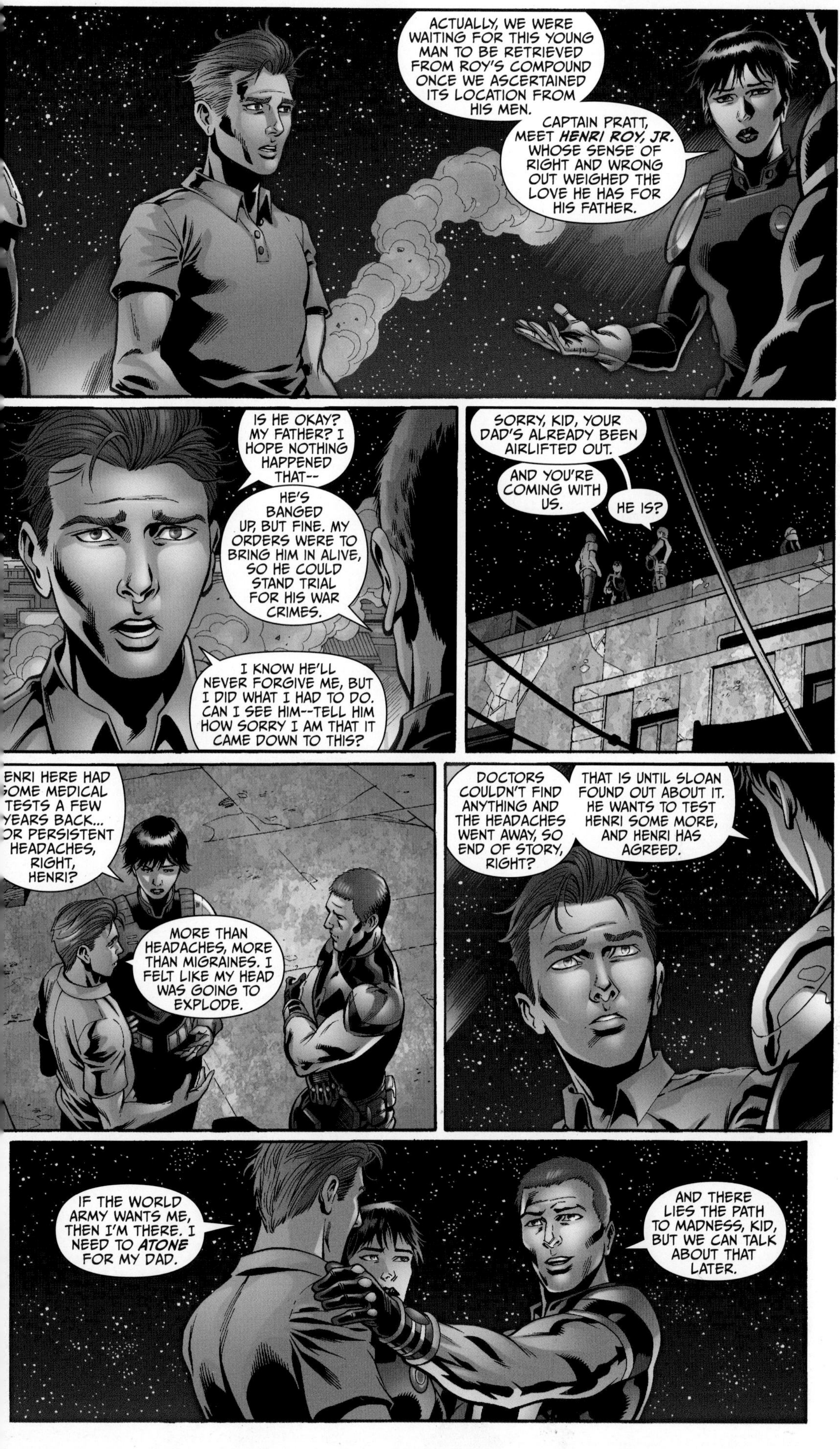

ACTUALLY, WE WERE WAITING FOR THIS YOUNG MAN TO BE RETRIEVED FROM ROY'S COMPOUND ONCE WE ASCERTAINED ITS LOCATION FROM HIS MEN.
CAPTAIN PRATT, MEET HENRI ROY, JR. WHOSE SENSE OF RIGHT AND WRONG OUT WEIGHED THE LOVE HE HAS FOR HIS FATHER.
IS HE OKAY? MY FATHER? I HOPE NOTHING HAPPENED THAT--
HE'S BANGED UP, BUT FINE. MY ORDERS WERE TO BRING HIM IN ALIVE, SO HE COULD STAND TRIAL FOR HIS WAR CRIMES.
I KNOW HE'LL NEVER FORGIVE ME, BUT I DID WHAT I HAD TO DO. CAN I SEE HIM--TELL HIM HOW SORRY I AM THAT IT CAME DOWN TO THIS?
SORRY, KID, YOUR DAD'S ALREADY BEEN AIRLIFTED OUT.
AND YOU'RE COMING WITH US.
HE IS?
HENRI HERE HAD SOME MEDICAL TESTS A FEW YEARS BACK... FOR PERSISTENT HEADACHES, RIGHT, HENRI?
MORE THAN HEADACHES, MORE THAN MIGRAINES. I FELT LIKE MY HEAD WAS GOING TO EXPLODE.
DOCTORS COULDN'T FIND ANYTHING AND THE HEADACHES WENT AWAY, SO END OF STORY, RIGHT?
THAT IS UNTIL SLOAN FOUND OUT ABOUT IT. HE WANTS TO TEST HENRI SOME MORE, AND HENRI HAS AGREED.
IF THE WORLD ARMY WANTS ME, THEN I'M THERE. I NEED TO ATONE FOR MY DAD.
AND THERE LIES THE PATH TO MADNESS, KID, BUT WE CAN TALK ABOUT THAT LATER.

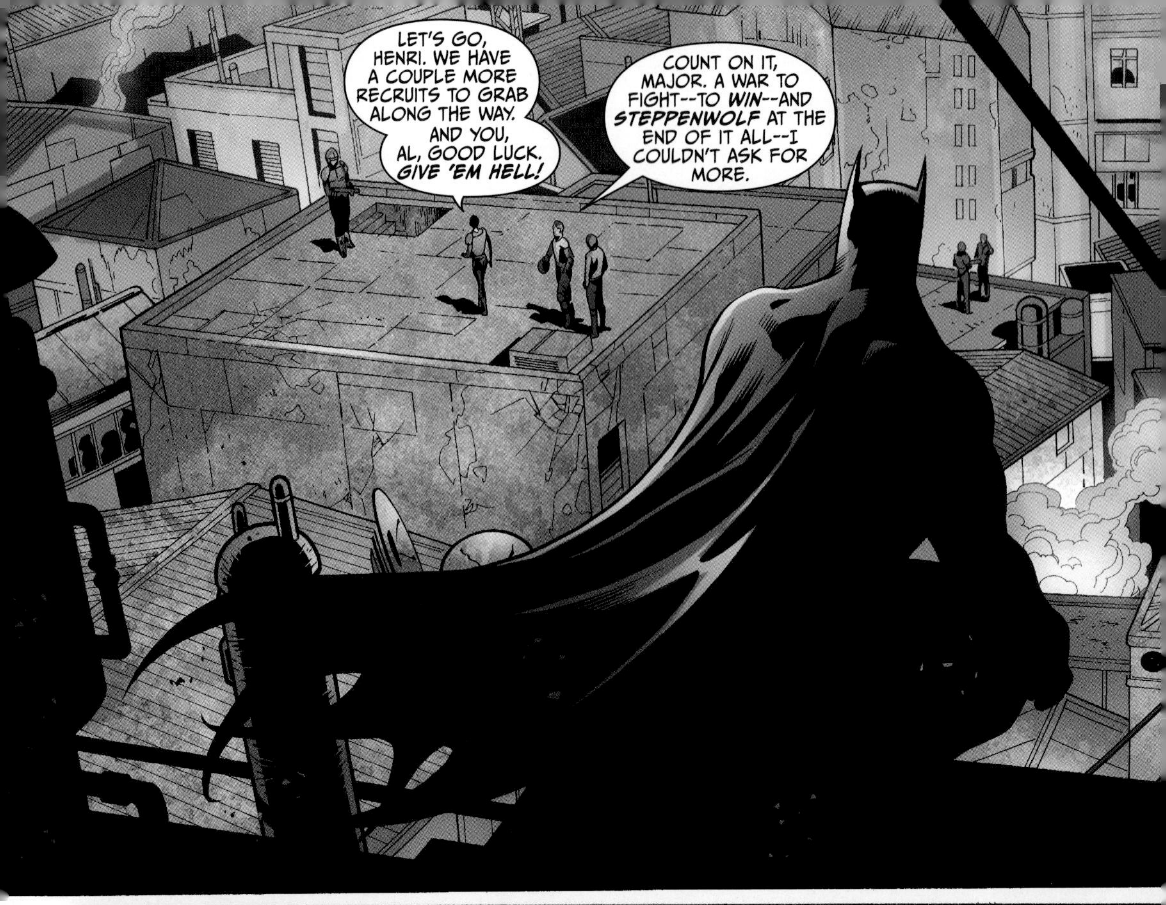
LET'S GO, HENRI. WE HAVE A COUPLE MORE RECRUITS TO GRAB ALONG THE WAY.
AND YOU, AL, GOOD LUCK. GIVE 'EM HELL!
COUNT ON IT, MAJOR. A WAR TO FIGHT--TO WIN--AND STEPPENWOLF AT THE END OF IT ALL--I COULDN'T ASK FOR MORE.

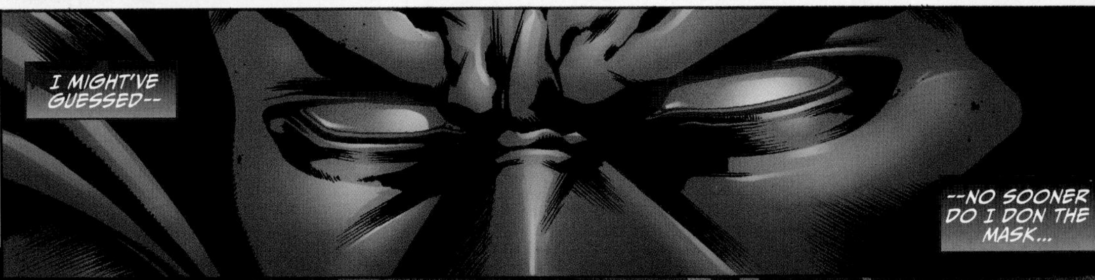
I MIGHT'VE GUESSED--
--NO SOONER DO I DON THE MASK...

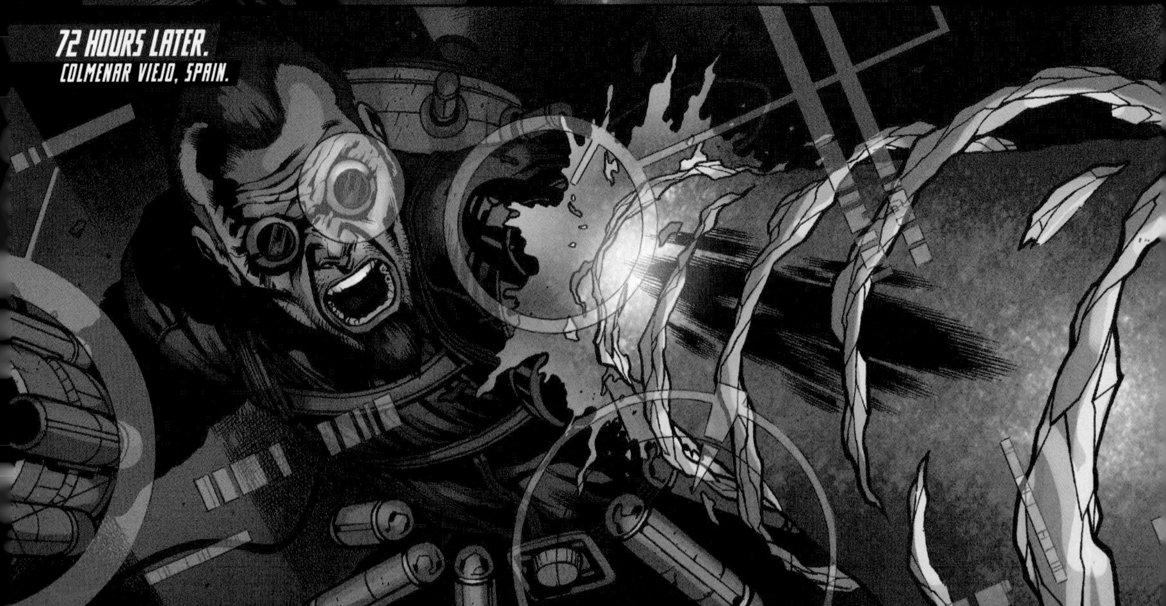
72 HOURS LATER.
COLMENAR VIEJO, SPAIN.
...I'M IN IT UP TO MY NECK.

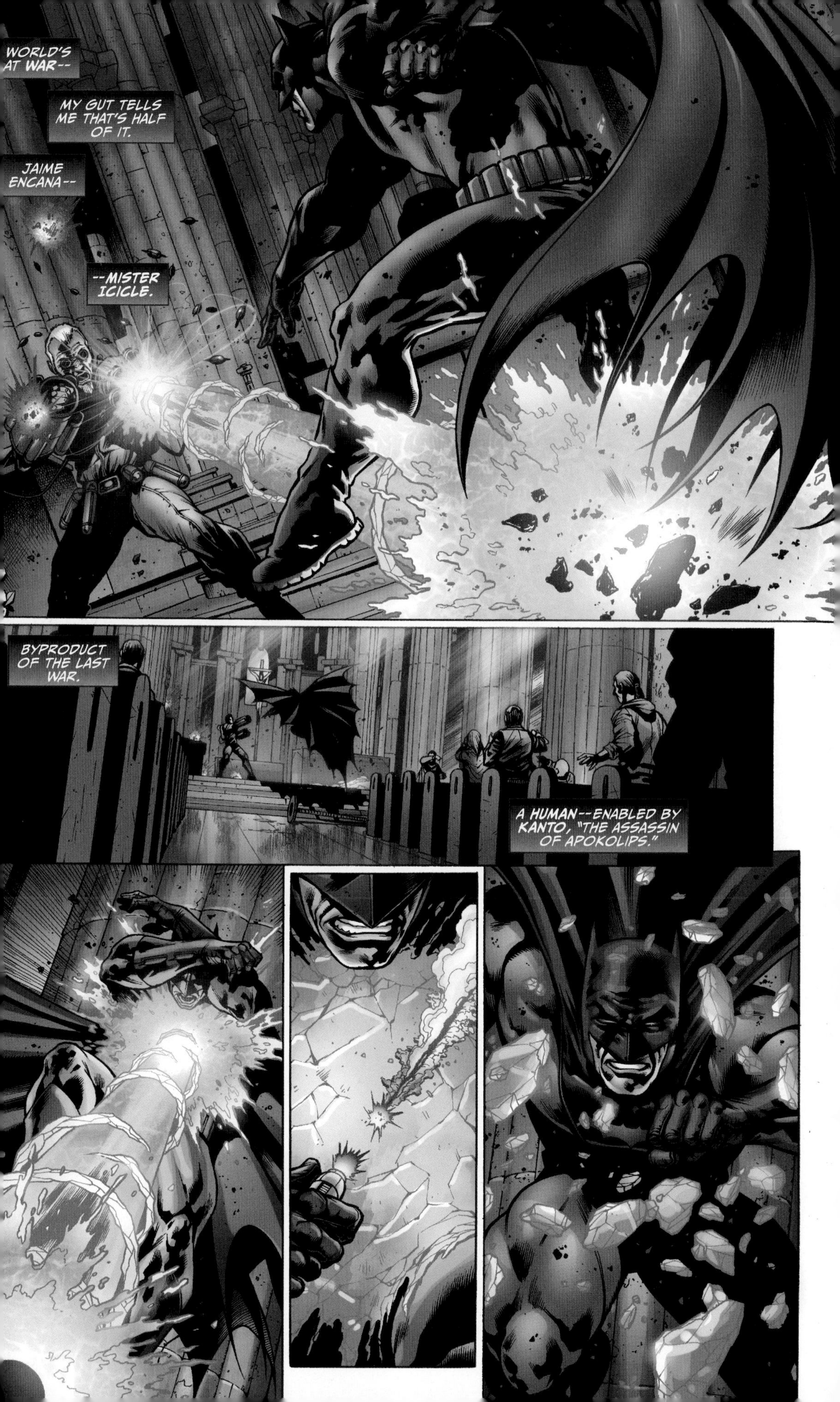
WORLD'S AT WAR--
MY GUT TELLS ME THAT'S HALF OF IT.
JAIME ENCANA--
--MISTER ICICLE.
BYPRODUCT OF THE LAST WAR.
A HUMAN--ENABLED BY KANTO, "THE ASSASSIN OF APOKOLIPS."

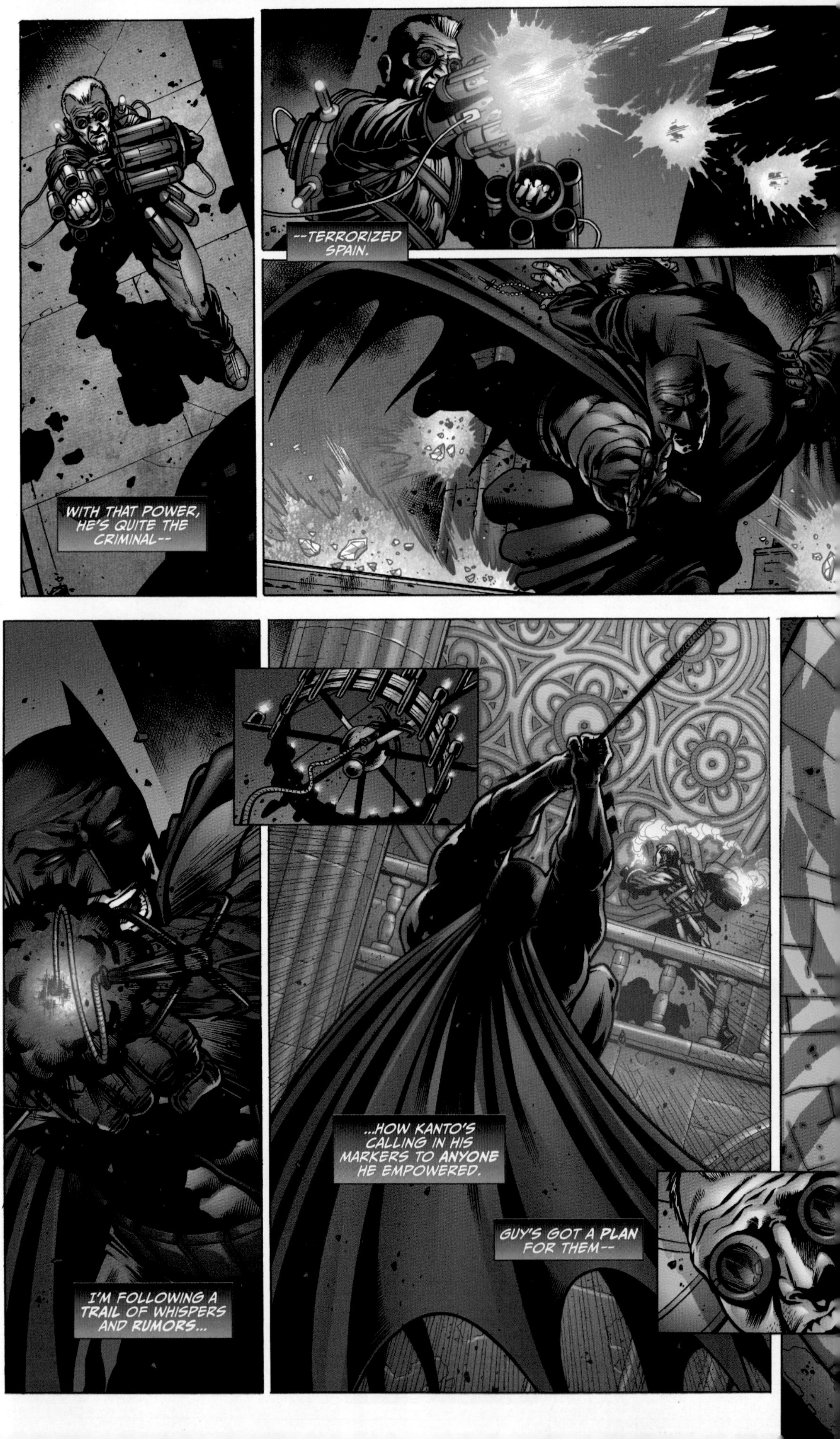
WITH THAT POWER, HE'S QUITE THE CRIMINAL--
--TERRORIZED SPAIN.
I'M FOLLOWING A TRAIL OF WHISPERS AND RUMORS...
...HOW KANTO'S CALLING IN HIS MARKERS TO ANYONE HE EMPOWERED.
GUY'S GOT A PLAN FOR THEM--

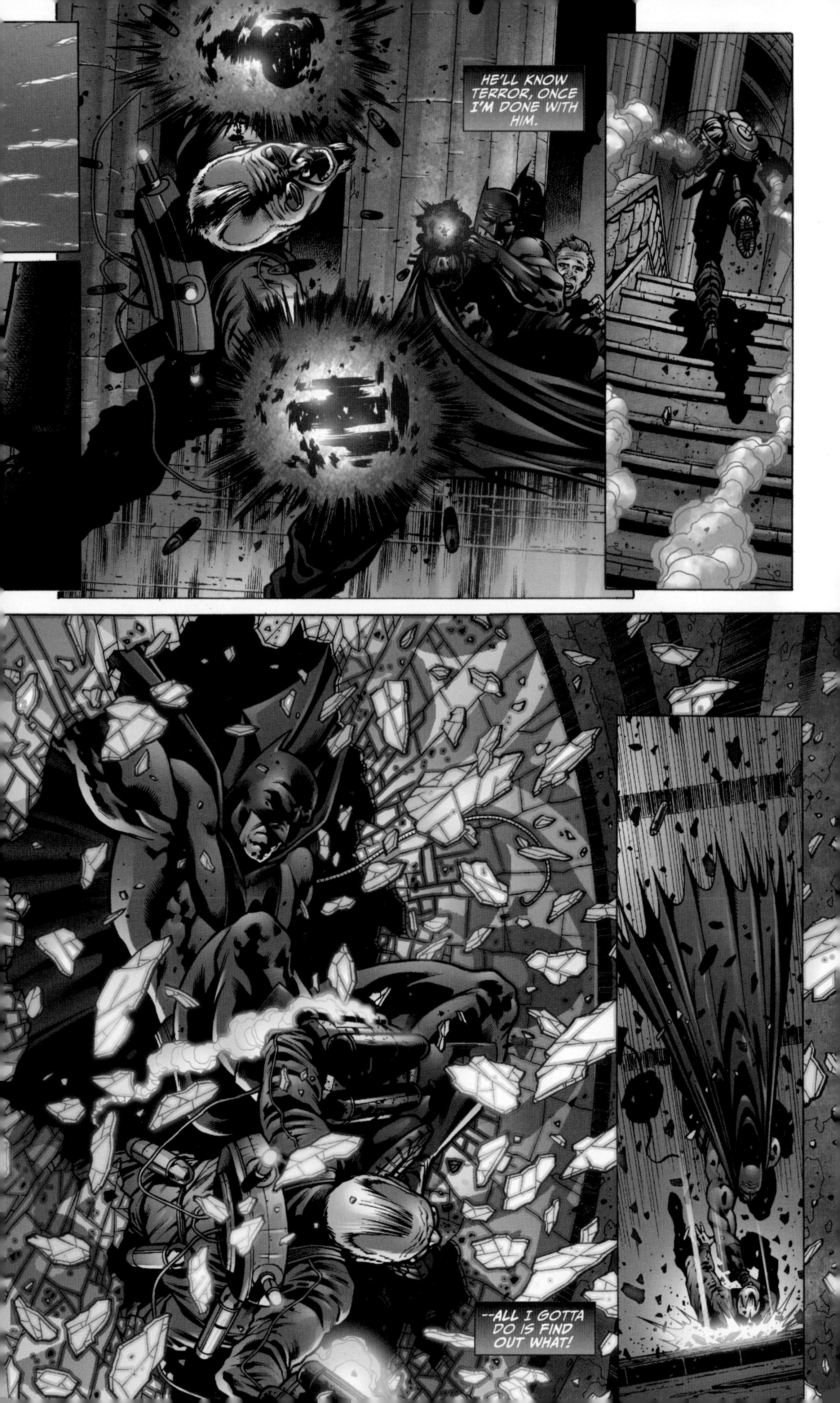
HE'LL KNOW TERROR, ONCE I'M DONE WITH HIM.
--ALL I GOTTA DO IS FIND OUT WHAT!

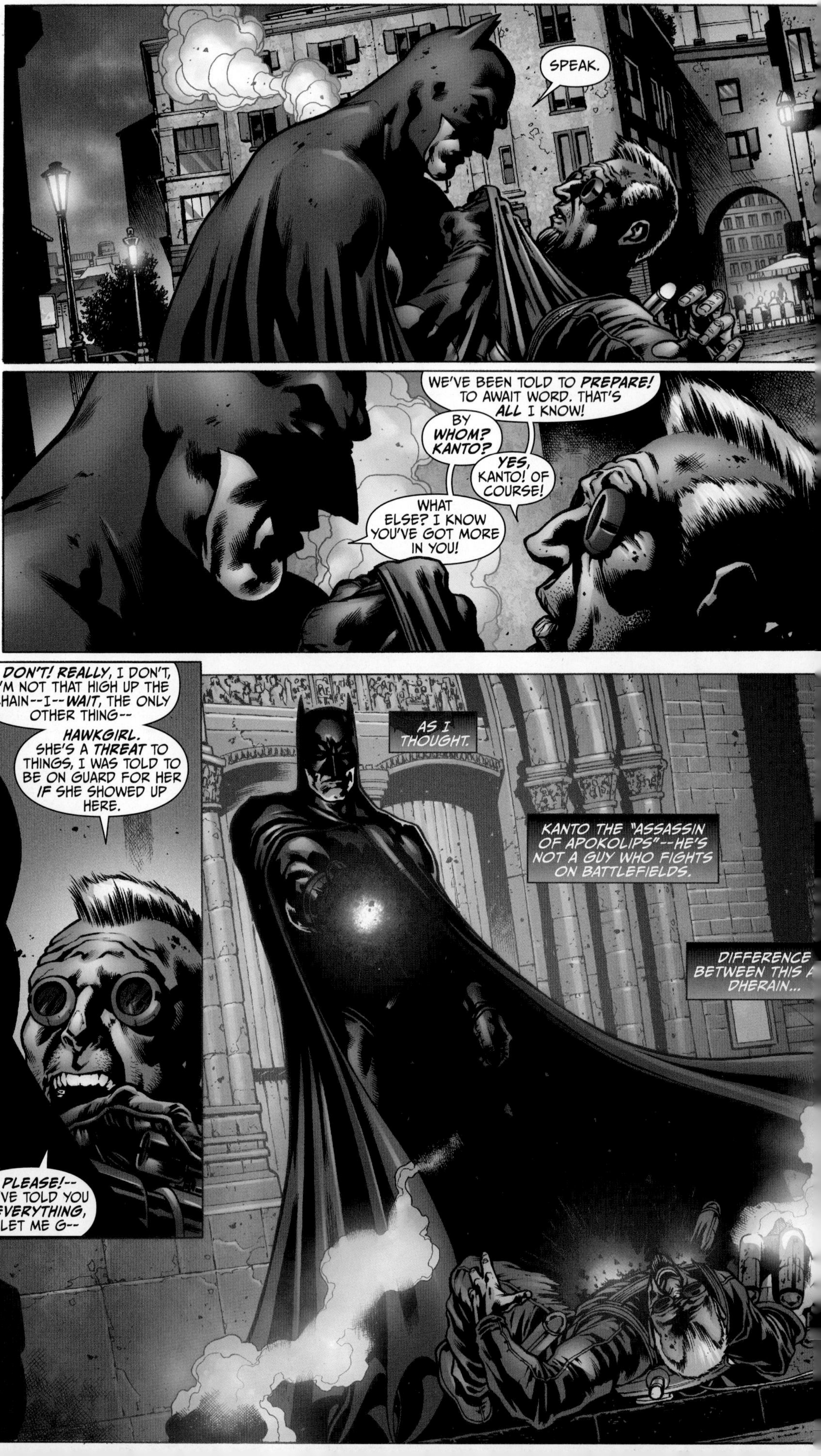

SPEAK.
WE'VE BEEN TOLD TO PREPARE! TO AWAIT WORD. THAT'S ALL I KNOW!
BY WHOM? KANTO?
YES, KANTO! OF COURSE!
WHAT ELSE? I KNOW YOU'VE GOT MORE IN YOU!
I DON'T! REALLY, I DON'T, I'M NOT THAT HIGH UP THE CHAIN--I--WAIT, THE ONLY OTHER THING--
HAWKGIRL. SHE'S A THREAT TO THINGS, I WAS TOLD TO BE ON GUARD FOR HER IF SHE SHOWED UP HERE.
PLEASE!--I'VE TOLD YOU EVERYTHING, LET ME G--
AS I THOUGHT.
KANTO THE "ASSASSIN OF APOKOLIPS"--HE'S NOT A GUY WHO FIGHTS ON BATTLEFIELDS.
DIFFERENCE BETWEEN THIS A
DHERAIN...

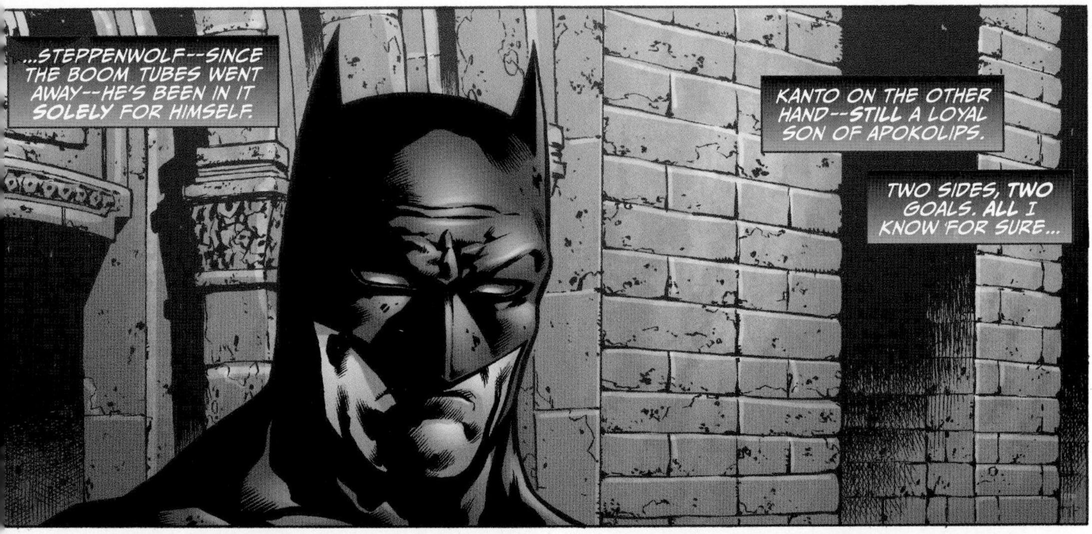
...STEPPENWOLF--SINCE THE BOOM TUBES WENT AWAY--HE'S BEEN IN IT SOLELY FOR HIMSELF.
KANTO ON THE OTHER HAND--STILL A LOYAL SON OF APOKOLIPS.
TWO SIDES, TWO GOALS. ALL I KNOW FOR SURE...
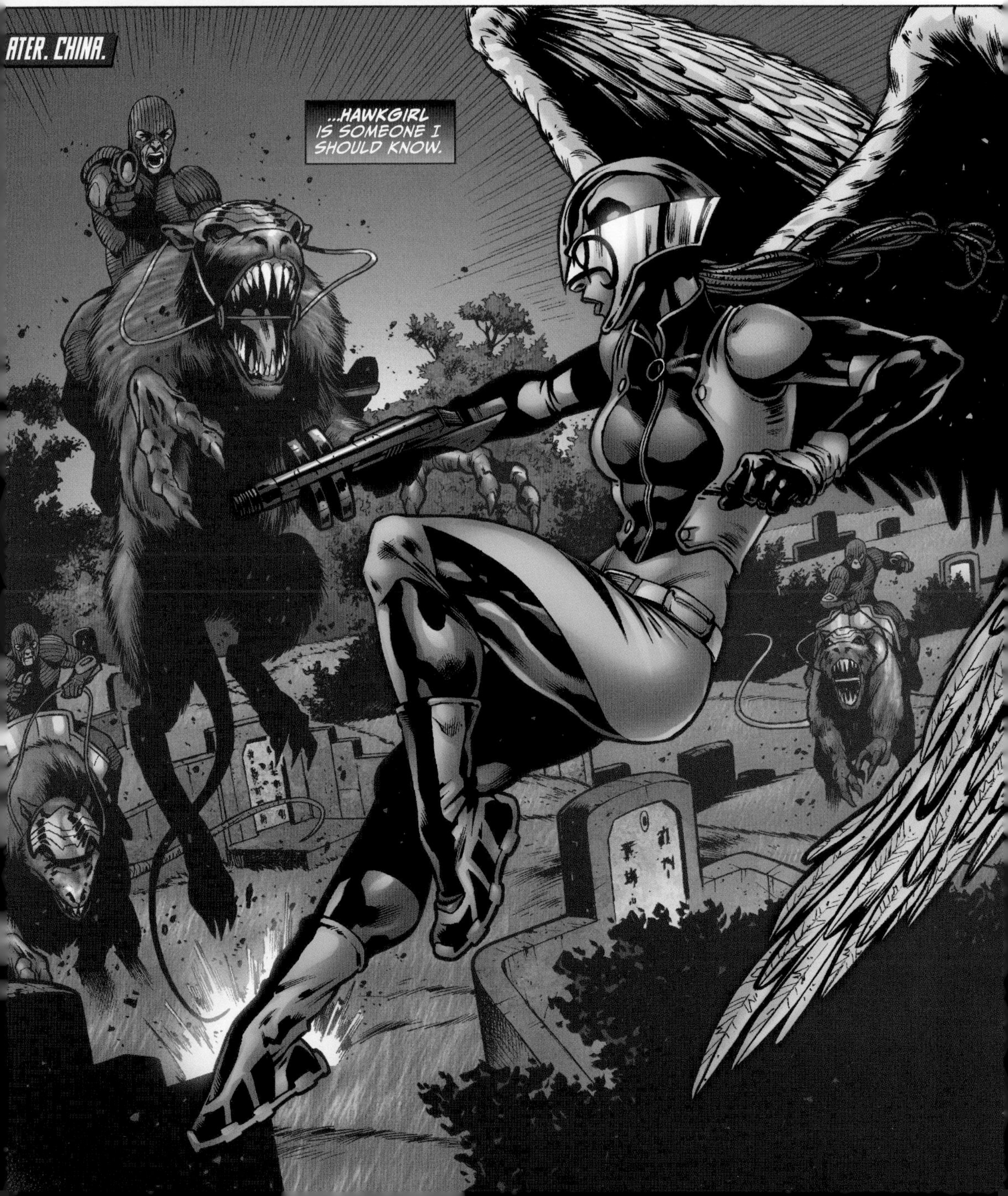
ATER. CHINA.
...HAWKGIRL IS SOMEONE I SHOULD KNOW.

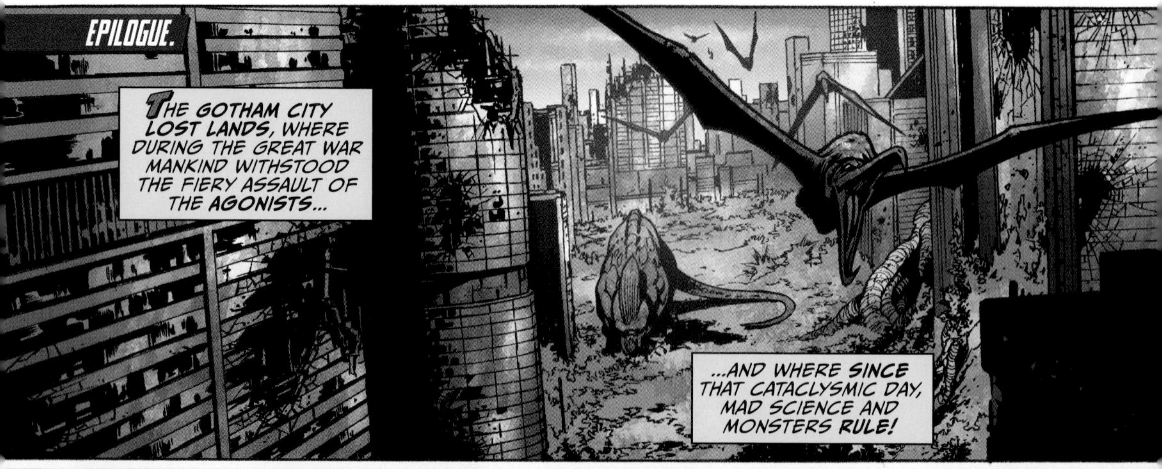
EPILOGUE.
THE GOTHAM CITY LOST LANDS, WHERE DURING THE GREAT WAR MANKIND WITHSTOOD THE FIERY ASSAULT OF THE AGONISTS...
...AND WHERE SINCE THAT CATACLYSMIC DAY, MAD SCIENCE AND MONSTERS RULE!

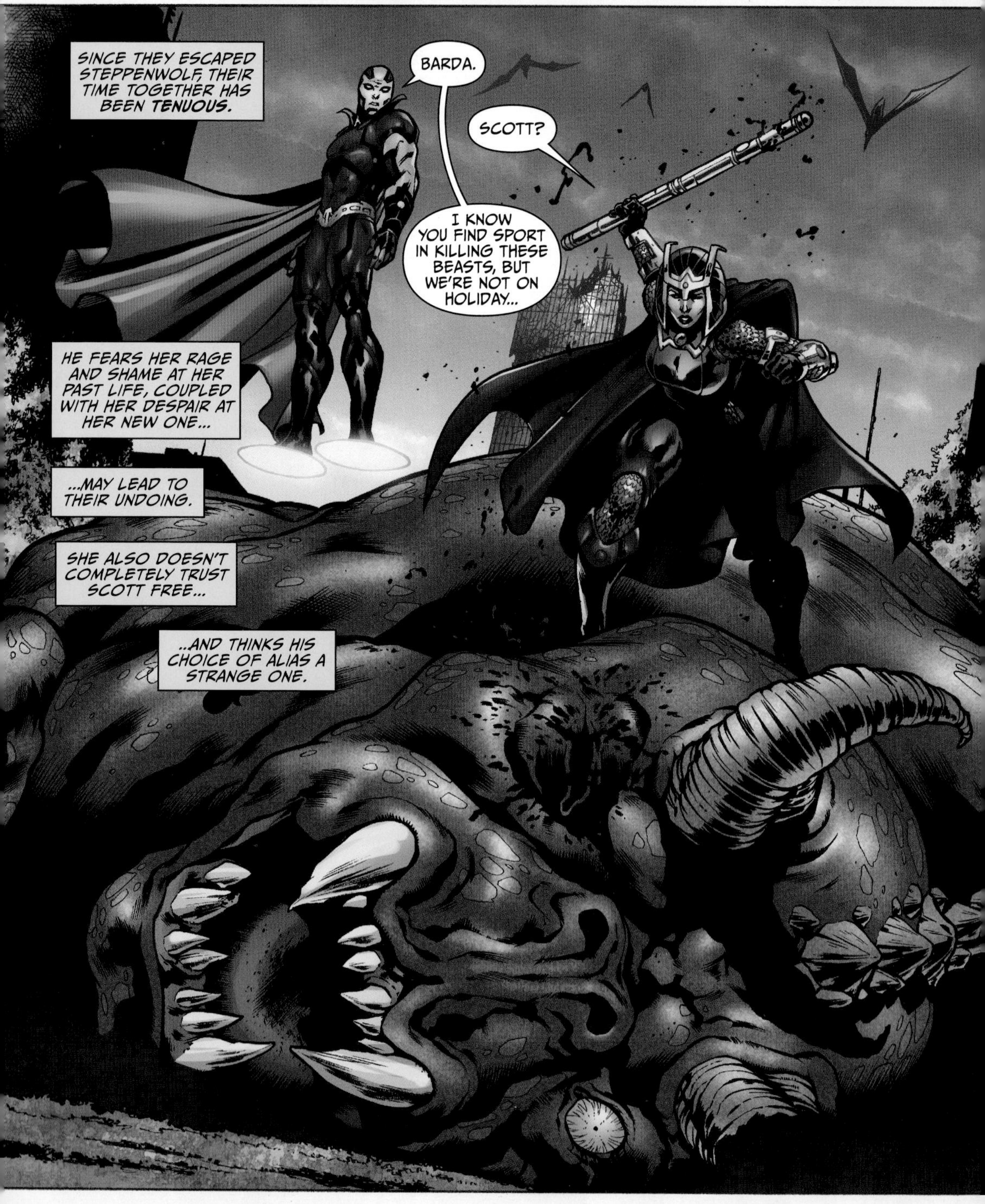
SINCE THEY ESCAPED STEPPENWOLF, THEIR TIME TOGETHER HAS BEEN TENUOUS.
BARDA.
SCOTT?
I KNOW YOU FIND SPORT IN KILLING THESE BEASTS, BUT WE'RE NOT ON HOLIDAY...
HE FEARS HER RAGE AND SHAME AT HER PAST LIFE, COUPLED WITH HER DESPAIR AT HER NEW ONE...
...MAY LEAD TO THEIR UNDOING.
SHE ALSO DOESN'T COMPLETELY TRUST SCOTT FREE...
...AND THINKS HIS CHOICE OF ALIAS A STRANGE ONE.

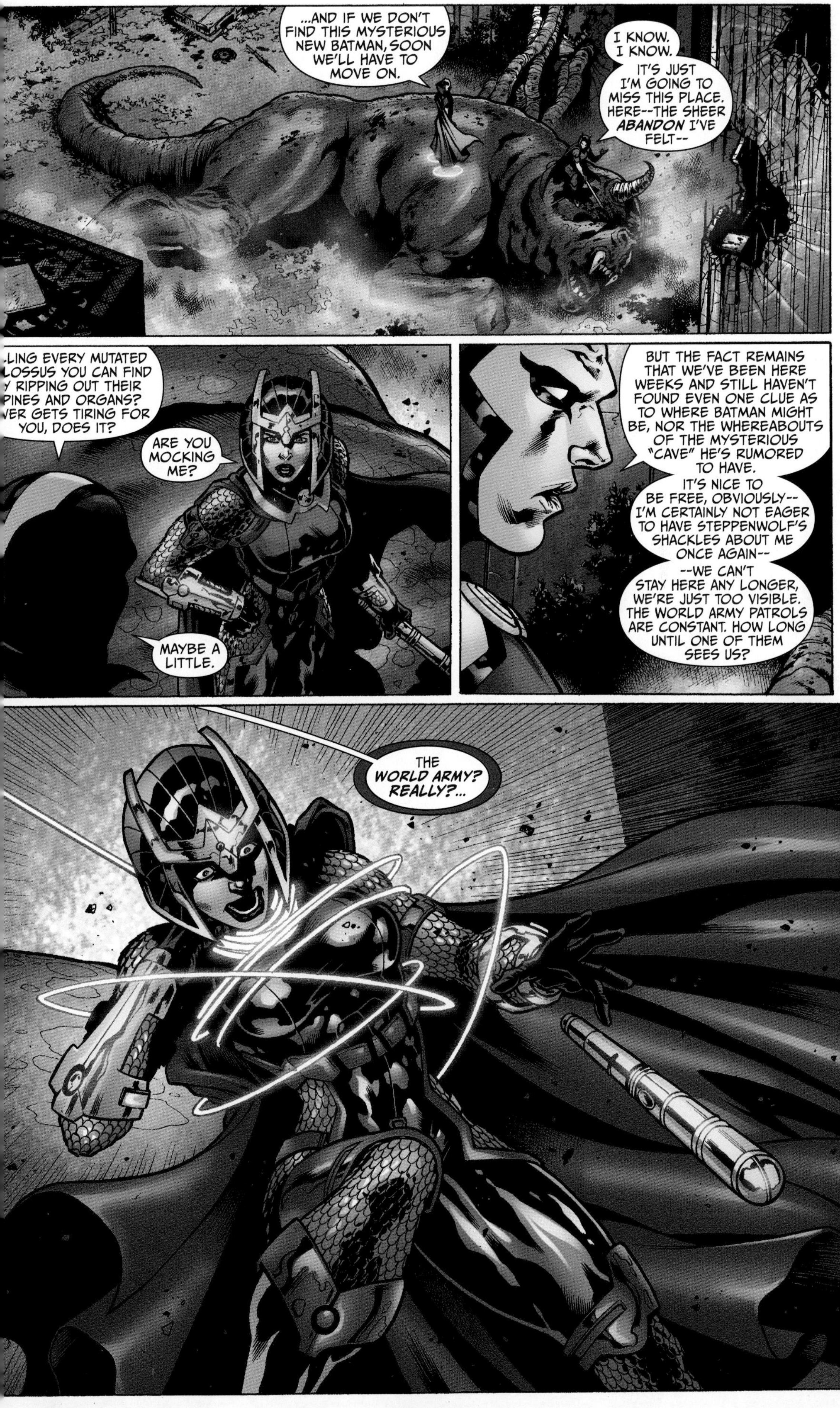
...AND IF WE DON'T FIND THIS MYSTERIOUS NEW BATMAN, SOON WE'LL HAVE TO MOVE ON.
I KNOW. I KNOW.
IT'S JUST I'M GOING TO MISS THIS PLACE. HERE--THE SHEER *ABANDON* I'VE FELT--
LLING EVERY MUTATED LOSSUS YOU CAN FIND Y RIPPING OUT THEIR PINES AND ORGANS? VER GETS TIRING FOR YOU, DOES IT?
ARE YOU MOCKING ME?
MAYBE A LITTLE.
BUT THE FACT REMAINS THAT WE'VE BEEN HERE WEEKS AND STILL HAVEN'T FOUND EVEN ONE CLUE AS TO WHERE BATMAN MIGHT BE, NOR THE WHEREABOUTS OF THE MYSTERIOUS "CAVE" HE'S RUMORED TO HAVE.
IT'S NICE TO BE FREE, OBVIOUSLY-- I'M CERTAINLY NOT EAGER TO HAVE STEPPENWOLF'S SHACKLES ABOUT ME ONCE AGAIN--
--WE CAN'T STAY HERE ANY LONGER, WE'RE JUST TOO VISIBLE. THE WORLD ARMY PATROLS ARE CONSTANT. HOW LONG UNTIL ONE OF THEM SEES US?
THE *WORLD ARMY? REALLY?...*

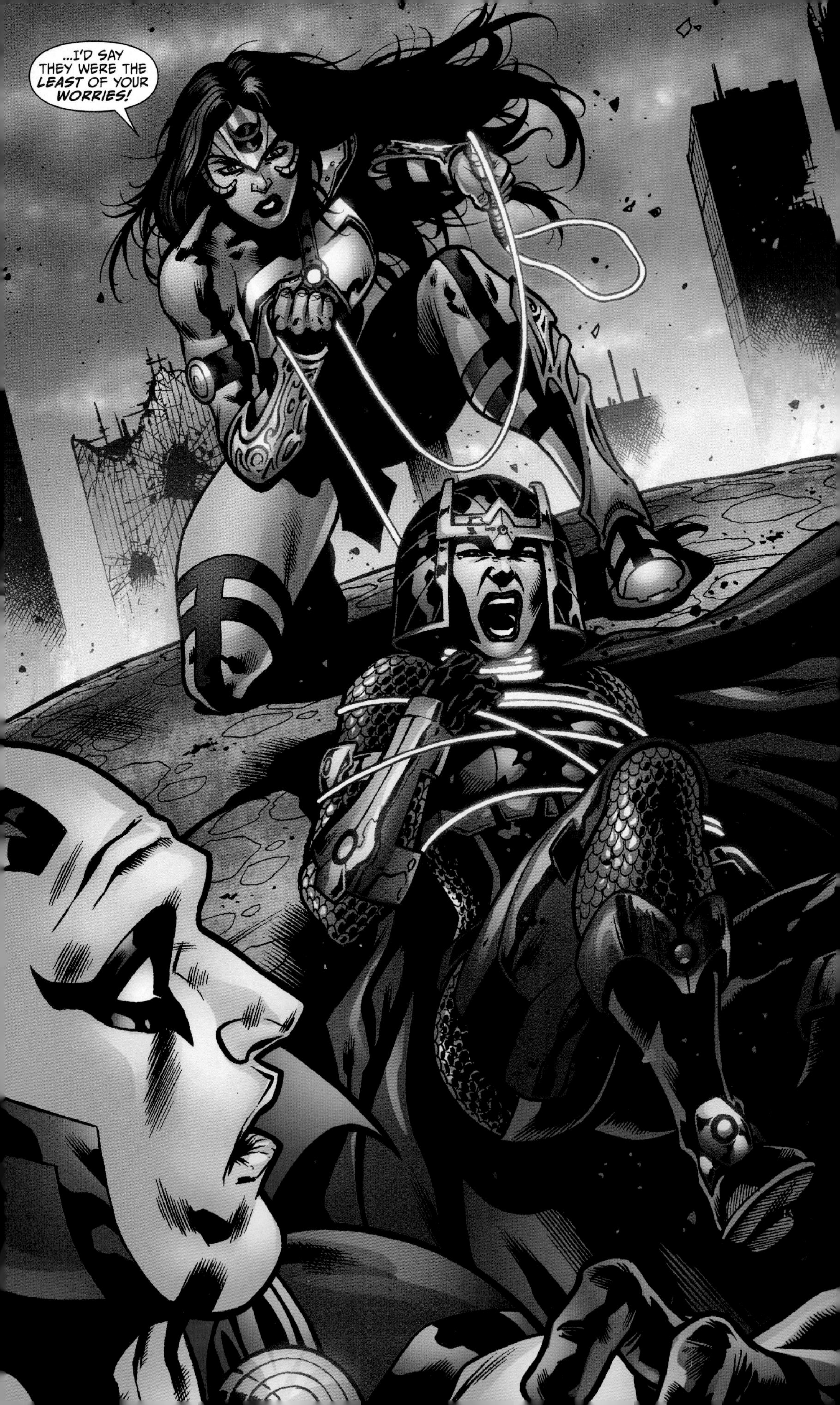
...I'D SAY THEY WERE THE LEAST OF YOUR WORRIES!

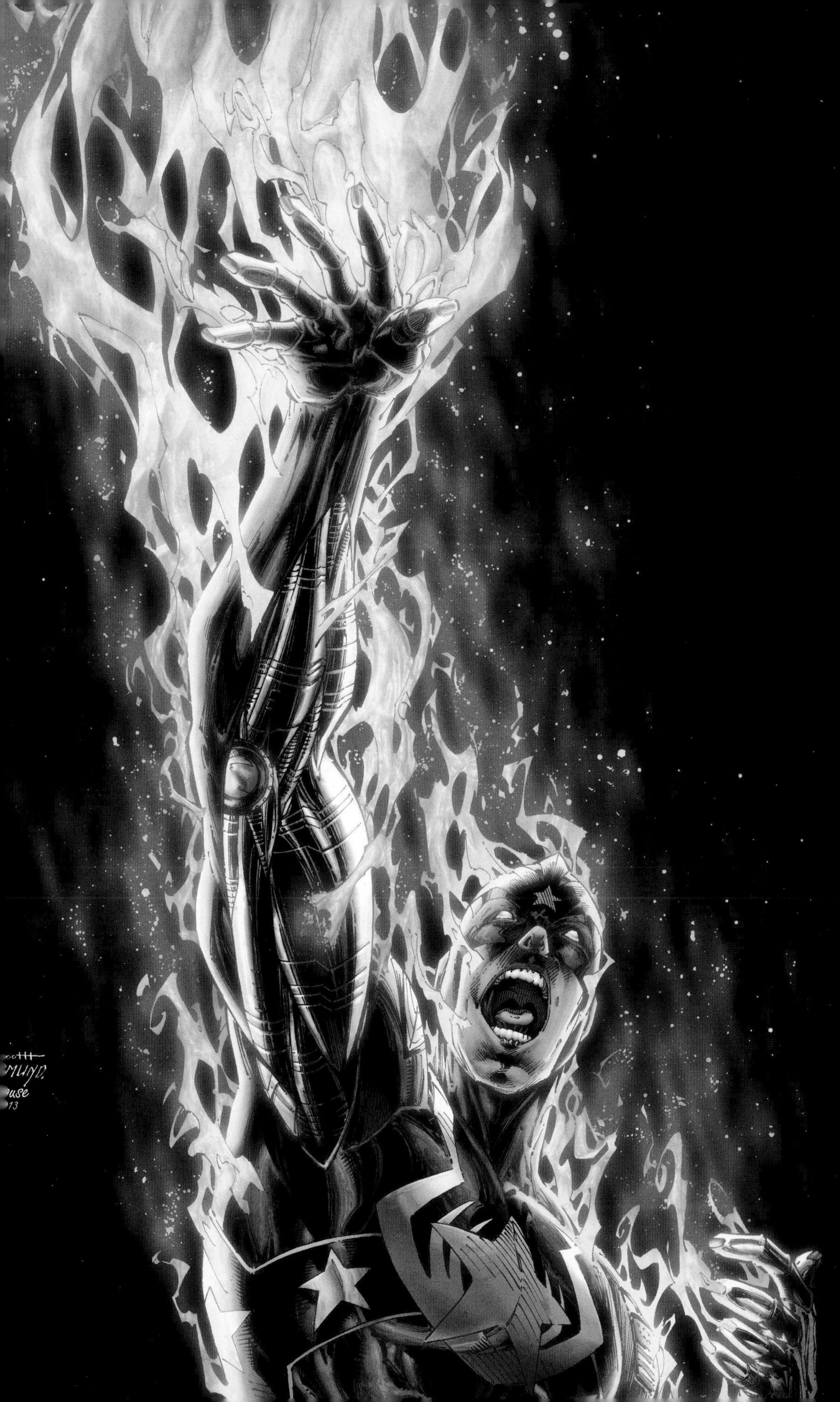

JAMES ROBINSON
writer

YILDIRAY CINAR
penciller

ROB HUNTER
inker

PETE PANTAZIS
colorist

BRETT BOOTH, NORM RAPMUND
& ANDREW DALHOUSE
cover artists

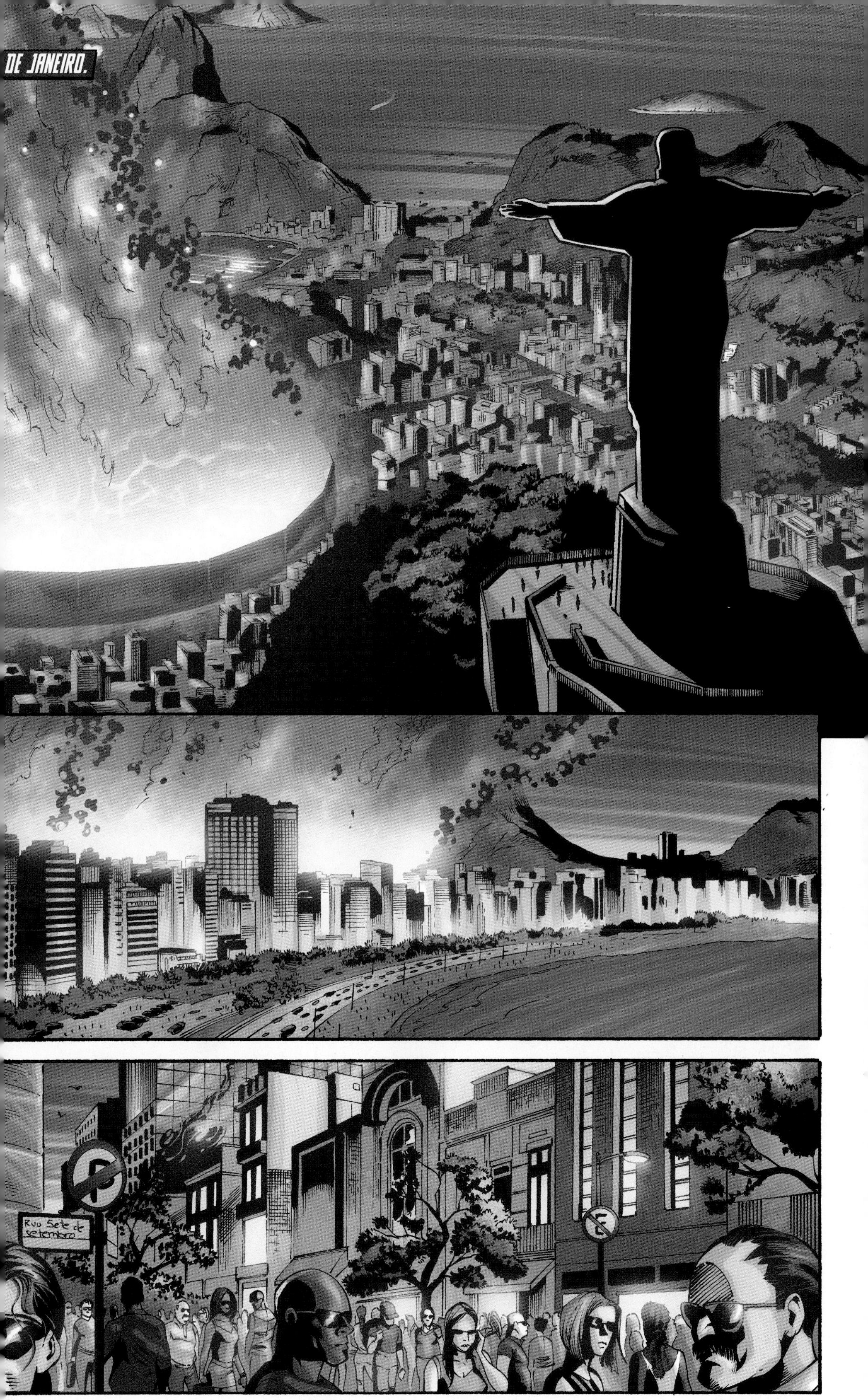
DE JANEIRO.
Ruo Sete de setembro

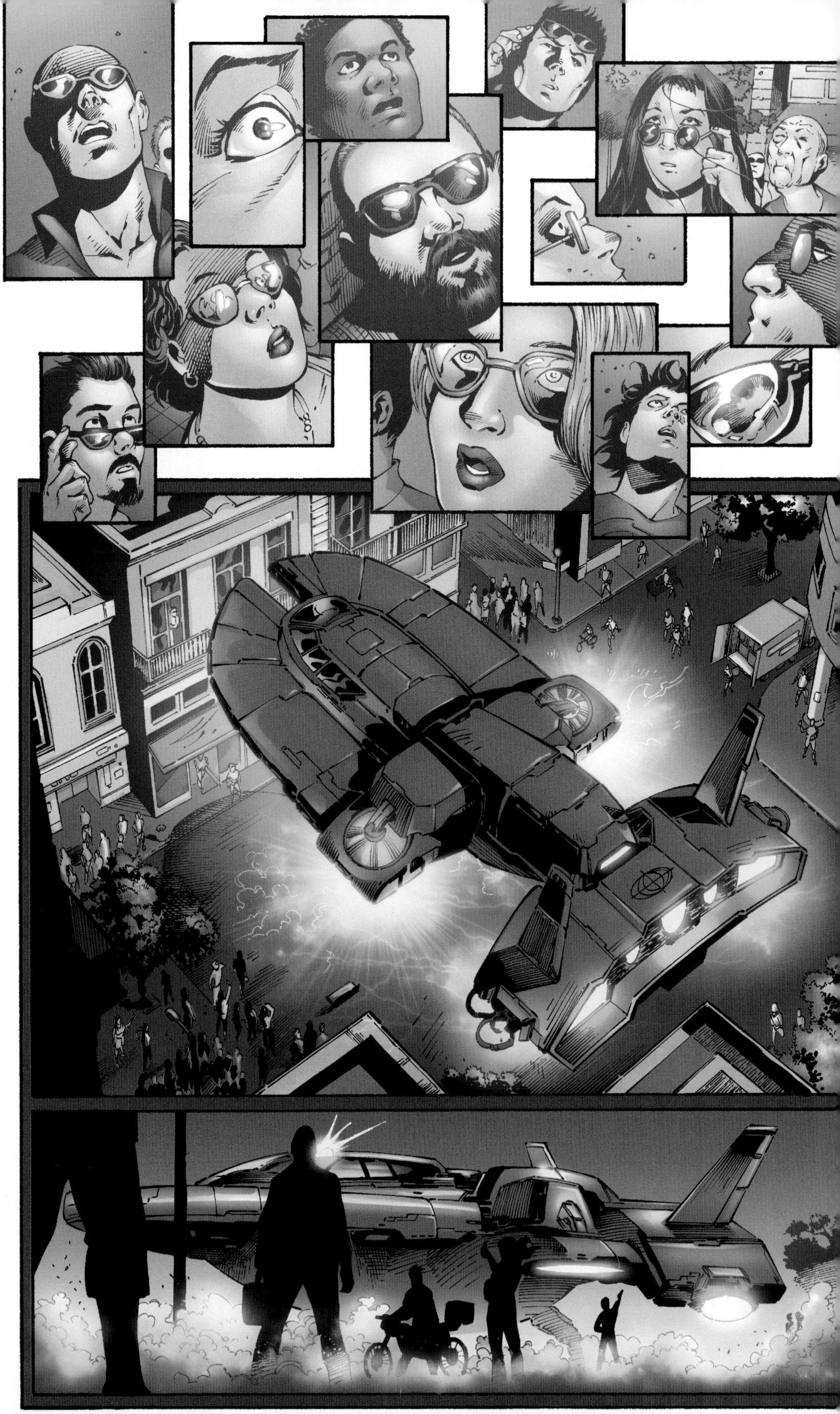

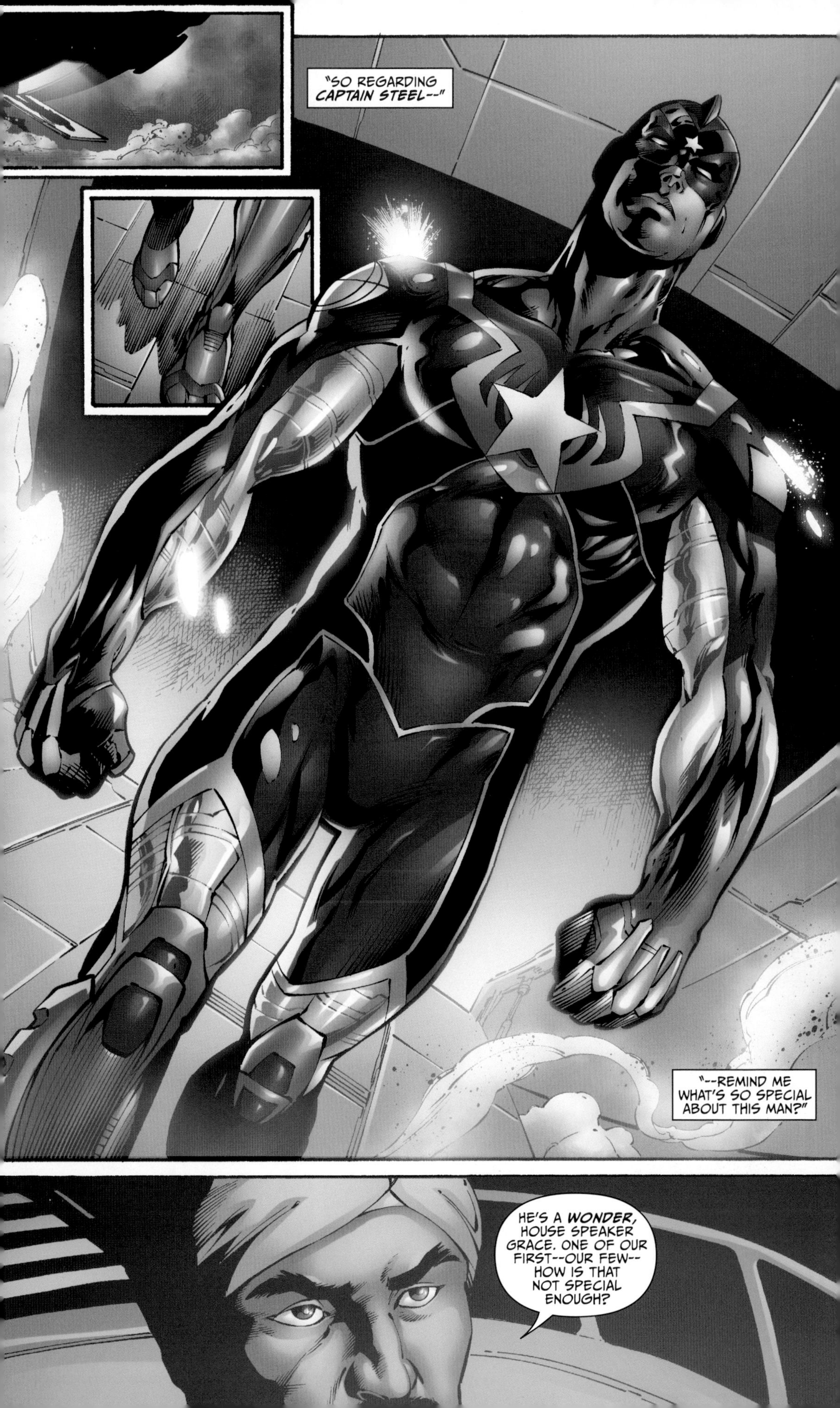
"SO REGARDING *CAPTAIN STEEL*--"
"--REMIND ME WHAT'S SO SPECIAL ABOUT THIS MAN?"
HE'S A ***WONDER***, HOUSE SPEAKER GRACE. ONE OF OUR FIRST--OUR FEW--HOW IS THAT NOT SPECIAL ENOUGH?

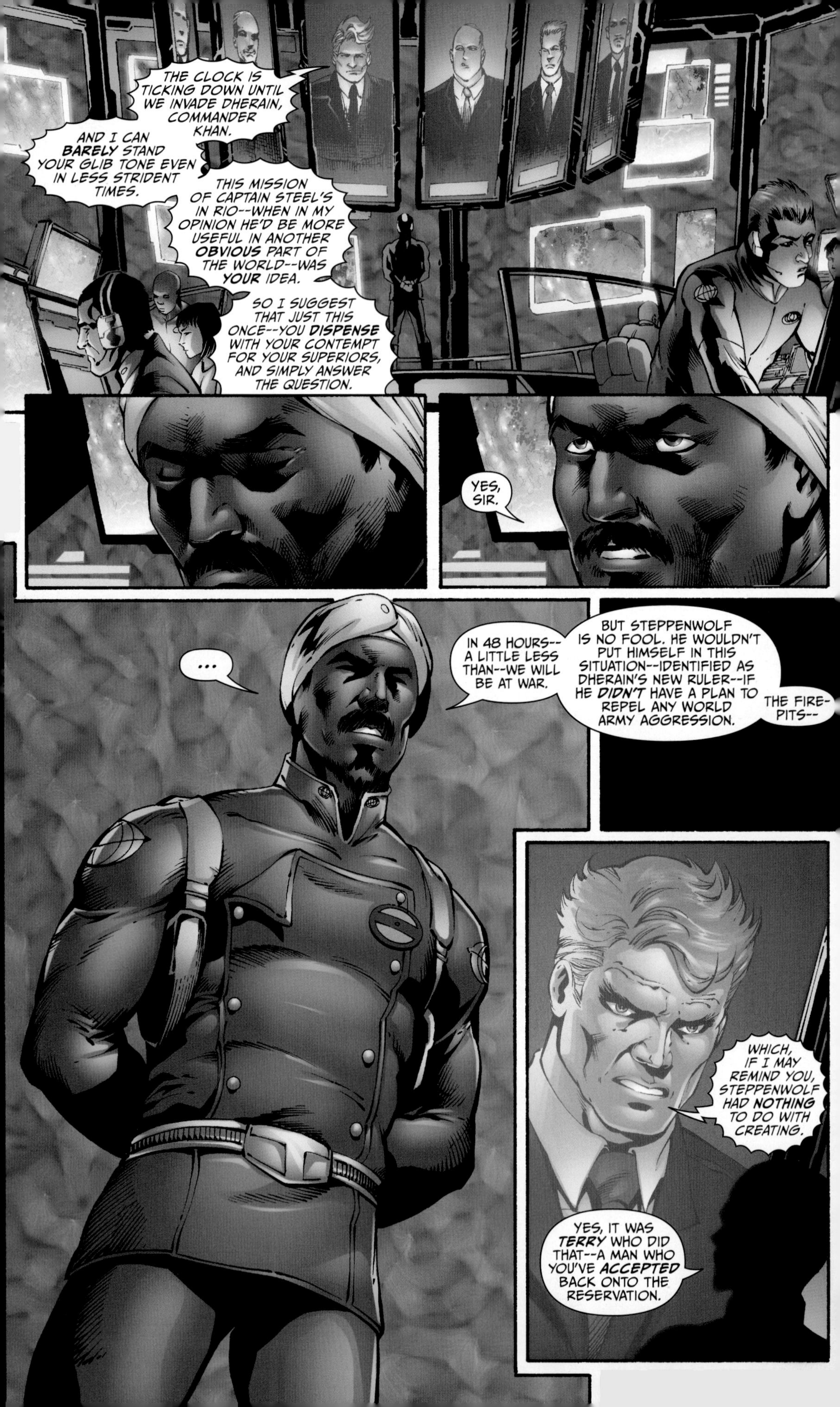
THE CLOCK IS TICKING DOWN UNTIL WE INVADE DHERAIN, COMMANDER KHAN.
AND I CAN BARELY STAND YOUR GLIB TONE EVEN IN LESS STRIDENT TIMES.
THIS MISSION OF CAPTAIN STEEL'S IN RIO--WHEN IN MY OPINION HE'D BE MORE USEFUL IN ANOTHER OBVIOUS PART OF THE WORLD--WAS YOUR IDEA.
SO I SUGGEST THAT JUST THIS ONCE--YOU DISPENSE WITH YOUR CONTEMPT FOR YOUR SUPERIORS, AND SIMPLY ANSWER THE QUESTION.
YES, SIR.
...
IN 48 HOURS-- A LITTLE LESS THAN--WE WILL BE AT WAR.
BUT STEPPENWOLF IS NO FOOL. HE WOULDN'T PUT HIMSELF IN THIS SITUATION--IDENTIFIED AS DHERAIN'S NEW RULER--IF HE DIDN'T HAVE A PLAN TO REPEL ANY WORLD ARMY AGGRESSION.
THE FIRE-PITS--
WHICH, IF I MAY REMIND YOU, STEPPENWOLF HAD NOTHING TO DO WITH CREATING.
YES, IT WAS TERRY WHO DID THAT--A MAN WHO YOU'VE ACCEPTED BACK ONTO THE RESERVATION.

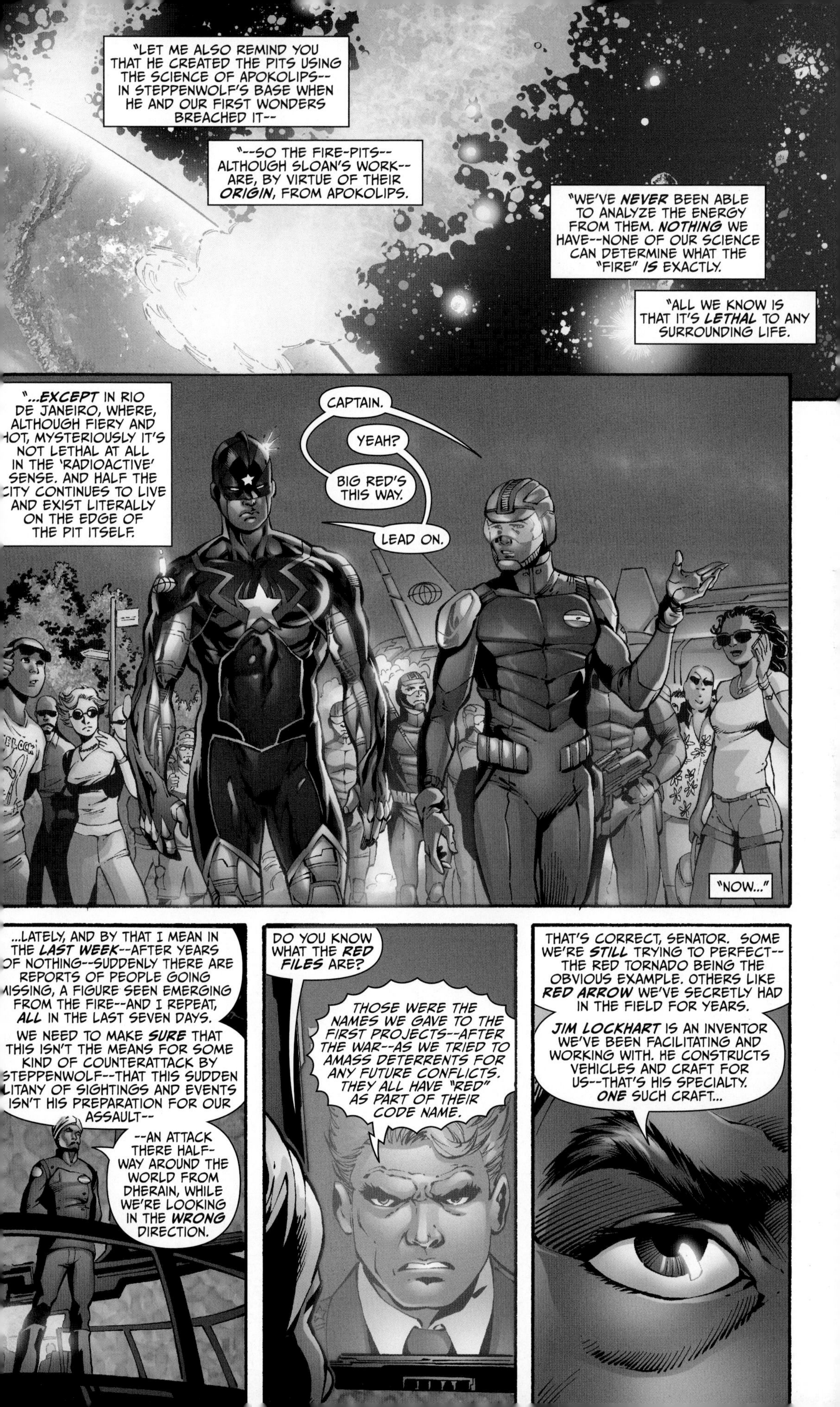
"LET ME ALSO REMIND YOU THAT HE CREATED THE PITS USING THE SCIENCE OF APOKOLIPS-- IN STEPPENWOLF'S BASE WHEN HE AND OUR FIRST WONDERS BREACHED IT--
"--SO THE FIRE-PITS-- ALTHOUGH SLOAN'S WORK-- ARE, BY VIRTUE OF THEIR ORIGIN, FROM APOKOLIPS.
"WE'VE NEVER BEEN ABLE TO ANALYZE THE ENERGY FROM THEM. NOTHING WE HAVE--NONE OF OUR SCIENCE CAN DETERMINE WHAT THE "FIRE" IS EXACTLY.
"ALL WE KNOW IS THAT IT'S LETHAL TO ANY SURROUNDING LIFE.
"...EXCEPT IN RIO DE JANEIRO, WHERE, ALTHOUGH FIERY AND HOT, MYSTERIOUSLY IT'S NOT LETHAL AT ALL IN THE 'RADIOACTIVE' SENSE. AND HALF THE CITY CONTINUES TO LIVE AND EXIST LITERALLY ON THE EDGE OF THE PIT ITSELF.
CAPTAIN.
YEAH?
BIG RED'S THIS WAY.
LEAD ON.
"NOW..."
...LATELY, AND BY THAT I MEAN IN THE LAST WEEK--AFTER YEARS OF NOTHING--SUDDENLY THERE ARE REPORTS OF PEOPLE GOING MISSING, A FIGURE SEEN EMERGING FROM THE FIRE--AND I REPEAT, ALL IN THE LAST SEVEN DAYS.
WE NEED TO MAKE SURE THAT THIS ISN'T THE MEANS FOR SOME KIND OF COUNTERATTACK BY STEPPENWOLF--THAT THIS SUDDEN LITANY OF SIGHTINGS AND EVENTS ISN'T HIS PREPARATION FOR OUR ASSAULT--
--AN ATTACK THERE HALF-WAY AROUND THE WORLD FROM DHERAIN, WHILE WE'RE LOOKING IN THE WRONG DIRECTION.
DO YOU KNOW WHAT THE RED FILES ARE?
THOSE WERE THE NAMES WE GAVE TO THE FIRST PROJECTS--AFTER THE WAR--AS WE TRIED TO AMASS DETERRENTS FOR ANY FUTURE CONFLICTS. THEY ALL HAVE "RED" AS PART OF THEIR CODE NAME.
THAT'S CORRECT, SENATOR. SOME WE'RE STILL TRYING TO PERFECT-- THE RED TORNADO BEING THE OBVIOUS EXAMPLE. OTHERS LIKE RED ARROW WE'VE SECRETLY HAD IN THE FIELD FOR YEARS.
JIM LOCKHART IS AN INVENTOR WE'VE BEEN FACILITATING AND WORKING WITH. HE CONSTRUCTS VEHICLES AND CRAFT FOR US--THAT'S HIS SPECIALTY. ONE SUCH CRAFT...

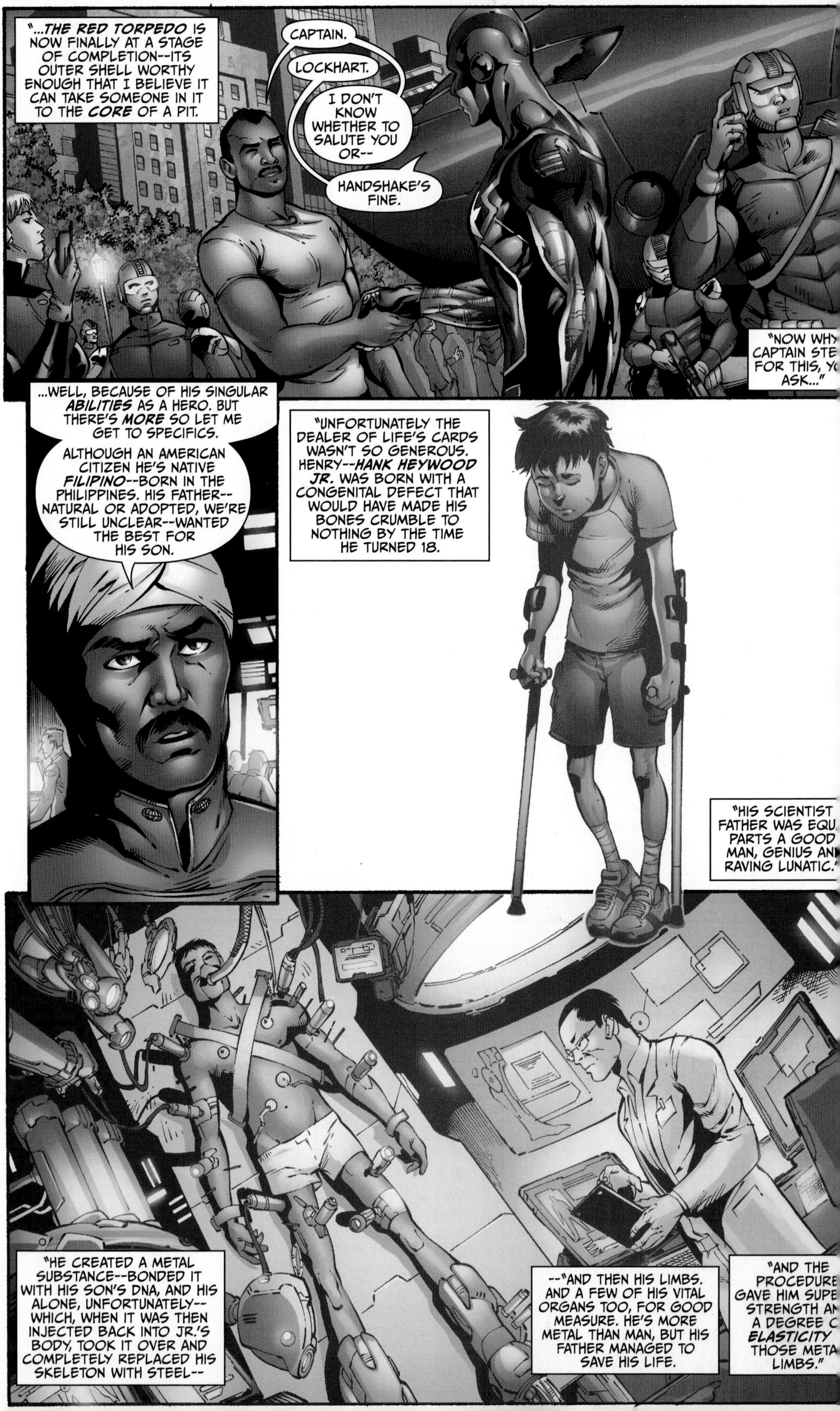

"...THE RED TORPEDO IS NOW FINALLY AT A STAGE OF COMPLETION--ITS OUTER SHELL WORTHY ENOUGH THAT I BELIEVE IT CAN TAKE SOMEONE IN IT TO THE CORE OF A PIT.
CAPTAIN.
LOCKHART.
I DON'T KNOW WHETHER TO SALUTE YOU OR--
HANDSHAKE'S FINE.
"NOW WHY CAPTAIN STE FOR THIS, YO ASK..."
...WELL, BECAUSE OF HIS SINGULAR ABILITIES AS A HERO. BUT THERE'S MORE SO LET ME GET TO SPECIFICS.
ALTHOUGH AN AMERICAN CITIZEN HE'S NATIVE FILIPINO--BORN IN THE PHILIPPINES. HIS FATHER--NATURAL OR ADOPTED, WE'RE STILL UNCLEAR--WANTED THE BEST FOR HIS SON.
"UNFORTUNATELY THE DEALER OF LIFE'S CARDS WASN'T SO GENEROUS. HENRY--HANK HEYWOOD JR. WAS BORN WITH A CONGENITAL DEFECT THAT WOULD HAVE MADE HIS BONES CRUMBLE TO NOTHING BY THE TIME HE TURNED 18.
"HIS SCIENTIST FATHER WAS EQU PARTS A GOOD MAN, GENIUS AN RAVING LUNATIC."
"HE CREATED A METAL SUBSTANCE--BONDED IT WITH HIS SON'S DNA, AND HIS ALONE, UNFORTUNATELY--WHICH, WHEN IT WAS THEN INJECTED BACK INTO JR.'S BODY, TOOK IT OVER AND COMPLETELY REPLACED HIS SKELETON WITH STEEL--
--"AND THEN HIS LIMBS. AND A FEW OF HIS VITAL ORGANS TOO, FOR GOOD MEASURE. HE'S MORE METAL THAN MAN, BUT HIS FATHER MANAGED TO SAVE HIS LIFE.
"AND THE PROCEDURE GAVE HIM SUPE STRENGTH AN A DEGREE O ELASTICITY THOSE META LIMBS."

"HEYWOOD WAS IN CONTACT WITH US, 'BOUT TO TURN OVER HIS WORK TO OUR SCIENTISTS--WE *COULD* HAVE HAD AN *ARMY* OF CAPTAIN STEELS--

"--WHEN APOKOLIPS'S FORCES DISCOVERED HIS WORK--THIS WAS RIGHT IN THE MIDDLE OF THE WAR, REMEMBER-- AND THEY ATTACKED."

"HEYWOOD'S SON REPELLED OR KILLED HALF OF THEM THAT DAY, BUT COULDN'T SAVE HIS FATHER...

"...WHO KILLED HIMSELF AND DESTROYED HIS RESEARCH--RIGHT BEFORE STEPPENWOLF'S MONSTERS COULD GET IT.

"JR. ESCAPED, CAME TO US... AND FROM OUT OF NOWHERE THE WORLD ARMY HAD ITS *FIRST* NEW WONDER."

SO, TO ANSWER YOUR QUESTION, FINALLY--AND THANK YOU FOR YOUR PATIENCE, GENTLEMEN... THE REASON I'M SENDING CAPTAIN STEEL TO RIO AND NOT THE ATOM OR--OR--WELL, I CAN ONLY THINK OF THE ATOM AS A *POSSIBLE* REPLACEMENT FOR THIS--

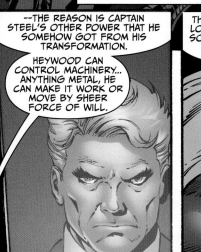

--THE REASON IS CAPTAIN STEEL'S OTHER POWER THAT HE SOMEHOW GOT FROM HIS TRANSFORMATION.

HEYWOOD CAN CONTROL MACHINERY... ANYTHING METAL, HE CAN MAKE IT WORK OR MOVE BY SHEER FORCE OF WILL.

THAT GIVES US INSURANCE...IF LOCKHART'S RED TORPEDO IS SOMEHOW COMPROMISED OR CORRUPTED BY THE PIT'S ENERGY...

...HEYWOOD HAS THE POWER TO KEEP THE CRAFT IN MOTION...

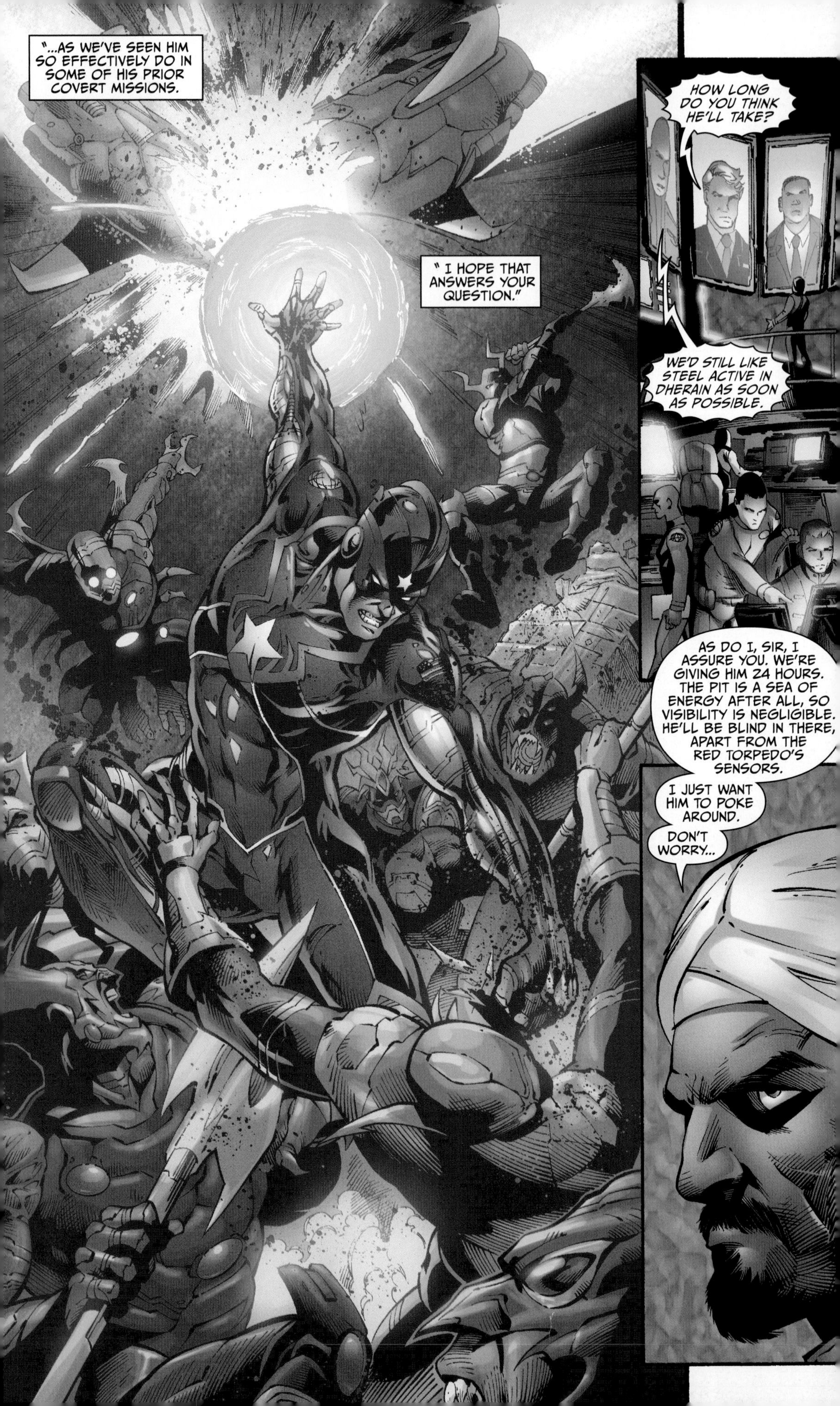
"...AS WE'VE SEEN HIM SO EFFECTIVELY DO IN SOME OF HIS PRIOR COVERT MISSIONS.
" I HOPE THAT ANSWERS YOUR QUESTION."
HOW LONG DO YOU THINK HE'LL TAKE?
WE'D STILL LIKE STEEL ACTIVE IN DHERAIN AS SOON AS POSSIBLE.
AS DO I, SIR, I ASSURE YOU. WE'RE GIVING HIM 24 HOURS. THE PIT IS A SEA OF ENERGY AFTER ALL, SO VISIBILITY IS NEGLIGIBLE. HE'LL BE BLIND IN THERE, APART FROM THE RED TORPEDO'S SENSORS.
I JUST WANT HIM TO POKE AROUND.
DON'T WORRY...

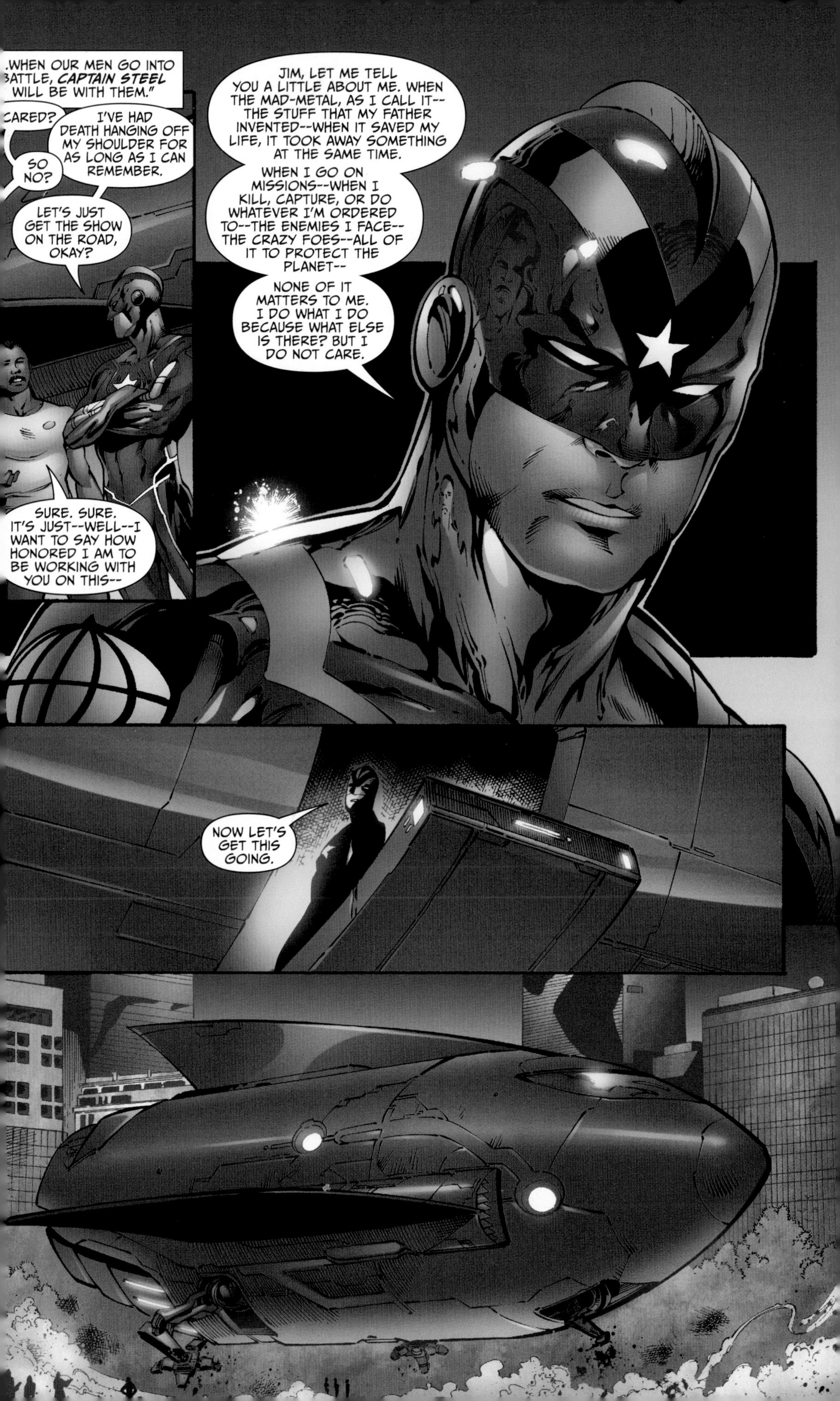

..WHEN OUR MEN GO INTO BATTLE, CAPTAIN STEEL WILL BE WITH THEM."
..CARED?
I'VE HAD DEATH HANGING OFF MY SHOULDER FOR AS LONG AS I CAN REMEMBER.
SO NO?
LET'S JUST GET THE SHOW ON THE ROAD, OKAY?
SURE. SURE. IT'S JUST--WELL--I WANT TO SAY HOW HONORED I AM TO BE WORKING WITH YOU ON THIS--
JIM, LET ME TELL YOU A LITTLE ABOUT ME. WHEN THE MAD-METAL, AS I CALL IT--THE STUFF THAT MY FATHER INVENTED--WHEN IT SAVED MY LIFE, IT TOOK AWAY SOMETHING AT THE SAME TIME.
WHEN I GO ON MISSIONS--WHEN I KILL, CAPTURE, OR DO WHATEVER I'M ORDERED TO--THE ENEMIES I FACE--THE CRAZY FOES--ALL OF IT TO PROTECT THE PLANET--
NONE OF IT MATTERS TO ME. I DO WHAT I DO BECAUSE WHAT ELSE IS THERE? BUT I DO NOT CARE.
NOW LET'S GET THIS GOING.

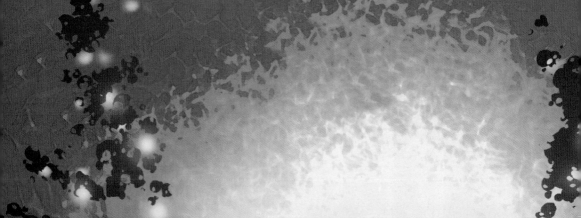

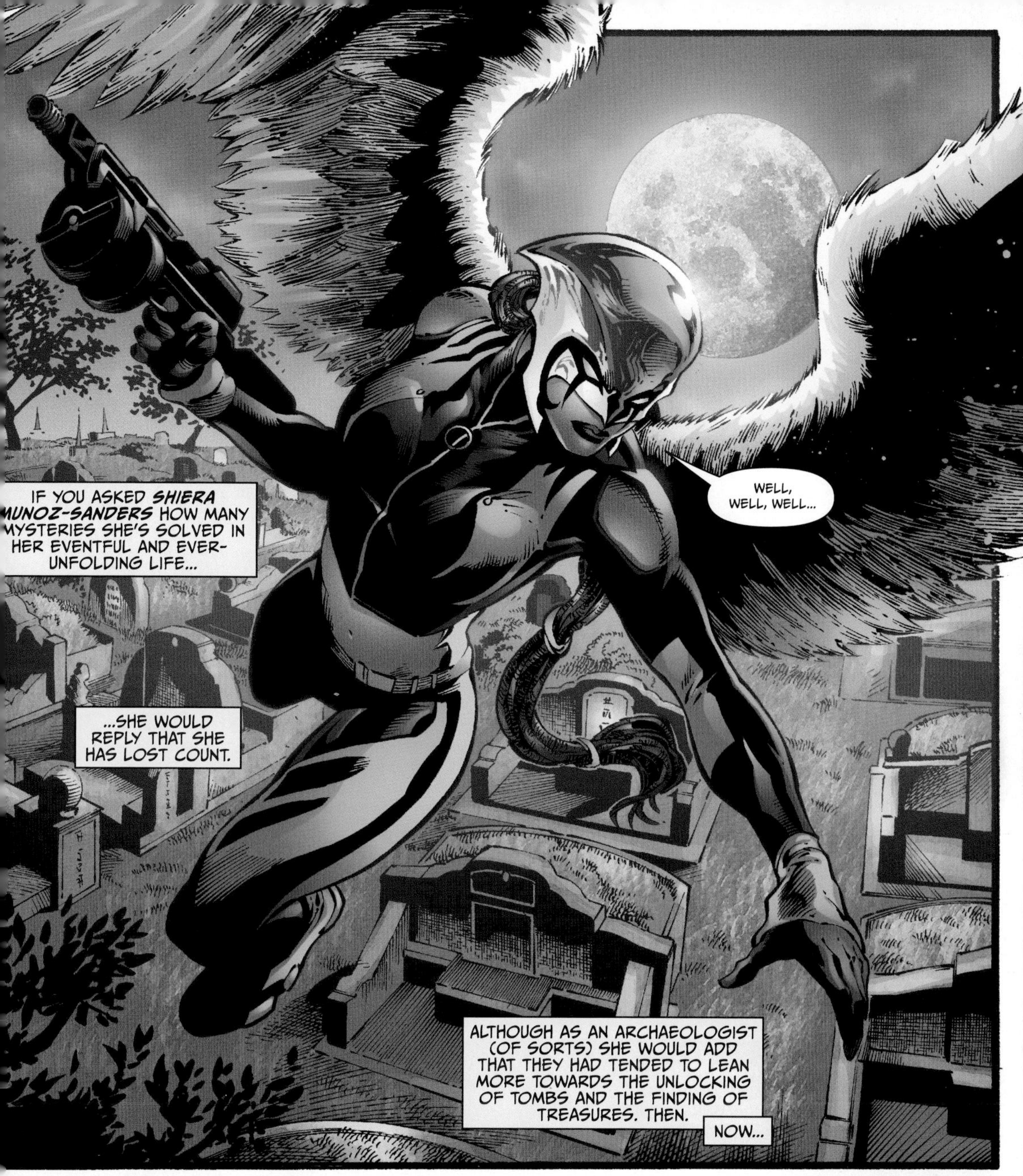
IF YOU ASKED SHIERA MUNOZ-SANDERS HOW MANY MYSTERIES SHE'S SOLVED IN HER EVENTFUL AND EVER-UNFOLDING LIFE...
WELL, WELL, WELL...
...SHE WOULD REPLY THAT SHE HAS LOST COUNT.
ALTHOUGH AS AN ARCHAEOLOGIST (OF SORTS) SHE WOULD ADD THAT THEY HAD TENDED TO LEAN MORE TOWARDS THE UNLOCKING OF TOMBS AND THE FINDING OF TREASURES. THEN.
NOW...

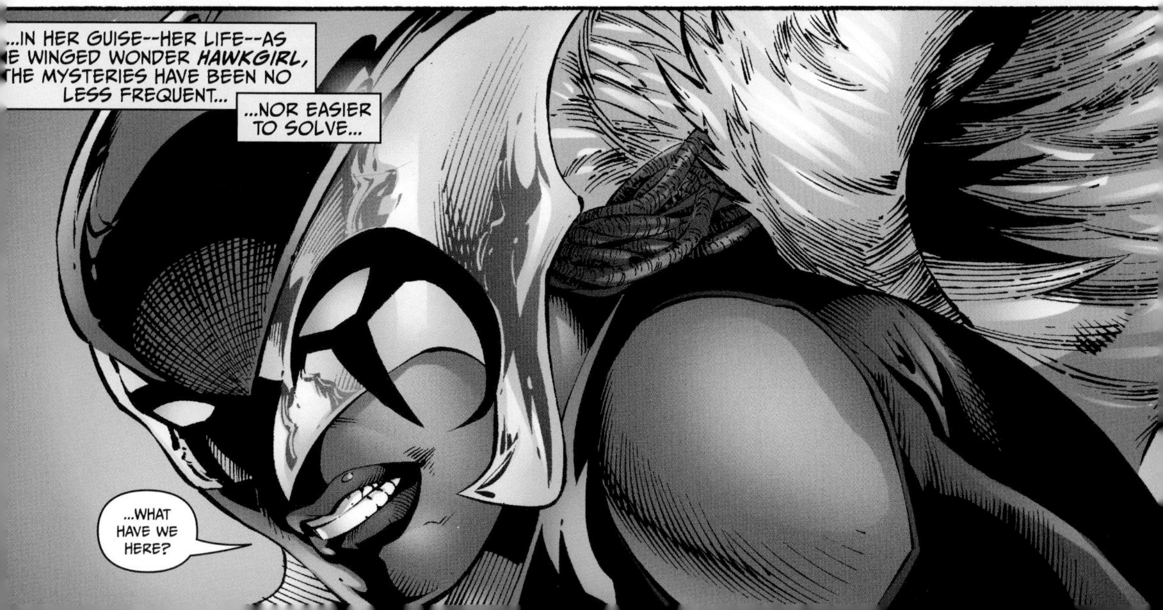
...IN HER GUISE--HER LIFE--AS E WINGED WONDER HAWKGIRL, THE MYSTERIES HAVE BEEN NO LESS FREQUENT...
...NOR EASIER TO SOLVE...
...WHAT HAVE WE HERE?

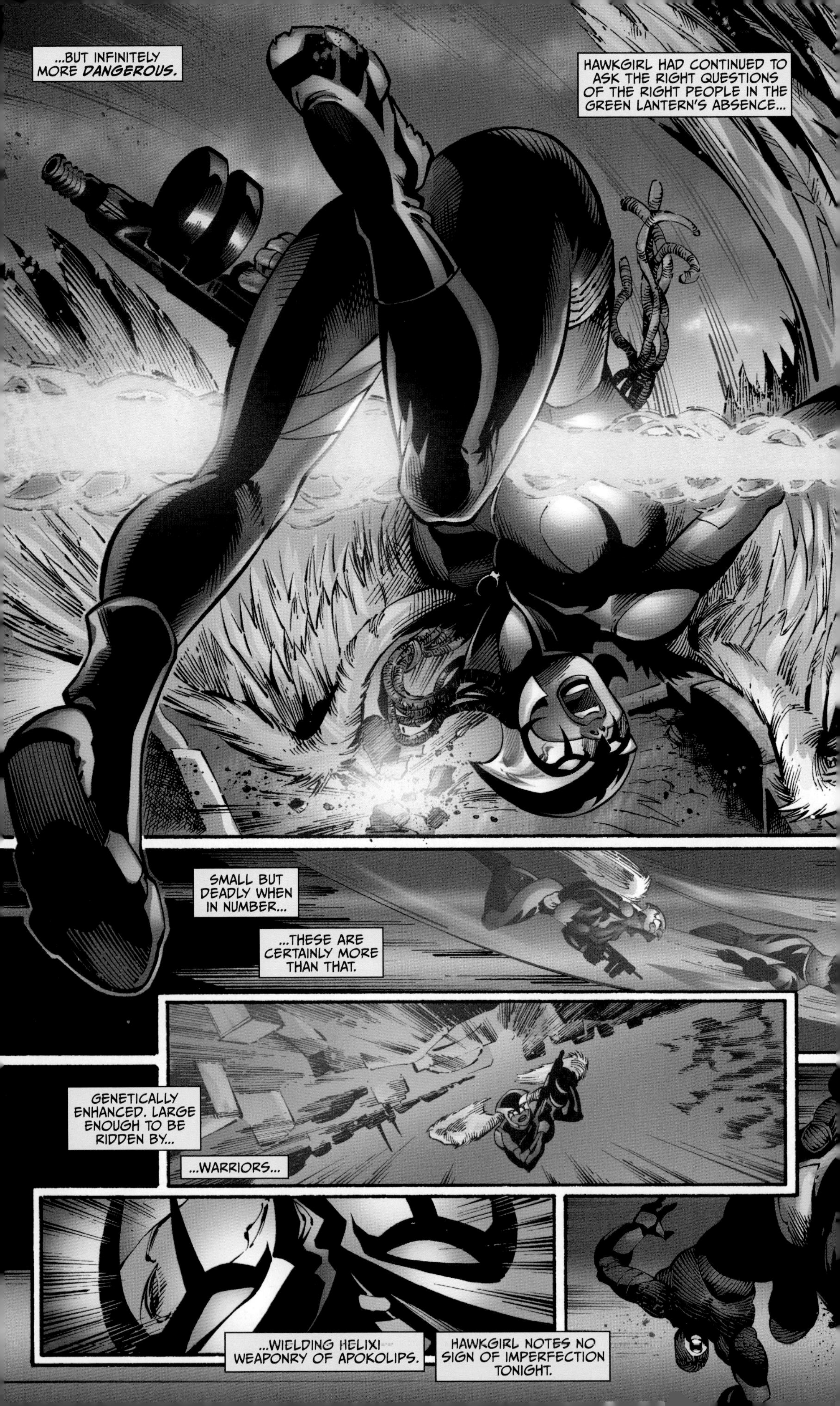
...BUT INFINITELY MORE **DANGEROUS.**
HAWKGIRL HAD CONTINUED TO ASK THE RIGHT QUESTIONS OF THE RIGHT PEOPLE IN THE GREEN LANTERN'S ABSENCE...
SMALL BUT DEADLY WHEN IN NUMBER...
...THESE ARE CERTAINLY MORE THAN THAT.
GENETICALLY ENHANCED. LARGE ENOUGH TO BE RIDDEN BY...
...WARRIORS...
...WIELDING HELIXI WEAPONRY OF APOKOLIPS.
HAWKGIRL NOTES NO SIGN OF IMPERFECTION TONIGHT.

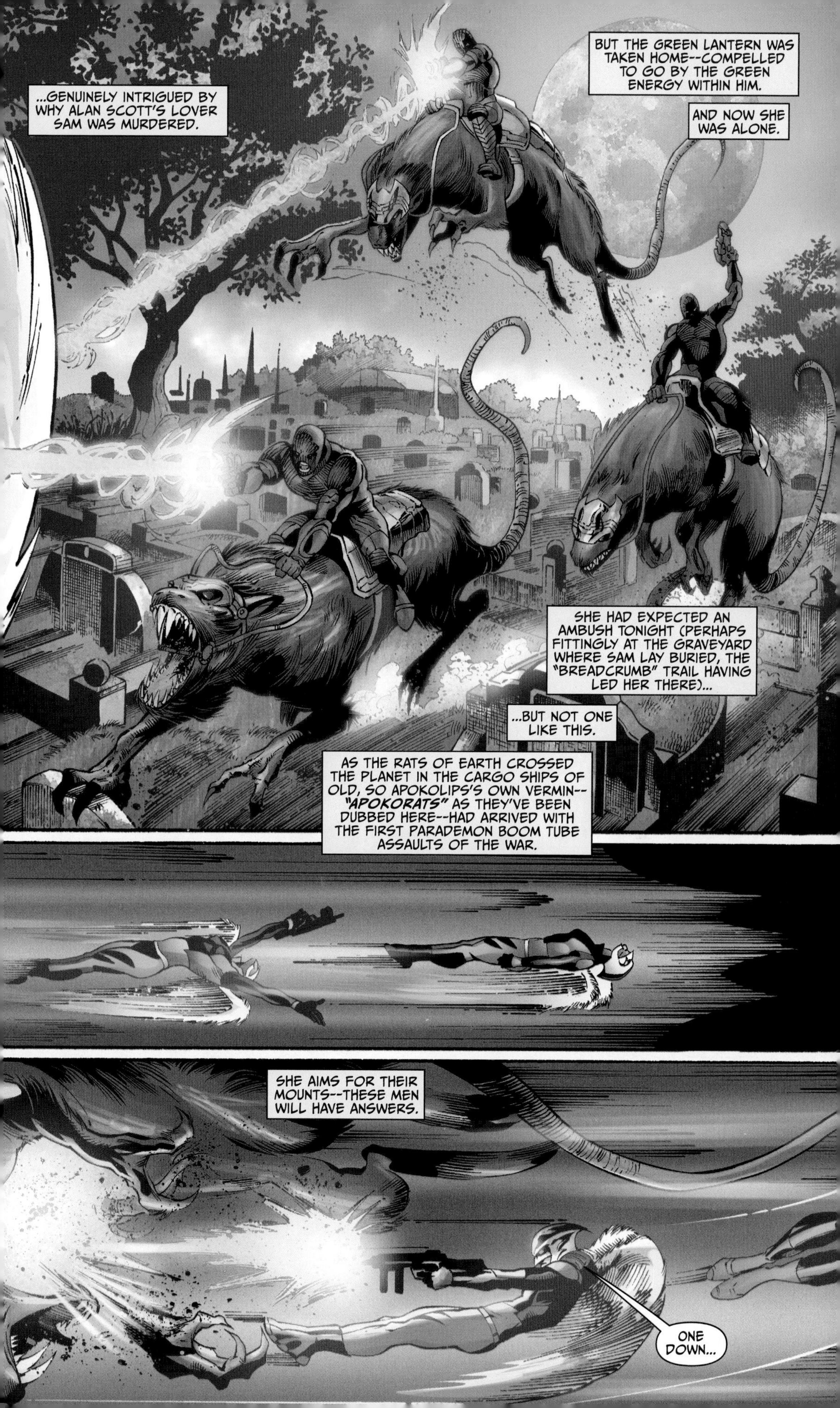
...GENUINELY INTRIGUED BY WHY ALAN SCOTT'S LOVER SAM WAS MURDERED.
BUT THE GREEN LANTERN WAS TAKEN HOME--COMPELLED TO GO BY THE GREEN ENERGY WITHIN HIM.
AND NOW SHE WAS ALONE.
SHE HAD EXPECTED AN AMBUSH TONIGHT (PERHAPS FITTINGLY AT THE GRAVEYARD WHERE SAM LAY BURIED, THE "BREADCRUMB" TRAIL HAVING LED HER THERE)...
...BUT NOT ONE LIKE THIS.
AS THE RATS OF EARTH CROSSED THE PLANET IN THE CARGO SHIPS OF OLD, SO APOKOLIPS'S OWN VERMIN-- *"APOKORATS"* AS THEY'VE BEEN DUBBED HERE--HAD ARRIVED WITH THE FIRST PARADEMON BOOM TUBE ASSAULTS OF THE WAR.
SHE AIMS FOR THEIR MOUNTS--THESE MEN WILL HAVE ANSWERS.
ONE DOWN...

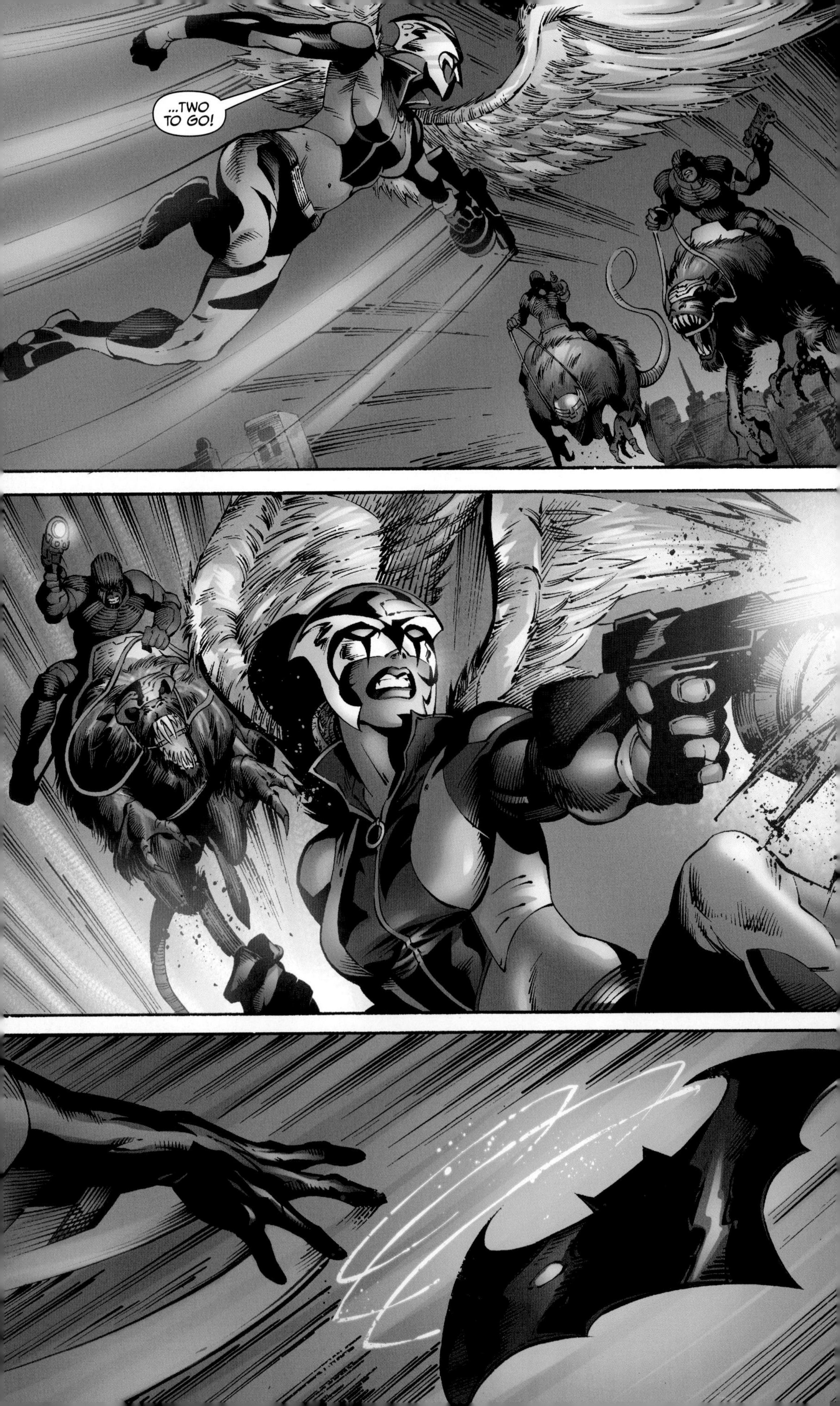
...TWO TO GO!

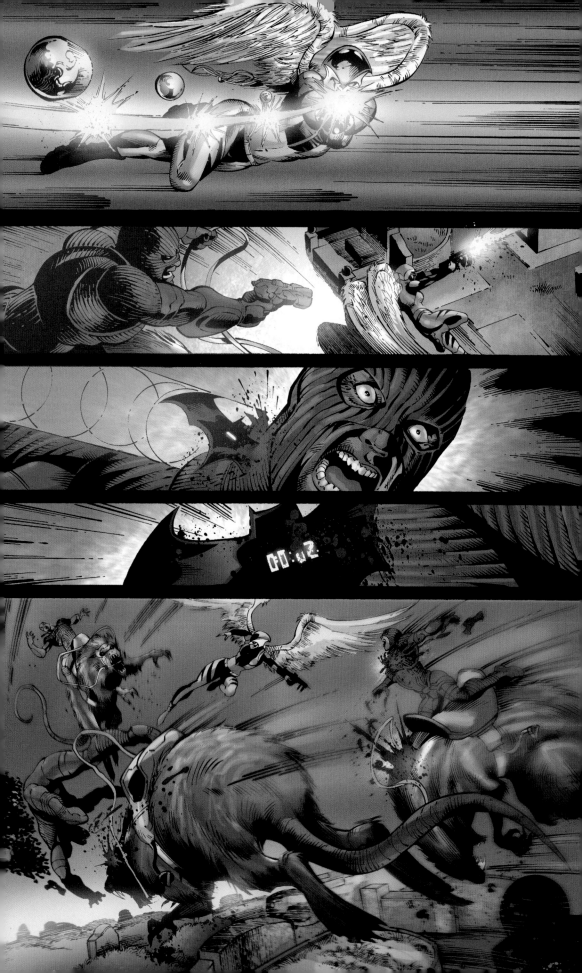

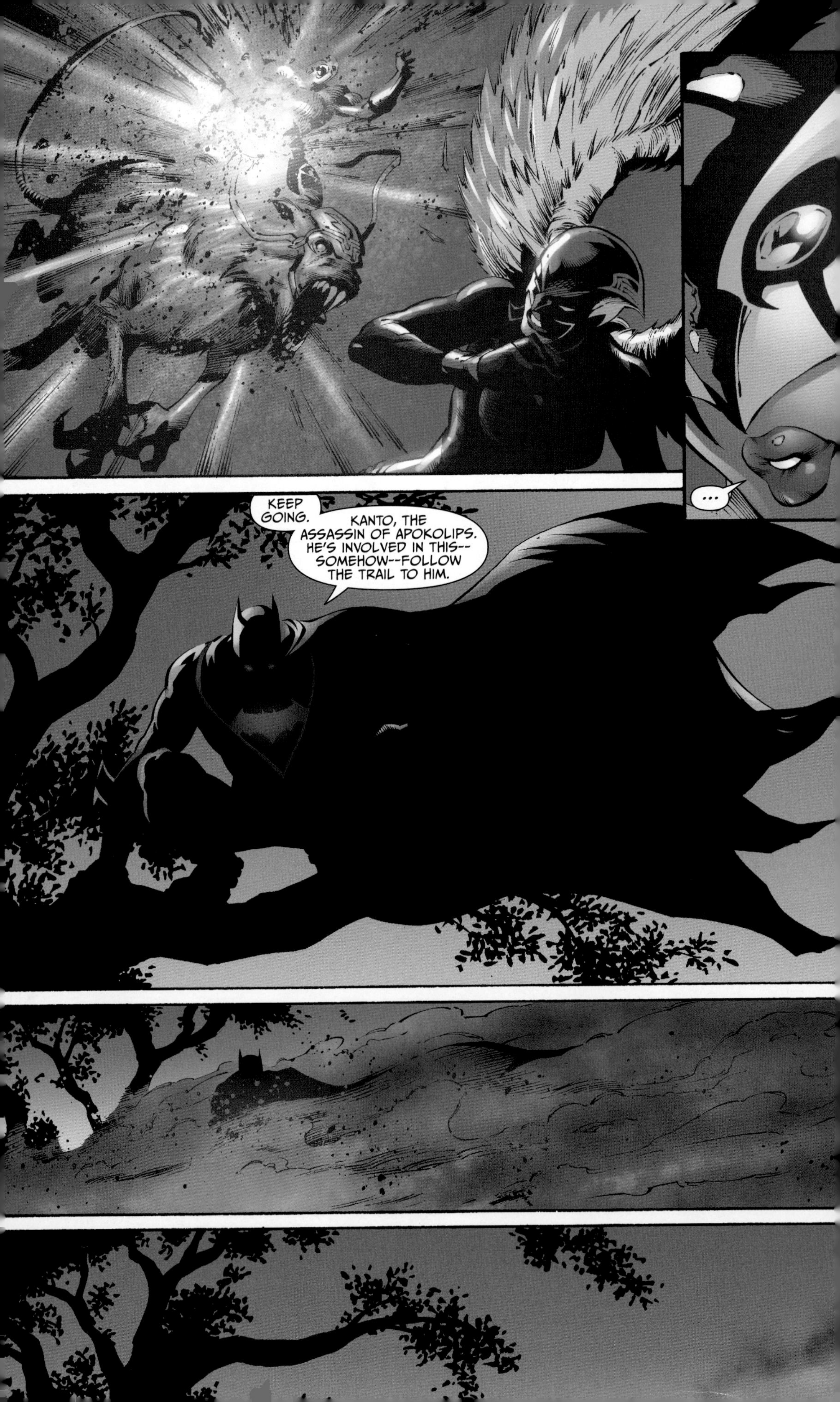
...
KEEP GOING.
KANTO, THE ASSASSIN OF APOKOLIPS. HE'S INVOLVED IN THIS-- SOMEHOW--FOLLOW THE TRAIL TO HIM.

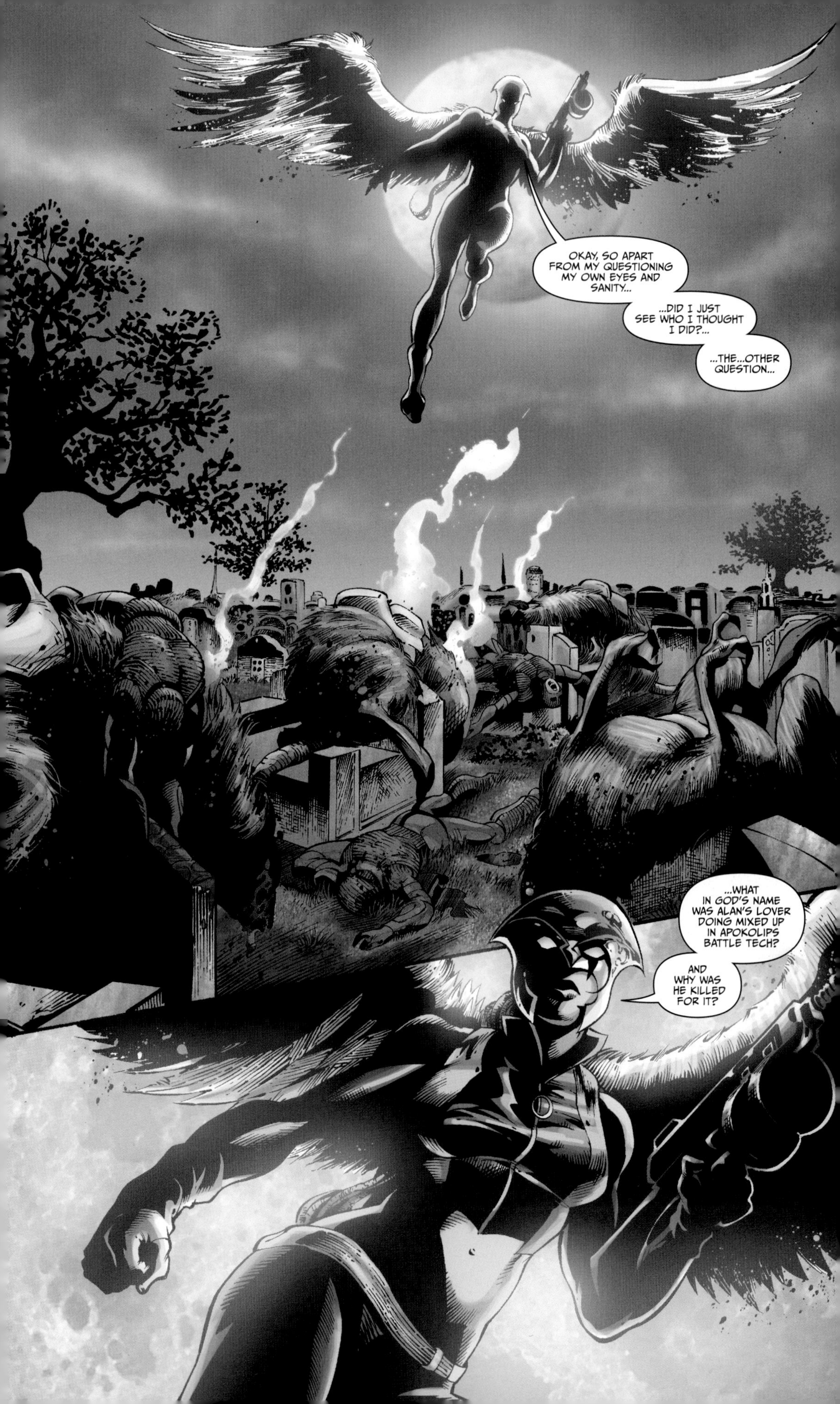
OKAY, SO APART FROM MY QUESTIONING MY OWN EYES AND SANITY...
...DID I JUST SEE WHO I THOUGHT I DID?...
...THE...OTHER QUESTION...
...WHAT IN GOD'S NAME WAS ALAN'S LOVER DOING MIXED UP IN APOKOLIPS BATTLE TECH?
AND WHY WAS HE KILLED FOR IT?

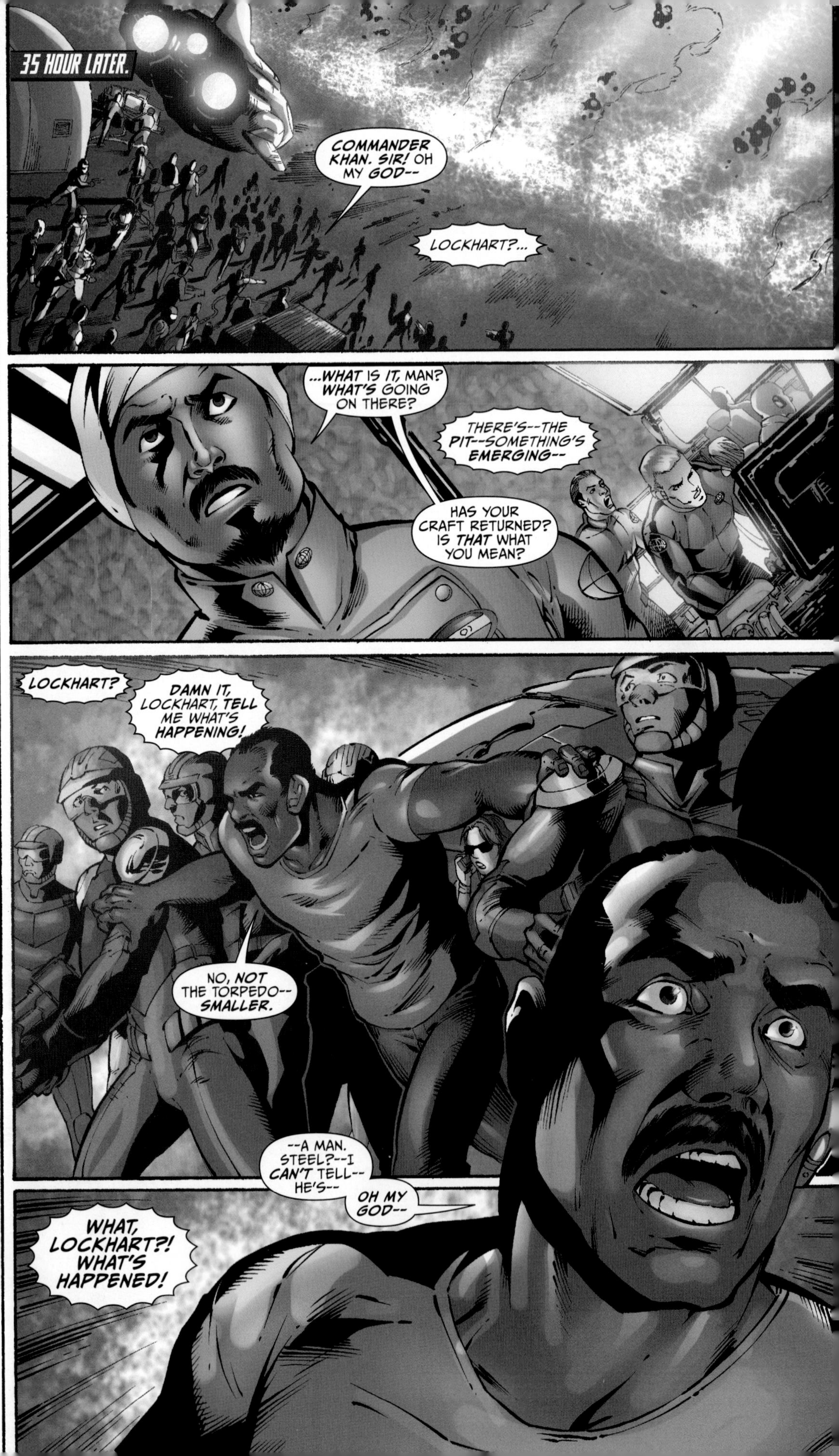
35 HOUR LATER.
COMMANDER KHAN. SIR! OH MY GOD--
LOCKHART?...
...WHAT IS IT, MAN? WHAT'S GOING ON THERE?
THERE'S--THE PIT--SOMETHING'S EMERGING--
HAS YOUR CRAFT RETURNED? IS THAT WHAT YOU MEAN?
LOCKHART?
DAMN IT, LOCKHART, TELL ME WHAT'S HAPPENING!
NO, NOT THE TORPEDO--SMALLER.
--A MAN. STEEL?--I CAN'T TELL--HE'S--
OH MY GOD--
WHAT, LOCKHART?! WHAT'S HAPPENED!

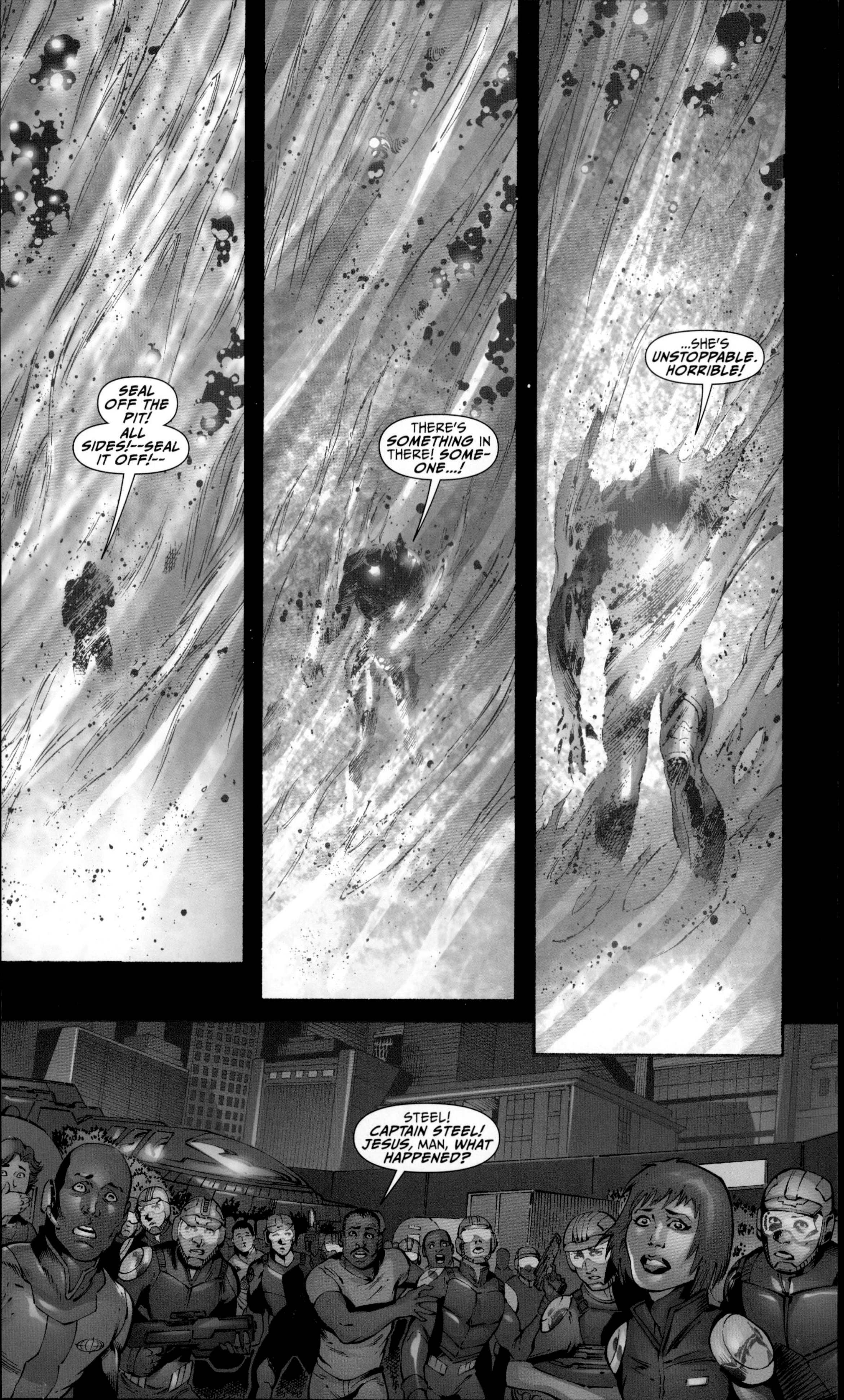
SEAL OFF THE PIT! ALL SIDES!--SEAL IT OFF!--
THERE'S SOMETHING IN THERE! SOME-ONE...!
...SHE'S UNSTOPPABLE. HORRIBLE!
STEEL! CAPTAIN STEEL! JESUS, MAN, WHAT HAPPENED?

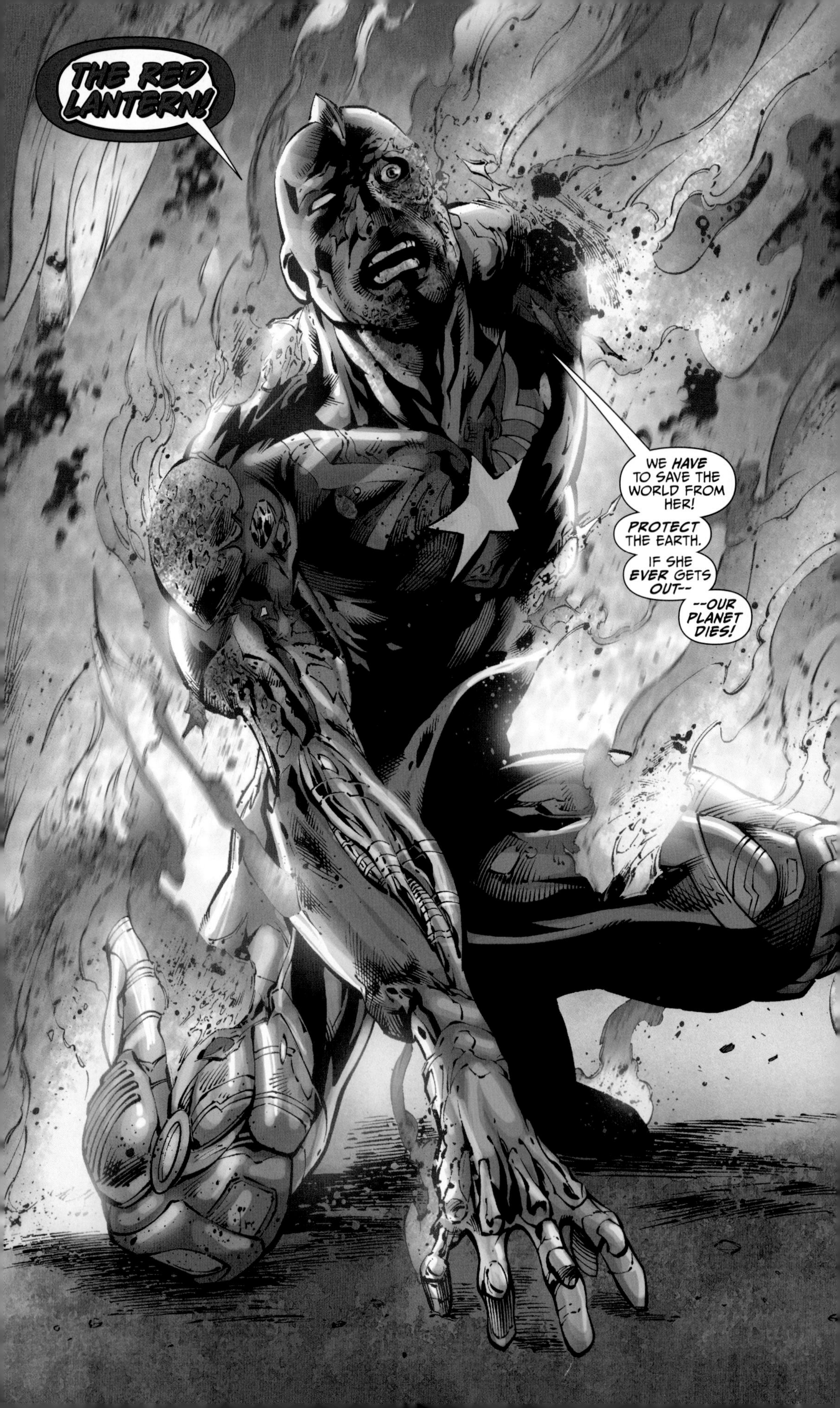
THE RED LANTERN!
WE HAVE TO SAVE THE WORLD FROM HER!
PROTECT THE EARTH.
IF SHE EVER GETS OUT--
--OUR PLANET DIES!

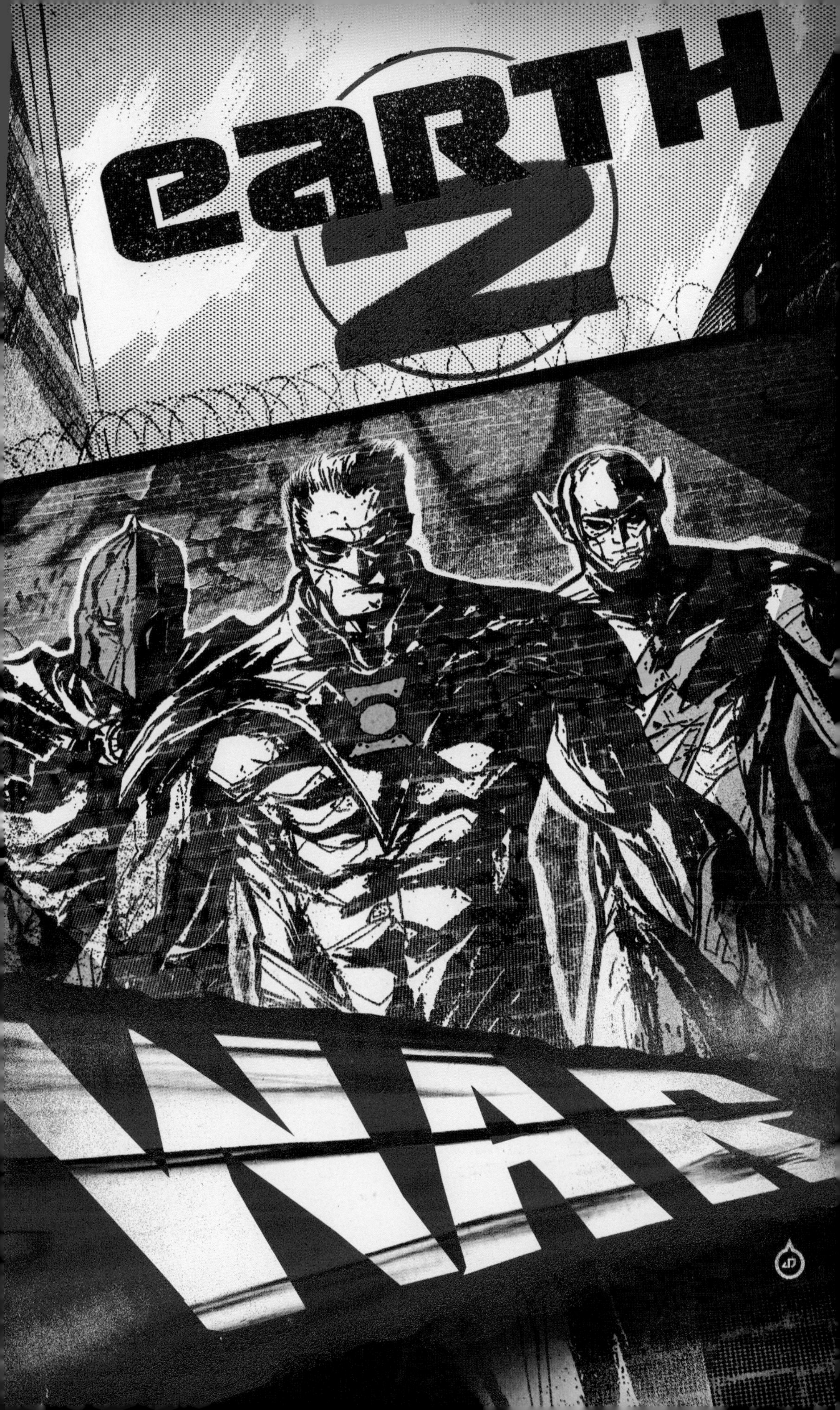
EARTH 2
WAR

JAMES ROBINSON
writer

NICOLA SCOTT
penciller

TREVOR SCOTT
inker

PETE PANTAZIS
colorist

JUAN DOE
cover artist

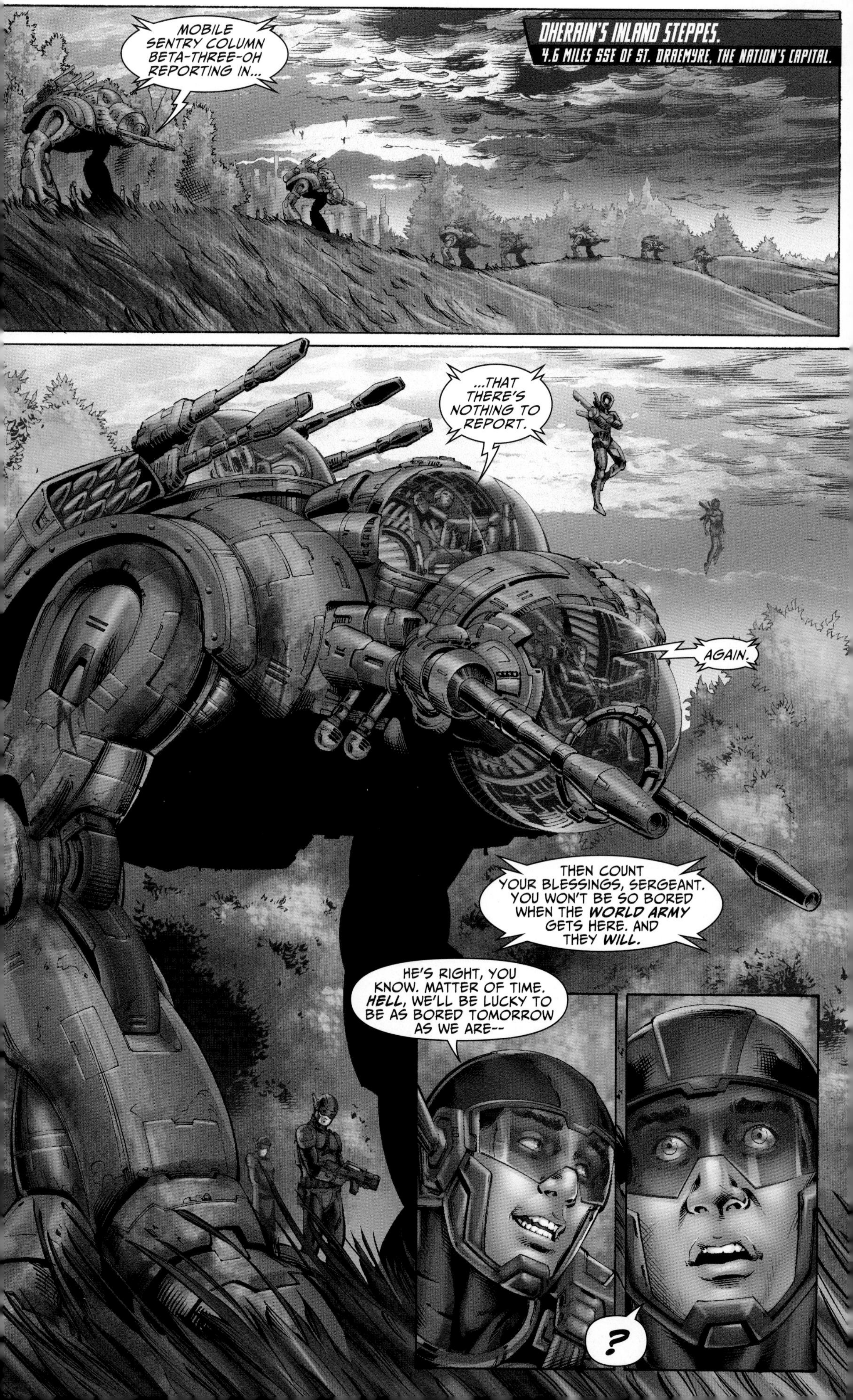
DHERAIN'S INLAND STEPPES.
4.6 MILES SSE OF ST. DRAEMYRE, THE NATION'S CAPITAL.
MOBILE SENTRY COLUMN BETA-THREE-OH REPORTING IN...
...THAT THERE'S NOTHING TO REPORT.
AGAIN.
THEN COUNT YOUR BLESSINGS, SERGEANT. YOU WON'T BE SO BORED WHEN THE WORLD ARMY GETS HERE. AND THEY WILL.
HE'S RIGHT, YOU KNOW. MATTER OF TIME. HELL, WE'LL BE LUCKY TO BE AS BORED TOMORROW AS WE ARE--
?

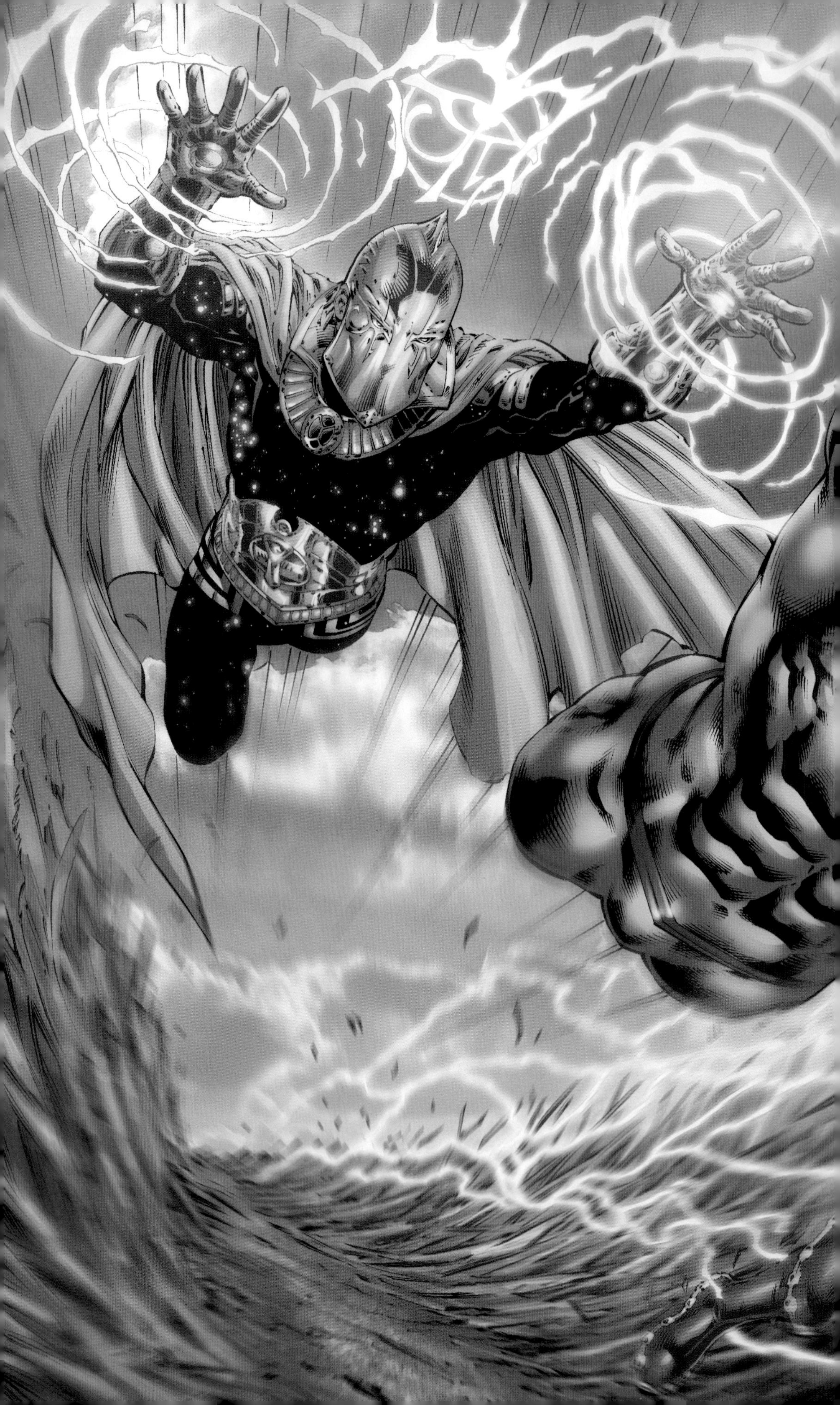

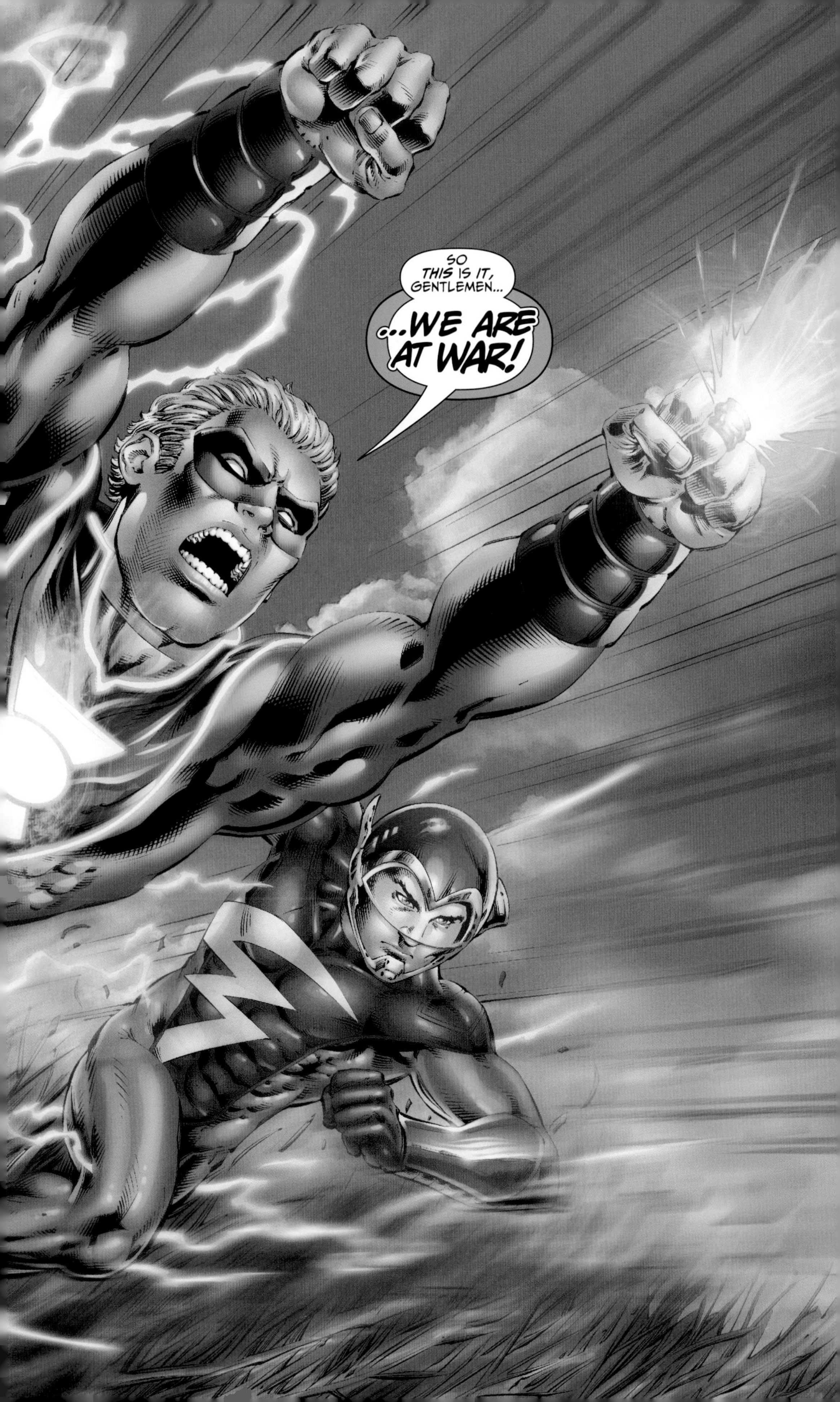
SO THIS IS IT, GENTLEMEN...
...WE ARE AT WAR!

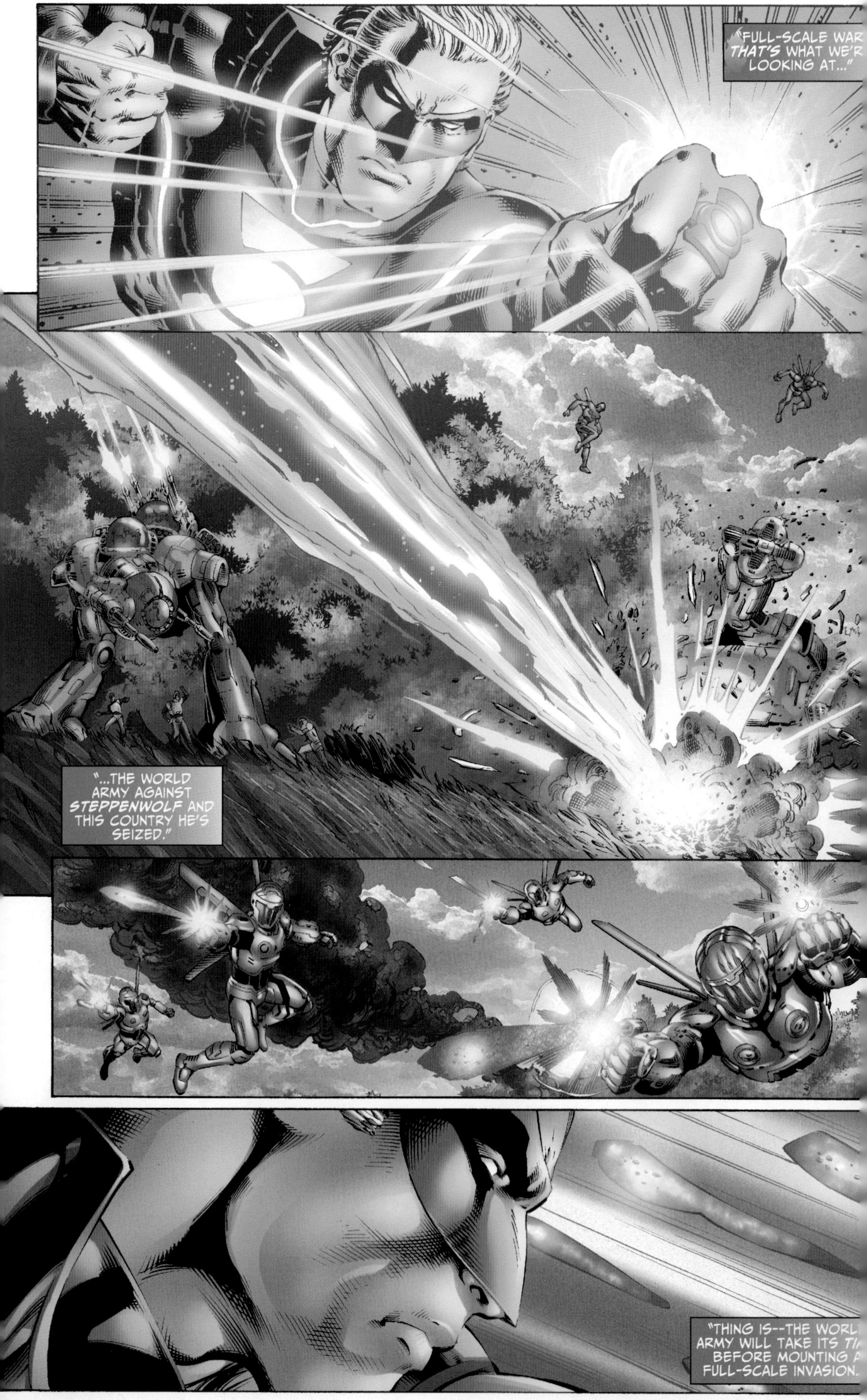

"FULL-SCALE WAR THAT'S WHAT WE'R LOOKING AT..."
"...THE WORLD ARMY AGAINST STEPPENWOLF AND THIS COUNTRY HE'S SEIZED."
"THING IS--THE WORL ARMY WILL TAKE ITS TI BEFORE MOUNTING A FULL-SCALE INVASION.

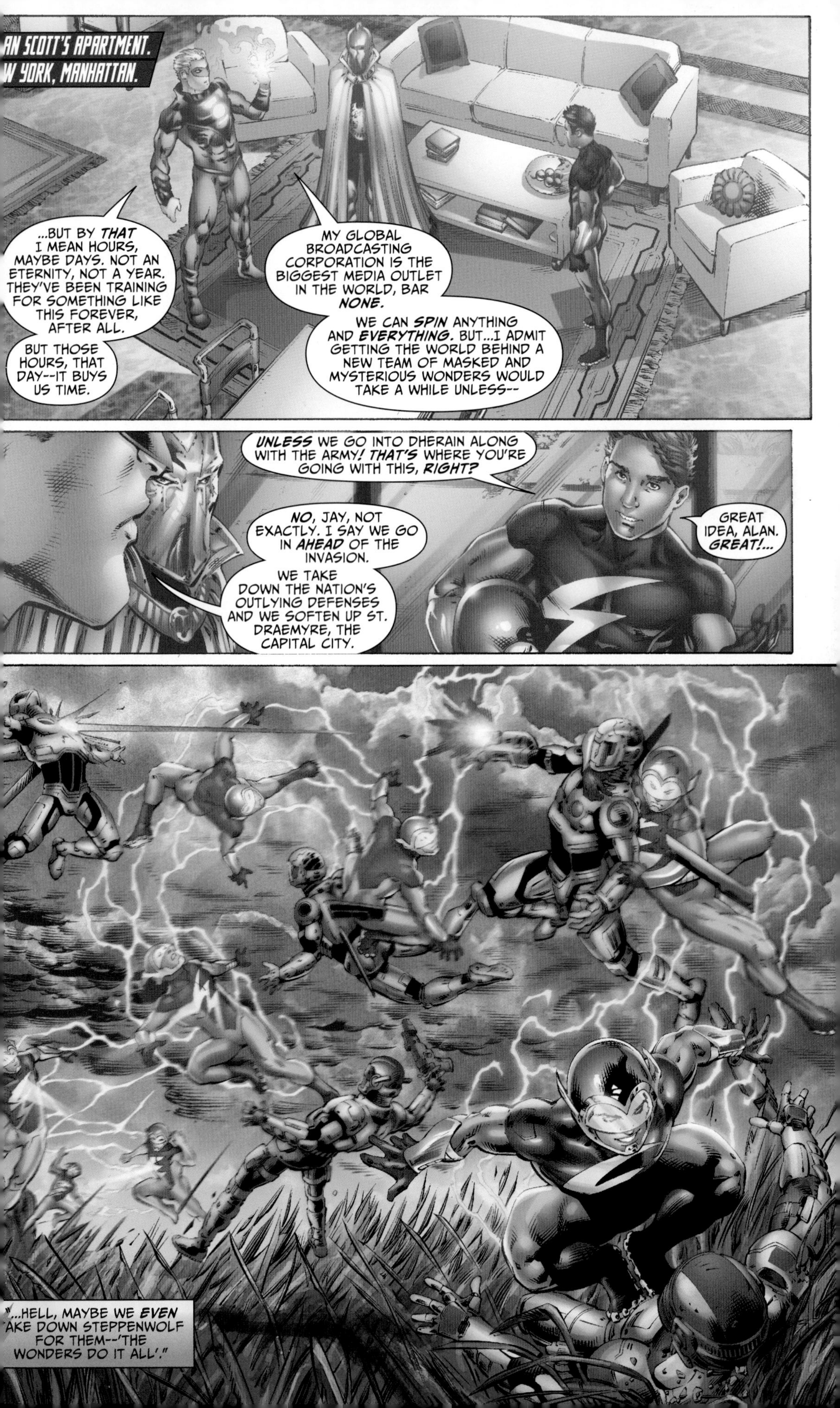
AN SCOTT'S APARTMENT. W YORK, MANHATTAN.
...BUT BY THAT I MEAN HOURS, MAYBE DAYS. NOT AN ETERNITY, NOT A YEAR. THEY'VE BEEN TRAINING FOR SOMETHING LIKE THIS FOREVER, AFTER ALL.
BUT THOSE HOURS, THAT DAY--IT BUYS US TIME.
MY GLOBAL BROADCASTING CORPORATION IS THE BIGGEST MEDIA OUTLET IN THE WORLD, BAR NONE.
WE CAN SPIN ANYTHING AND EVERYTHING. BUT...I ADMIT GETTING THE WORLD BEHIND A NEW TEAM OF MASKED AND MYSTERIOUS WONDERS WOULD TAKE A WHILE UNLESS--
UNLESS WE GO INTO DHERAIN ALONG WITH THE ARMY! THAT'S WHERE YOU'RE GOING WITH THIS, RIGHT?
NO, JAY, NOT EXACTLY. I SAY WE GO IN AHEAD OF THE INVASION.
WE TAKE DOWN THE NATION'S OUTLYING DEFENSES AND WE SOFTEN UP ST. DRAEMYRE, THE CAPITAL CITY.
GREAT IDEA, ALAN. GREAT!...
"...HELL, MAYBE WE EVEN AKE DOWN STEPPENWOLF FOR THEM--'THE WONDERS DO IT ALL'."

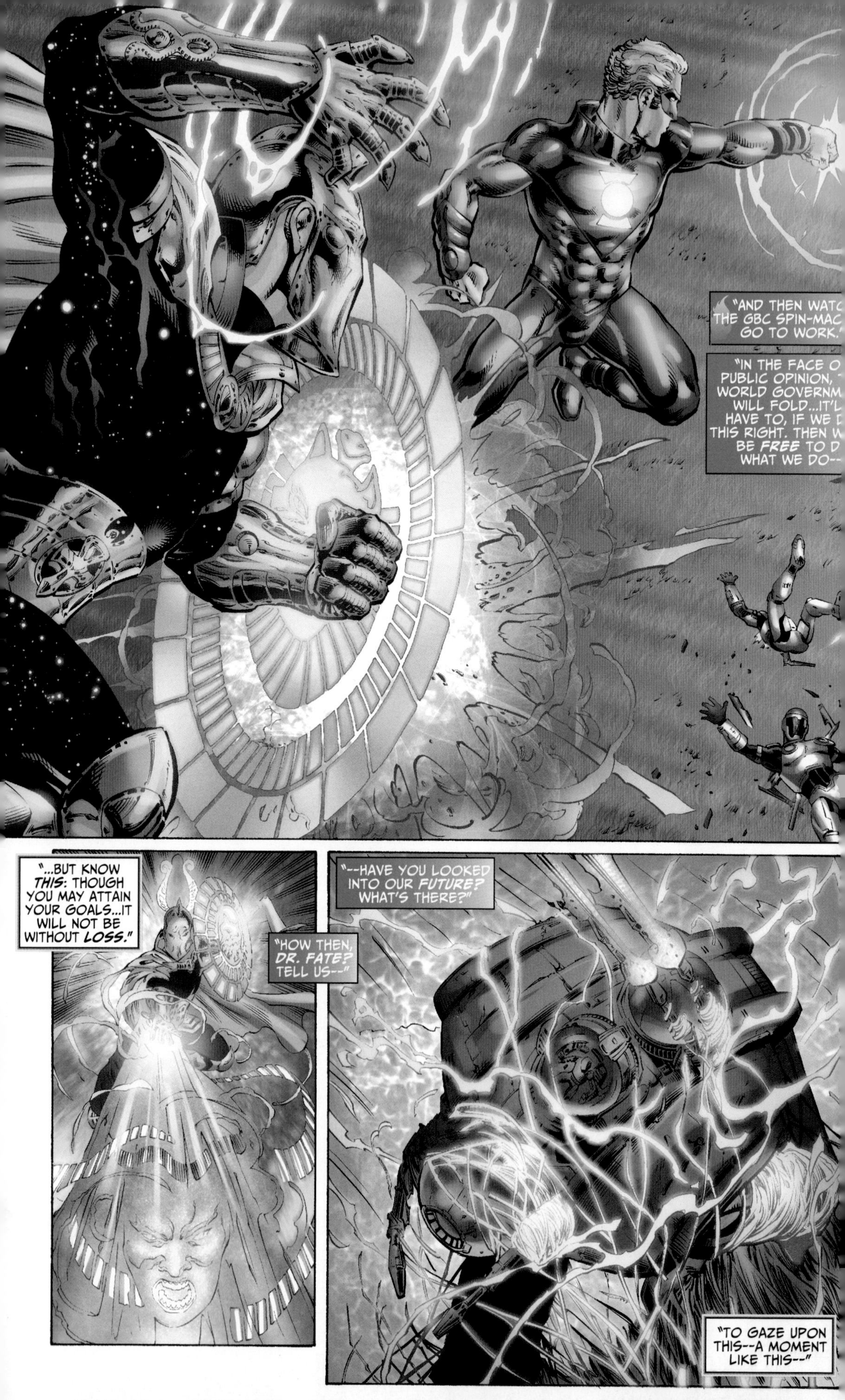
"AND THEN WATC
THE GBC SPIN-MAC
GO TO WORK."
"IN THE FACE O
PUBLIC OPINION,
WORLD GOVERNM
WILL FOLD...IT'L
HAVE TO, IF WE D
THIS RIGHT. THEN W
BE FREE TO D
WHAT WE DO--
"...BUT KNOW THIS: THOUGH YOU MAY ATTAIN YOUR GOALS...IT WILL NOT BE WITHOUT LOSS."
"HOW THEN, DR. FATE? TELL US--"
"--HAVE YOU LOOKED INTO OUR FUTURE? WHAT'S THERE?"
"TO GAZE UPON THIS--A MOMENT LIKE THIS--"

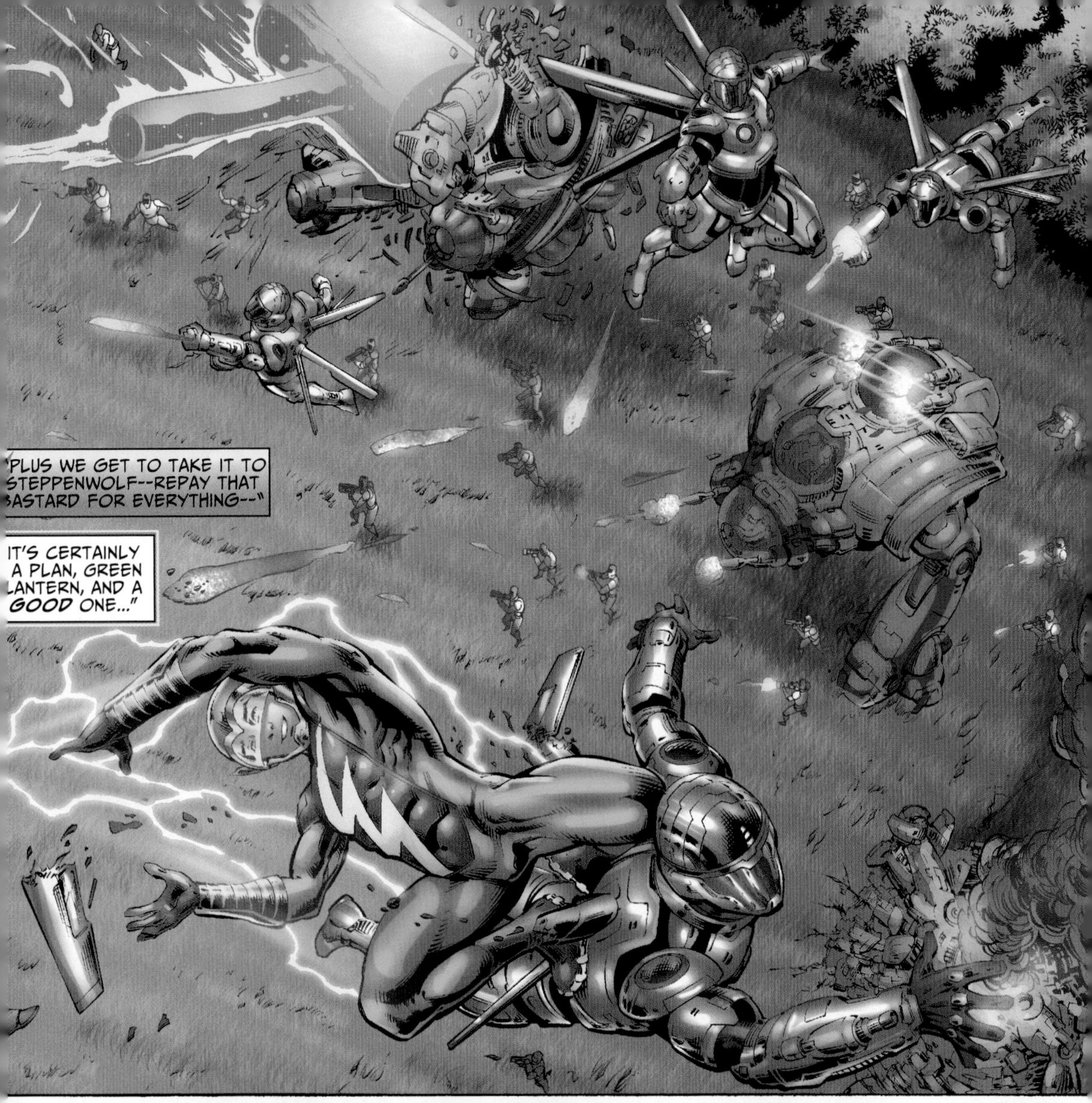
"PLUS WE GET TO TAKE IT TO STEPPENWOLF--REPAY THAT BASTARD FOR EVERYTHING--"
IT'S CERTAINLY A PLAN, GREEN LANTERN, AND A *GOOD* ONE..."

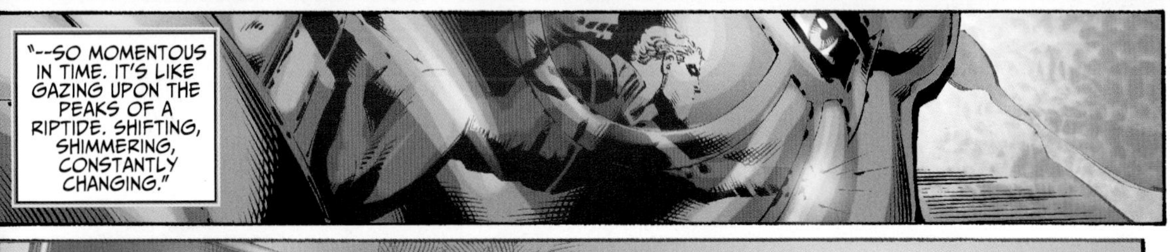
"--SO MOMENTOUS IN TIME. IT'S LIKE GAZING UPON THE PEAKS OF A RIPTIDE. SHIFTING, SHIMMERING, CONSTANTLY CHANGING."

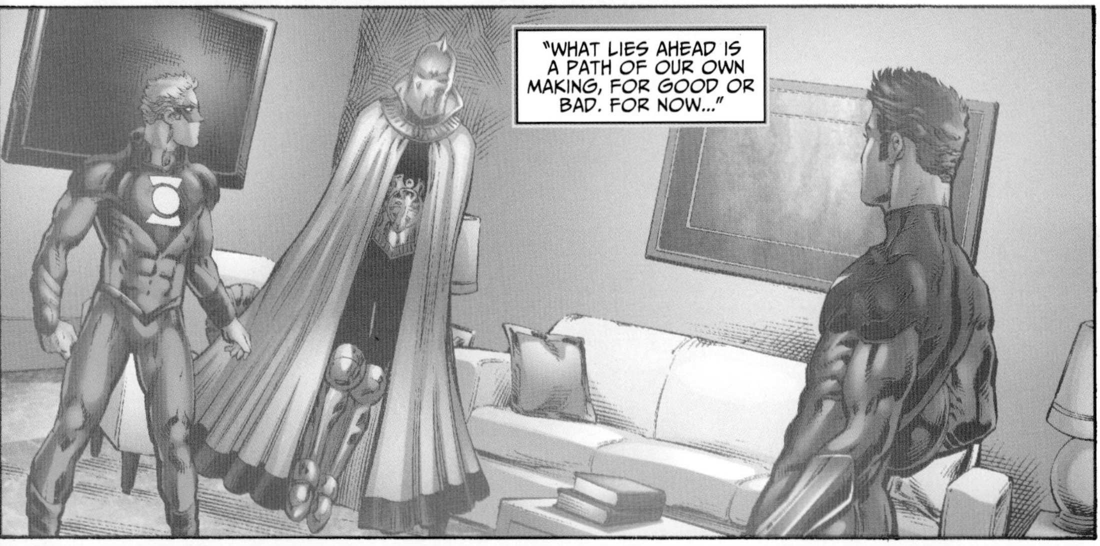
"WHAT LIES AHEAD IS A PATH OF OUR OWN MAKING, FOR GOOD OR BAD. FOR NOW..."

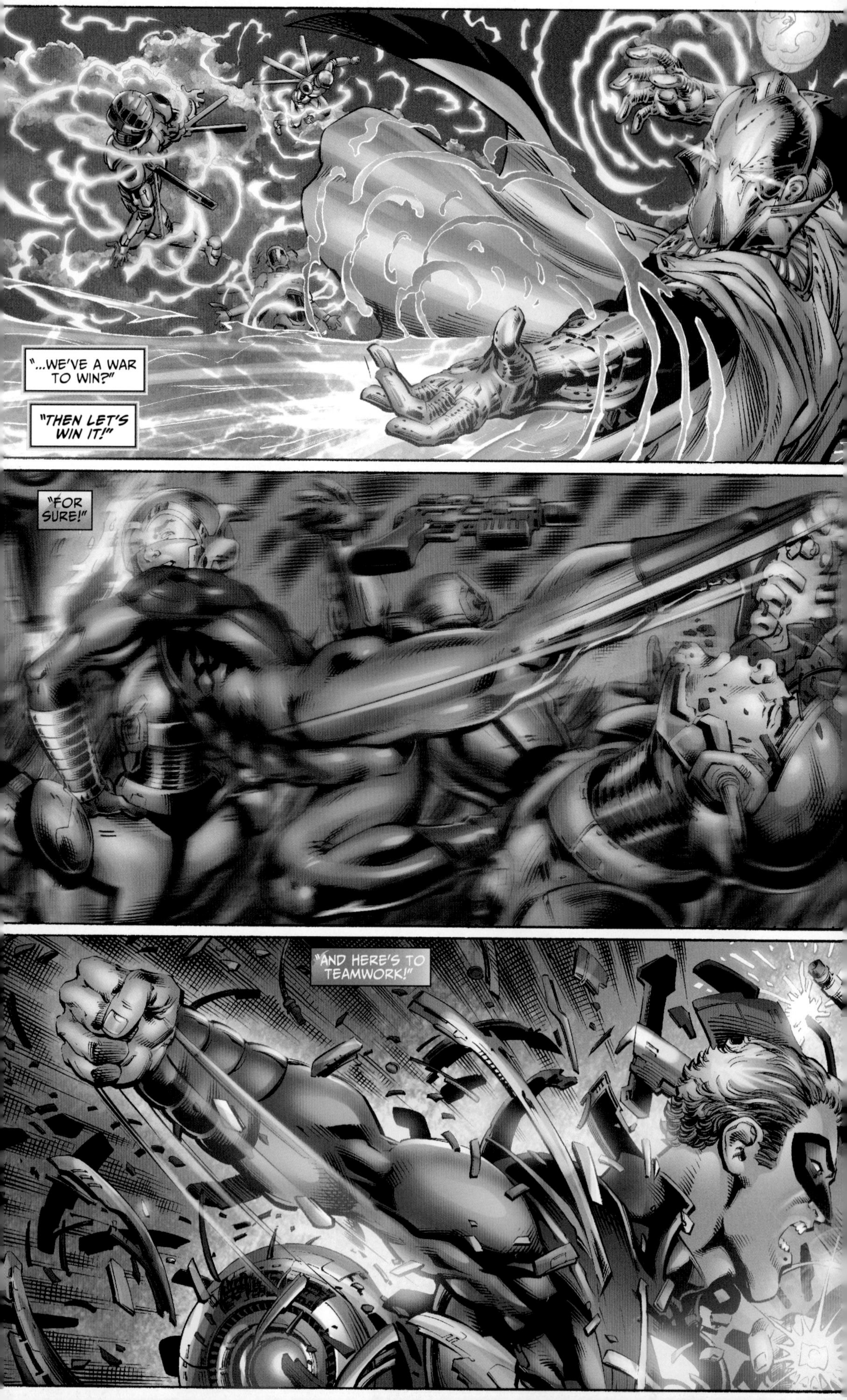
"...WE'VE A WAR TO WIN?"
"THEN LET'S WIN IT!"
"FOR SURE!"
"AND HERE'S TO TEAMWORK!"

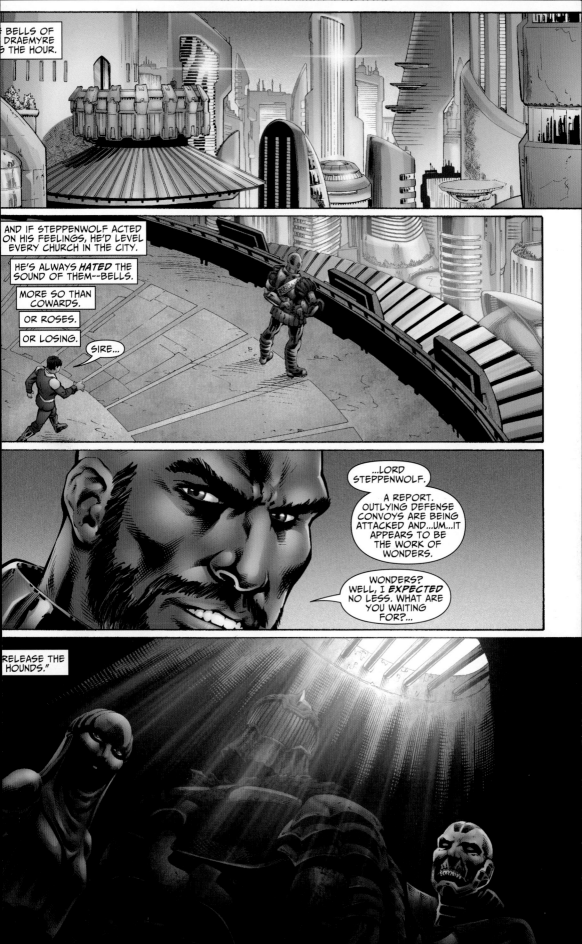

BELLS OF
DRAEMYRE
S THE HOUR.

AND IF STEPPENWOLF ACTED ON HIS FEELINGS, HE'D LEVEL EVERY CHURCH IN THE CITY.

HE'S ALWAYS *HATED* THE SOUND OF THEM--BELLS.

MORE SO THAN COWARDS.

OR ROSES.

OR LOSING.

SIRE...

...LORD STEPPENWOLF.

A REPORT. OUTLYING DEFENSE CONVOYS ARE BEING ATTACKED AND...UM...IT APPEARS TO BE THE WORK OF WONDERS.

WONDERS? WELL, I *EXPECTED* NO LESS. WHAT ARE YOU WAITING FOR?...

RELEASE THE HOUNDS."

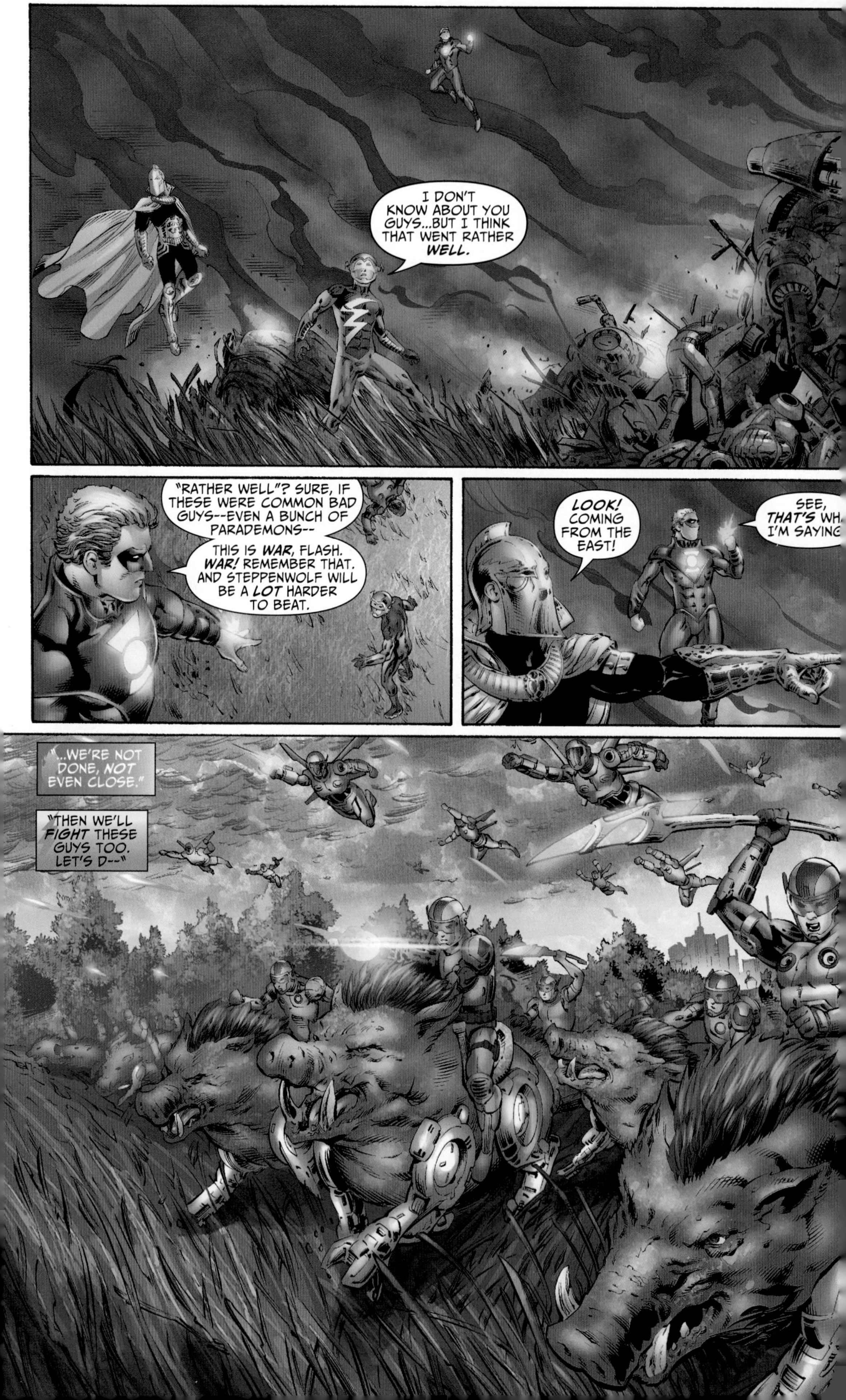
I DON'T KNOW ABOUT YOU GUYS...BUT I THINK THAT WENT RATHER WELL.
"RATHER WELL"? SURE, IF THESE WERE COMMON BAD GUYS--EVEN A BUNCH OF PARADEMONS--
THIS IS WAR, FLASH. WAR! REMEMBER THAT. AND STEPPENWOLF WILL BE A LOT HARDER TO BEAT.
LOOK! COMING FROM THE EAST!
SEE, THAT'S WHA I'M SAYING
"...WE'RE NOT DONE, NOT EVEN CLOSE."
"THEN WE'LL FIGHT THESE GUYS TOO. LET'S D--"

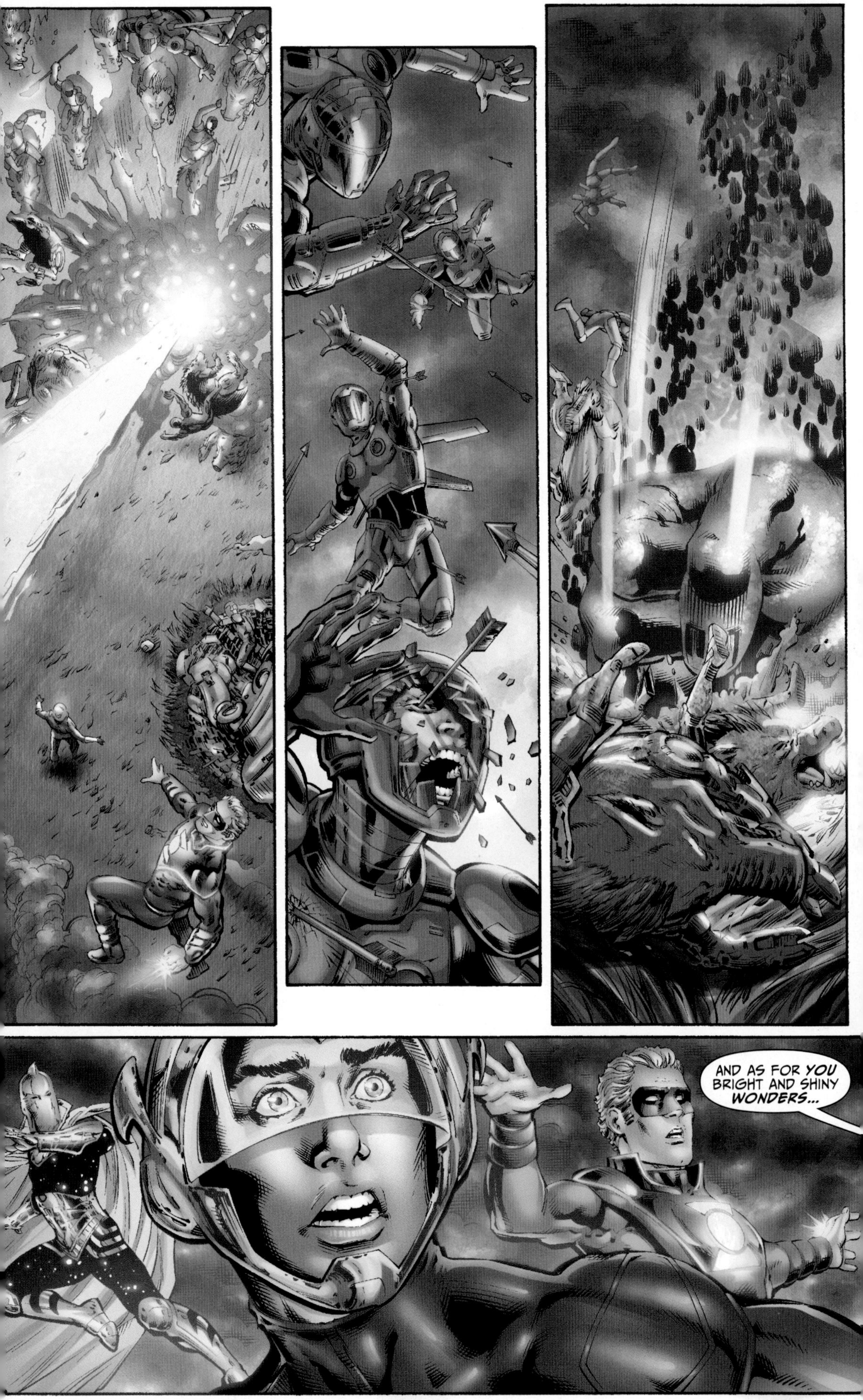
AND AS FOR YOU BRIGHT AND SHINY WONDERS...

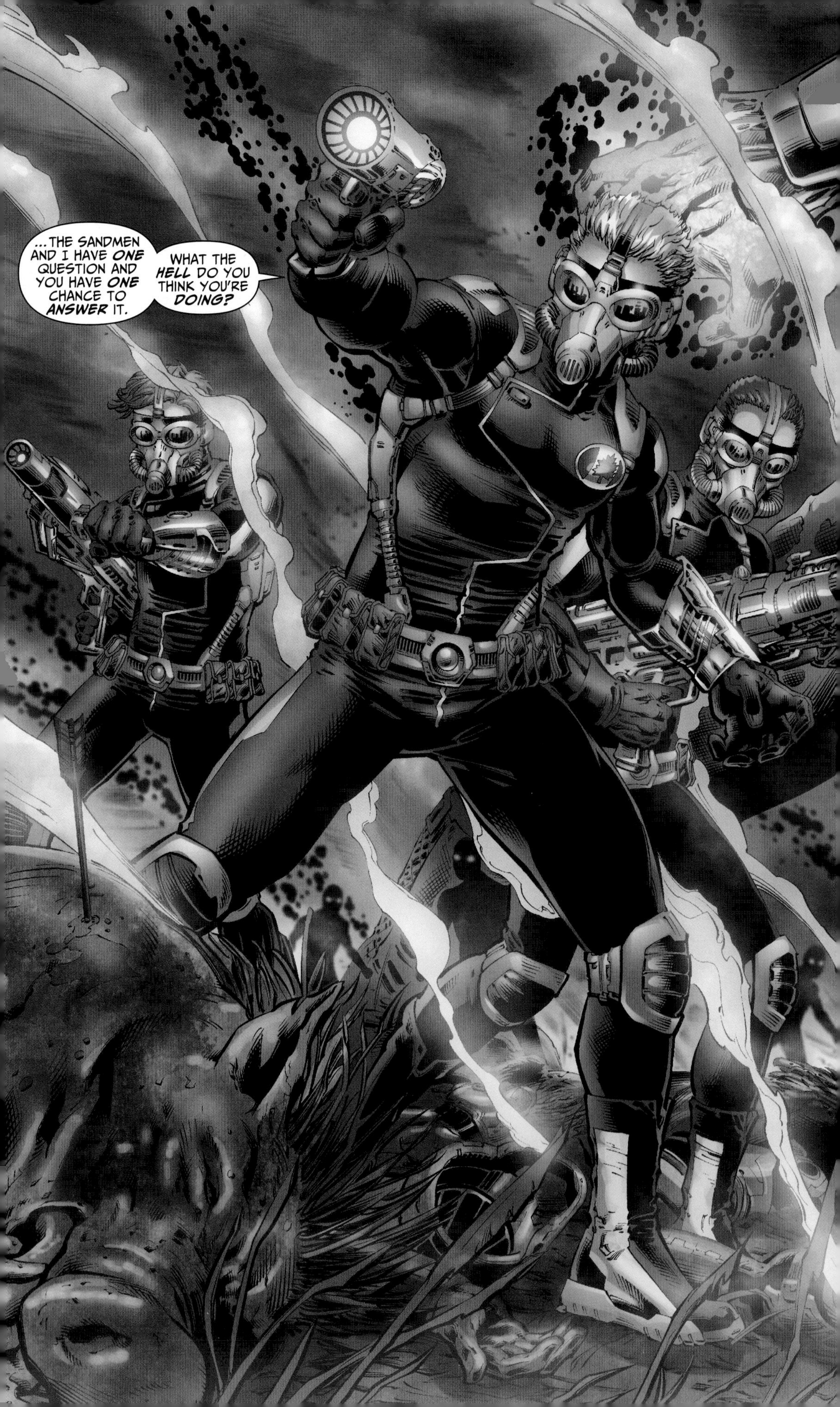
...THE SANDMEN AND I HAVE ONE QUESTION AND YOU HAVE ONE CHANCE TO ANSWER IT.
WHAT THE HELL DO YOU THINK YOU'RE DOING?

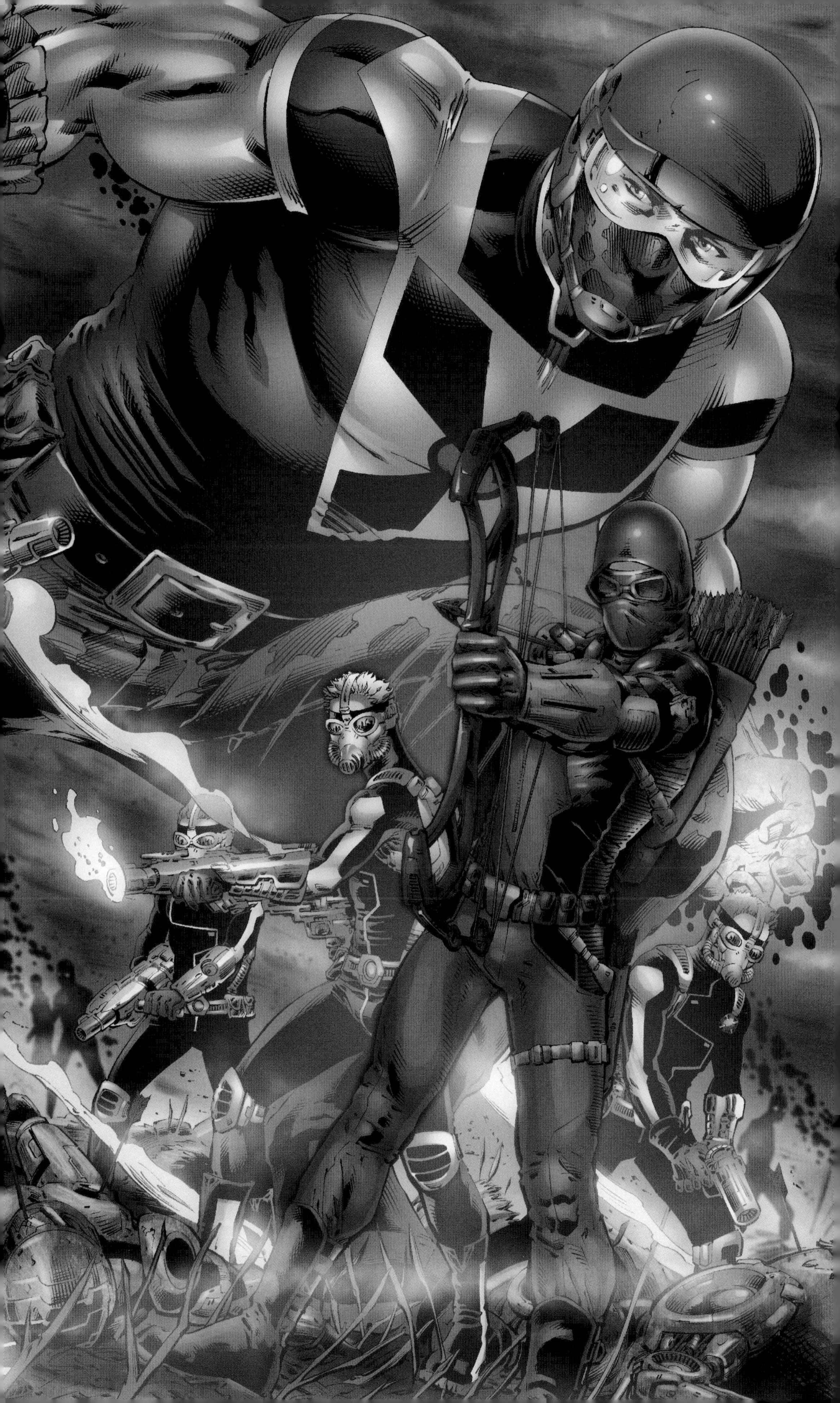

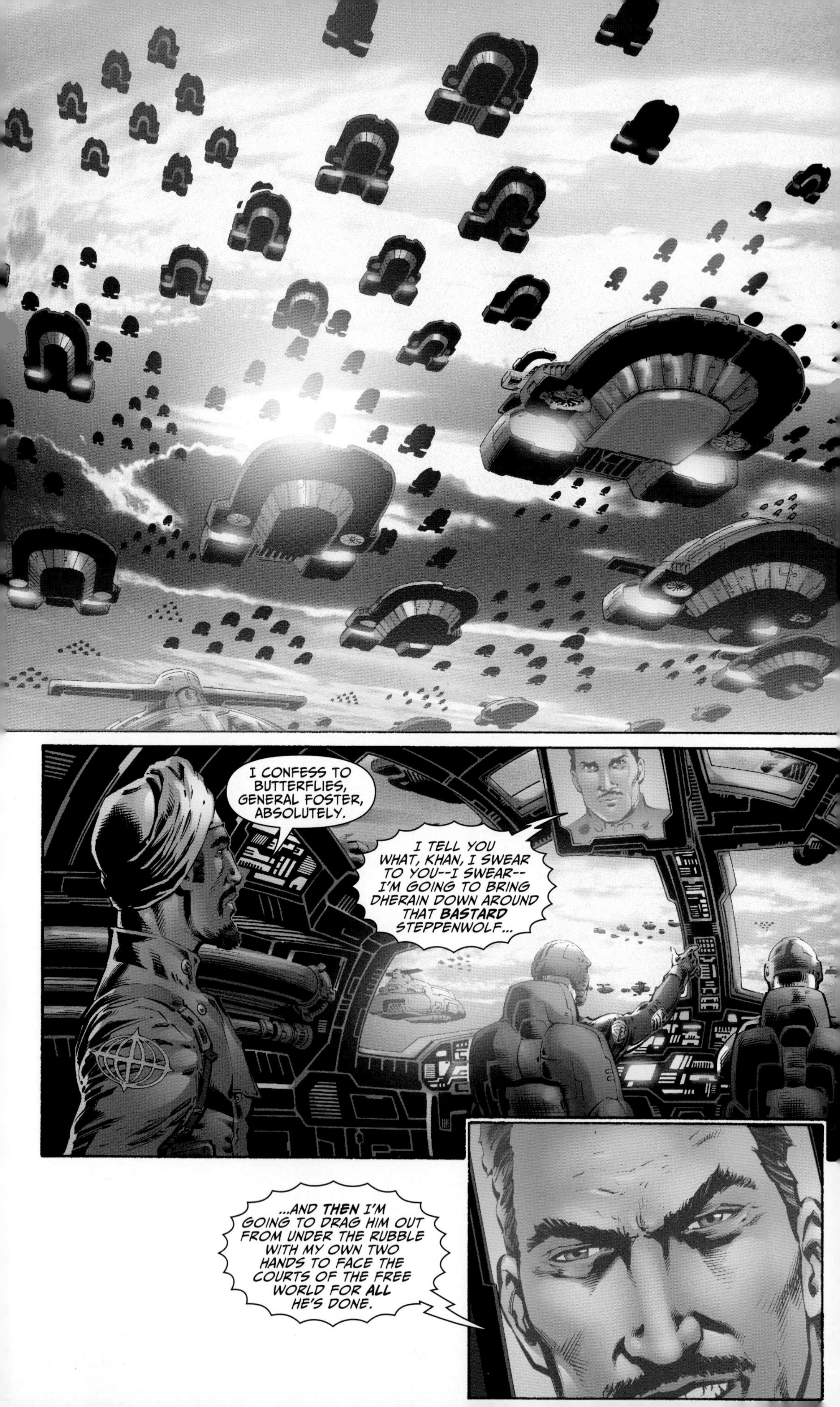
I CONFESS TO BUTTERFLIES, GENERAL FOSTER, ABSOLUTELY.
I TELL YOU WHAT, KHAN, I SWEAR TO YOU--I SWEAR-- I'M GOING TO BRING DHERAIN DOWN AROUND THAT **BASTARD** STEPPENWOLF...
...AND **THEN** I'M GOING TO DRAG HIM OUT FROM UNDER THE RUBBLE WITH MY OWN TWO HANDS TO FACE THE COURTS OF THE FREE WORLD FOR **ALL** HE'S DONE.

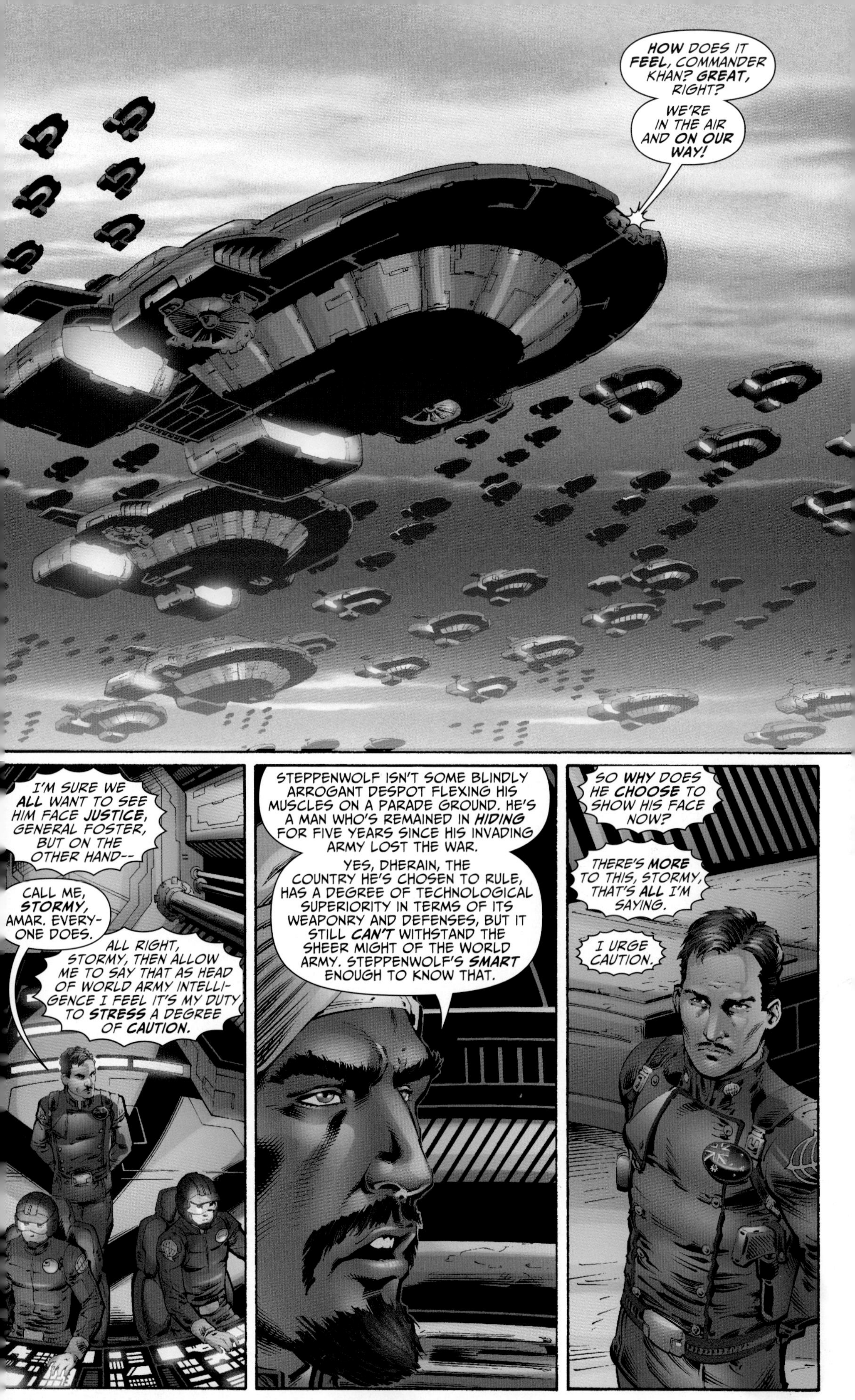

HOW DOES IT FEEL, COMMANDER KHAN? GREAT, RIGHT?
WE'RE IN THE AIR AND ON OUR WAY!
I'M SURE WE ALL WANT TO SEE HIM FACE JUSTICE, GENERAL FOSTER, BUT ON THE OTHER HAND--
CALL ME, STORMY, AMAR. EVERY-ONE DOES.
ALL RIGHT, STORMY, THEN ALLOW ME TO SAY THAT AS HEAD OF WORLD ARMY INTELLI-GENCE I FEEL IT'S MY DUTY TO STRESS A DEGREE OF CAUTION.
STEPPENWOLF ISN'T SOME BLINDLY ARROGANT DESPOT FLEXING HIS MUSCLES ON A PARADE GROUND. HE'S A MAN WHO'S REMAINED IN HIDING FOR FIVE YEARS SINCE HIS INVADING ARMY LOST THE WAR.
YES, DHERAIN, THE COUNTRY HE'S CHOSEN TO RULE, HAS A DEGREE OF TECHNOLOGICAL SUPERIORITY IN TERMS OF ITS WEAPONRY AND DEFENSES, BUT IT STILL CAN'T WITHSTAND THE SHEER MIGHT OF THE WORLD ARMY. STEPPENWOLF'S SMART ENOUGH TO KNOW THAT.
SO WHY DOES HE CHOOSE TO SHOW HIS FACE NOW?
THERE'S MORE TO THIS, STORMY, THAT'S ALL I'M SAYING.
I URGE CAUTION.

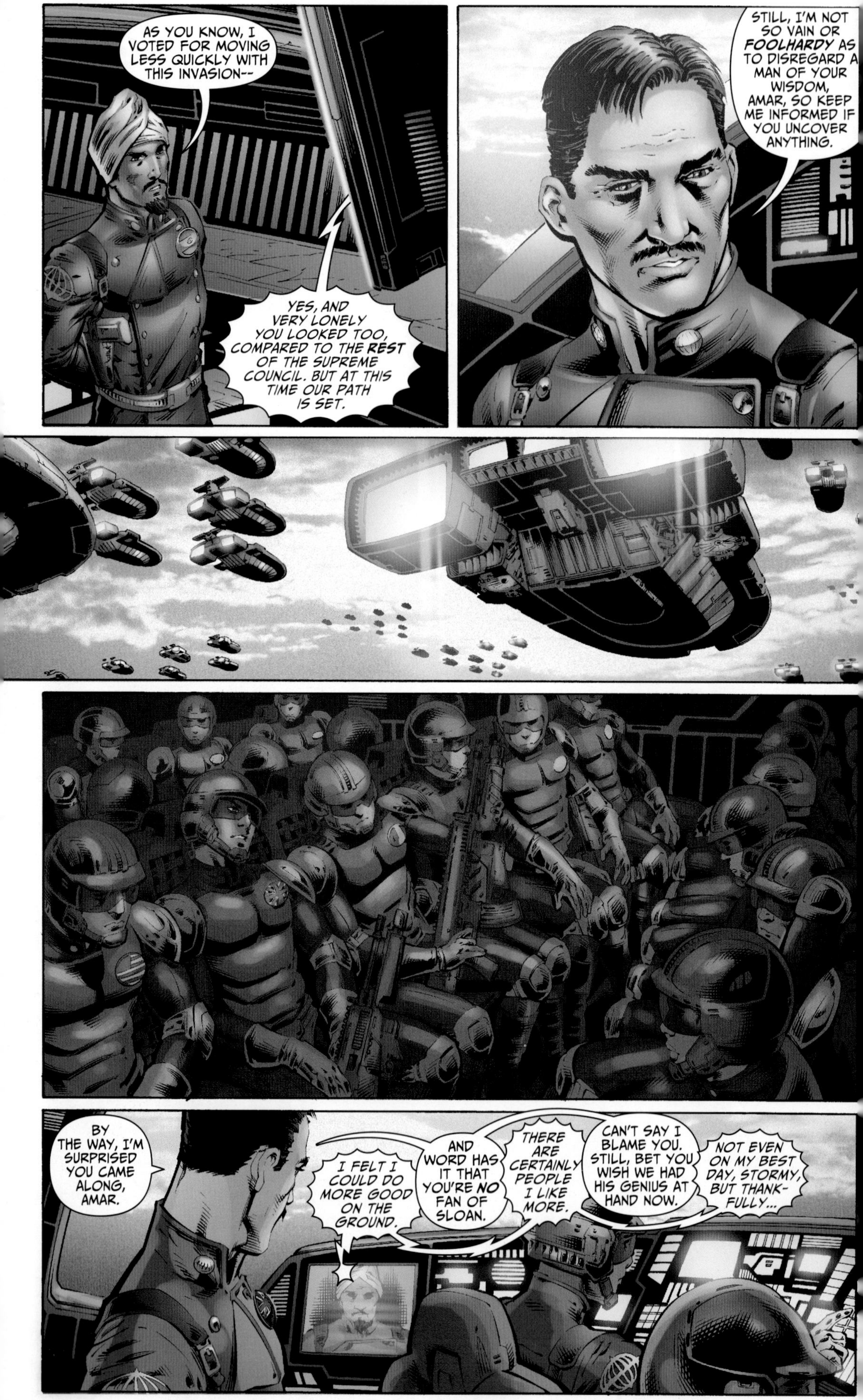
AS YOU KNOW, I VOTED FOR MOVING LESS QUICKLY WITH THIS INVASION--
YES, AND VERY LONELY YOU LOOKED TOO, COMPARED TO THE REST OF THE SUPREME COUNCIL. BUT AT THIS TIME OUR PATH IS SET.
STILL, I'M NOT SO VAIN OR FOOLHARDY AS TO DISREGARD A MAN OF YOUR WISDOM, AMAR, SO KEEP ME INFORMED IF YOU UNCOVER ANYTHING.
BY THE WAY, I'M SURPRISED YOU CAME ALONG, AMAR.
I FELT I COULD DO MORE GOOD ON THE GROUND.
AND WORD HAS IT THAT YOU'RE NO FAN OF SLOAN.
THERE ARE CERTAINLY PEOPLE I LIKE MORE.
CAN'T SAY I BLAME YOU. STILL, BET YOU WISH WE HAD HIS GENIUS AT HAND NOW.
NOT EVEN ON MY BEST DAY, STORMY, BUT THANK-FULLY...

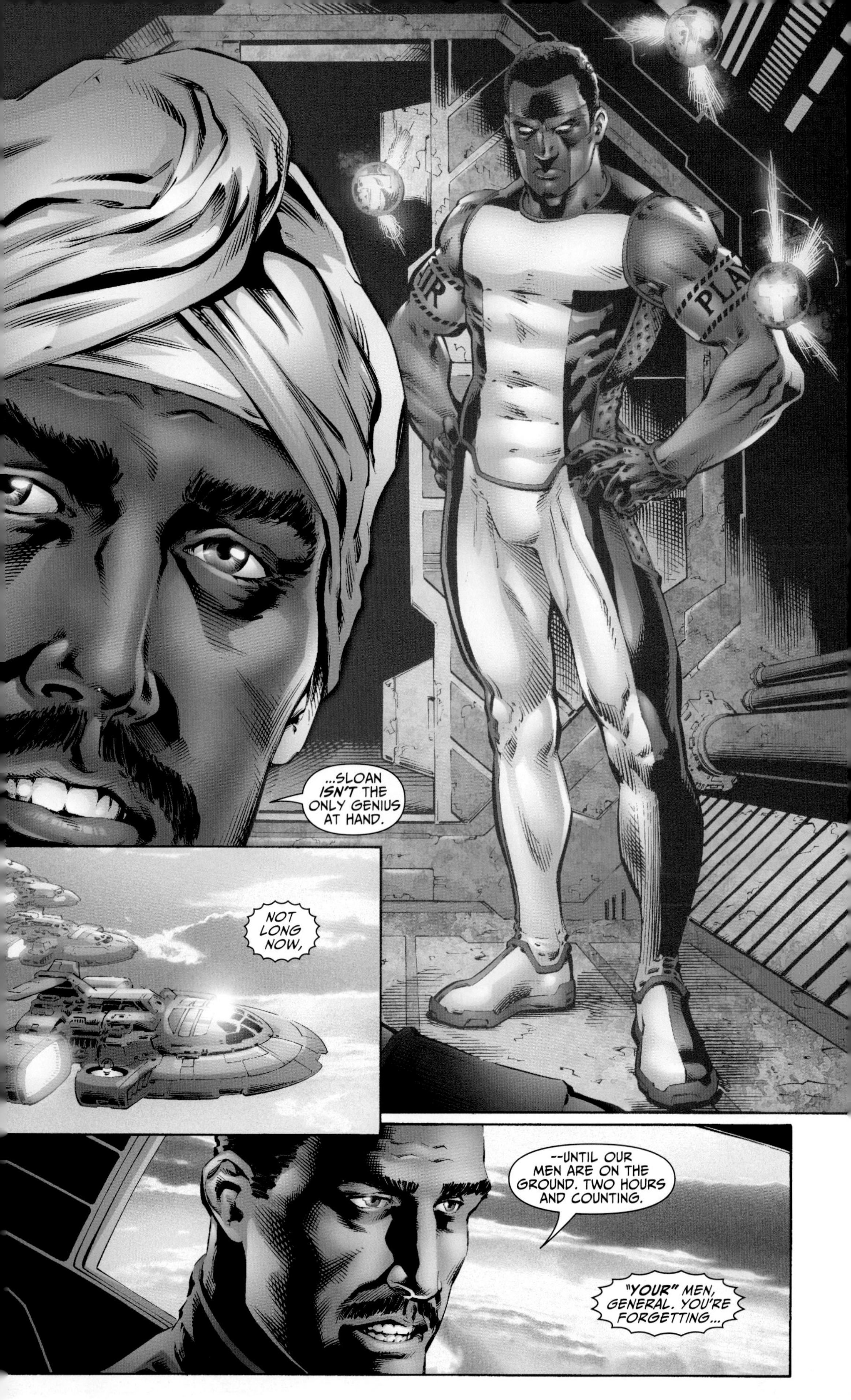
...SLOAN ISN'T THE ONLY GENIUS AT HAND.
NOT LONG NOW,
--UNTIL OUR MEN ARE ON THE GROUND. TWO HOURS AND COUNTING.
"YOUR" MEN, GENERAL. YOU'RE FORGETTING...

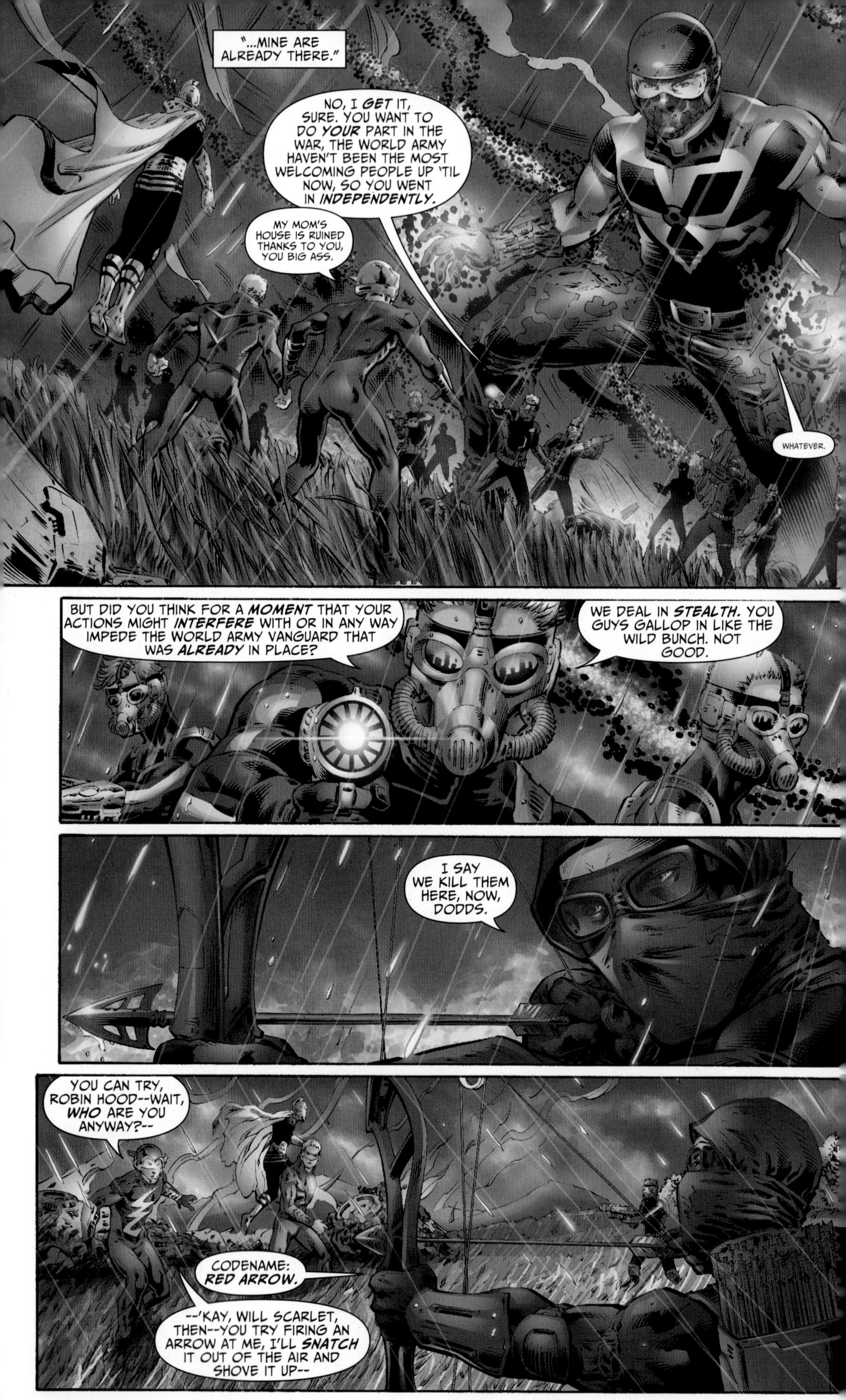
"...MINE ARE ALREADY THERE."
NO, I GET IT, SURE. YOU WANT TO DO YOUR PART IN THE WAR, THE WORLD ARMY HAVEN'T BEEN THE MOST WELCOMING PEOPLE UP 'TIL NOW, SO YOU WENT IN INDEPENDENTLY.
MY MOM'S HOUSE IS RUINED THANKS TO YOU, YOU BIG ASS.
WHATEVER.
BUT DID YOU THINK FOR A MOMENT THAT YOUR ACTIONS MIGHT INTERFERE WITH OR IN ANY WAY IMPEDE THE WORLD ARMY VANGUARD THAT WAS ALREADY IN PLACE?
WE DEAL IN STEALTH. YOU GUYS GALLOP IN LIKE THE WILD BUNCH. NOT GOOD.
I SAY WE KILL THEM HERE, NOW, DODDS.
YOU CAN TRY, ROBIN HOOD--WAIT, WHO ARE YOU ANYWAY?--
CODENAME: RED ARROW.
--'KAY, WILL SCARLET, THEN--YOU TRY FIRING AN ARROW AT ME, I'LL SNATCH IT OUT OF THE AIR AND SHOVE IT UP--

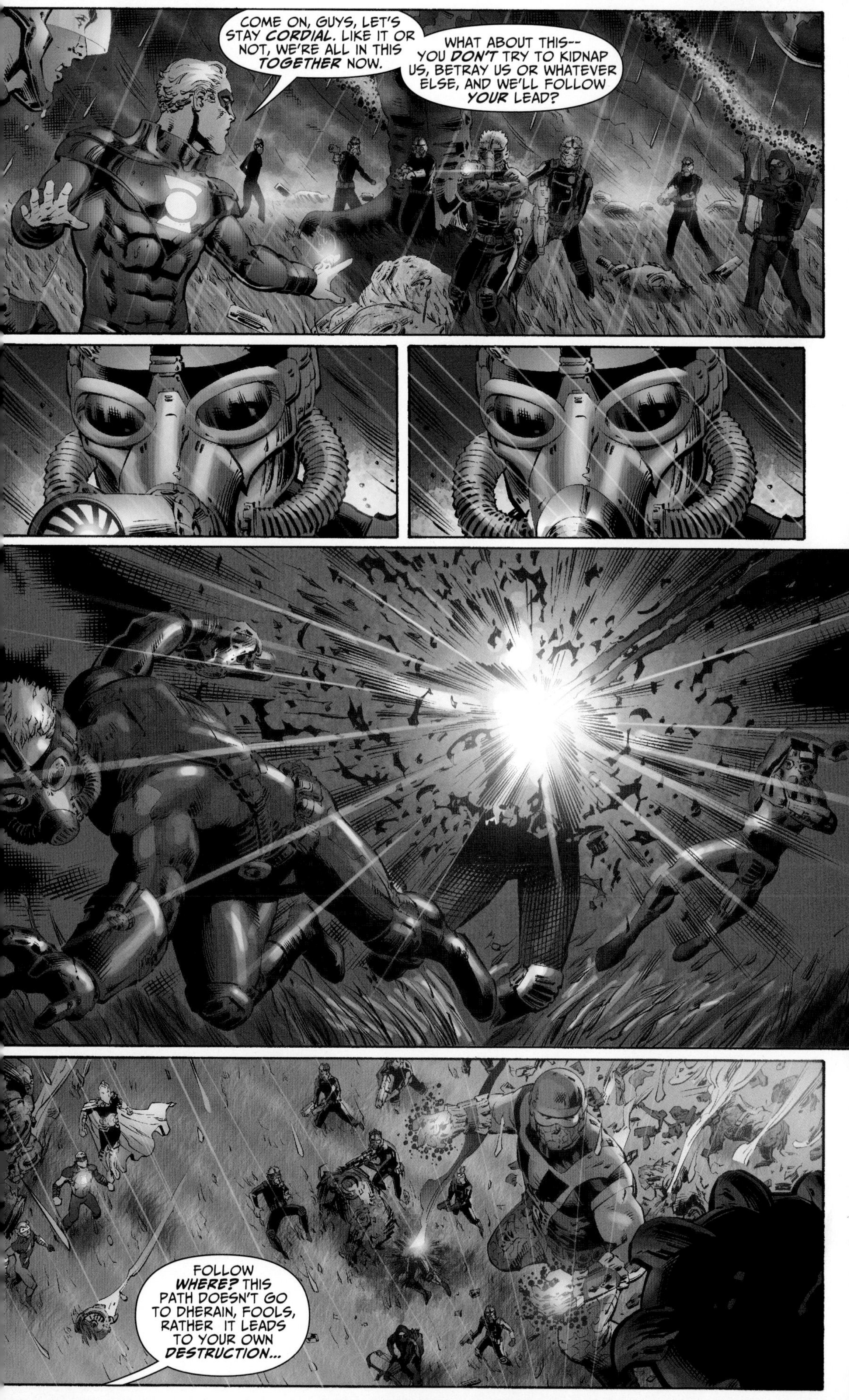

COME ON, GUYS, LET'S STAY CORDIAL. LIKE IT OR NOT, WE'RE ALL IN THIS TOGETHER NOW.
WHAT ABOUT THIS-- YOU DON'T TRY TO KIDNAP US, BETRAY US OR WHATEVER ELSE, AND WE'LL FOLLOW YOUR LEAD?
FOLLOW WHERE? THIS PATH DOESN'T GO TO DHERAIN, FOOLS, RATHER IT LEADS TO YOUR OWN DESTRUCTION...

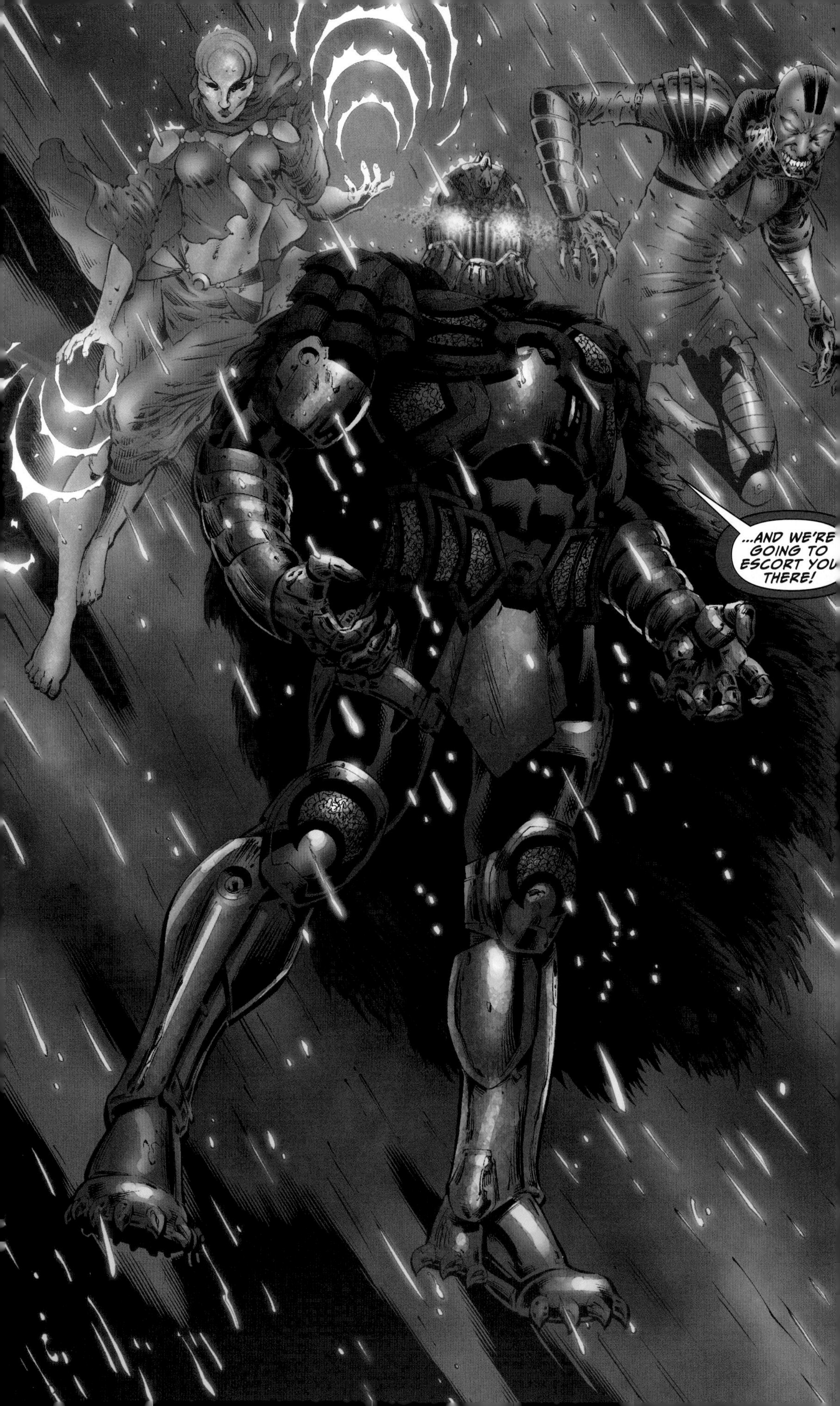
...AND WE'RE GOING TO ESCORT YOU THERE!

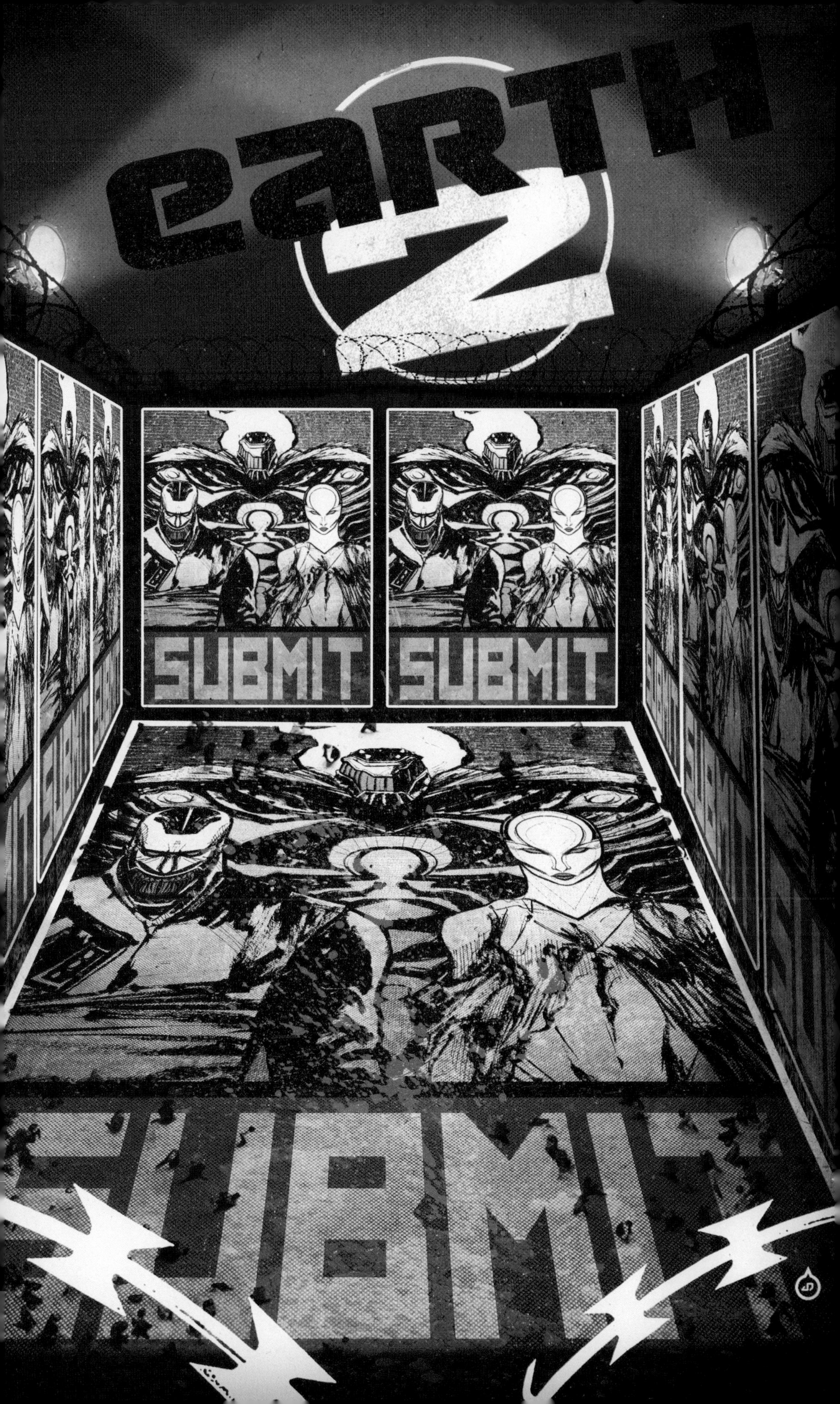

EARTH 2
SUBMIT
SUBMIT

JAMES ROBINSON
writer

NICOLA SCOTT
penciller

TREVOR SCOTT
inker

PETE PANTAZIS
colorist

JUAN DOE
cover artist

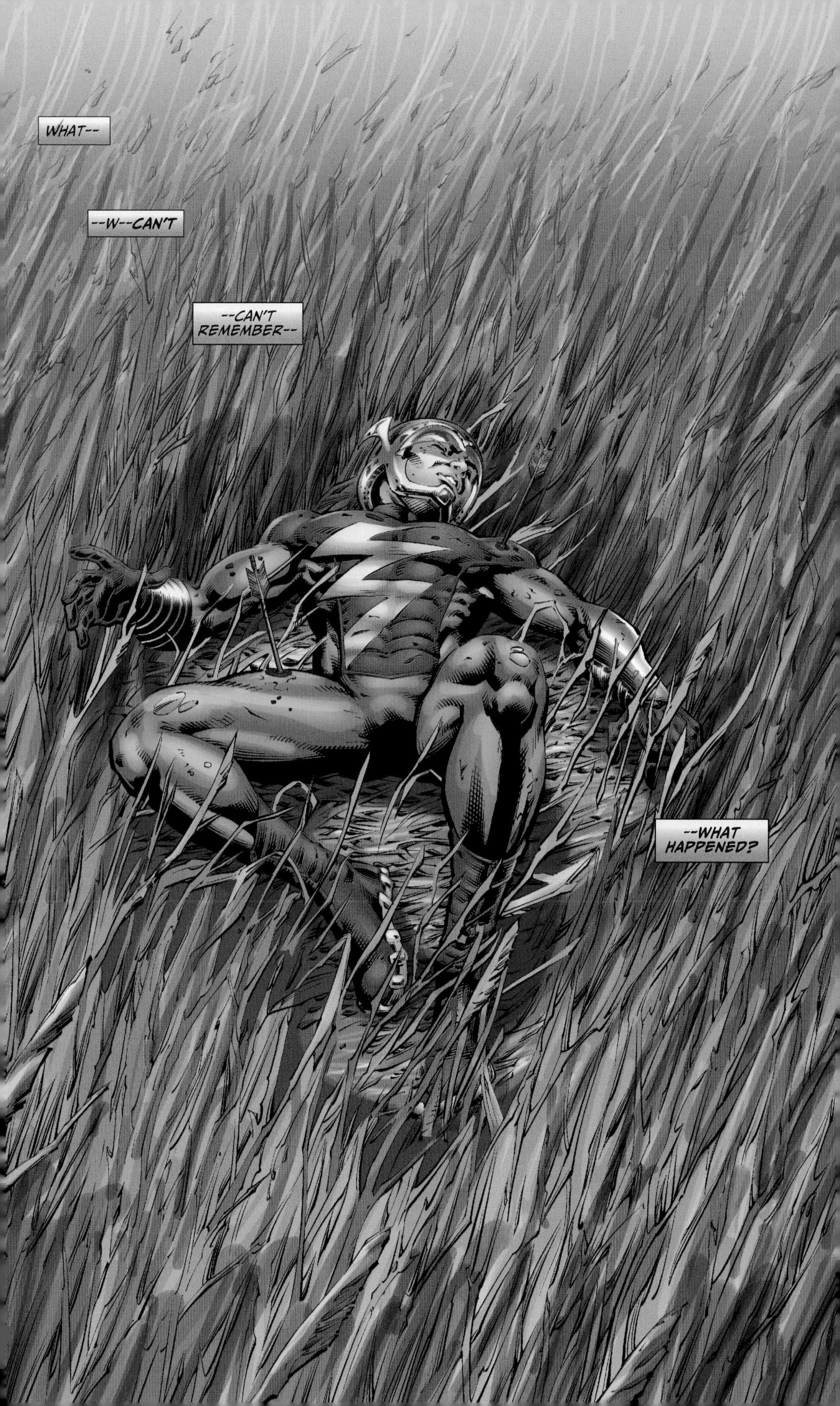
WHAT--
--W--CAN'T
--CAN'T REMEMBER--
--WHAT HAPPENED?

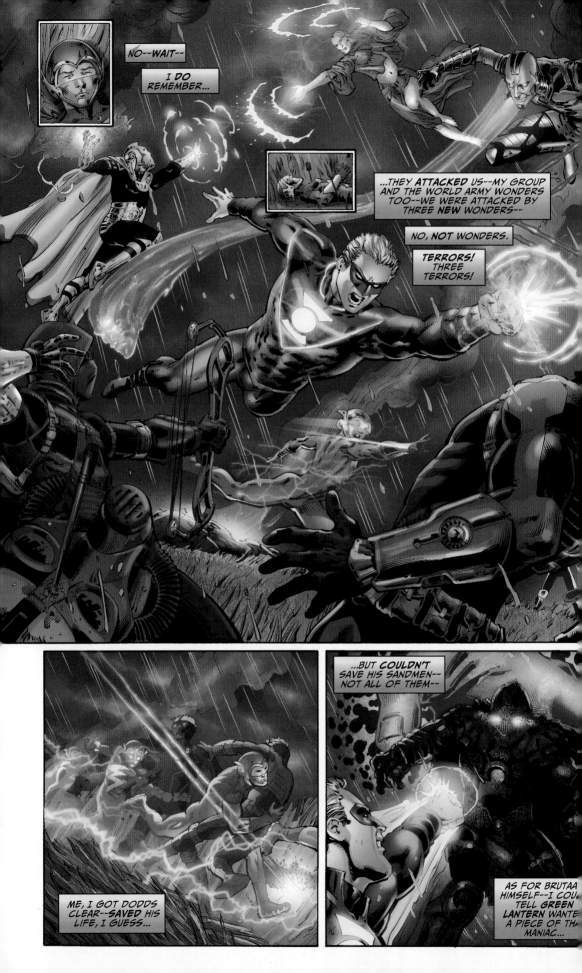

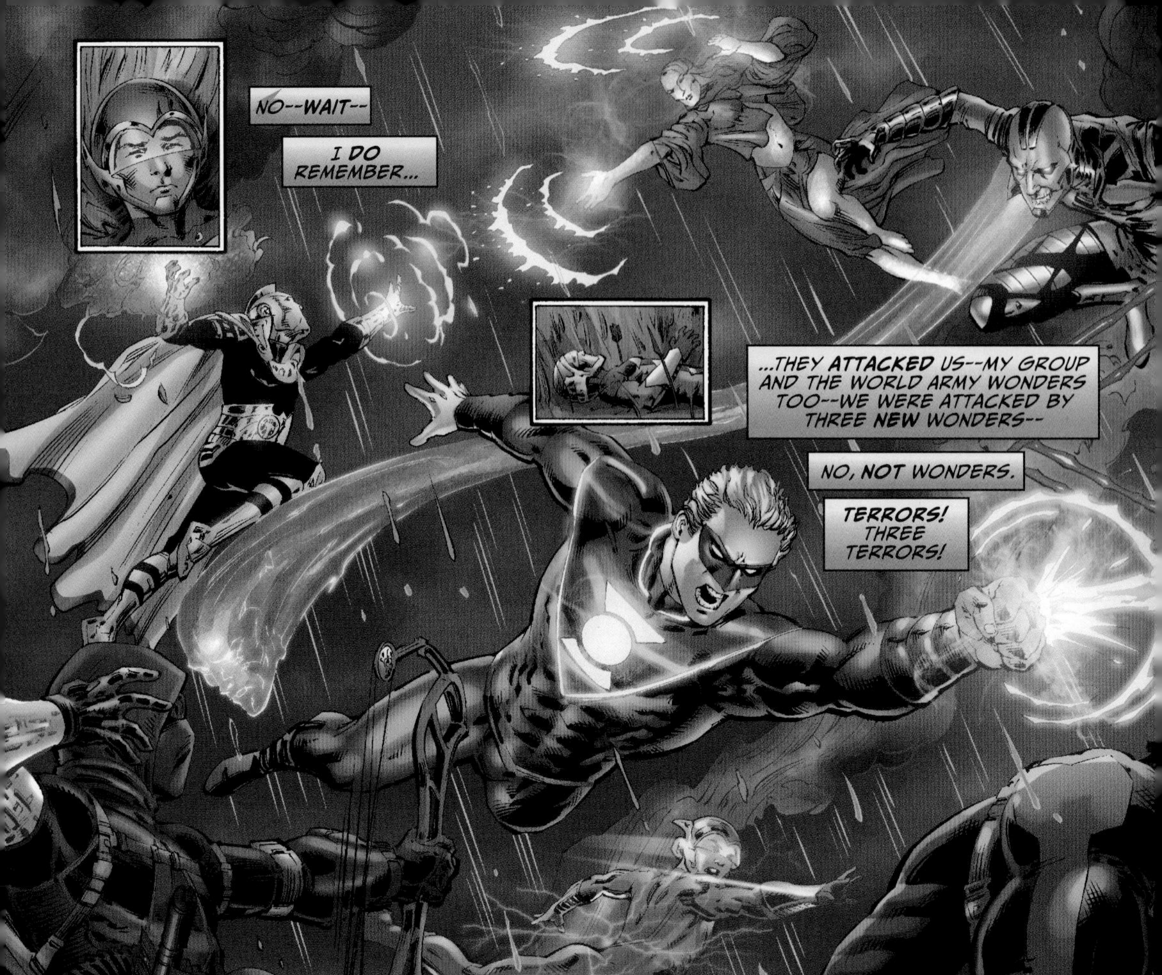
NO--WAIT--
I DO REMEMBER...
...THEY ATTACKED US--MY GROUP AND THE WORLD ARMY WONDERS TOO--WE WERE ATTACKED BY THREE NEW WONDERS--
NO, NOT WONDERS.
TERRORS! THREE TERRORS!

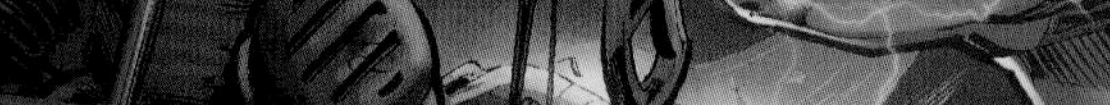
ME, I GOT DODDS CLEAR--SAVED HIS LIFE, I GUESS...

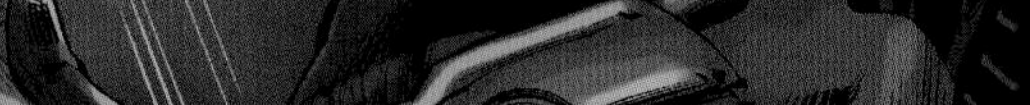
...BUT COULDN'T SAVE HIS SANDMEN--NOT ALL OF THEM--
AS FOR BRUTAA
HIMSELF--I COU
TELL GREEN
LANTERN WANTE
A PIECE OF TH
MANIAC...

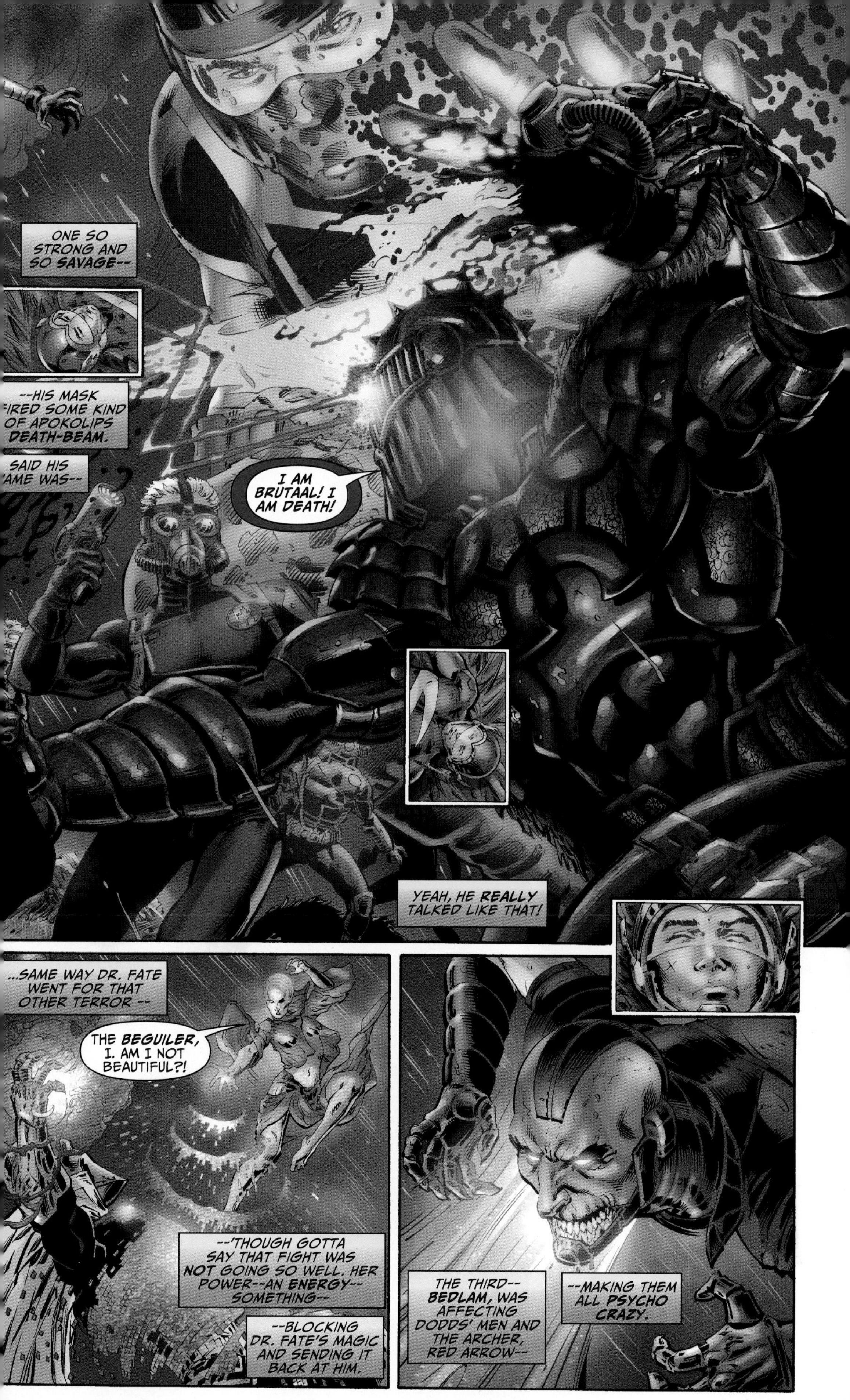
ONE SO STRONG AND SO SAVAGE--
--HIS MASK FIRED SOME KIND OF APOKOLIPS DEATH-BEAM.
SAID HIS NAME WAS--
I AM BRUTAAL! I AM DEATH!
YEAH, HE REALLY TALKED LIKE THAT!
...SAME WAY DR. FATE WENT FOR THAT OTHER TERROR --
THE BEGUILER, I. AM I NOT BEAUTIFUL?!
--'THOUGH GOTTA SAY THAT FIGHT WAS NOT GOING SO WELL. HER POWER--AN ENERGY--SOMETHING--
--BLOCKING DR. FATE'S MAGIC AND SENDING IT BACK AT HIM.
THE THIRD--BEDLAM, WAS AFFECTING DODDS' MEN AND THE ARCHER, RED ARROW--
--MAKING THEM ALL PSYCHO CRAZY.

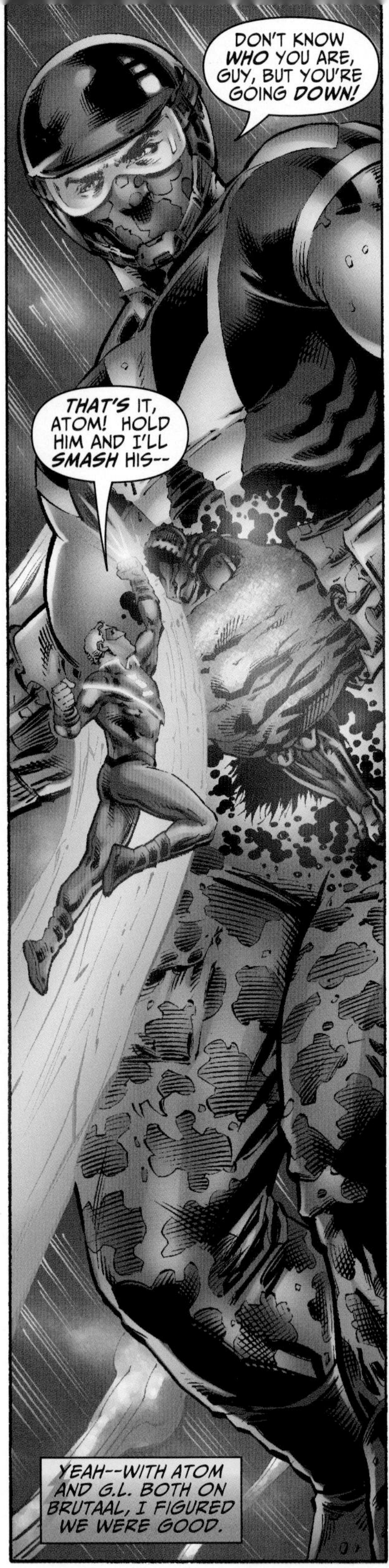
DON'T KNOW WHO YOU ARE, GUY, BUT YOU'RE GOING DOWN!
THAT'S IT, ATOM! HOLD HIM AND I'LL SMASH HIS--
YEAH--WITH ATOM AND G.L. BOTH ON BRUTAAL, I FIGURED WE WERE GOOD.
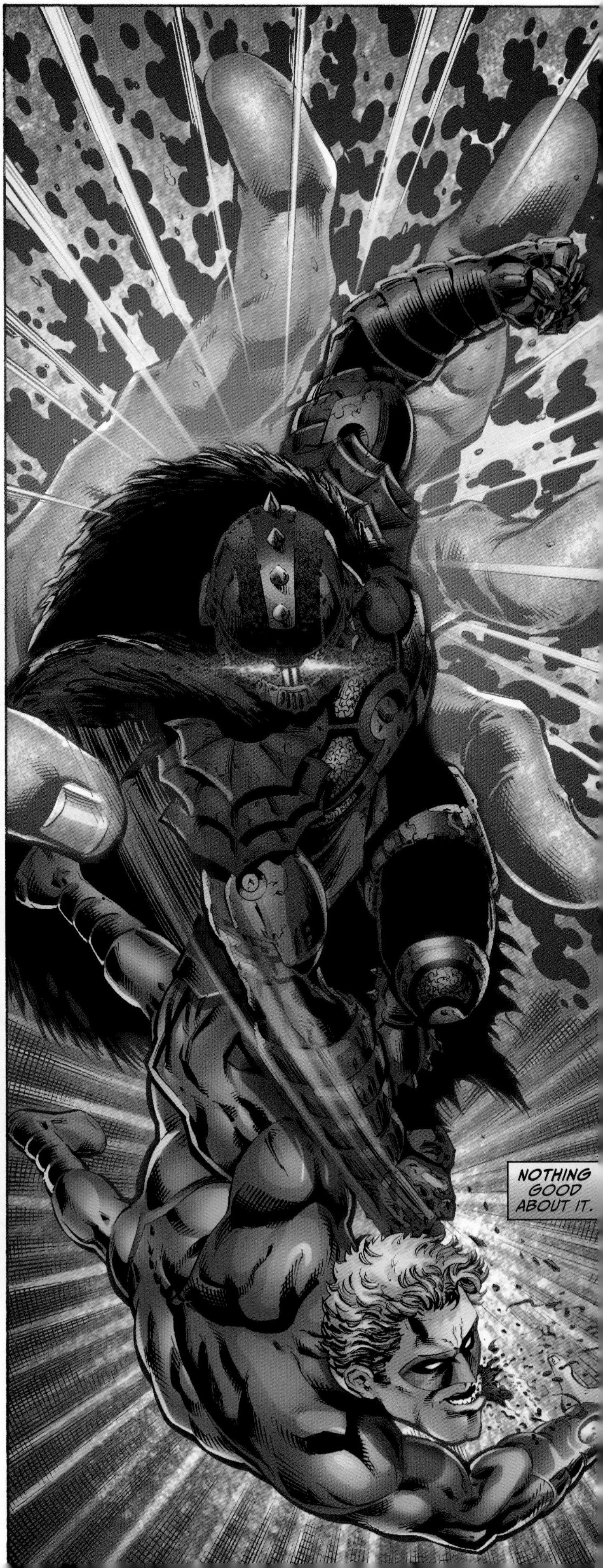
NOTHING GOOD ABOUT IT.

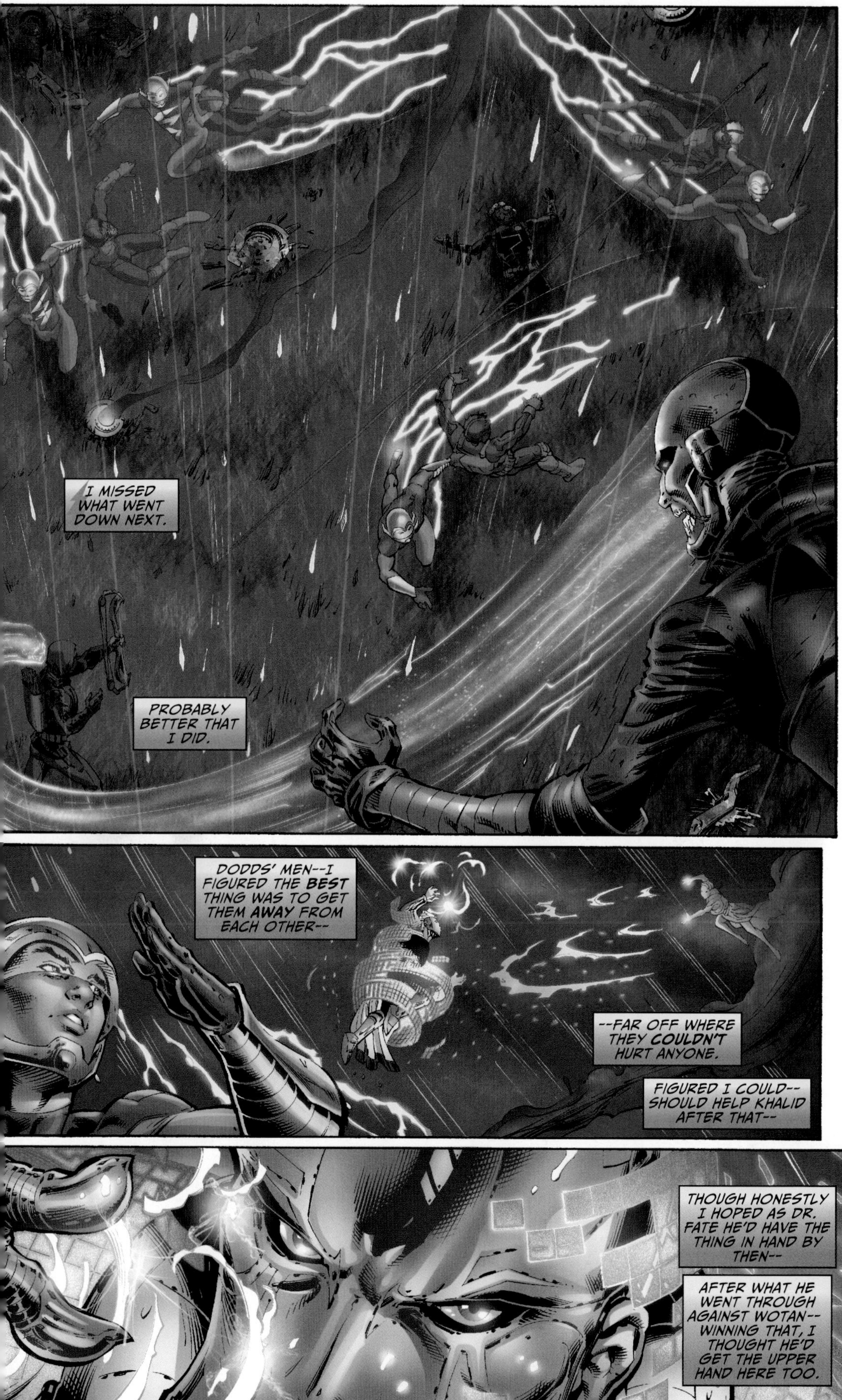

I MISSED WHAT WENT DOWN NEXT.
PROBABLY BETTER THAT I DID.
DODDS' MEN--I FIGURED THE BEST THING WAS TO GET THEM AWAY FROM EACH OTHER--
--FAR OFF WHERE THEY COULDN'T HURT ANYONE.
FIGURED I COULD--SHOULD HELP KHALID AFTER THAT--
THOUGH HONESTLY I HOPED AS DR. FATE HE'D HAVE THE THING IN HAND BY THEN--
AFTER WHAT HE WENT THROUGH AGAINST WOTAN--WINNING THAT, I THOUGHT HE'D GET THE UPPER HAND HERE TOO.

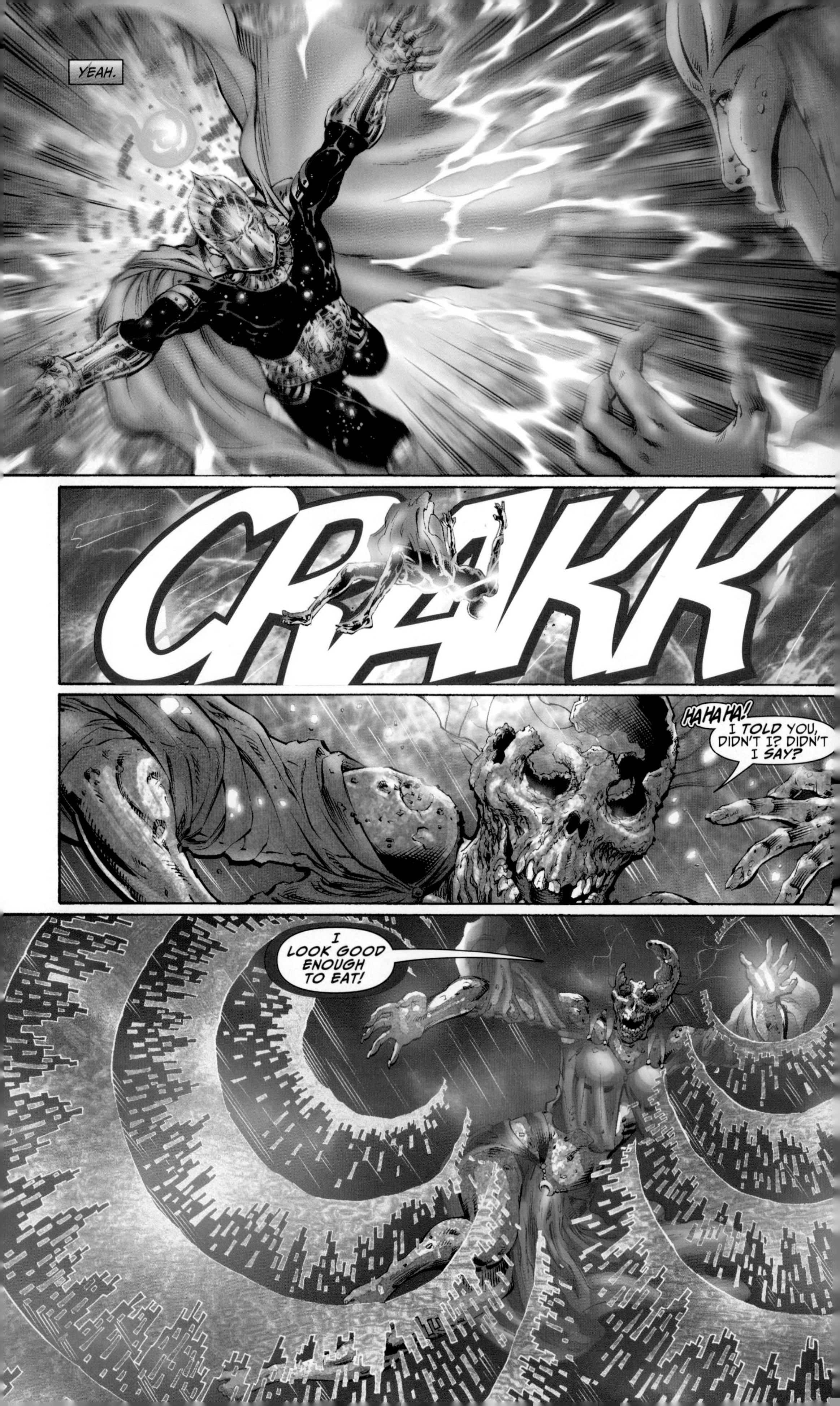
YEAH.
CRAKK
HAHAHA!
I TOLD YOU, DIDN'T I? DIDN'T I SAY?
I LOOK GOOD ENOUGH TO EAT!

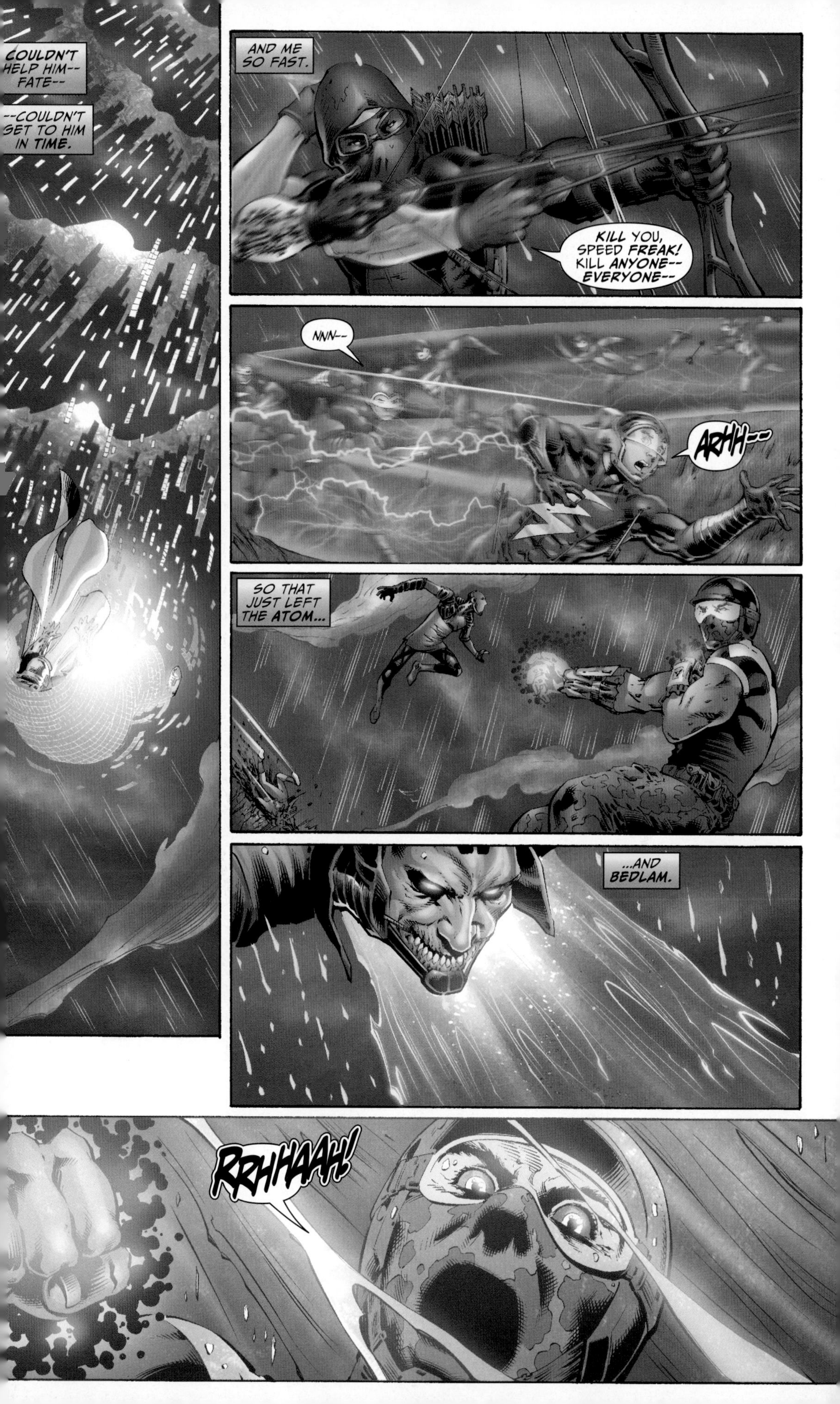
COULDN'T HELP HIM-- FATE--
--COULDN'T GET TO HIM IN TIME.
AND ME SO FAST.
KILL YOU, SPEED FREAK! KILL ANYONE-- EVERYONE--
NNN--
ARHH--
SO THAT JUST LEFT THE ATOM...
...AND BEDLAM.
RRHHAAH!

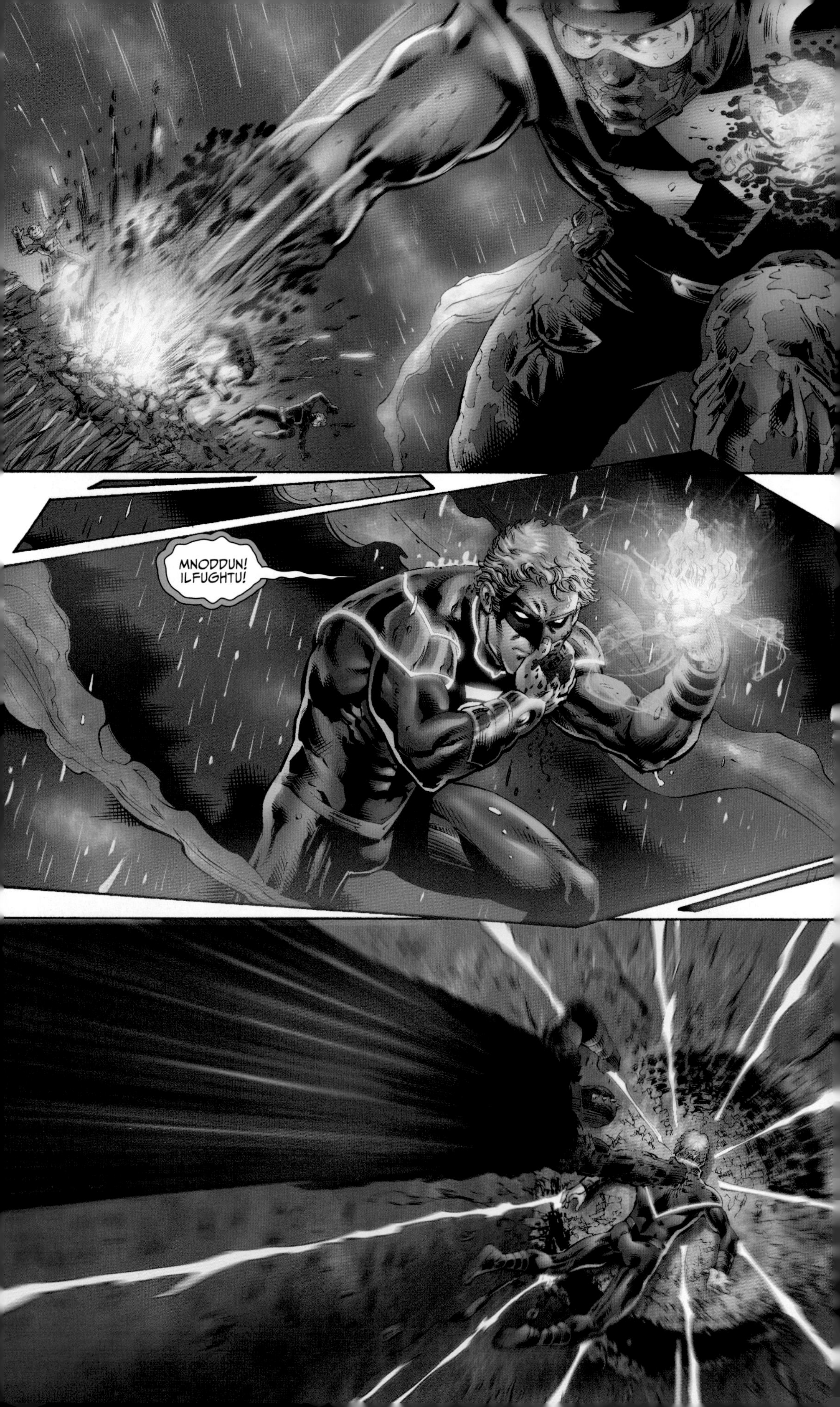
MNODDUN! ILFUGHTU!

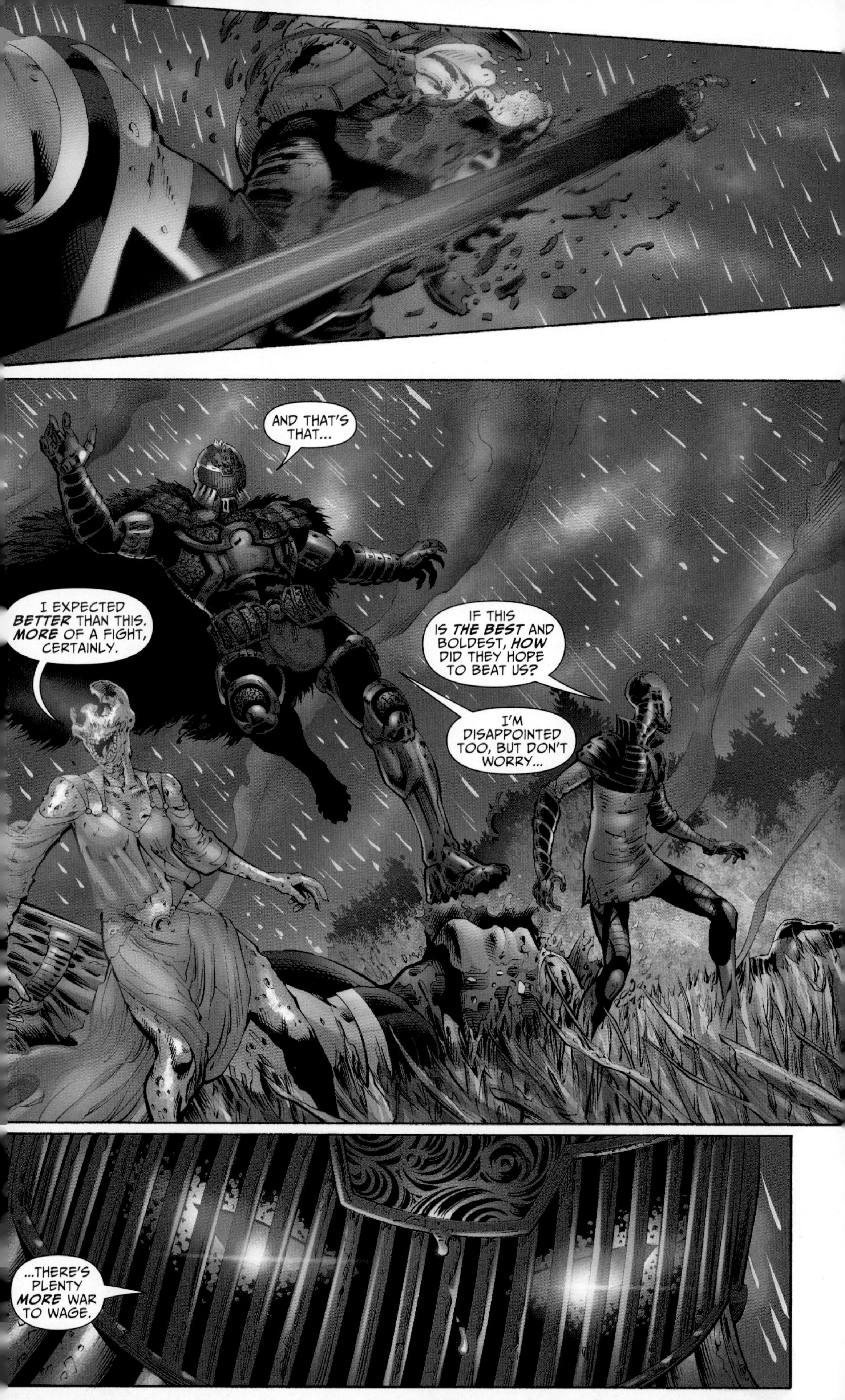
AND THAT'S THAT...
I EXPECTED BETTER THAN THIS. MORE OF A FIGHT, CERTAINLY.
IF THIS IS THE BEST AND BOLDEST, HOW DID THEY HOPE TO BEAT US?
I'M DISAPPOINTED TOO, BUT DON'T WORRY...
...THERE'S PLENTY MORE WAR TO WAGE.

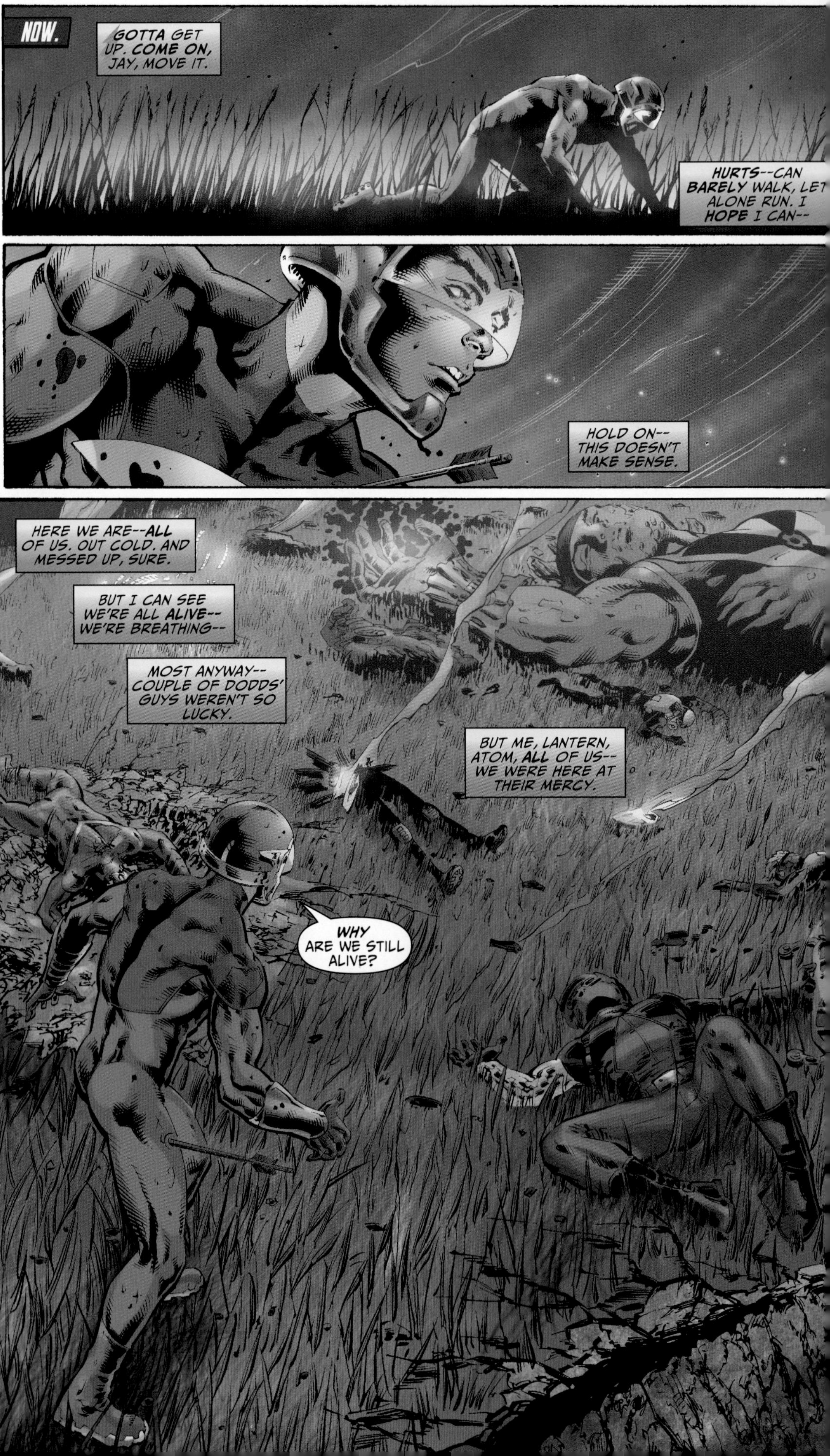
NOW.
GOTTA GET UP. COME ON, JAY, MOVE IT.
HURTS--CAN BARELY WALK, LET ALONE RUN. I HOPE I CAN--
HOLD ON-- THIS DOESN'T MAKE SENSE.
HERE WE ARE--ALL OF US. OUT COLD. AND MESSED UP, SURE.
BUT I CAN SEE WE'RE ALL ALIVE-- WE'RE BREATHING--
MOST ANYWAY-- COUPLE OF DODDS' GUYS WEREN'T SO LUCKY.
BUT ME, LANTERN, ATOM, ALL OF US-- WE WERE HERE AT THEIR MERCY.
WHY ARE WE STILL ALIVE?

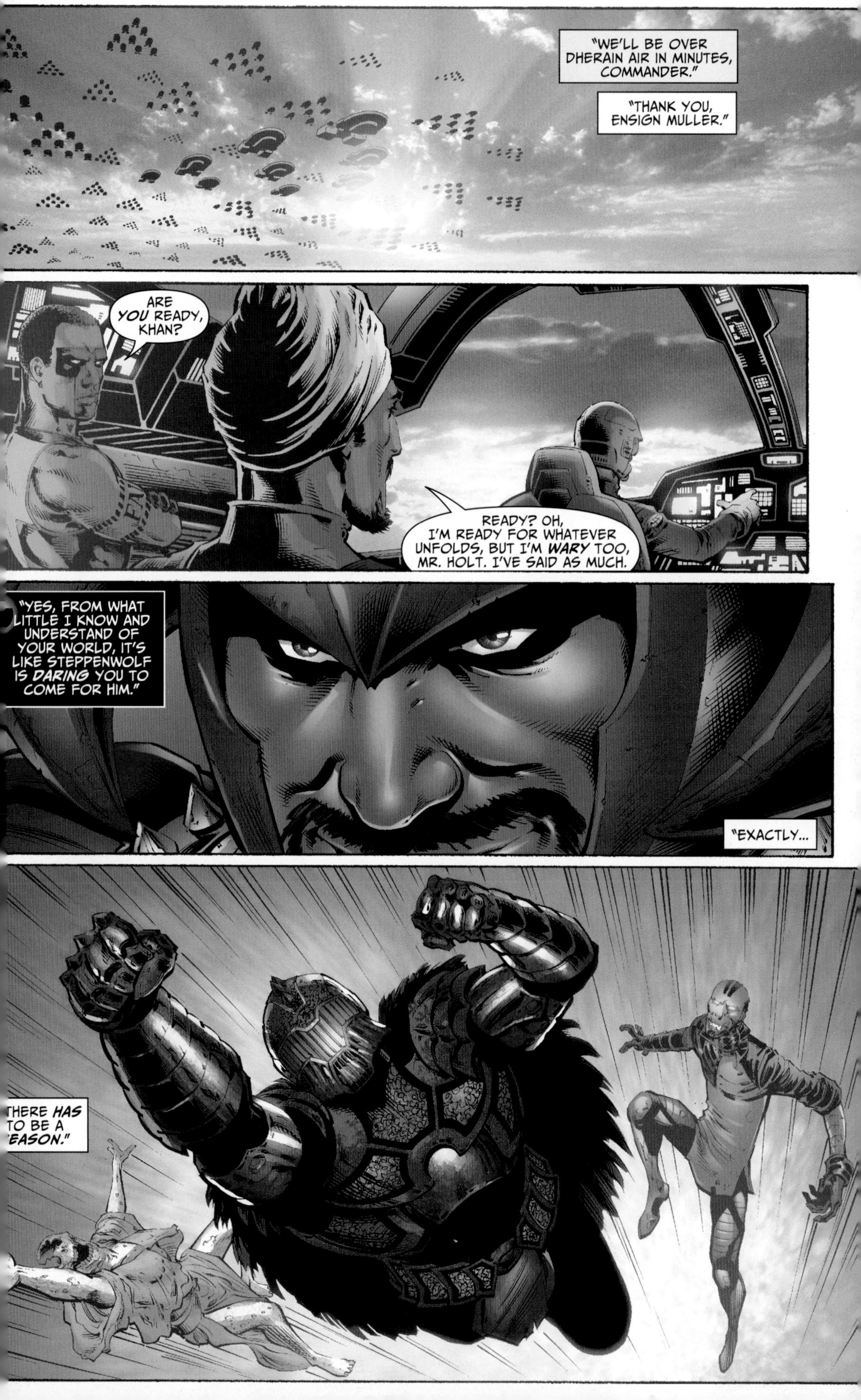
"WE'LL BE OVER DHERAIN AIR IN MINUTES, COMMANDER."
"THANK YOU, ENSIGN MULLER."
ARE *YOU* READY, KHAN?
READY? OH, I'M READY FOR WHATEVER UNFOLDS, BUT I'M *WARY* TOO, MR. HOLT. I'VE SAID AS MUCH.
"YES, FROM WHAT LITTLE I KNOW AND UNDERSTAND OF YOUR WORLD, IT'S LIKE STEPPENWOLF IS *DARING* YOU TO COME FOR HIM."
"EXACTLY...
THERE *HAS* TO BE A EASON."

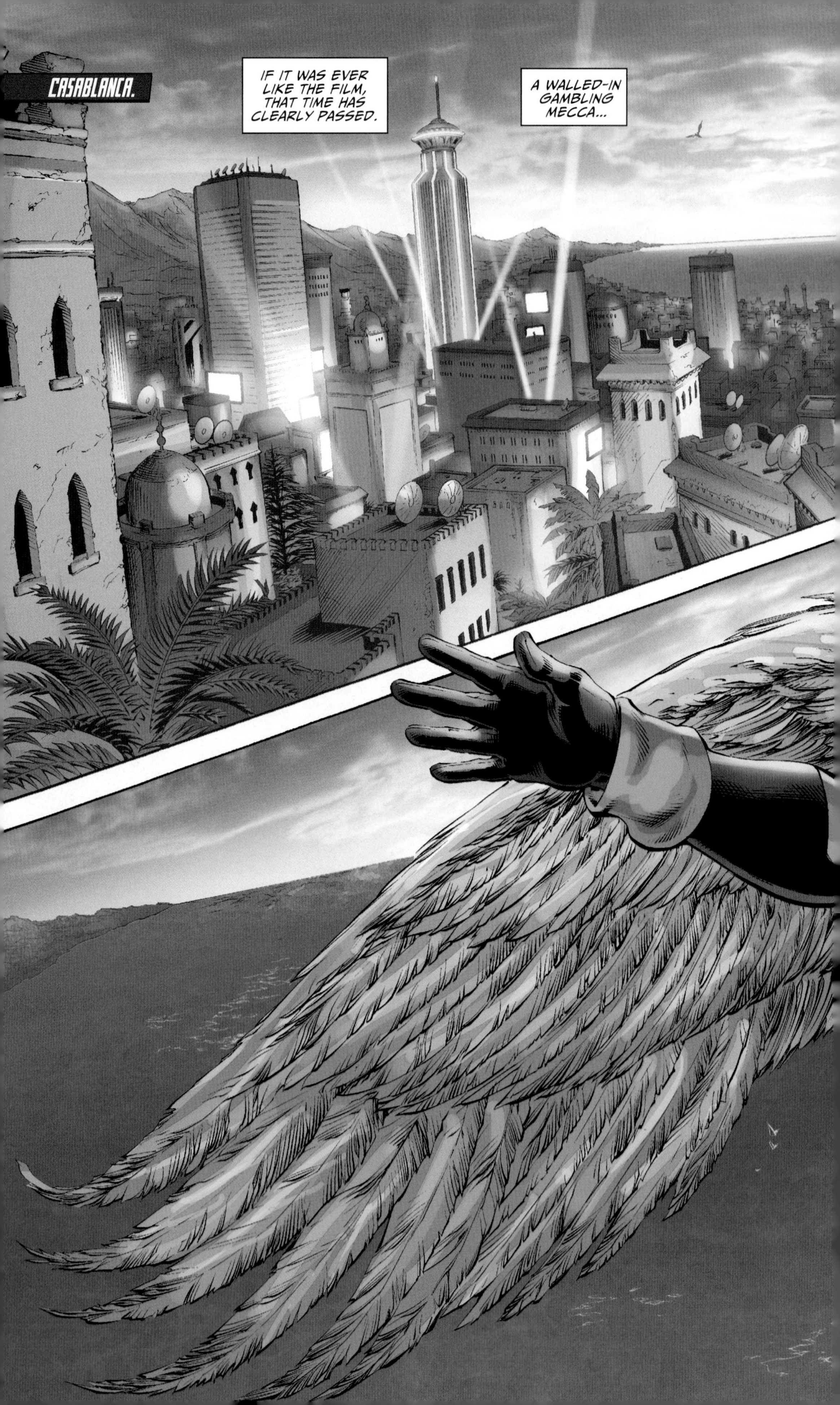
CASABLANCA.
IF IT WAS EVER LIKE THE FILM, THAT TIME HAS CLEARLY PASSED.
A WALLED-IN GAMBLING MECCA...

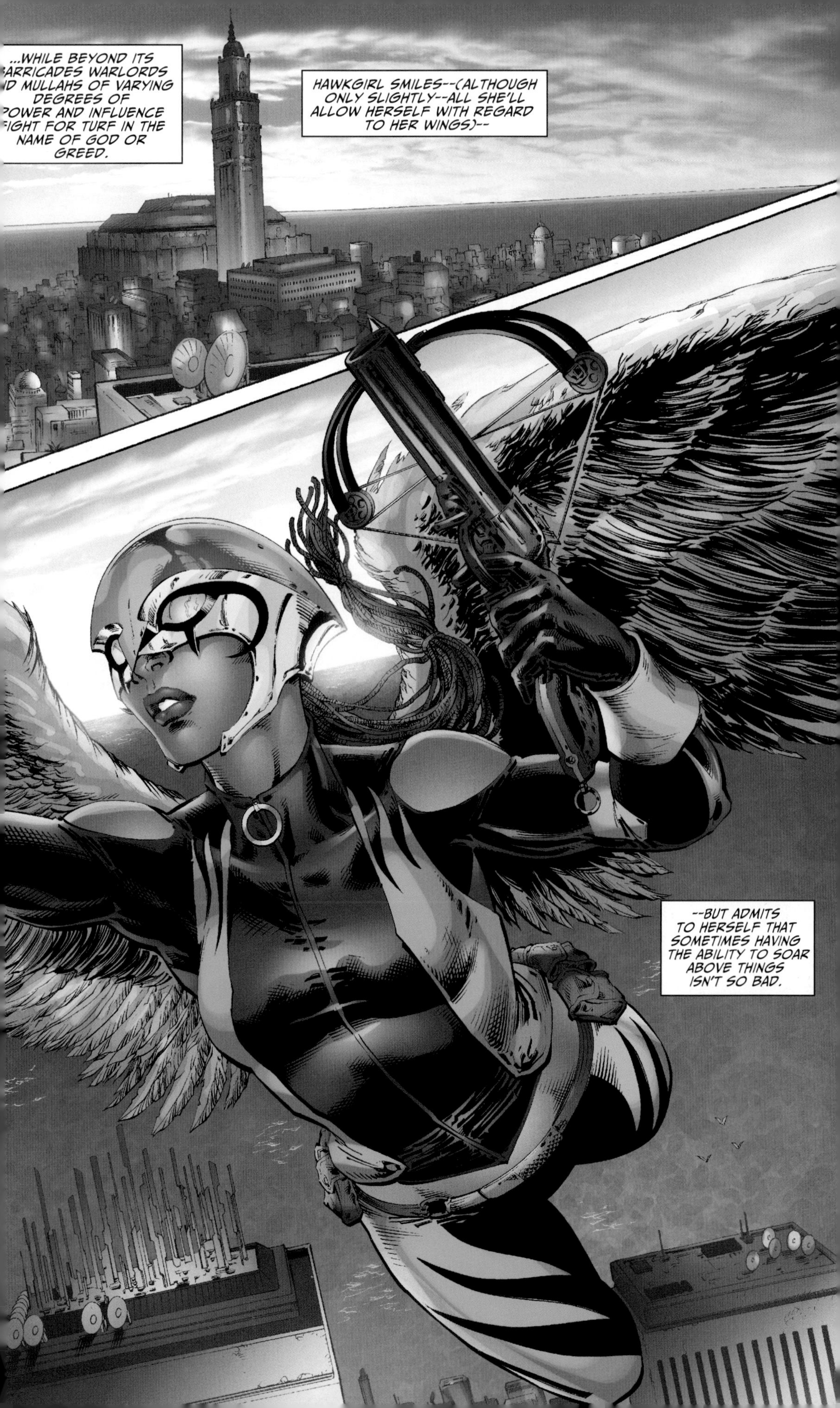

...WHILE BEYOND ITS BARRICADES WARLORDS AND MULLAHS OF VARYING DEGREES OF POWER AND INFLUENCE FIGHT FOR TURF IN THE NAME OF GOD OR GREED.
HAWKGIRL SMILES--(ALTHOUGH ONLY SLIGHTLY--ALL SHE'LL ALLOW HERSELF WITH REGARD TO HER WINGS)--
--BUT ADMITS TO HERSELF THAT SOMETIMES HAVING THE ABILITY TO SOAR ABOVE THINGS ISN'T SO BAD.

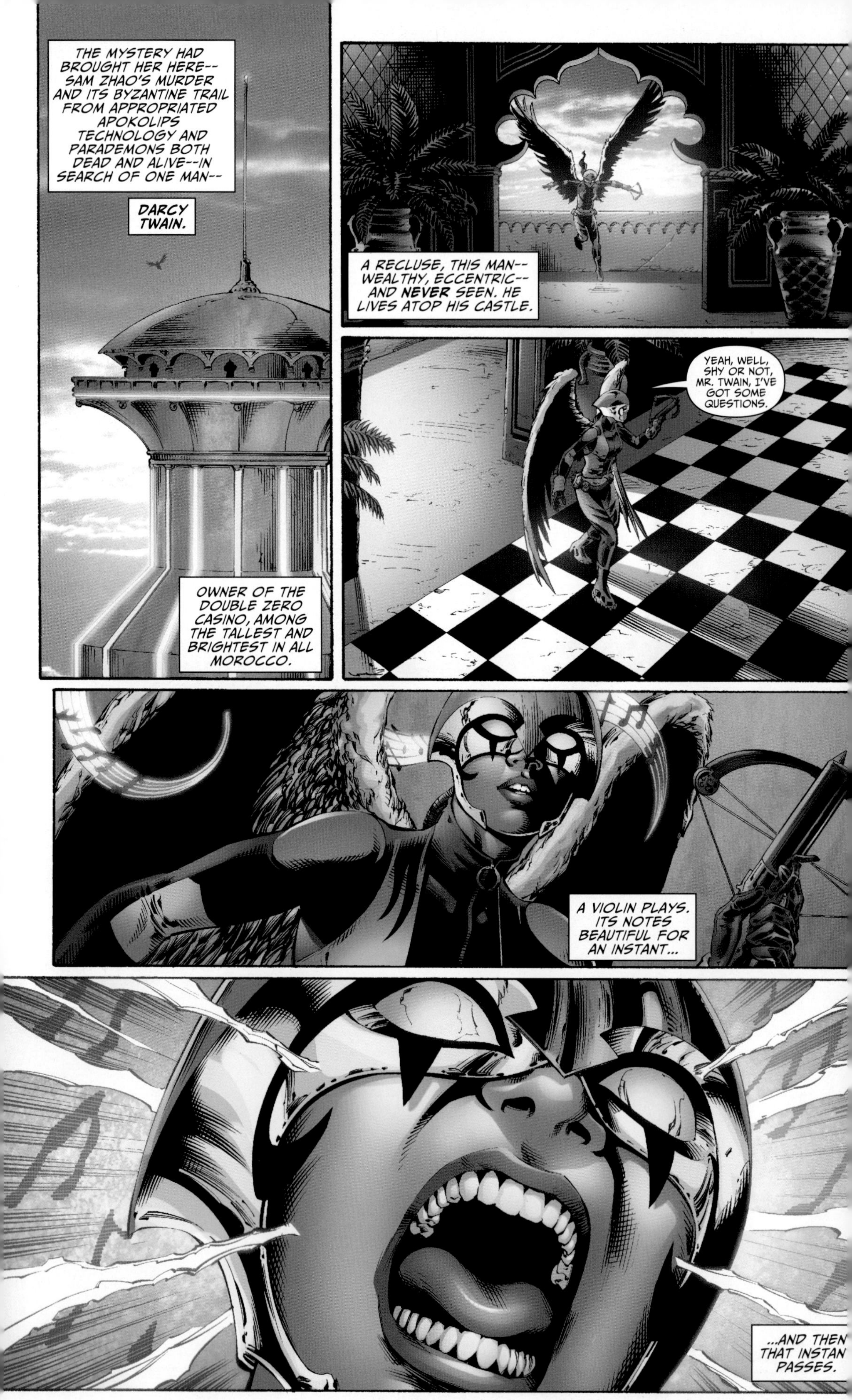

THE MYSTERY HAD BROUGHT HER HERE-- SAM ZHAO'S MURDER AND ITS BYZANTINE TRAIL FROM APPROPRIATED APOKOLIPS TECHNOLOGY AND PARADEMONS BOTH DEAD AND ALIVE--IN SEARCH OF ONE MAN--
DARCY TWAIN.
OWNER OF THE DOUBLE ZERO CASINO, AMONG THE TALLEST AND BRIGHTEST IN ALL MOROCCO.
A RECLUSE, THIS MAN-- WEALTHY, ECCENTRIC-- AND **NEVER** SEEN. HE LIVES ATOP HIS CASTLE.
YEAH, WELL, SHY OR NOT, MR. TWAIN, I'VE GOT SOME QUESTIONS.
A VIOLIN PLAYS. ITS NOTES BEAUTIFUL FOR AN INSTANT...
...AND THEN THAT INSTAN PASSES.

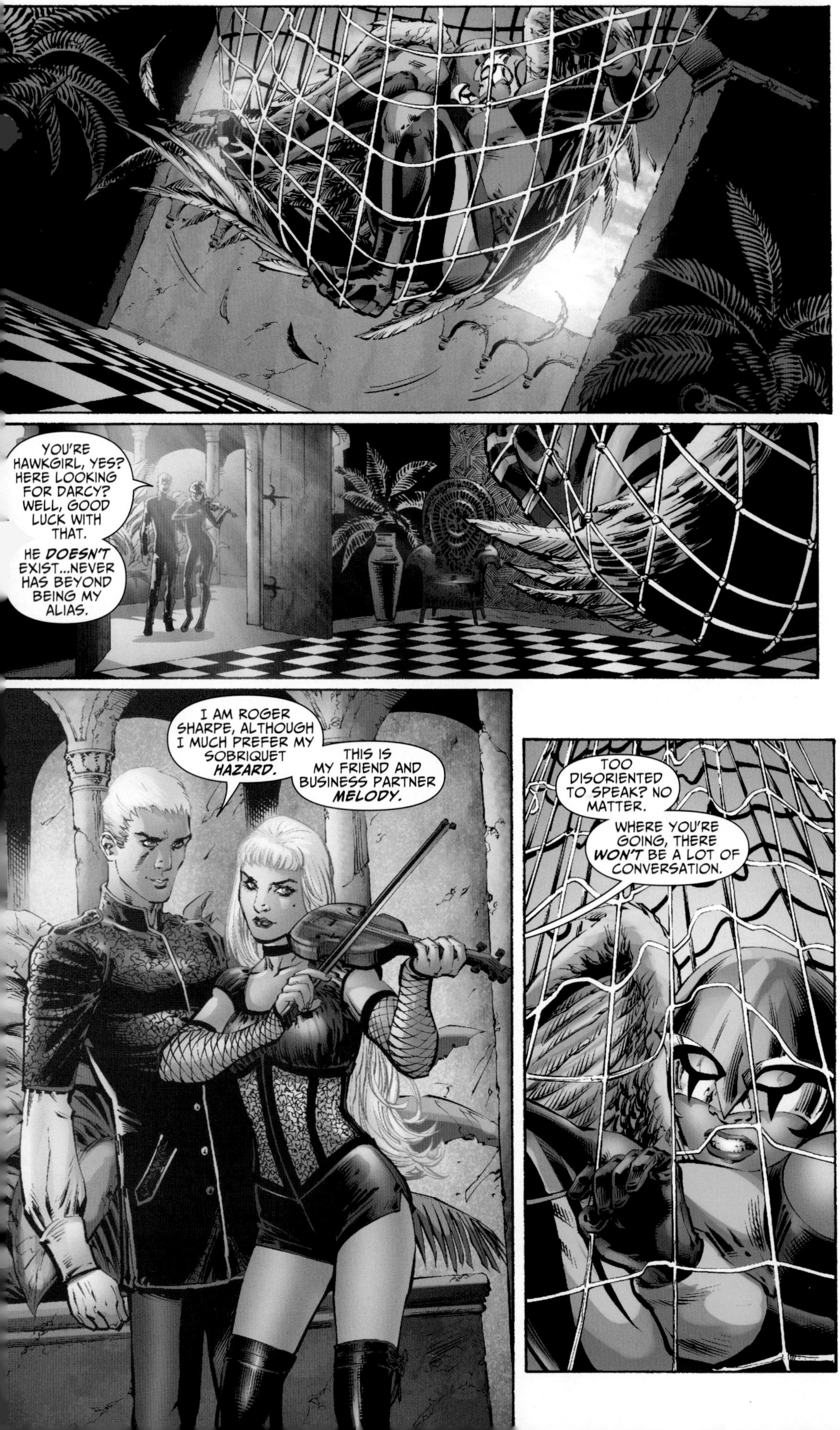
YOU'RE HAWKGIRL, YES? HERE LOOKING FOR DARCY? WELL, GOOD LUCK WITH THAT.
HE DOESN'T EXIST...NEVER HAS BEYOND BEING MY ALIAS.
I AM ROGER SHARPE, ALTHOUGH I MUCH PREFER MY SOBRIQUET HAZARD.
THIS IS MY FRIEND AND BUSINESS PARTNER MELODY.
TOO DISORIENTED TO SPEAK? NO MATTER.
WHERE YOU'RE GOING, THERE WON'T BE A LOT OF CONVERSATION.

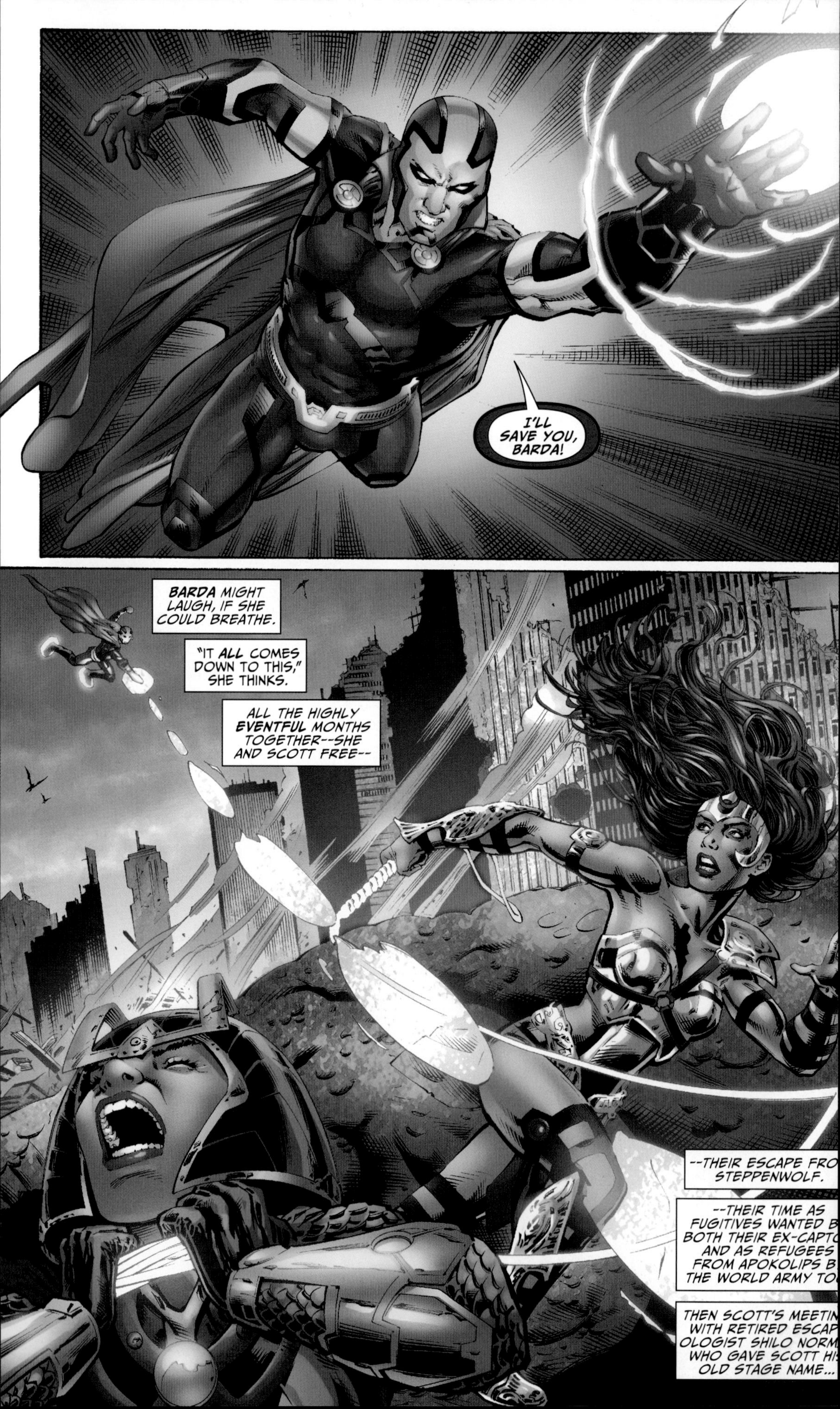
I'LL SAVE YOU, BARDA!
BARDA MIGHT LAUGH, IF SHE COULD BREATHE.
"IT ALL COMES DOWN TO THIS," SHE THINKS.
ALL THE HIGHLY EVENTFUL MONTHS TOGETHER--SHE AND SCOTT FREE--
--THEIR ESCAPE FRO STEPPENWOLF.
--THEIR TIME AS FUGITIVES WANTED B BOTH THEIR EX-CAPTO AND AS REFUGEES FROM APOKOLIPS B THE WORLD ARMY TO
THEN SCOTT'S MEETIN WITH RETIRED ESCAP OLOGIST SHILO NORM WHO GAVE SCOTT HI OLD STAGE NAME...

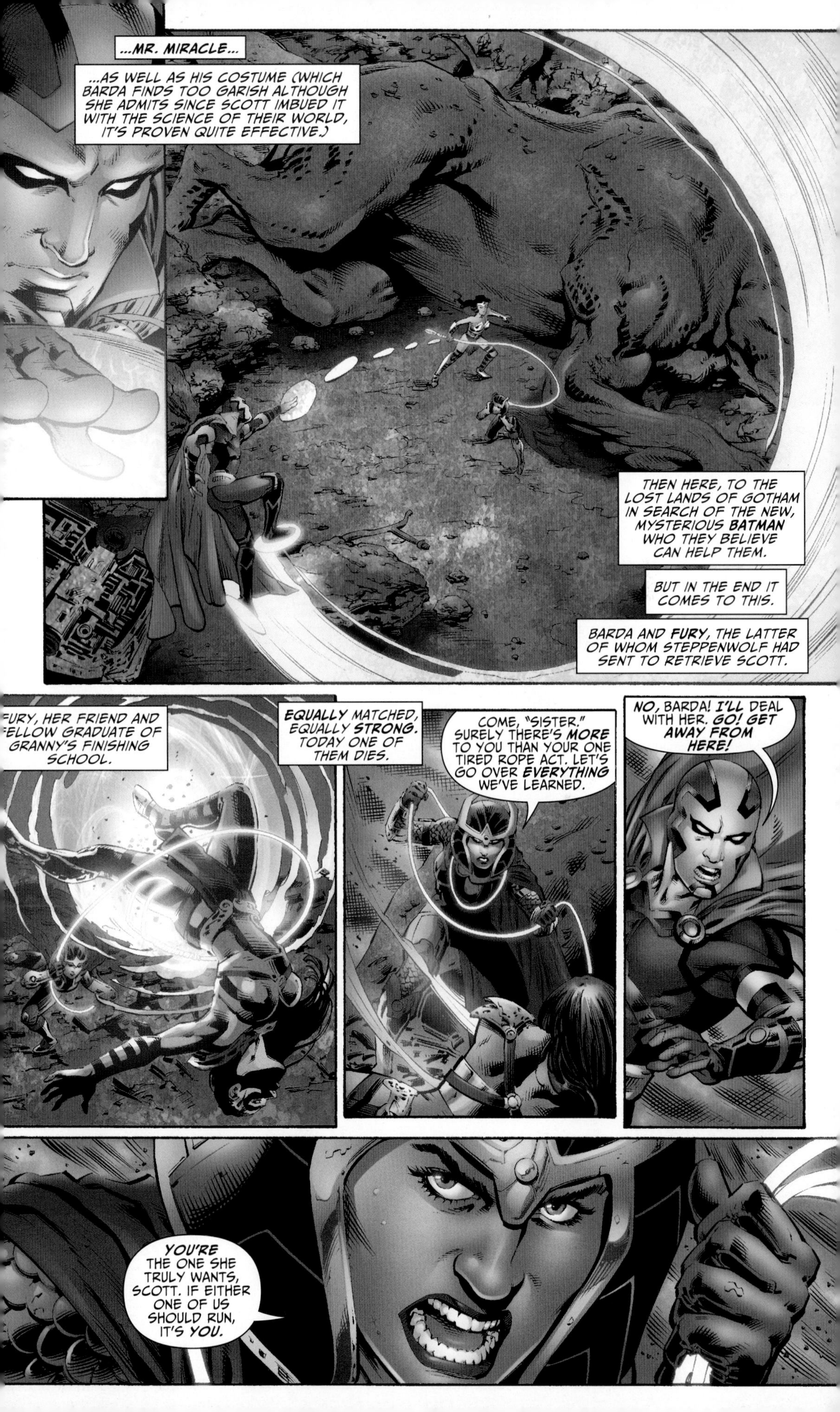

...MR. MIRACLE...
...AS WELL AS HIS COSTUME (WHICH BARDA FINDS TOO GARISH ALTHOUGH SHE ADMITS SINCE SCOTT IMBUED IT WITH THE SCIENCE OF THEIR WORLD, IT'S PROVEN QUITE EFFECTIVE.)
THEN HERE, TO THE LOST LANDS OF GOTHAM IN SEARCH OF THE NEW, MYSTERIOUS BATMAN WHO THEY BELIEVE CAN HELP THEM.
BUT IN THE END IT COMES TO THIS.
BARDA AND FURY, THE LATTER OF WHOM STEPPENWOLF HAD SENT TO RETRIEVE SCOTT.
FURY, HER FRIEND AND FELLOW GRADUATE OF GRANNY'S FINISHING SCHOOL.
EQUALLY MATCHED, EQUALLY STRONG. TODAY ONE OF THEM DIES.
COME, "SISTER." SURELY THERE'S MORE TO YOU THAN YOUR ONE TIRED ROPE ACT. LET'S GO OVER EVERYTHING WE'VE LEARNED.
NO, BARDA! I'LL DEAL WITH HER. GO! GET AWAY FROM HERE!
YOU'RE THE ONE SHE TRULY WANTS, SCOTT. IF EITHER ONE OF US SHOULD RUN, IT'S YOU.

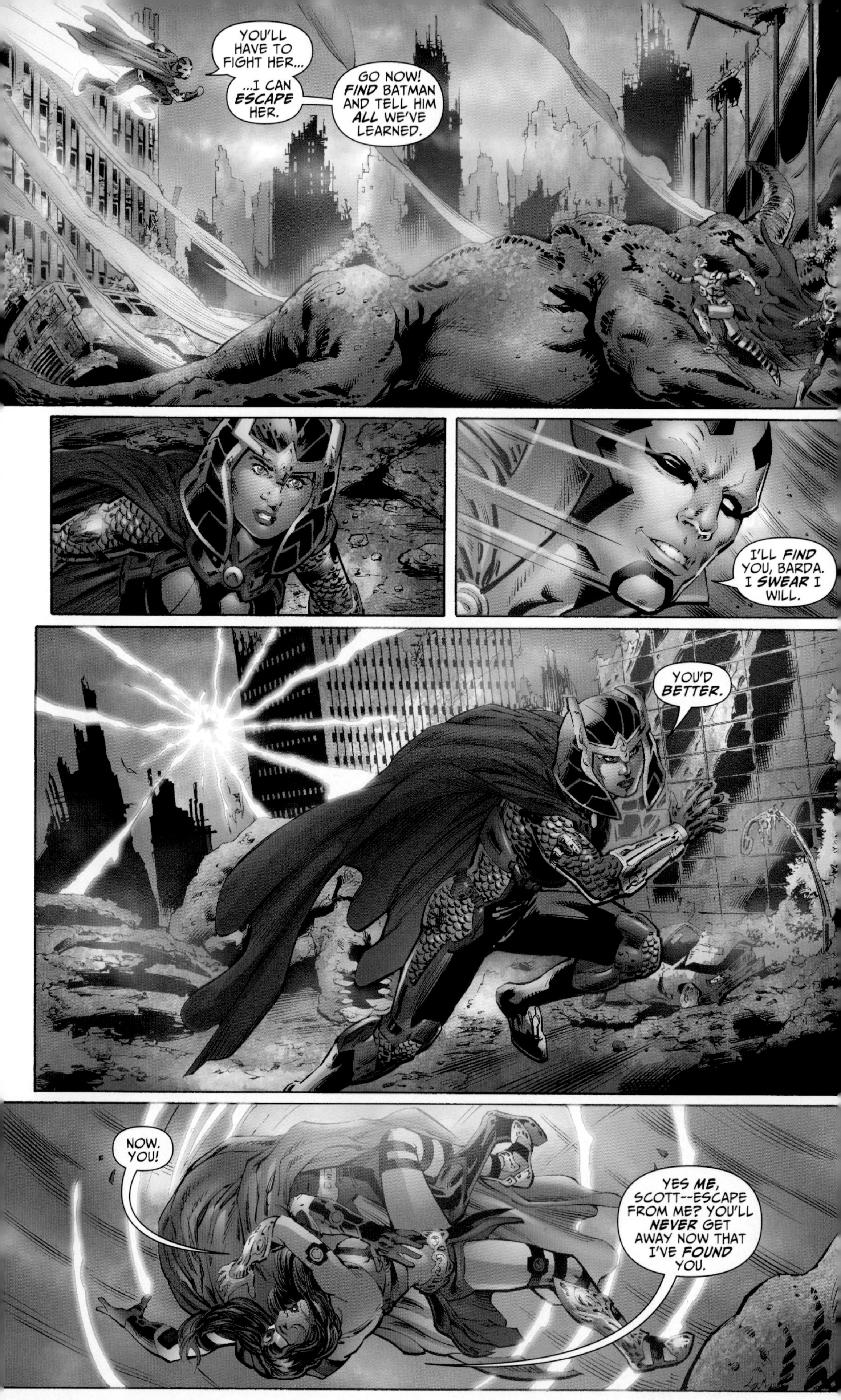
YOU'LL HAVE TO FIGHT HER...
...I CAN ESCAPE HER.
GO NOW! FIND BATMAN AND TELL HIM ALL WE'VE LEARNED.
I'LL FIND YOU, BARDA. I SWEAR I WILL.
YOU'D BETTER.
NOW. YOU!
YES ME, SCOTT--ESCAPE FROM ME? YOU'LL NEVER GET AWAY NOW THAT I'VE FOUND YOU.

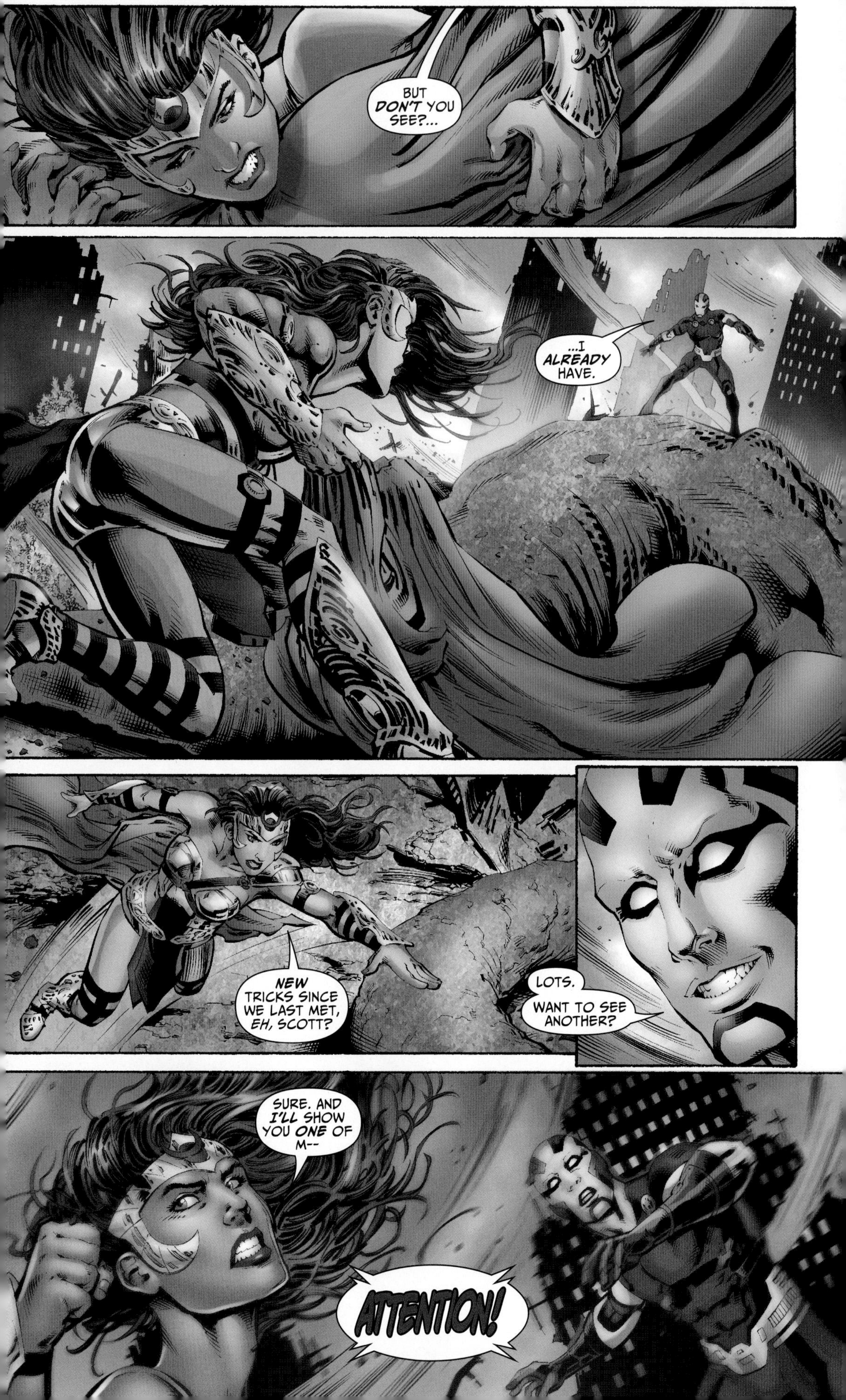
BUT DON'T YOU SEE?...
...I ALREADY HAVE.
NEW TRICKS SINCE WE LAST MET, EH, SCOTT?
LOTS.
WANT TO SEE ANOTHER?
SURE. AND I'LL SHOW YOU ONE OF M--
ATTENTION!

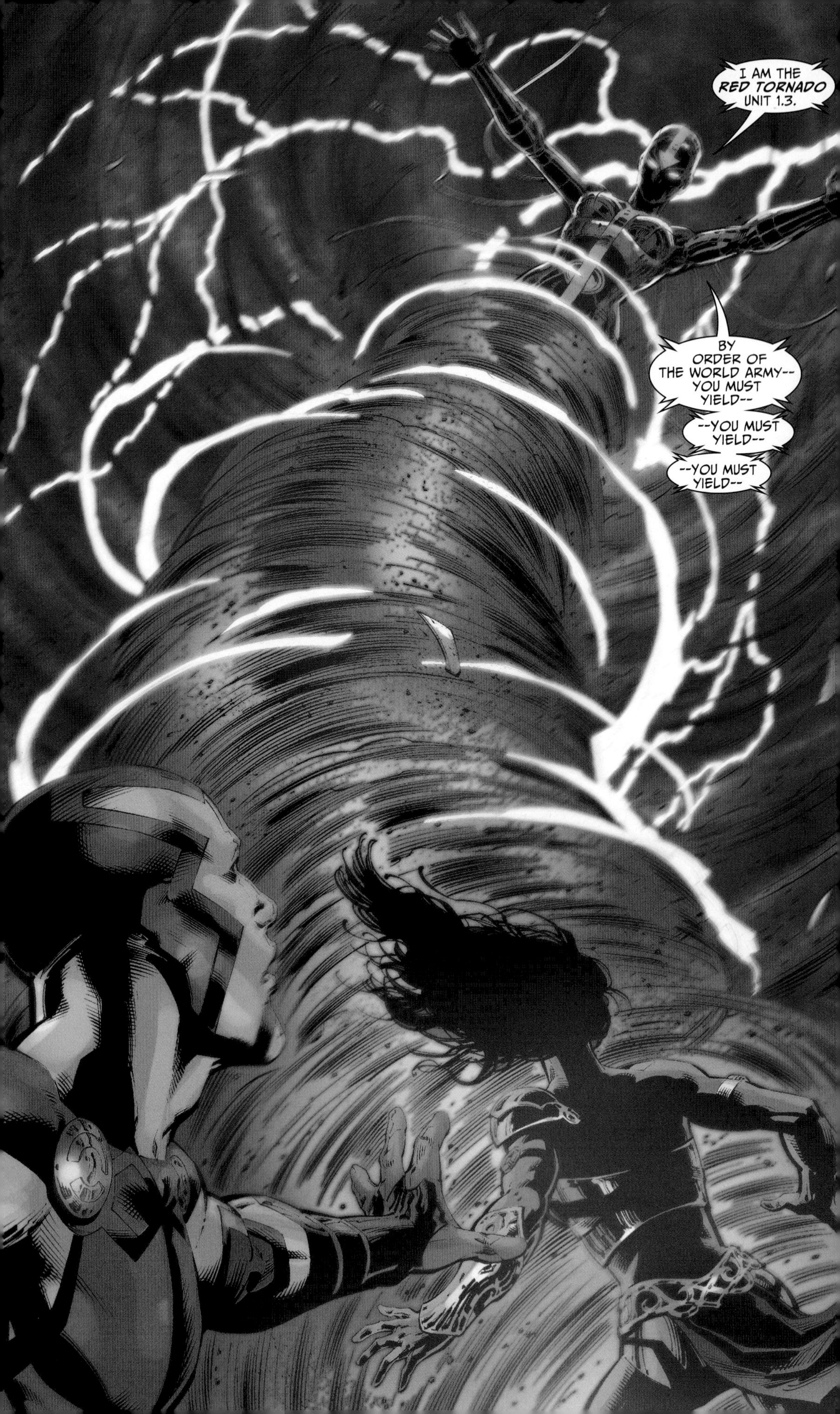
I AM THE *RED TORNADO* UNIT 1.3.
BY ORDER OF THE WORLD ARMY-- YOU MUST YIELD--
--YOU MUST YIELD--
--YOU MUST YIELD--

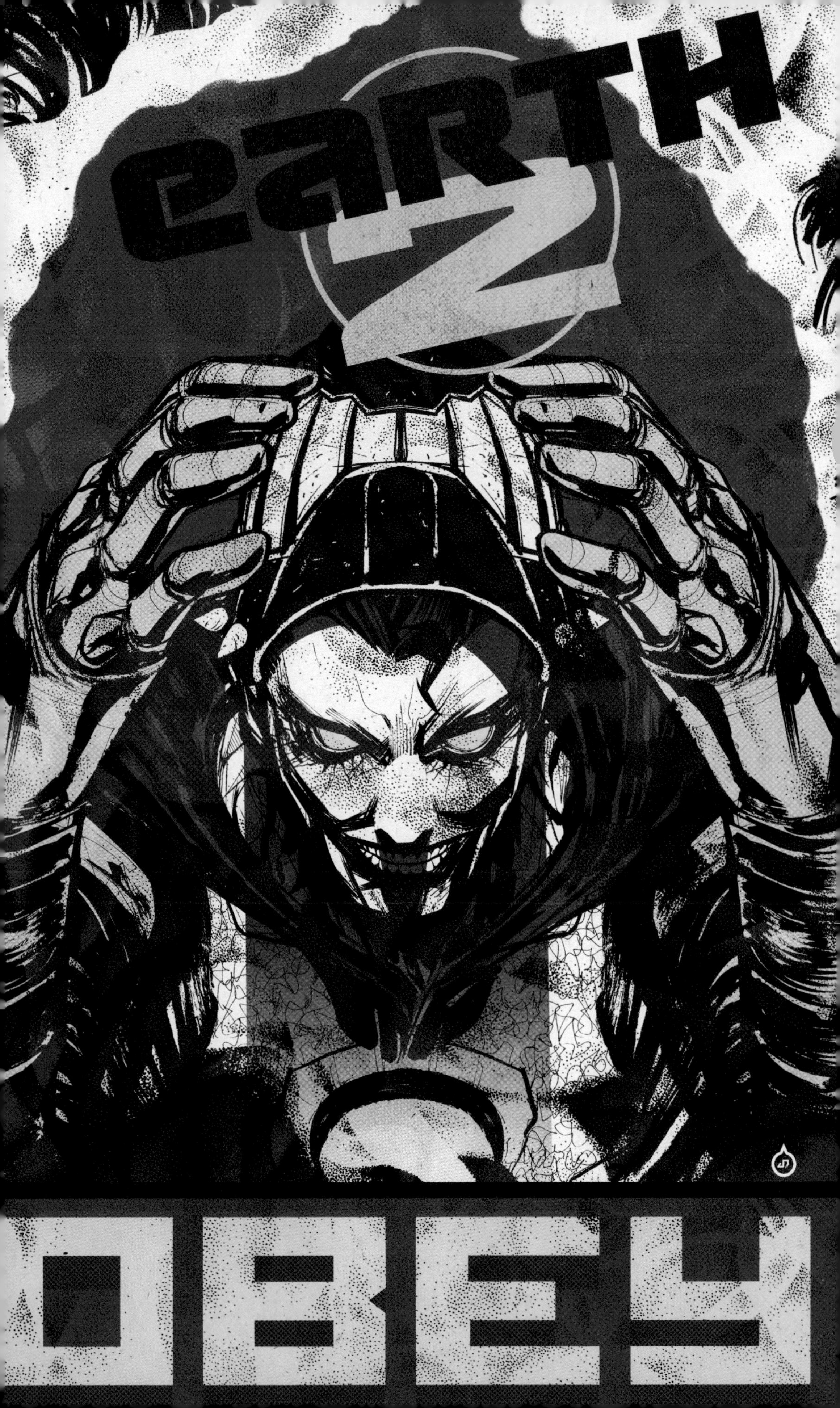

EARTH 2
OBEY

JAMES ROBINSON
writer

NICOLA SCOTT
penciller

TREVOR SCOTT
inker

PETE PANTAZIS
colorist

JUAN DOE
cover artist

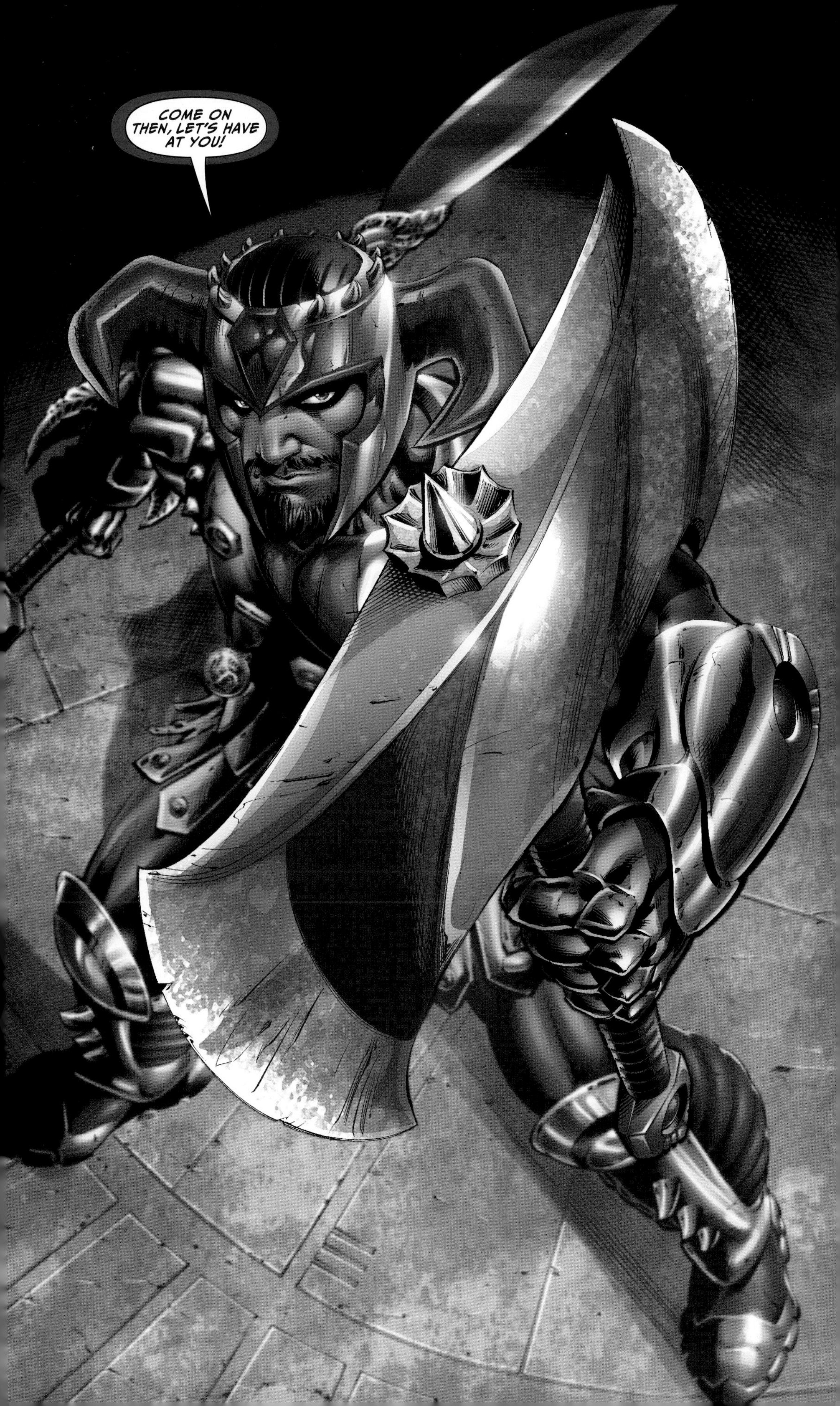
COME ON THEN, LET'S HAVE AT YOU!

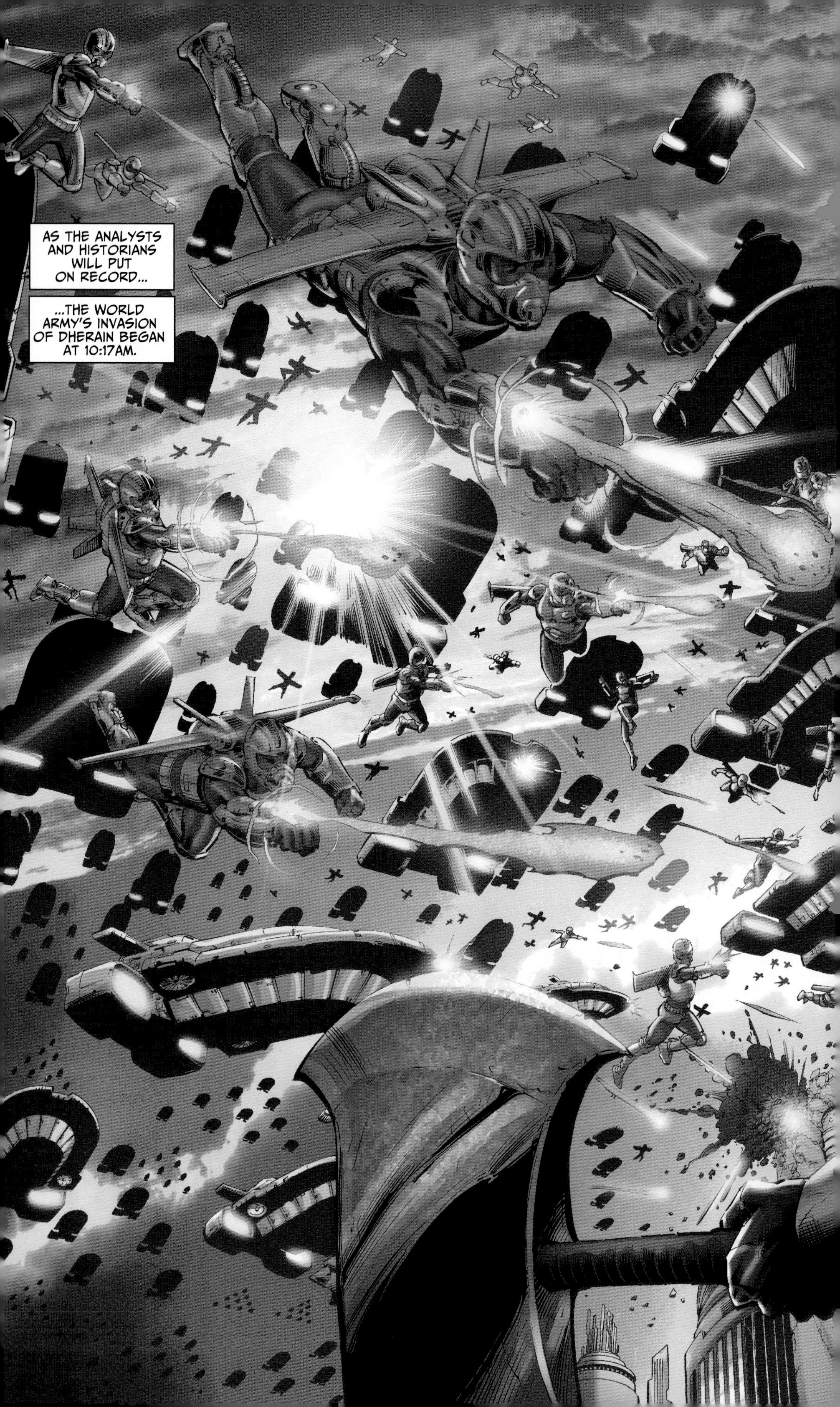
AS THE ANALYSTS AND HISTORIANS WILL PUT ON RECORD...
...THE WORLD ARMY'S INVASION OF DHERAIN BEGAN AT 10:17AM.

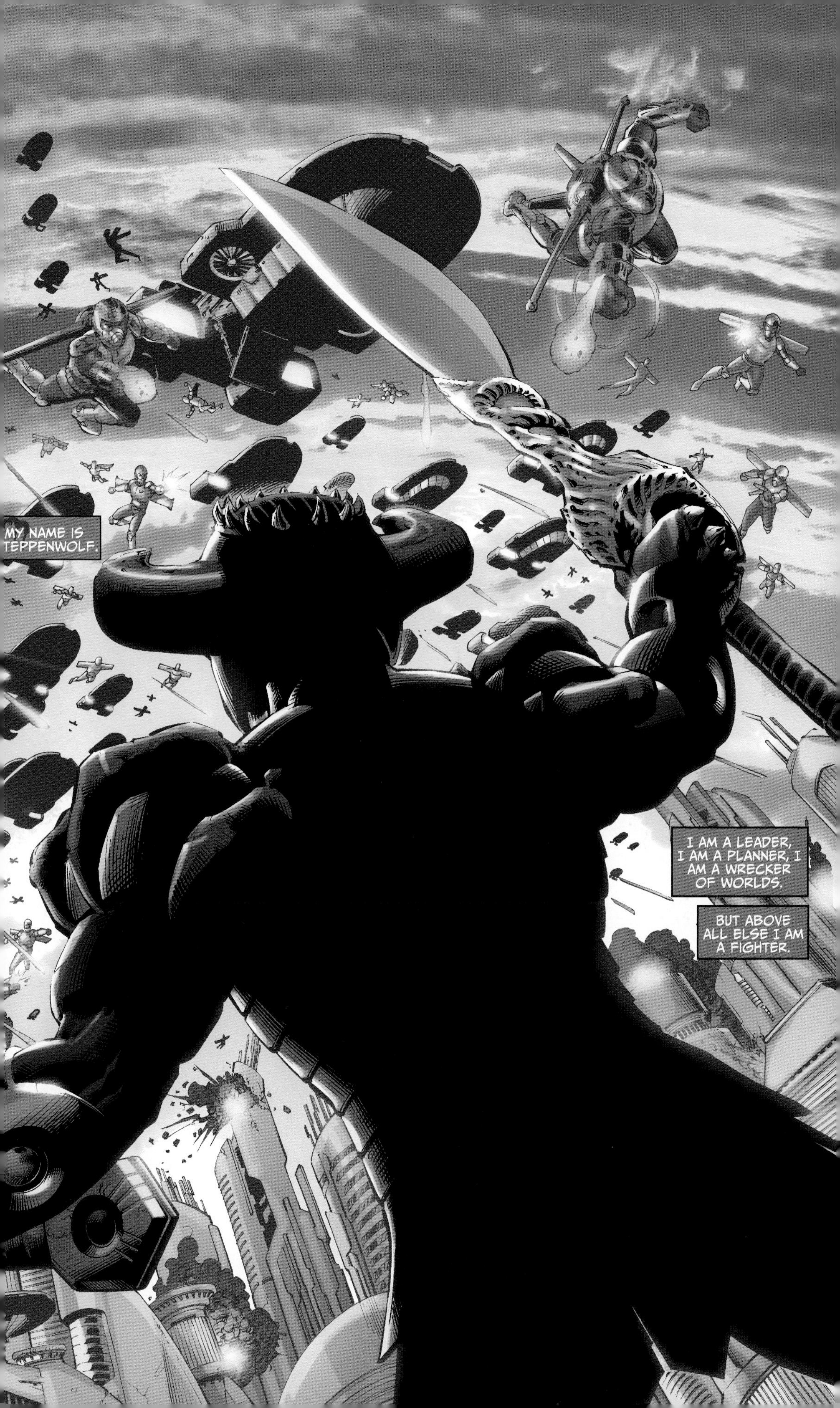
MY NAME IS TEPPENWOLF.
I AM A LEADER, I AM A PLANNER, I AM A WRECKER OF WORLDS.
BUT ABOVE ALL ELSE I AM A FIGHTER.

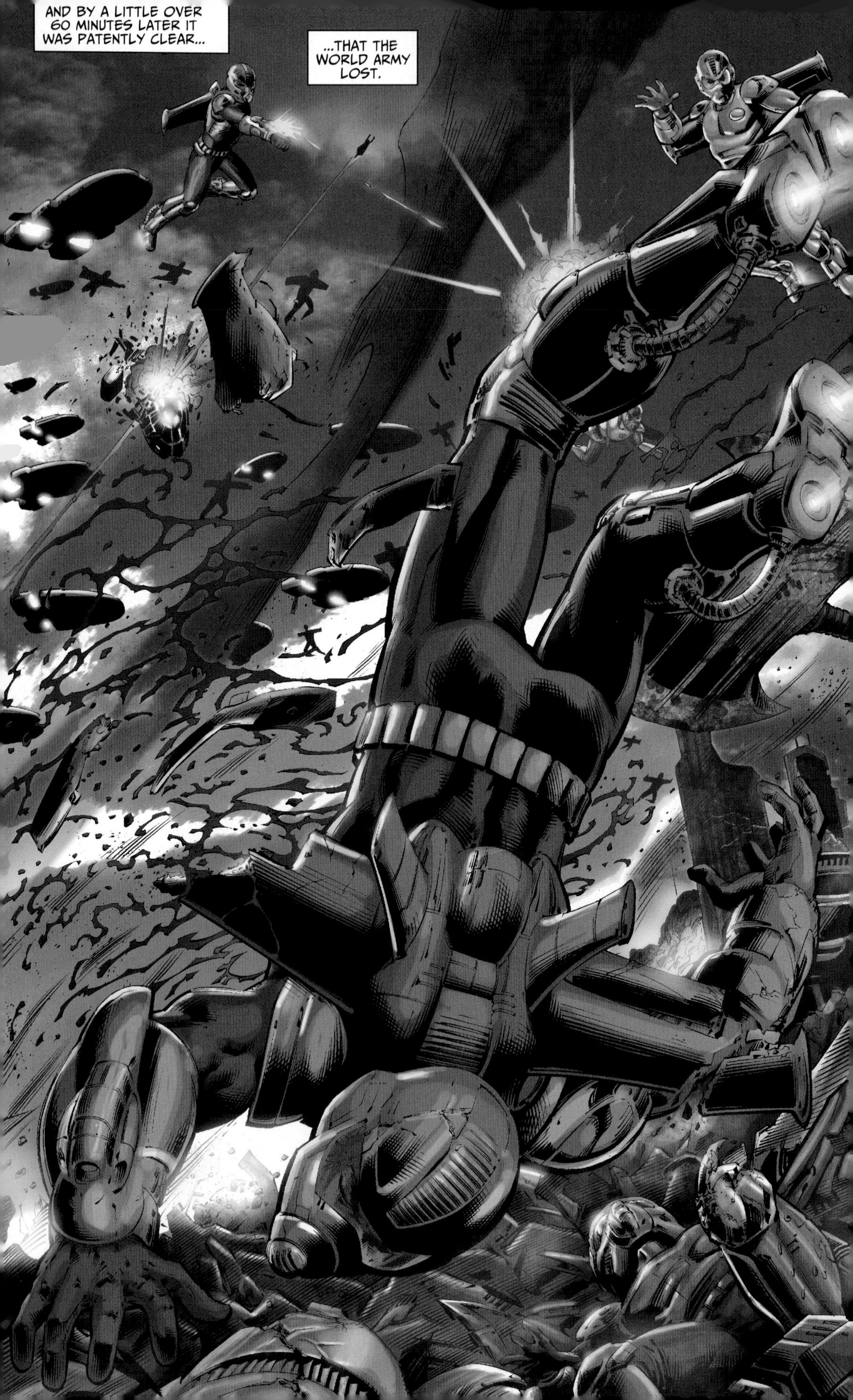
AND BY A LITTLE OVER 60 MINUTES LATER IT WAS PATENTLY CLEAR...
...THAT THE WORLD ARMY LOST.

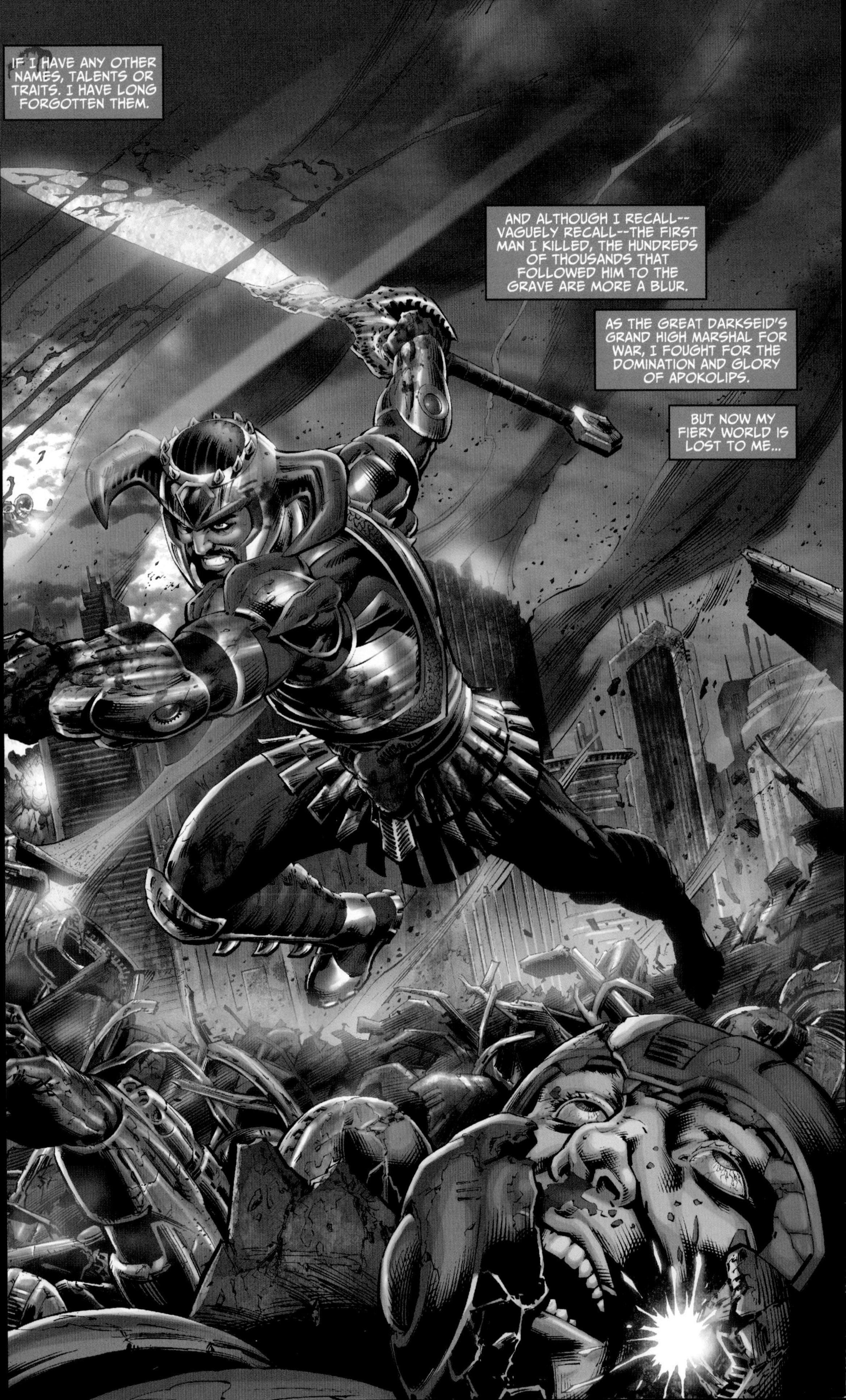
IF I HAVE ANY OTHER NAMES, TALENTS OR TRAITS. I HAVE LONG FORGOTTEN THEM.
AND ALTHOUGH I RECALL--VAGUELY RECALL--THE FIRST MAN I KILLED, THE HUNDREDS OF THOUSANDS THAT FOLLOWED HIM TO THE GRAVE ARE MORE A BLUR.
AS THE GREAT DARKSEID'S GRAND HIGH MARSHAL FOR WAR, I FOUGHT FOR THE DOMINATION AND GLORY OF APOKOLIPS.
BUT NOW MY FIERY WORLD IS LOST TO ME...

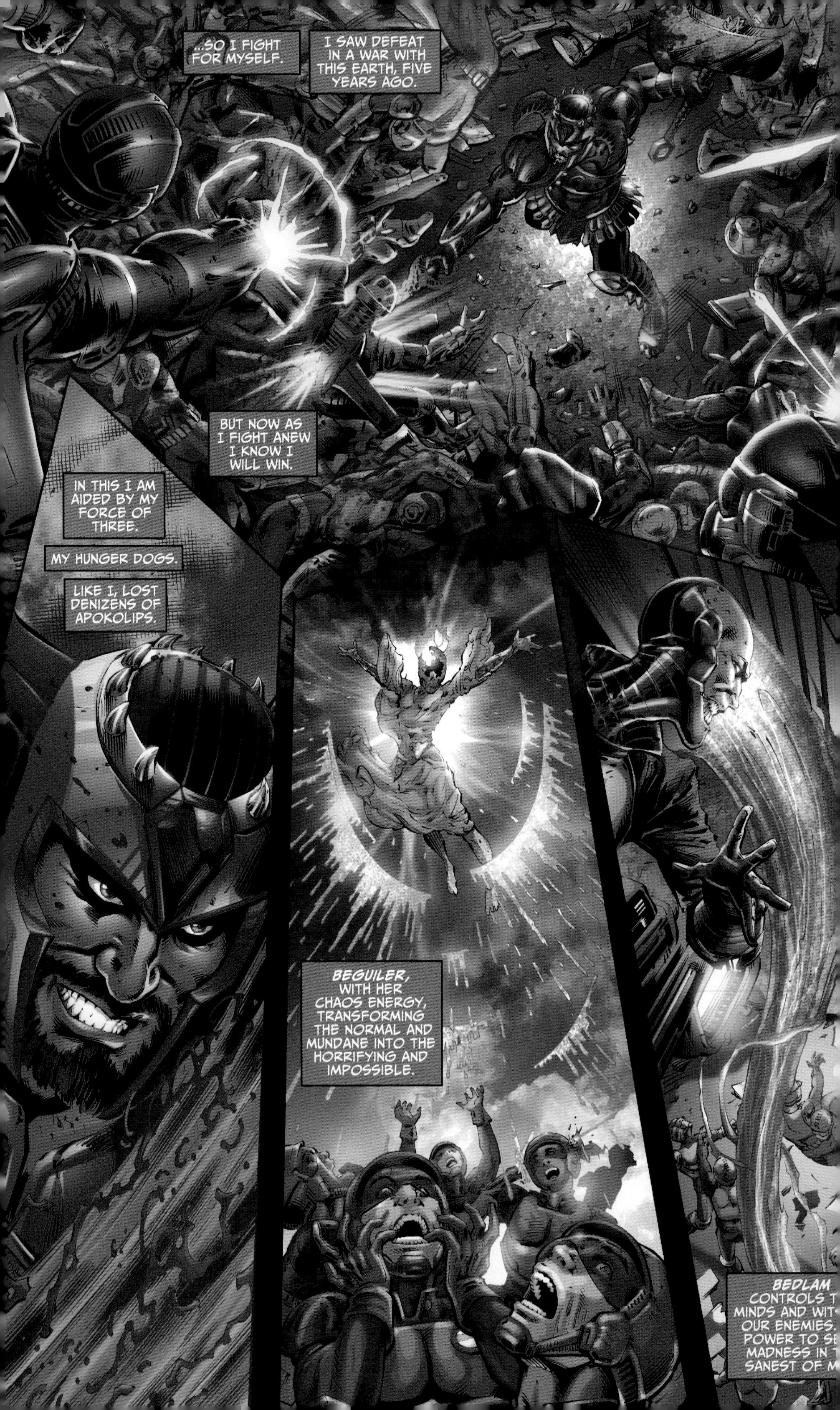

...SO I FIGHT FOR MYSELF.
I SAW DEFEAT IN A WAR WITH THIS EARTH, FIVE YEARS AGO.
BUT NOW AS I FIGHT ANEW I KNOW I WILL WIN.
IN THIS I AM AIDED BY MY FORCE OF THREE.
MY HUNGER DOGS.
LIKE I, LOST DENIZENS OF APOKOLIPS.
BEGUILER, WITH HER CHAOS ENERGY, TRANSFORMING THE NORMAL AND MUNDANE INTO THE HORRIFYING AND IMPOSSIBLE.
BEDLAM CONTROLS T MINDS AND WIT OUR ENEMIES. POWER TO SE MADNESS IN SANEST OF M

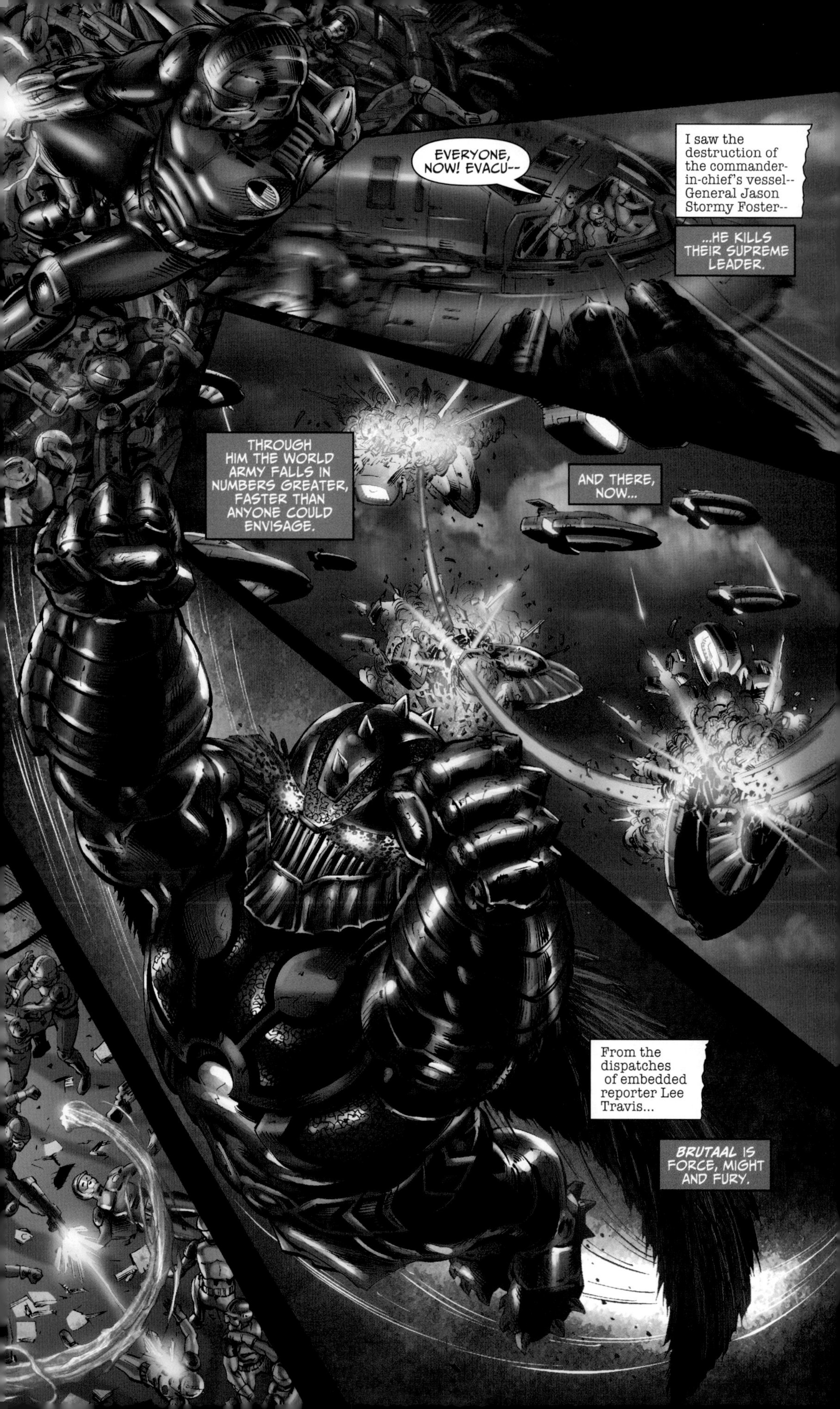
EVERYONE, NOW! EVACU--
I saw the destruction of the commander-in-chief's vessel--General Jason Stormy Foster--
...HE KILLS THEIR SUPREME LEADER.
THROUGH HIM THE WORLD ARMY FALLS IN NUMBERS GREATER, FASTER THAN ANYONE COULD ENVISAGE.
AND THERE, NOW...
From the dispatches of embedded reporter Lee Travis...
BRUTAAL IS FORCE, MIGHT AND FURY.

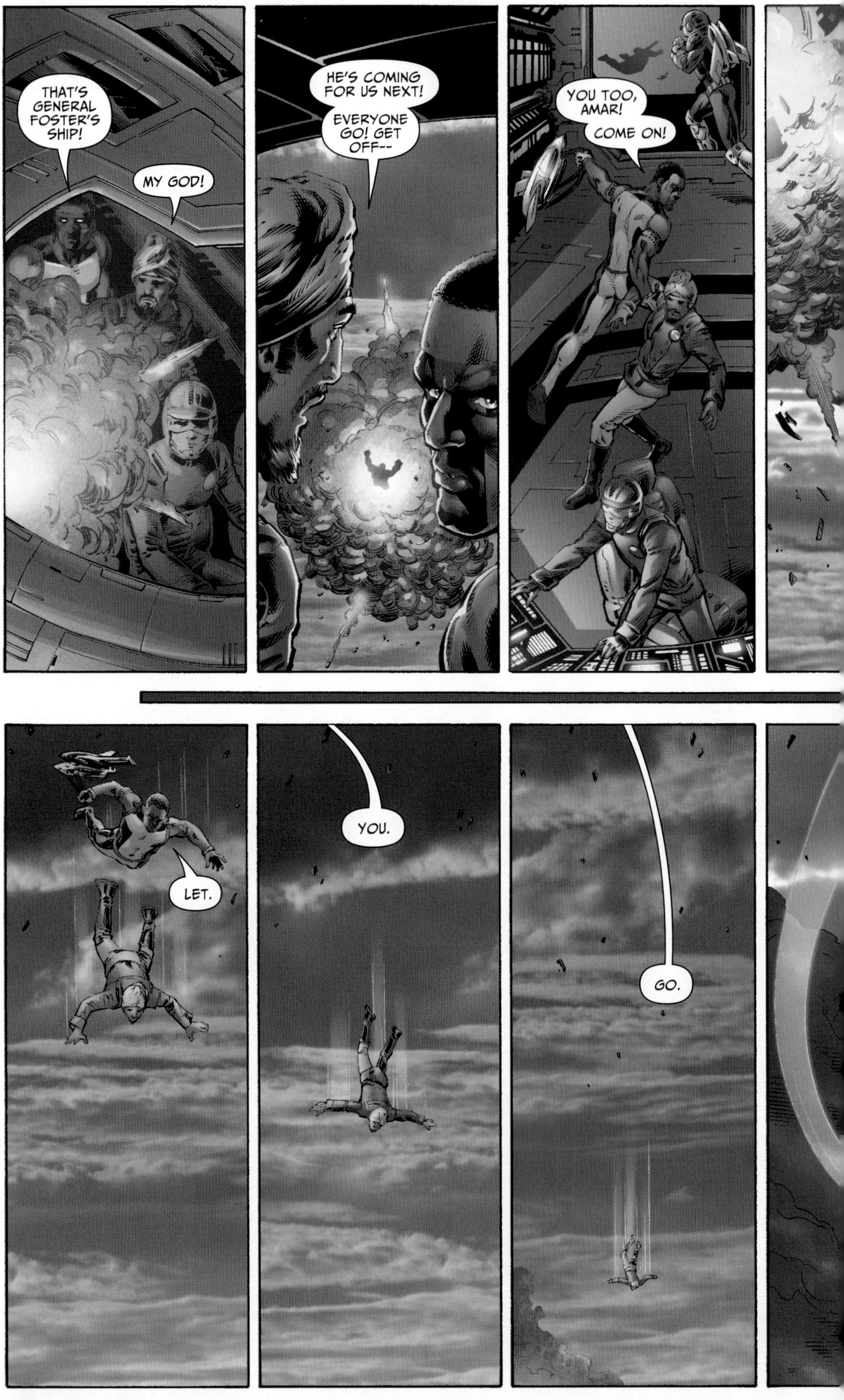

THAT'S GENERAL FOSTER'S SHIP!
MY GOD!
HE'S COMING FOR US NEXT!
EVERYONE GO! GET OFF--
YOU TOO, AMAR!
COME ON!
LET.
YOU.
GO.

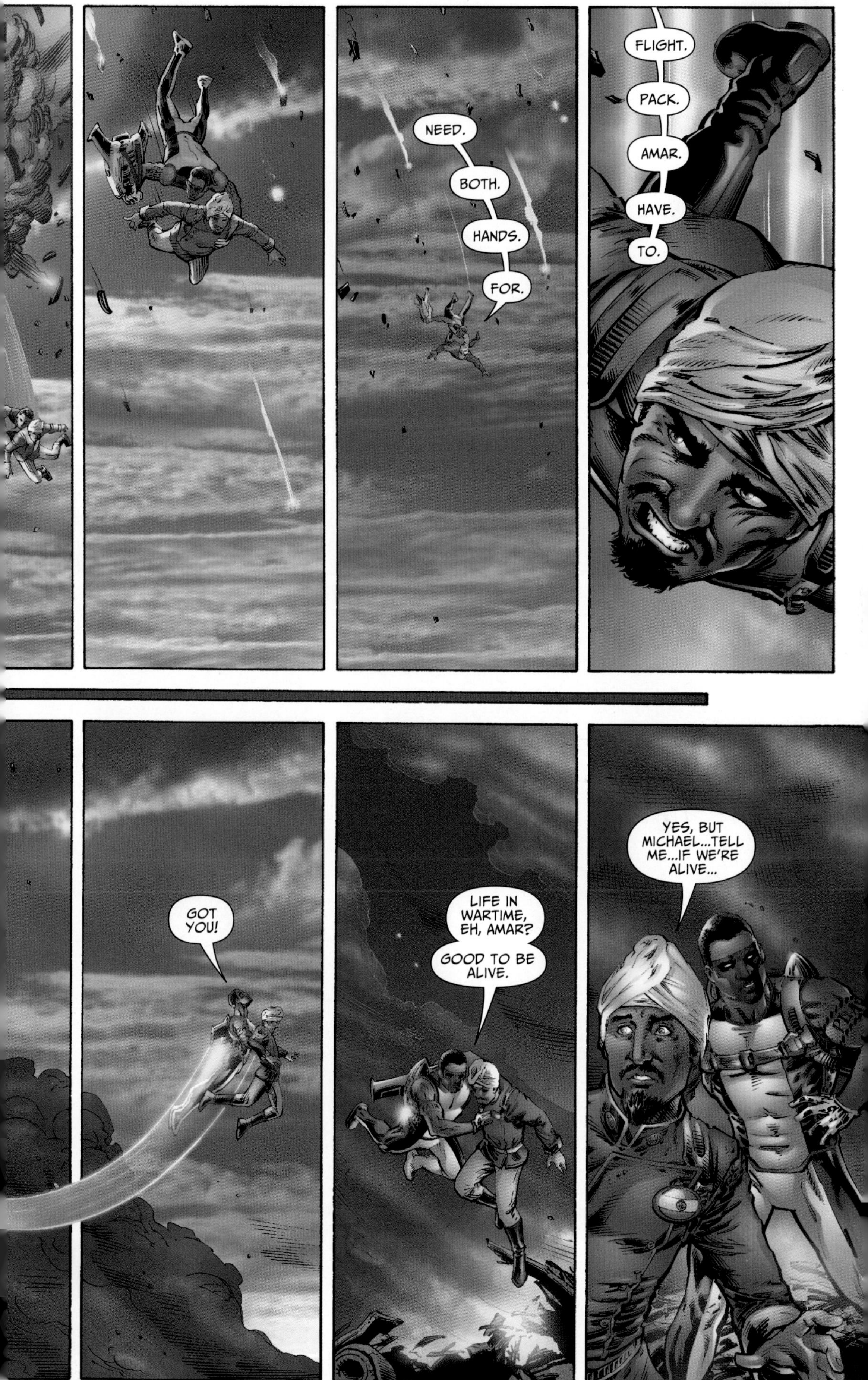
NEED.
BOTH.
HANDS.
FOR.
FLIGHT.
PACK.
AMAR.
HAVE.
TO.
GOT YOU!
LIFE IN WARTIME, EH, AMAR?
GOOD TO BE ALIVE.
YES, BUT MICHAEL...TELL ME...IF WE'RE ALIVE...

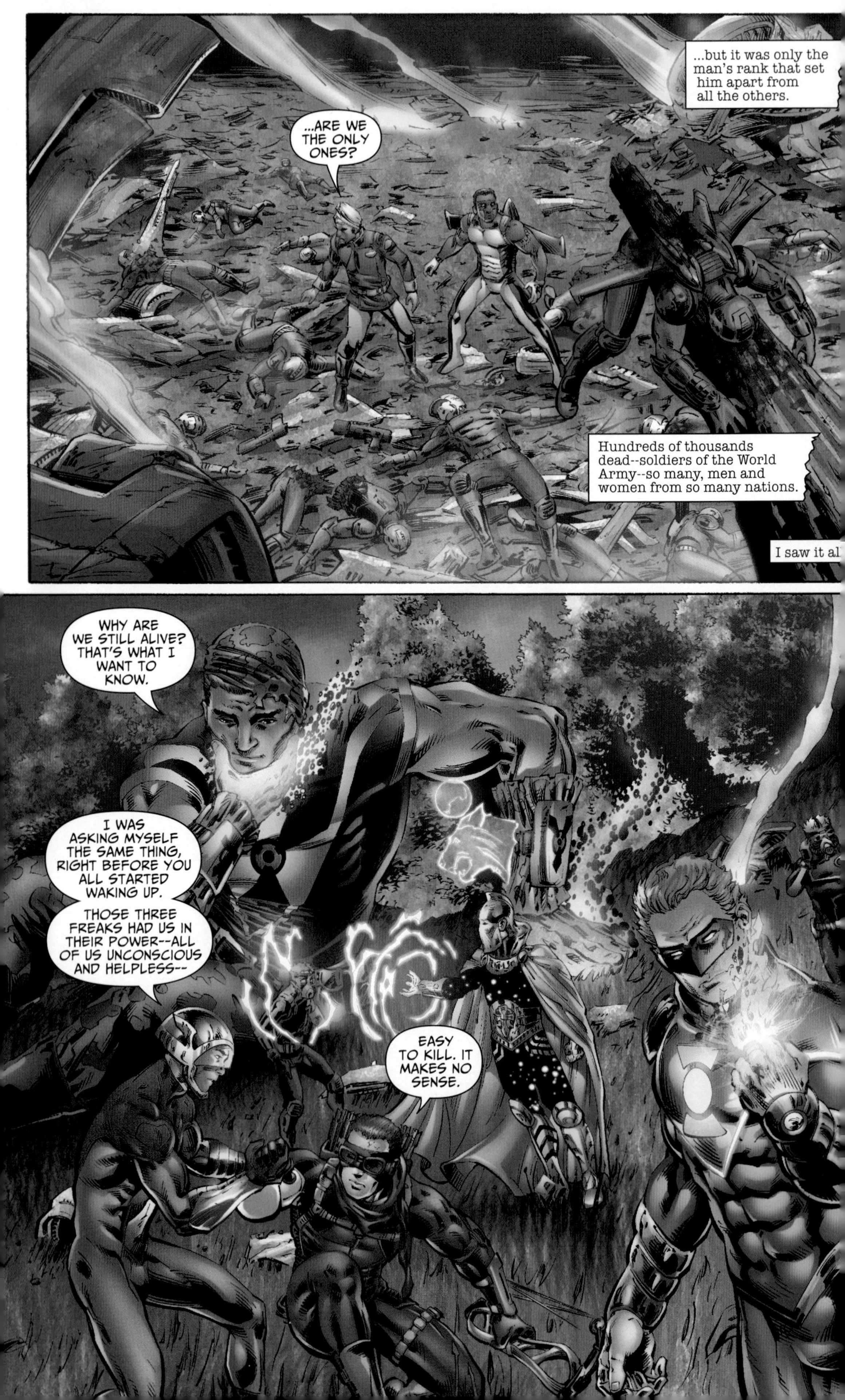
...but it was only the man's rank that set him apart from all the others.
...ARE WE THE ONLY ONES?
Hundreds of thousands dead--soldiers of the World Army--so many, men and women from so many nations.
I saw it al
WHY ARE WE STILL ALIVE? THAT'S WHAT I WANT TO KNOW.
I WAS ASKING MYSELF THE SAME THING, RIGHT BEFORE YOU ALL STARTED WAKING UP.
THOSE THREE FREAKS HAD US IN THEIR POWER--ALL OF US UNCONSCIOUS AND HELPLESS--
EASY TO KILL. IT MAKES NO SENSE.

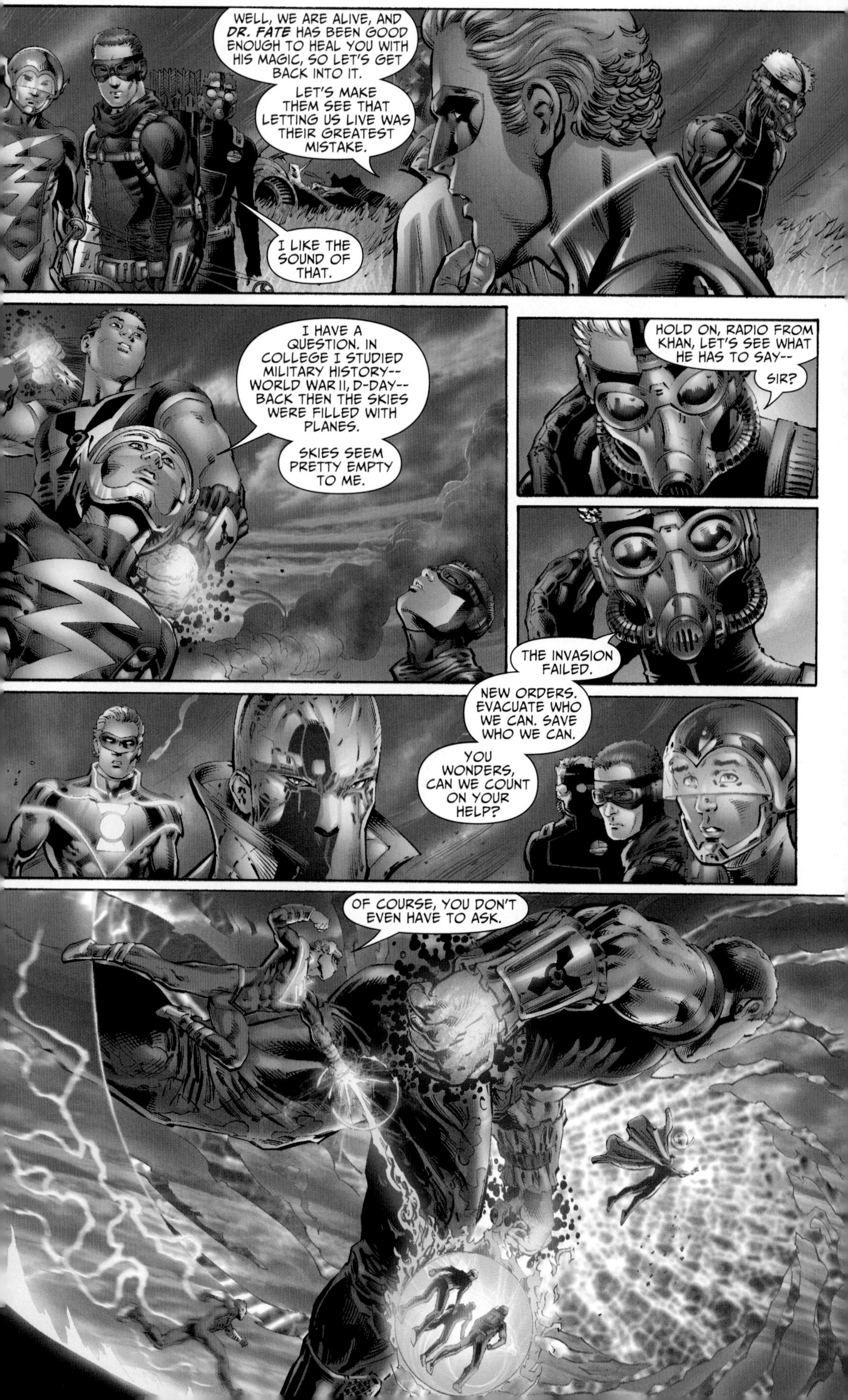
WELL, WE ARE ALIVE, AND ***DR. FATE*** HAS BEEN GOOD ENOUGH TO HEAL YOU WITH HIS MAGIC, SO LET'S GET BACK INTO IT.
LET'S MAKE THEM SEE THAT LETTING US LIVE WAS THEIR GREATEST MISTAKE.
I LIKE THE SOUND OF THAT.
I HAVE A QUESTION. IN COLLEGE I STUDIED MILITARY HISTORY-- WORLD WAR II, D-DAY-- BACK THEN THE SKIES WERE FILLED WITH PLANES.
SKIES SEEM PRETTY EMPTY TO ME.
HOLD ON, RADIO FROM KHAN, LET'S SEE WHAT HE HAS TO SAY--
SIR?
THE INVASION FAILED.
NEW ORDERS. EVACUATE WHO WE CAN. SAVE WHO WE CAN.
YOU WONDERS, CAN WE COUNT ON YOUR HELP?
OF COURSE, YOU DON'T EVEN HAVE TO ASK.

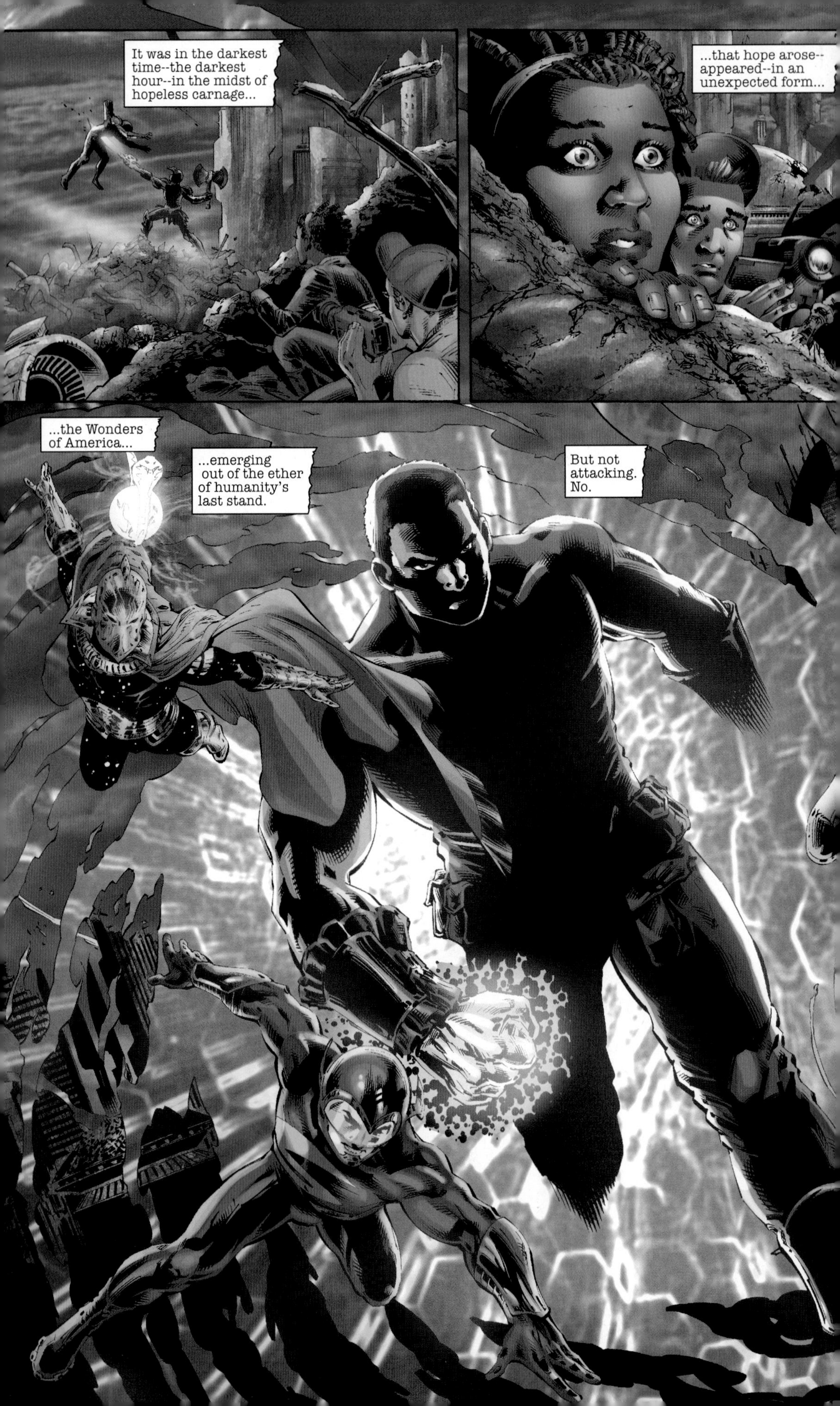
It was in the darkest time--the darkest hour--in the midst of hopeless carnage...
...that hope arose--appeared--in an unexpected form...
...the Wonders of America...
...emerging out of the ether of humanity's last stand.
But not attacking. No.

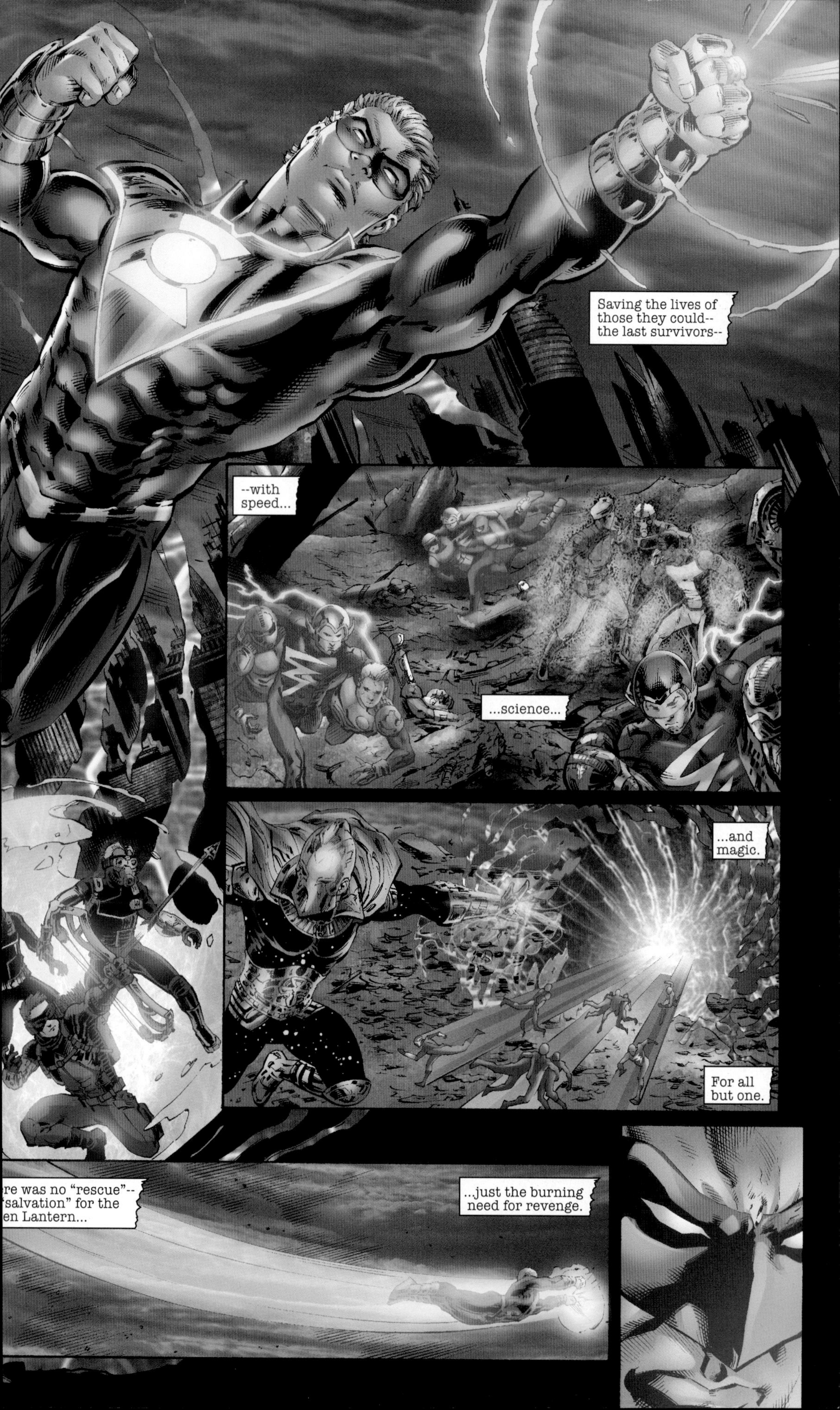
Saving the lives of those they could-- the last survivors--
--with speed...
...science...
...and magic.
For all but one.
re was no "rescue"-- "salvation" for the en Lantern...
...just the burning need for revenge.

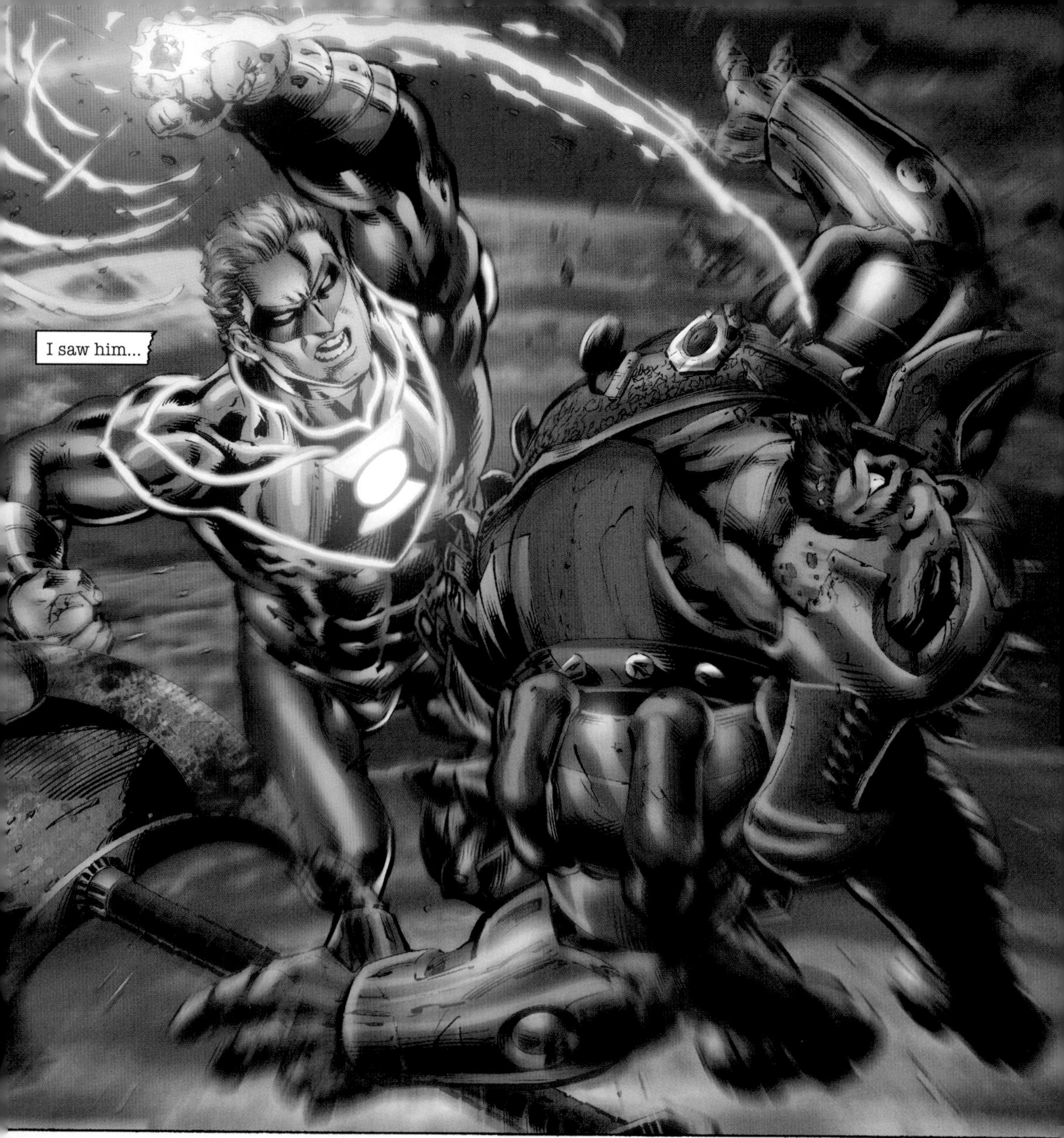
I saw him...

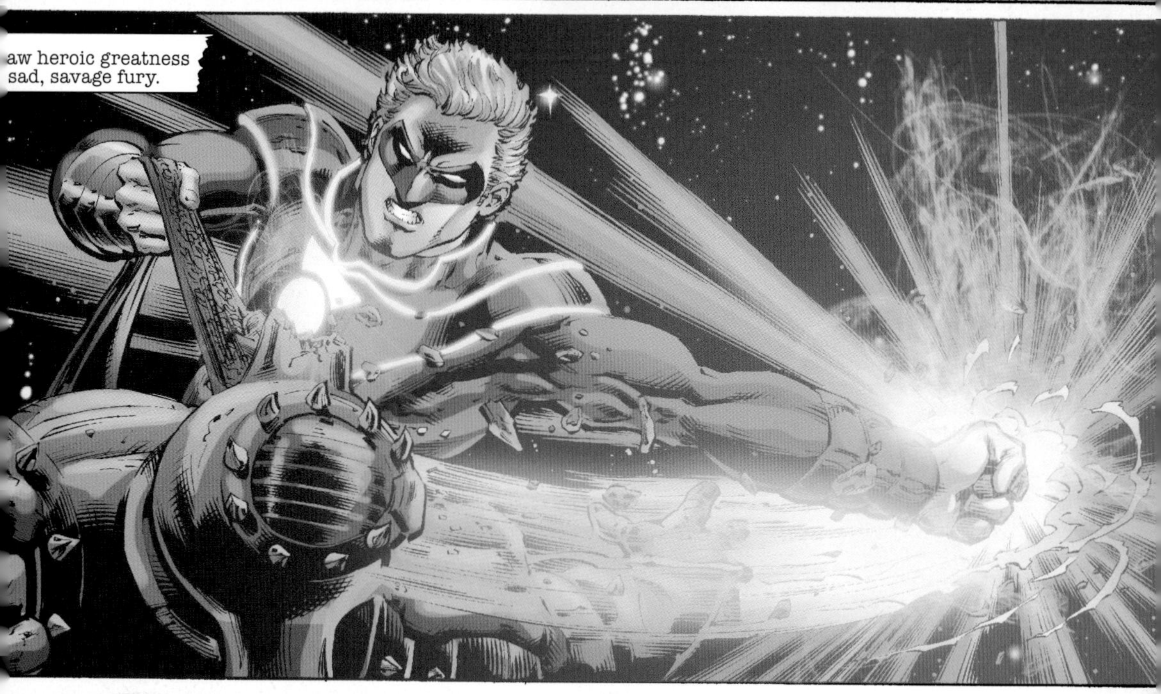
aw heroic greatness
sad, savage fury.

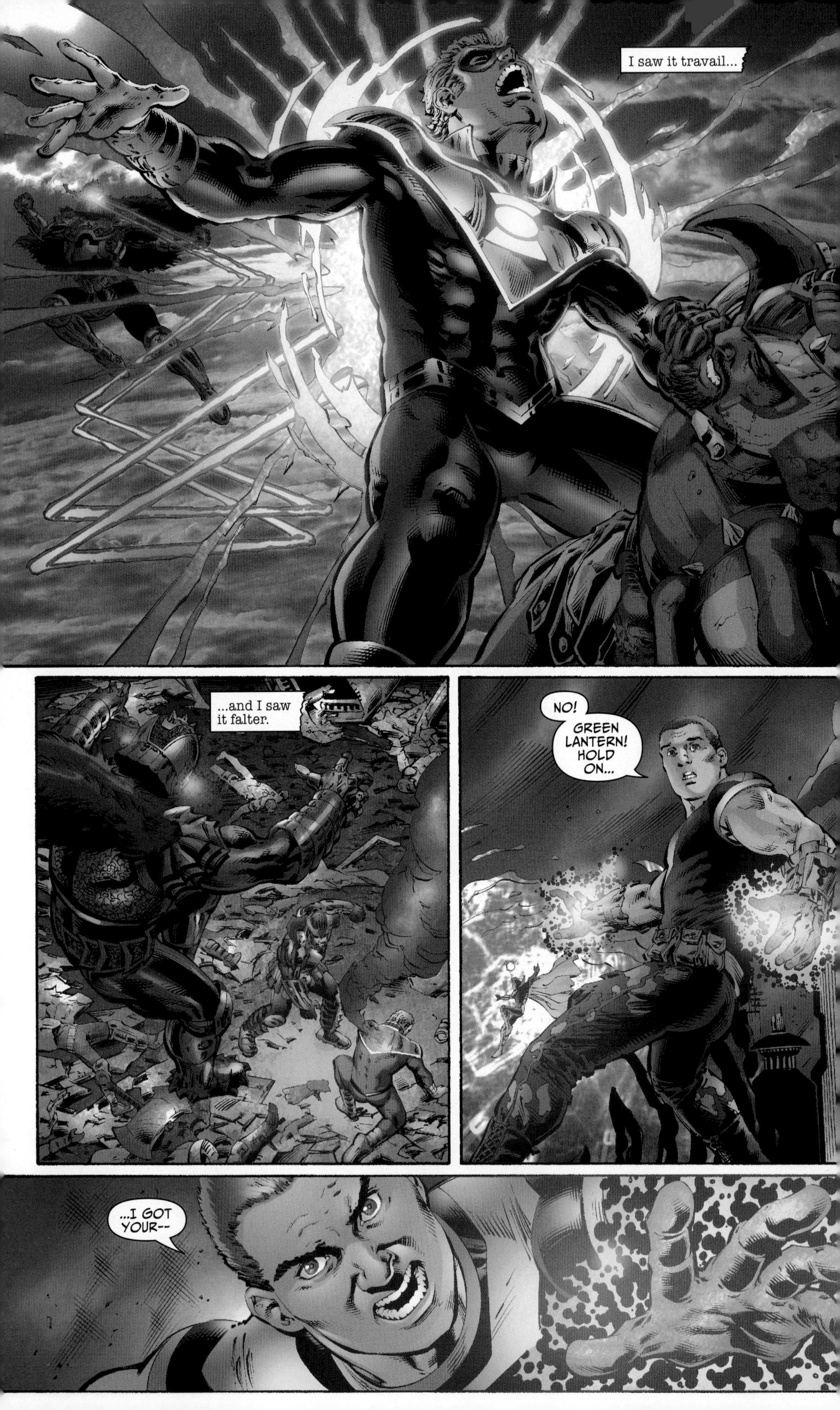
I saw it travail...
...and I saw it falter.
NO! GREEN LANTERN! HOLD ON...
...I GOT YOUR--

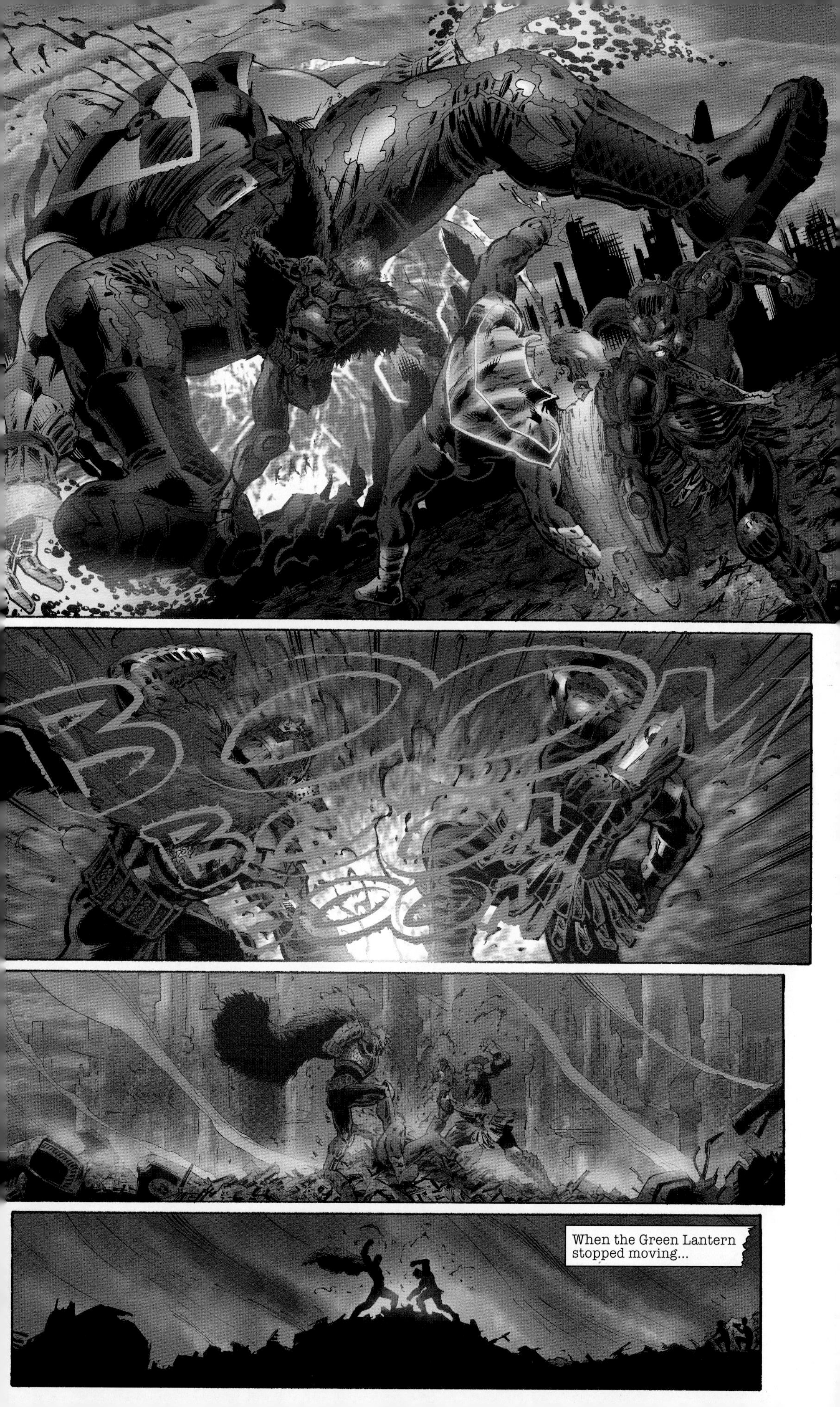
BOOM
BOOM
BOOM
When the Green Lantern stopped moving...

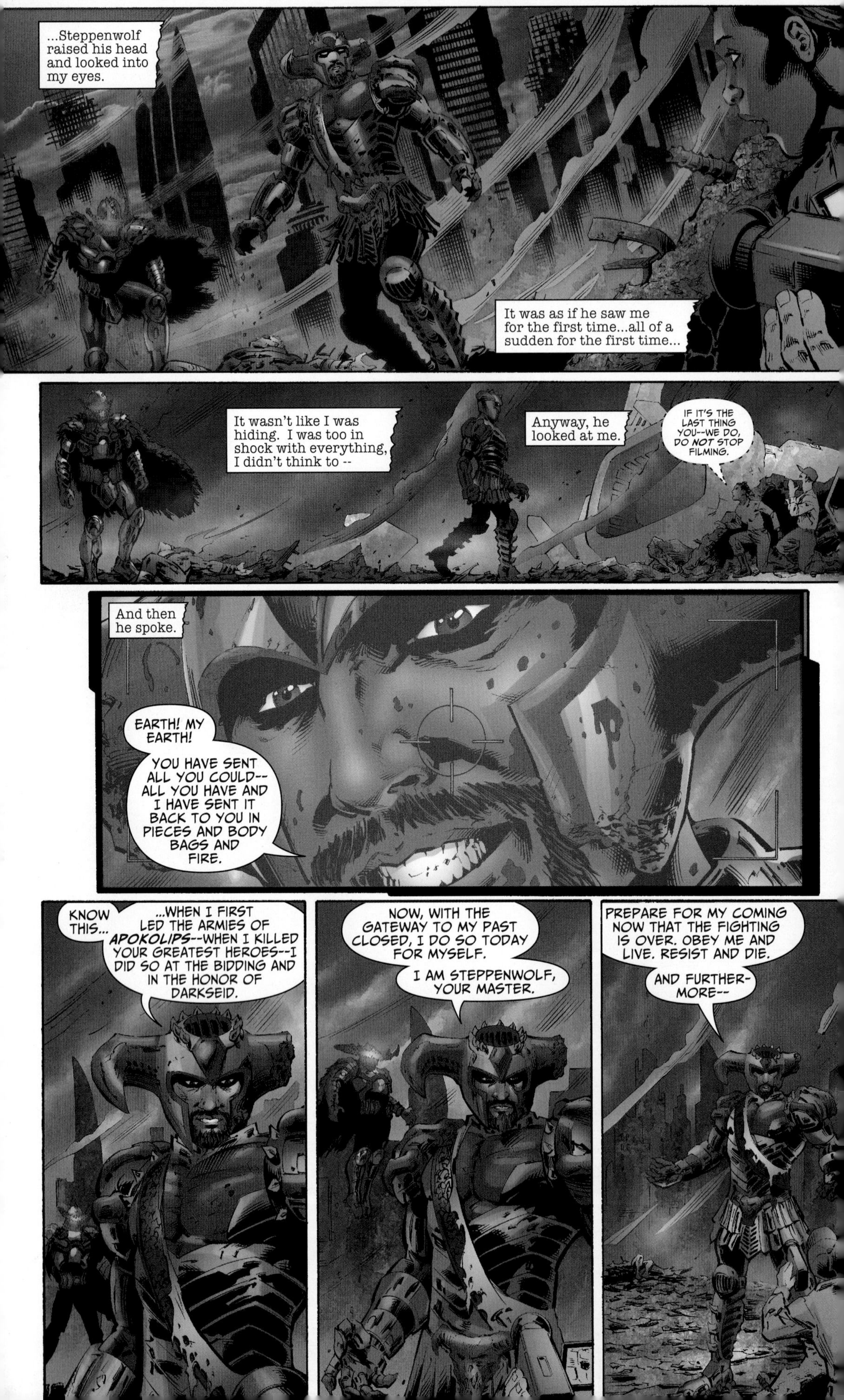

...Steppenwolf raised his head and looked into my eyes.
It was as if he saw me for the first time...all of a sudden for the first time...
It wasn't like I was hiding. I was too in shock with everything, I didn't think to --
Anyway, he looked at me.
IF IT'S THE LAST THING YOU--WE DO, DO NOT STOP FILMING.
And then he spoke.
EARTH! MY EARTH!
YOU HAVE SENT ALL YOU COULD--ALL YOU HAVE AND I HAVE SENT IT BACK TO YOU IN PIECES AND BODY BAGS AND FIRE.
KNOW THIS...
...WHEN I FIRST LED THE ARMIES OF APOKOLIPS--WHEN I KILLED YOUR GREATEST HEROES--I DID SO AT THE BIDDING AND IN THE HONOR OF DARKSEID.
NOW, WITH THE GATEWAY TO MY PAST CLOSED, I DO SO TODAY FOR MYSELF.
I AM STEPPENWOLF, YOUR MASTER.
PREPARE FOR MY COMING NOW THAT THE FIGHTING IS OVER. OBEY ME AND LIVE. RESIST AND DIE.
AND FURTHER-MORE--

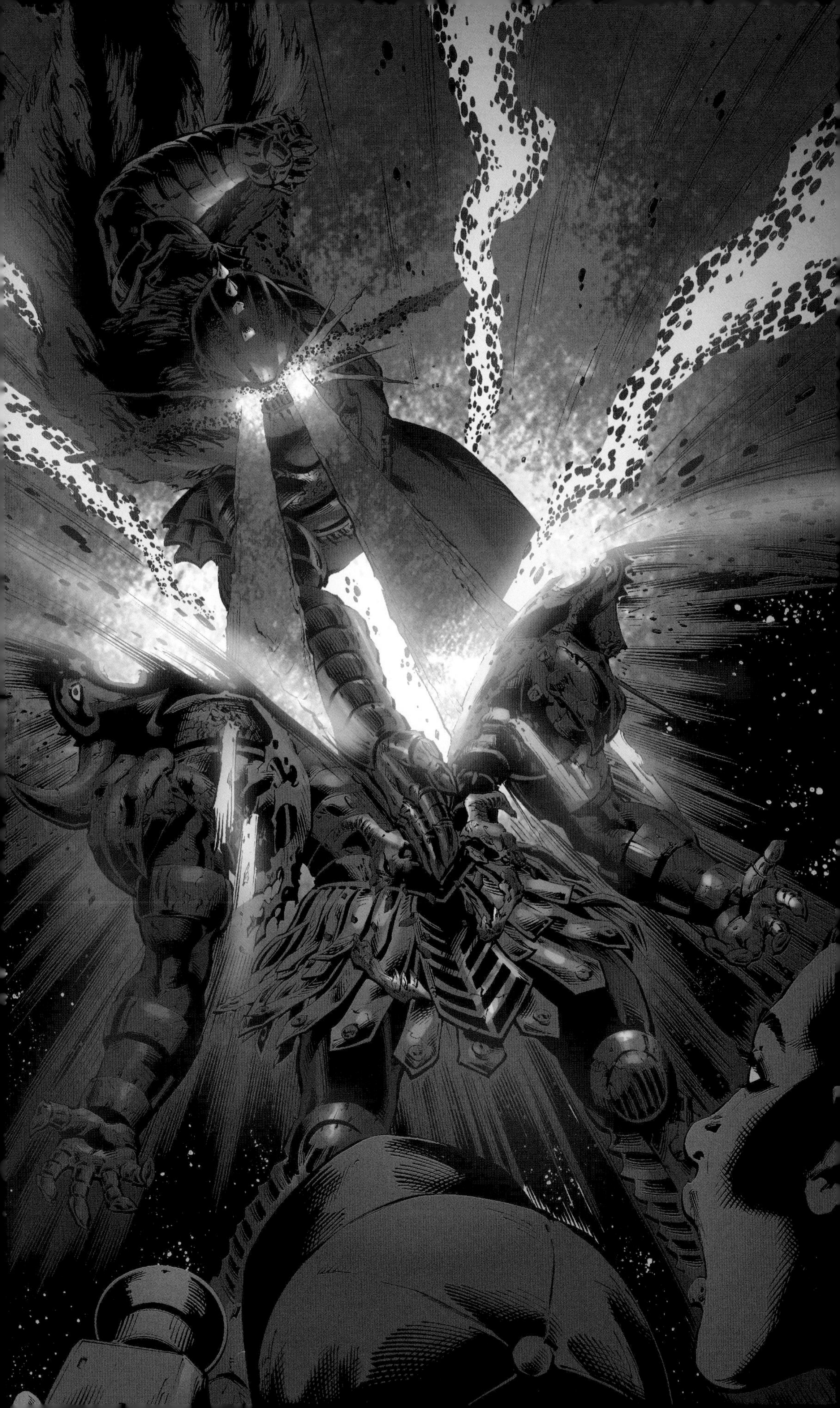

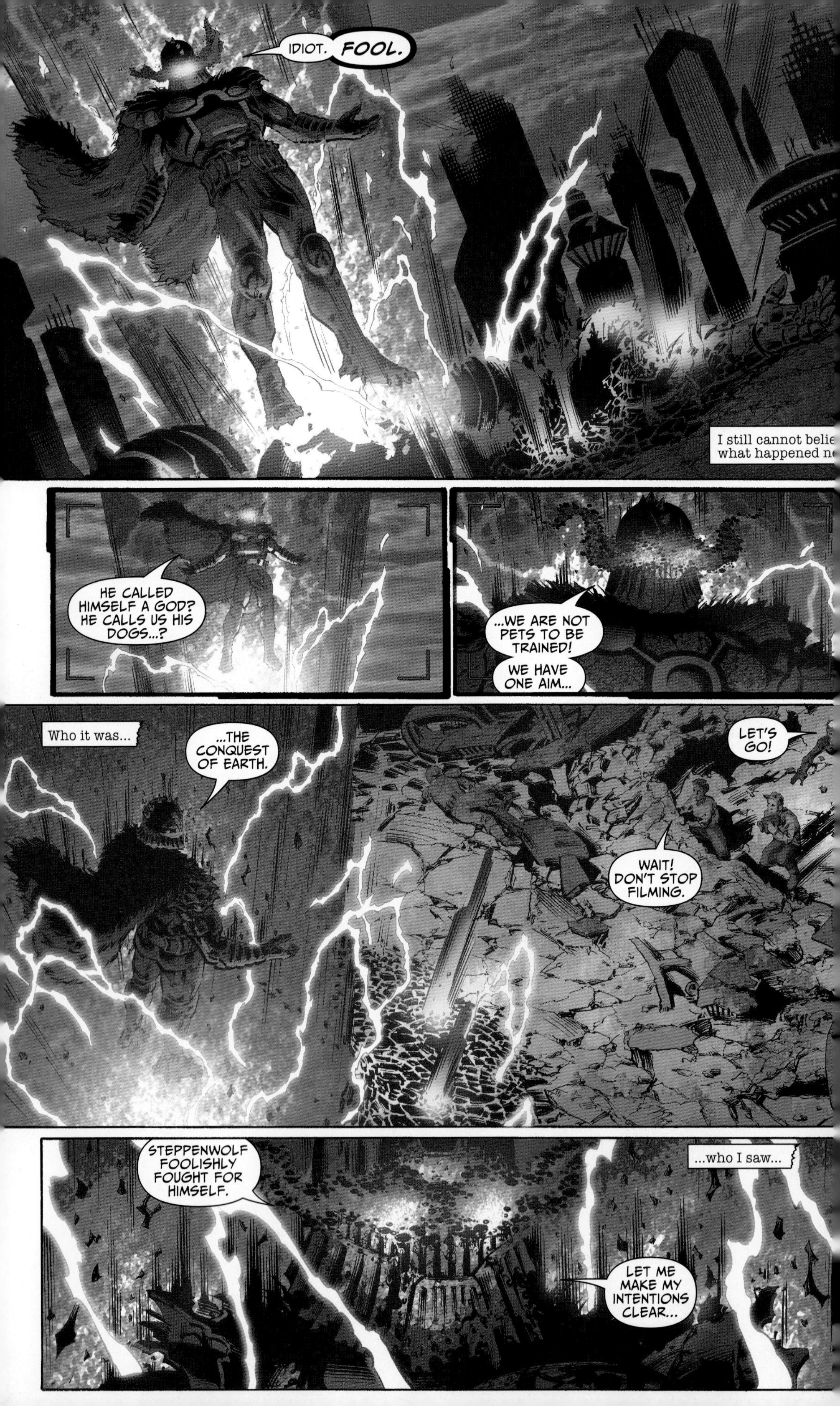
IDIOT.
FOOL.
I still cannot belie
what happened n
HE CALLED HIMSELF A GOD? HE CALLS US HIS DOGS...?
...WE ARE NOT PETS TO BE TRAINED!
WE HAVE ONE AIM...
Who it was...
...THE CONQUEST OF EARTH.
LET'S GO!
WAIT! DON'T STOP FILMING.
STEPPENWOLF FOOLISHLY FOUGHT FOR HIMSELF.
...who I saw...
LET ME MAKE MY INTENTIONS CLEAR...

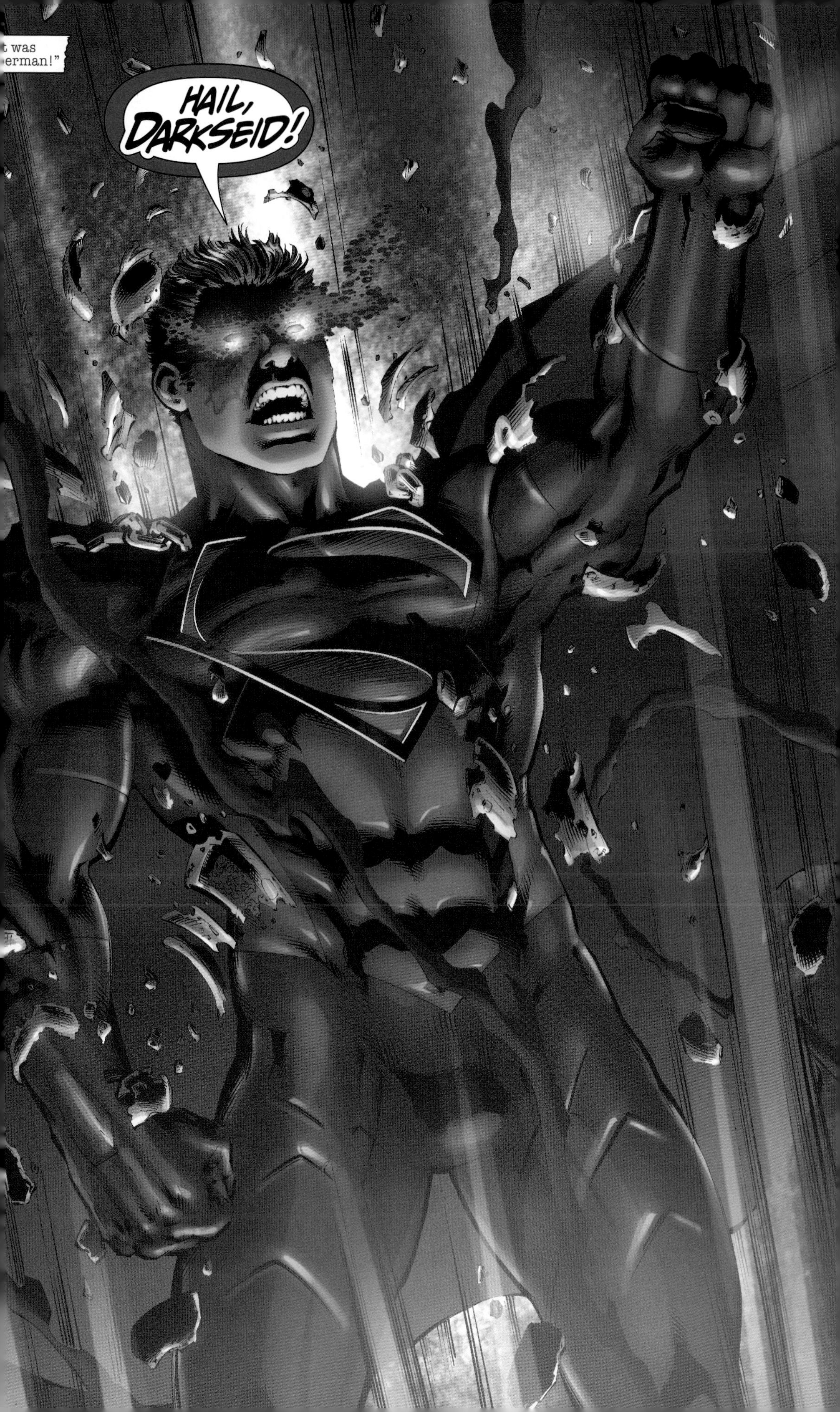
t was
erman!"
HAIL, DARKSEID!

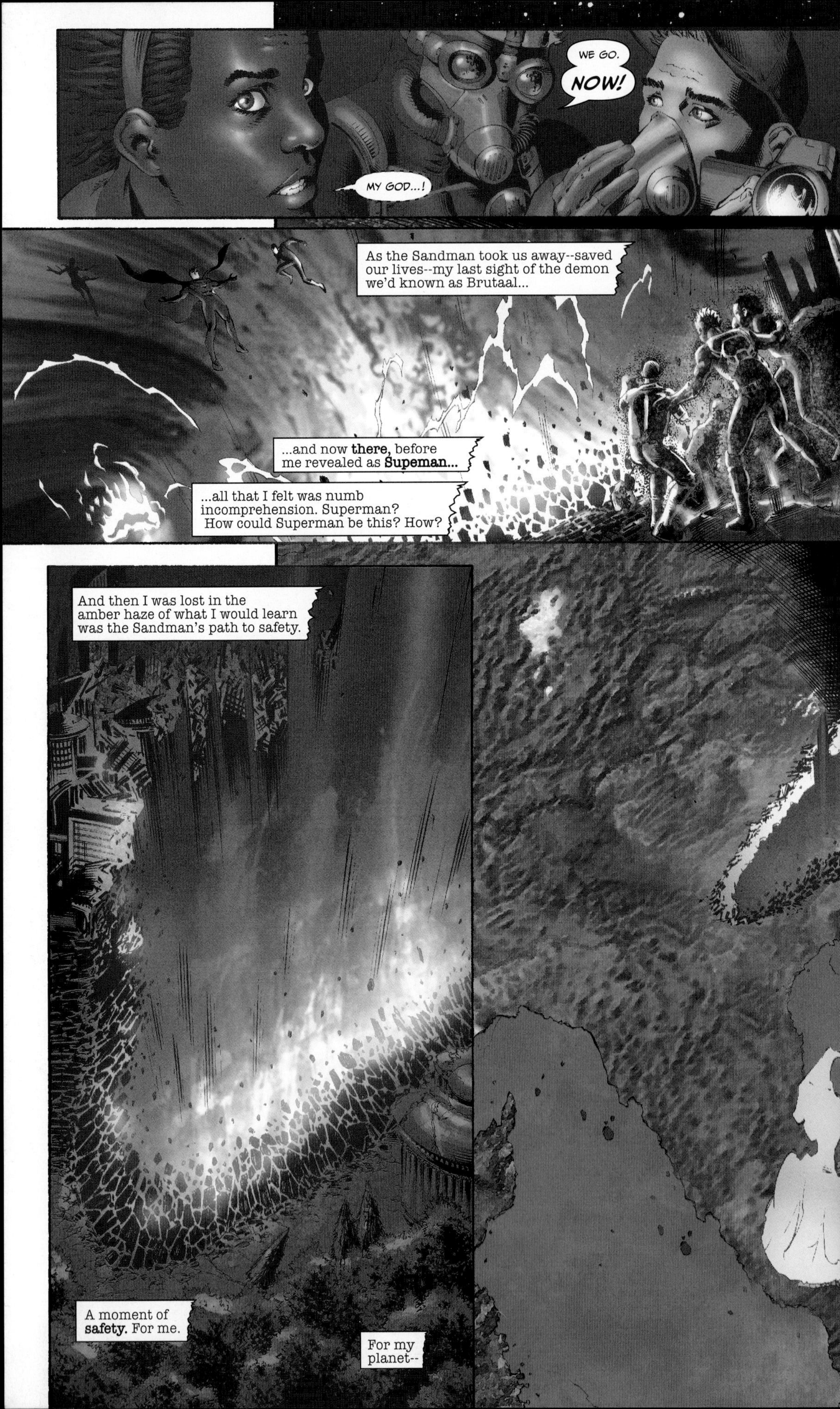

WE GO. NOW!
MY GOD...!
As the Sandman took us away--saved our lives--my last sight of the demon we'd known as Brutaal...
...and now there, before me revealed as Supeman...
...all that I felt was numb incomprehension. Superman? How could Superman be this? How?
And then I was lost in the amber haze of what I would learn was the Sandman's path to safety.
A moment of safety. For me.
For my planet--

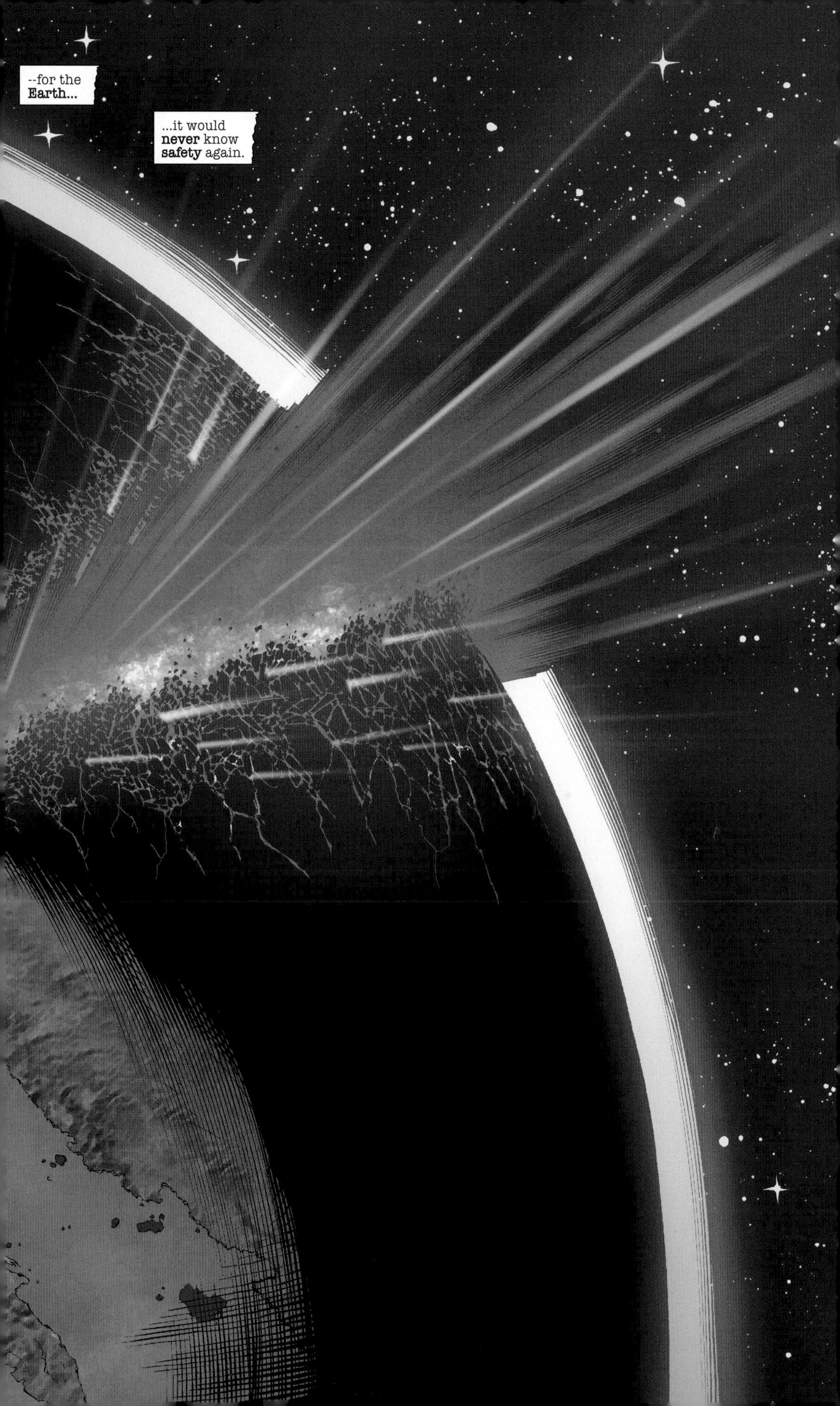
--for the **Earth...**
...it would **never** know **safety** again.

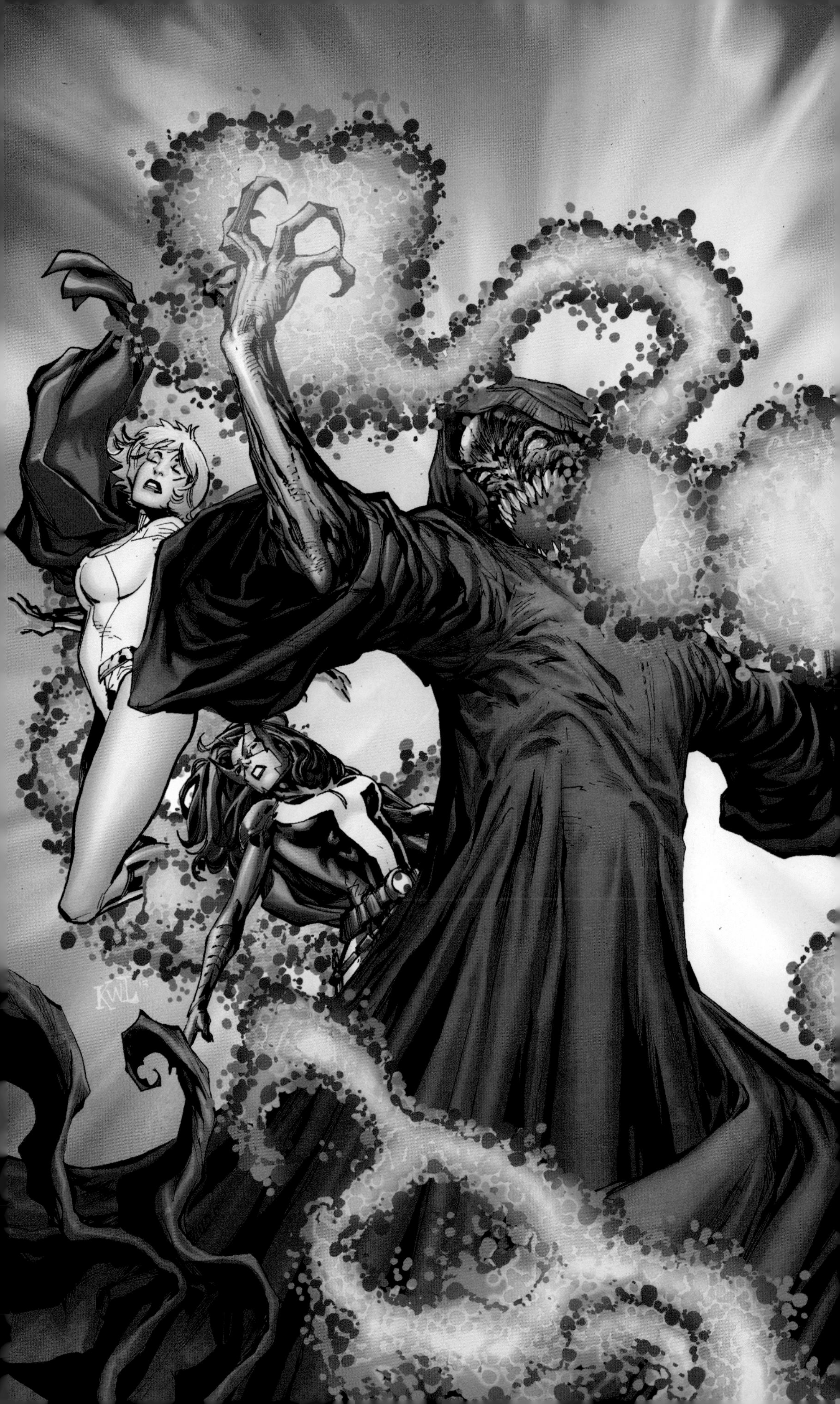

PAUL LEVITZ
writer

YILDIRAY CINAR
artist

JASON WRIGHT
colorist

KEN LASHLEY & JASON WRIGHT
cover artists

DESAAD created by JACK KIRBY

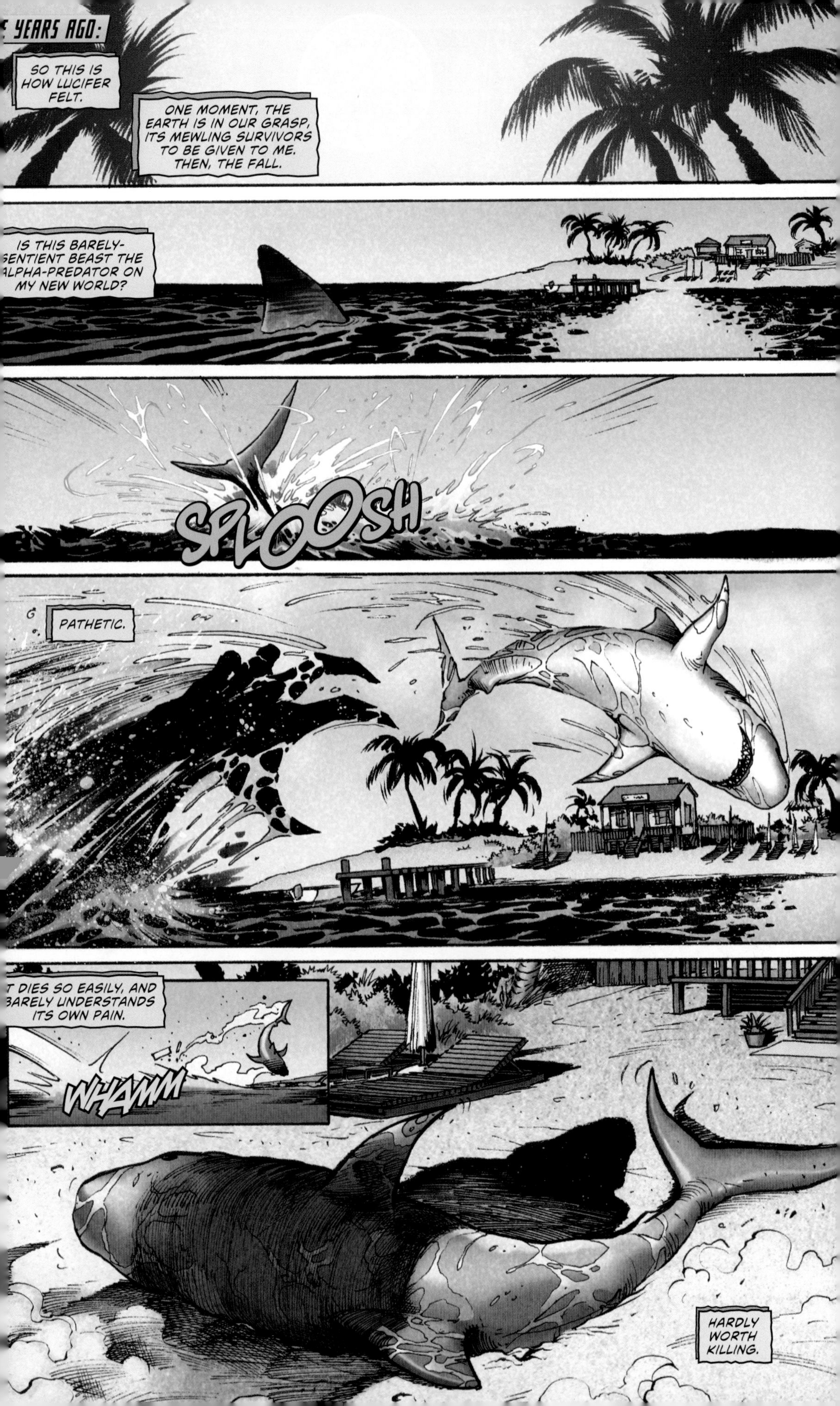
YEARS AGO:
SO THIS IS HOW LUCIFER FELT.
ONE MOMENT, THE EARTH IS IN OUR GRASP, ITS MEWLING SURVIVORS TO BE GIVEN TO ME. THEN, THE FALL.
IS THIS BARELY-SENTIENT BEAST THE ALPHA-PREDATOR ON MY NEW WORLD?
SPLOOSH
PATHETIC.
DIES SO EASILY, AND BARELY UNDERSTANDS ITS OWN PAIN.
WHAMM
HARDLY WORTH KILLING.

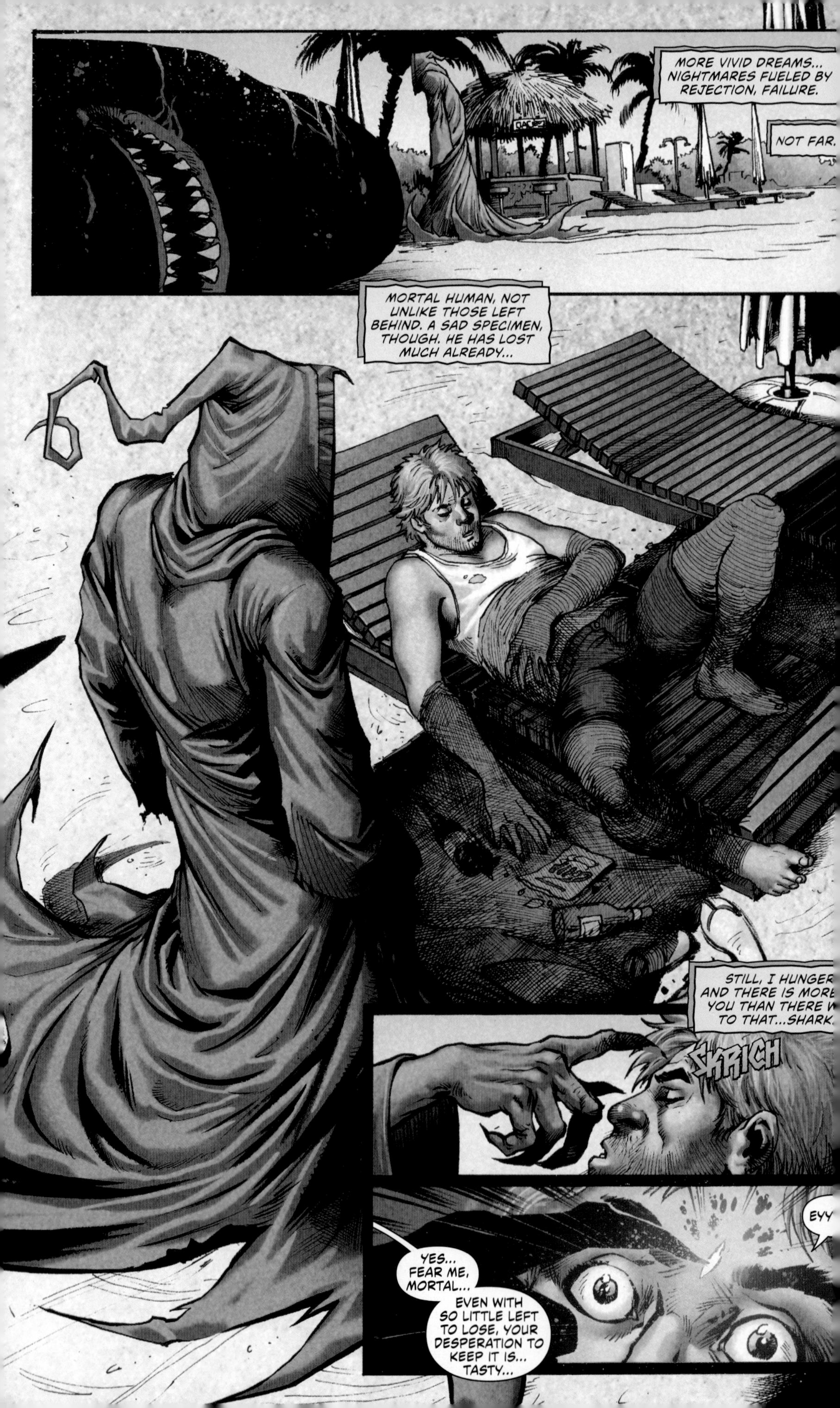
MORE VIVID DREAMS... NIGHTMARES FUELED BY REJECTION, FAILURE.
NOT FAR.
MORTAL HUMAN, NOT UNLIKE THOSE LEFT BEHIND. A SAD SPECIMEN, THOUGH. HE HAS LOST MUCH ALREADY...
STILL, I HUNGER AND THERE IS MORE YOU THAN THERE W TO THAT...SHARK.
SKRICH
EYY
YES... FEAR ME, MORTAL...
EVEN WITH SO LITTLE LEFT TO LOSE, YOUR DESPERATION TO KEEP IT IS... TASTY...

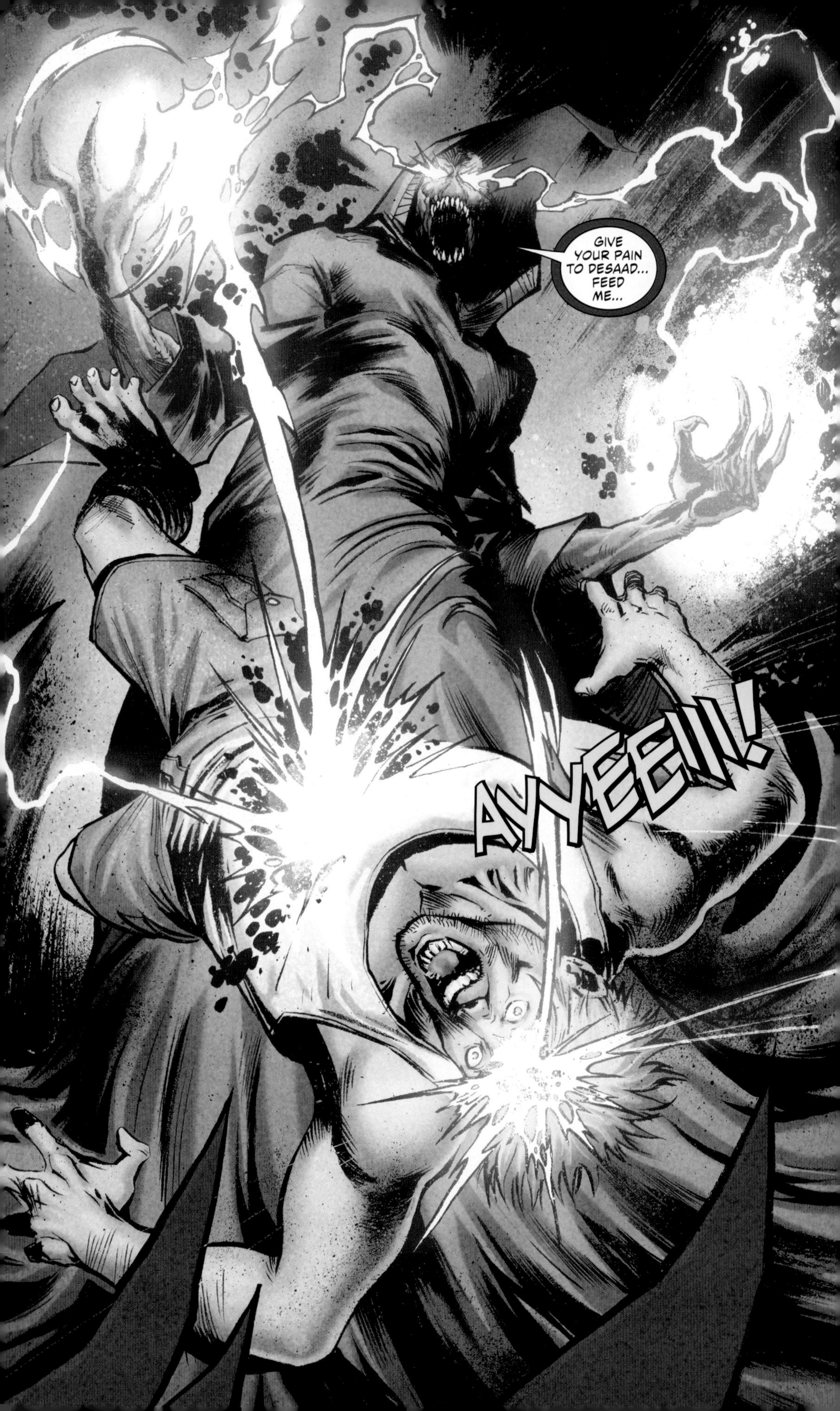
GIVE YOUR PAIN TO DESAAD... FEED ME...
AYYEEIII!

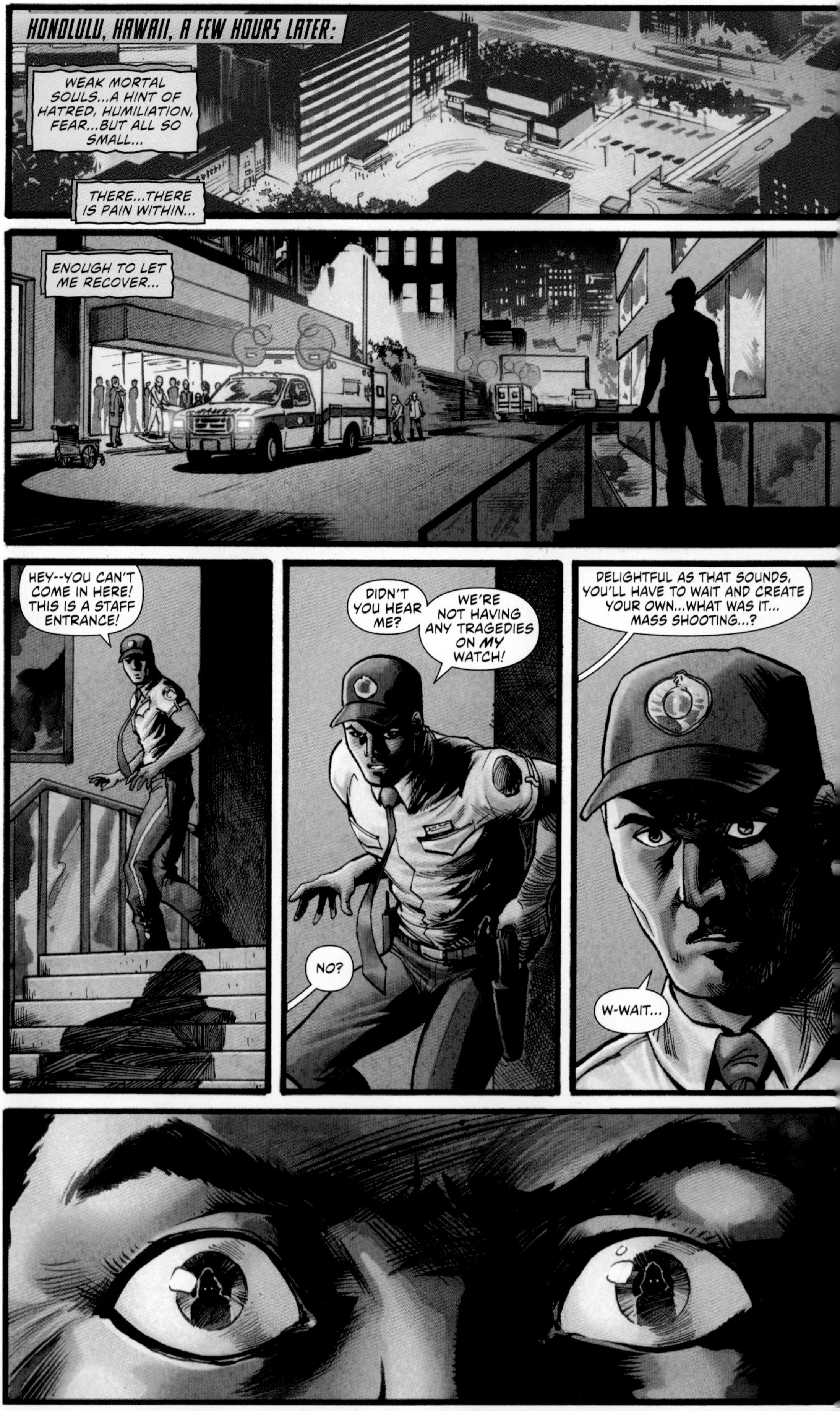
HONOLULU, HAWAII, A FEW HOURS LATER:
WEAK MORTAL SOULS...A HINT OF HATRED, HUMILIATION, FEAR...BUT ALL SO SMALL...
THERE...THERE IS PAIN WITHIN...
ENOUGH TO LET ME RECOVER...
HEY--YOU CAN'T COME IN HERE! THIS IS A STAFF ENTRANCE!
DIDN'T YOU HEAR ME?
WE'RE NOT HAVING ANY TRAGEDIES ON MY WATCH!
NO?
DELIGHTFUL AS THAT SOUNDS, YOU'LL HAVE TO WAIT AND CREATE YOUR OWN...WHAT WAS IT... MASS SHOOTING...?
W-WAIT...

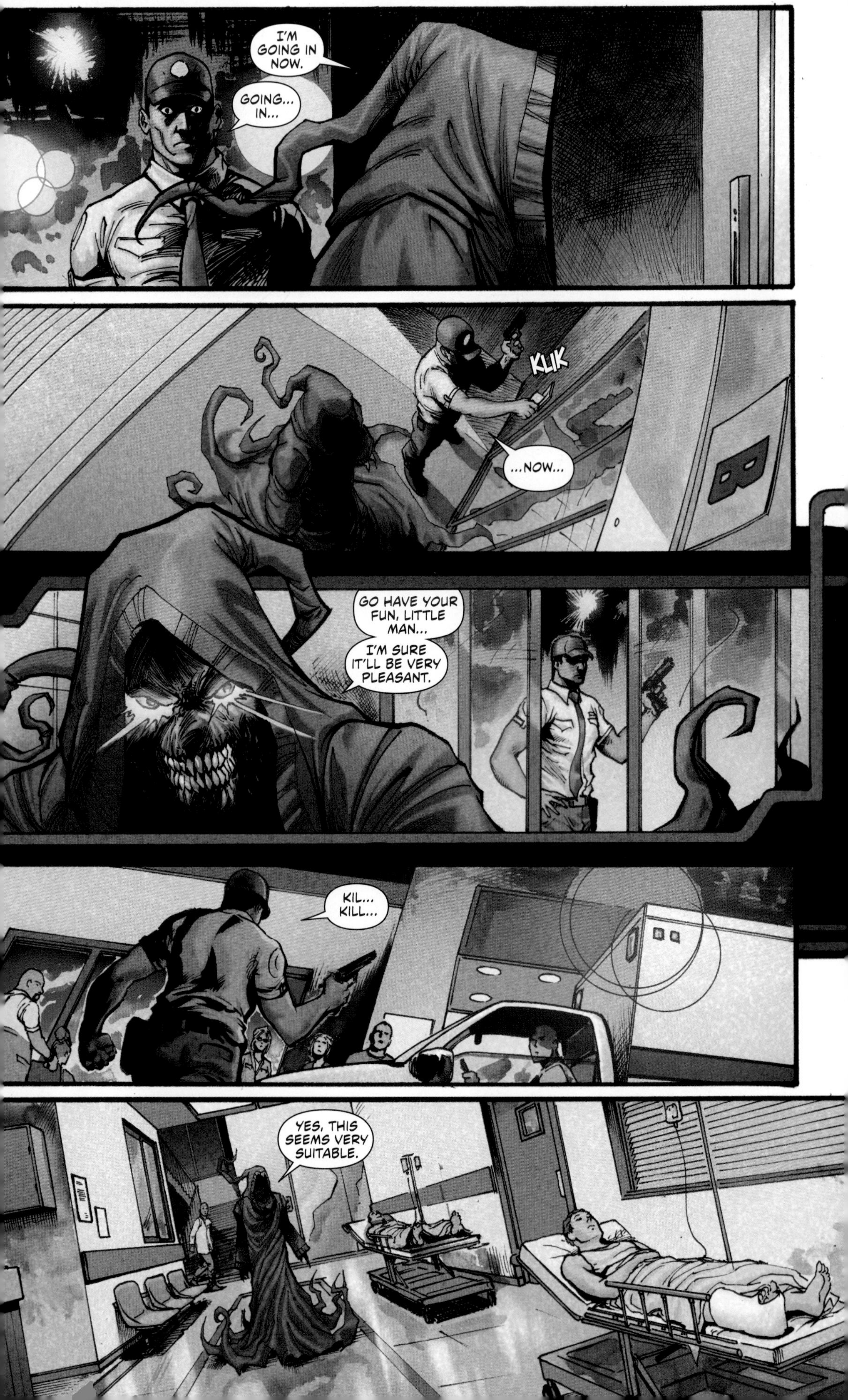

I'M GOING IN NOW.
GOING... IN...
KLIK
...NOW...
GO HAVE YOUR FUN, LITTLE MAN...
I'M SURE IT'LL BE VERY PLEASANT.
KIL... KILL...
YES, THIS SEEMS VERY SUITABLE.

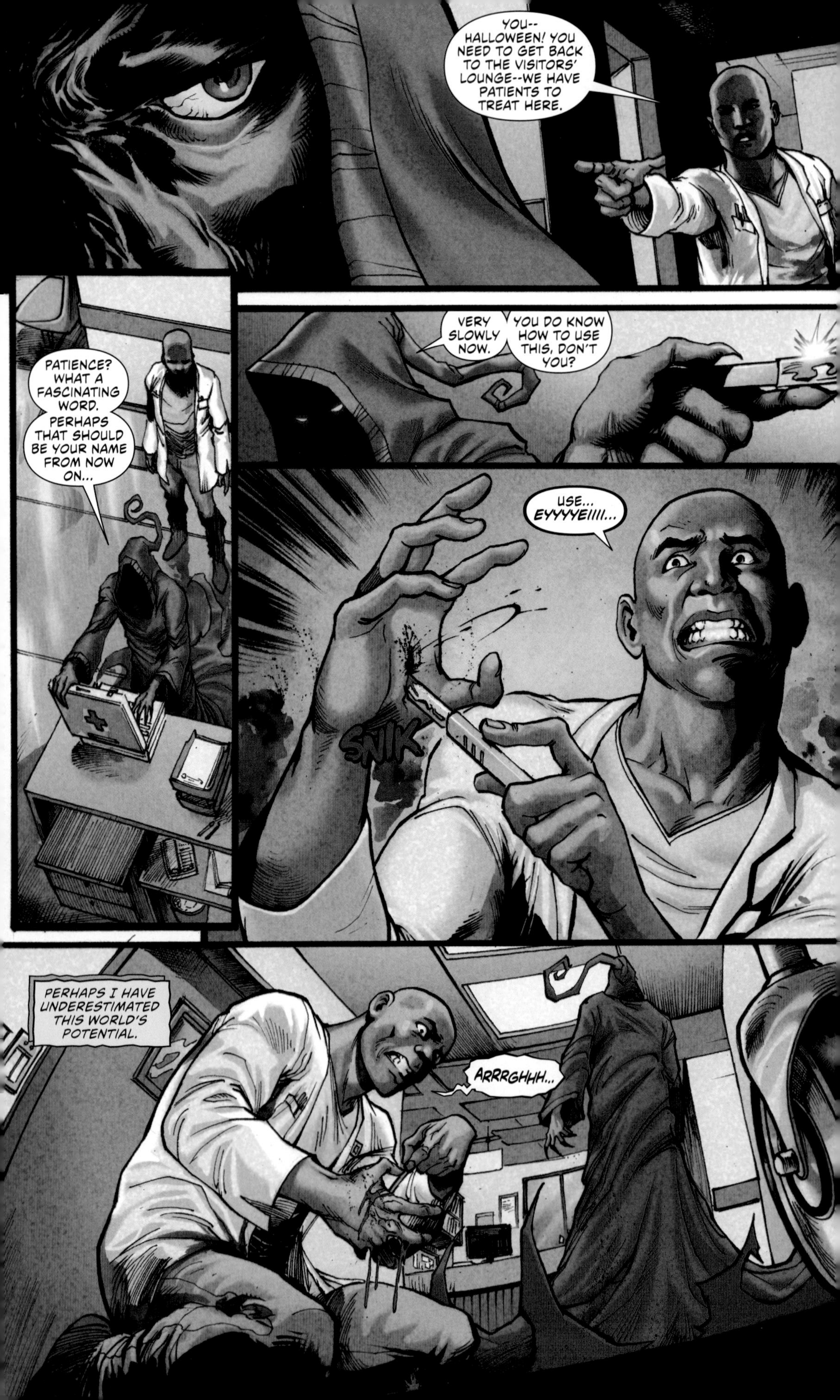

YOU-- HALLOWEEN! YOU NEED TO GET BACK TO THE VISITORS' LOUNGE--WE HAVE PATIENTS TO TREAT HERE.
PATIENCE? WHAT A FASCINATING WORD. PERHAPS THAT SHOULD BE YOUR NAME FROM NOW ON...
VERY SLOWLY NOW.
YOU DO KNOW HOW TO USE THIS, DON'T YOU?
USE... EYYYYEIIII...
SNIK
PERHAPS I HAVE UNDERESTIMATED THIS WORLD'S POTENTIAL.
ARRRGHHH...

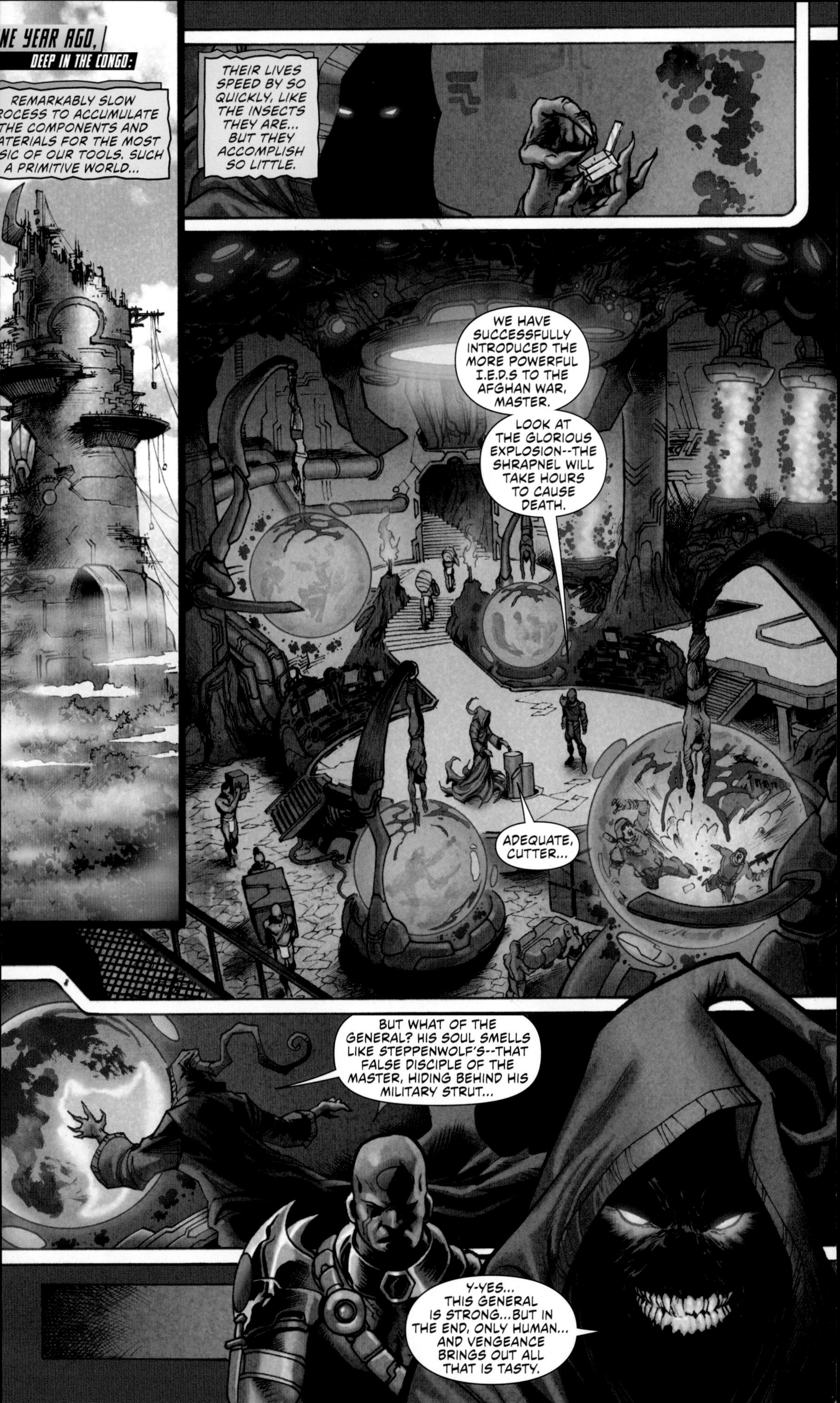
NE YEAR AGO,
DEEP IN THE CONGO:
REMARKABLY SLOW ROCESS TO ACCUMULATE THE COMPONENTS AND ATERIALS FOR THE MOST SIC OF OUR TOOLS. SUCH A PRIMITIVE WORLD...
THEIR LIVES SPEED BY SO QUICKLY, LIKE THE INSECTS THEY ARE... BUT THEY ACCOMPLISH SO LITTLE.
WE HAVE SUCCESSFULLY INTRODUCED THE MORE POWERFUL I.E.D.S TO THE AFGHAN WAR, MASTER.
LOOK AT THE GLORIOUS EXPLOSION--THE SHRAPNEL WILL TAKE HOURS TO CAUSE DEATH.
ADEQUATE, CUTTER...
BUT WHAT OF THE GENERAL? HIS SOUL SMELLS LIKE STEPPENWOLF'S--THAT FALSE DISCIPLE OF THE MASTER, HIDING BEHIND HIS MILITARY STRUT...
Y-YES... THIS GENERAL IS STRONG...BUT IN THE END, ONLY HUMAN... AND VENGEANCE BRINGS OUT ALL THAT IS TASTY.

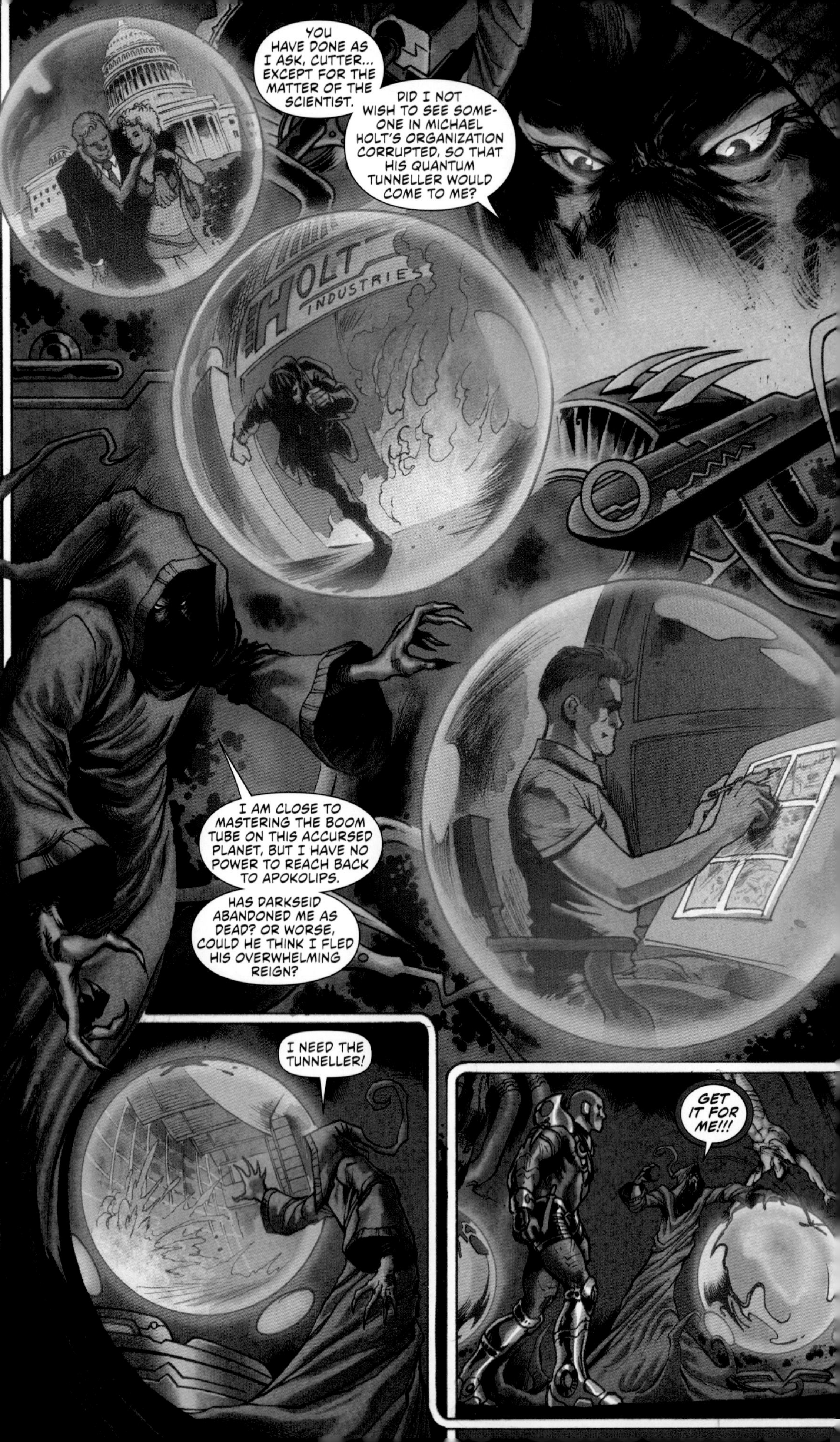
YOU HAVE DONE AS I ASK, CUTTER... EXCEPT FOR THE MATTER OF THE SCIENTIST.
DID I NOT WISH TO SEE SOME-ONE IN MICHAEL HOLT'S ORGANIZATION CORRUPTED, SO THAT HIS QUANTUM TUNNELLER WOULD COME TO ME?
HOLT INDUSTRIES
I AM CLOSE TO MASTERING THE BOOM TUBE ON THIS ACCURSED PLANET, BUT I HAVE NO POWER TO REACH BACK TO APOKOLIPS.
HAS DARKSEID ABANDONED ME AS DEAD? OR WORSE, COULD HE THINK I FLED HIS OVERWHELMING REIGN?
I NEED THE TUNNELLER!
GET IT FOR ME!!!

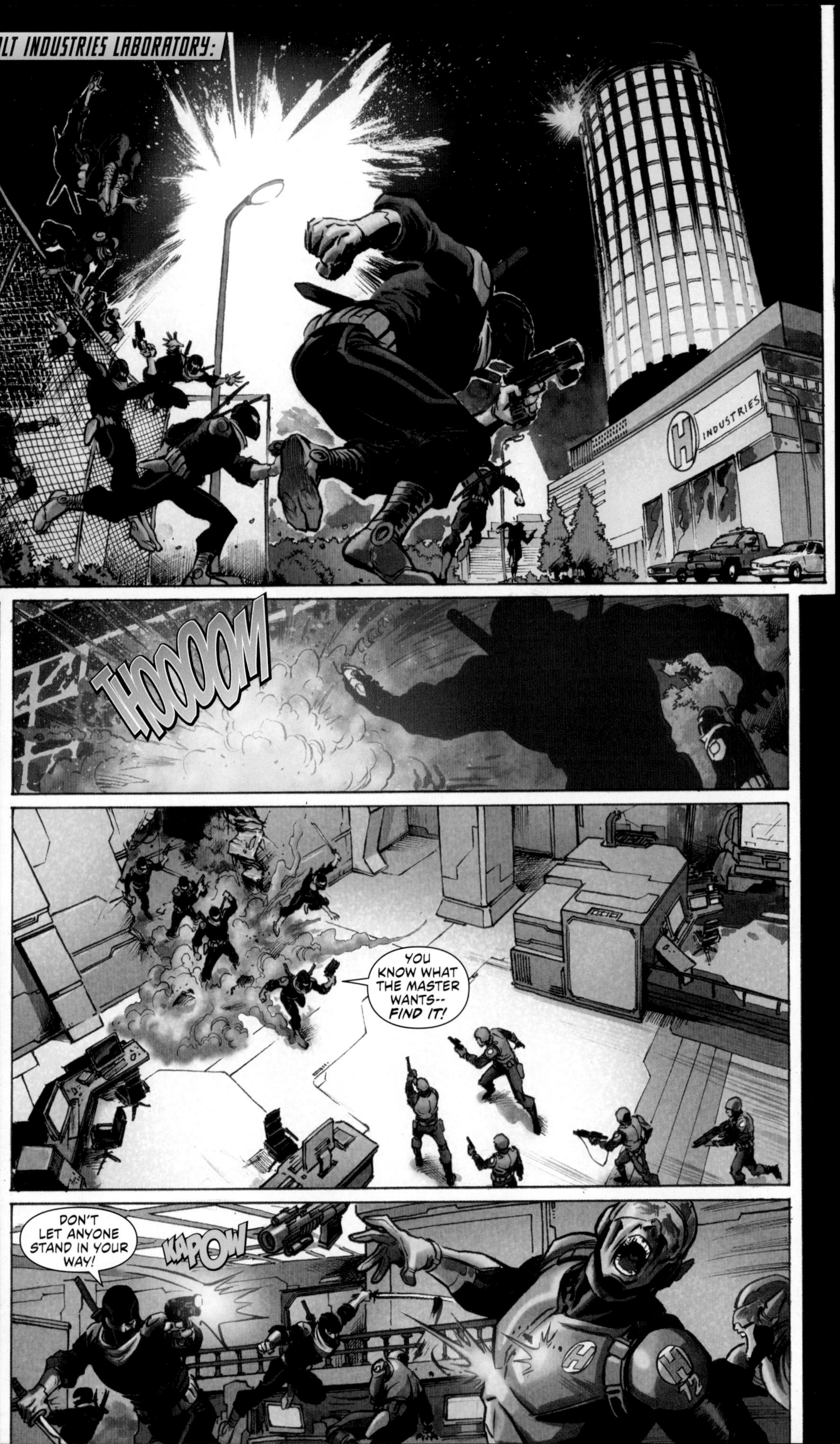
LT INDUSTRIES LABORATORY:
INDUSTRIES
THOOOOM
YOU KNOW WHAT THE MASTER WANTS-- FIND IT!
DON'T LET ANYONE STAND IN YOUR WAY!
KAPOW

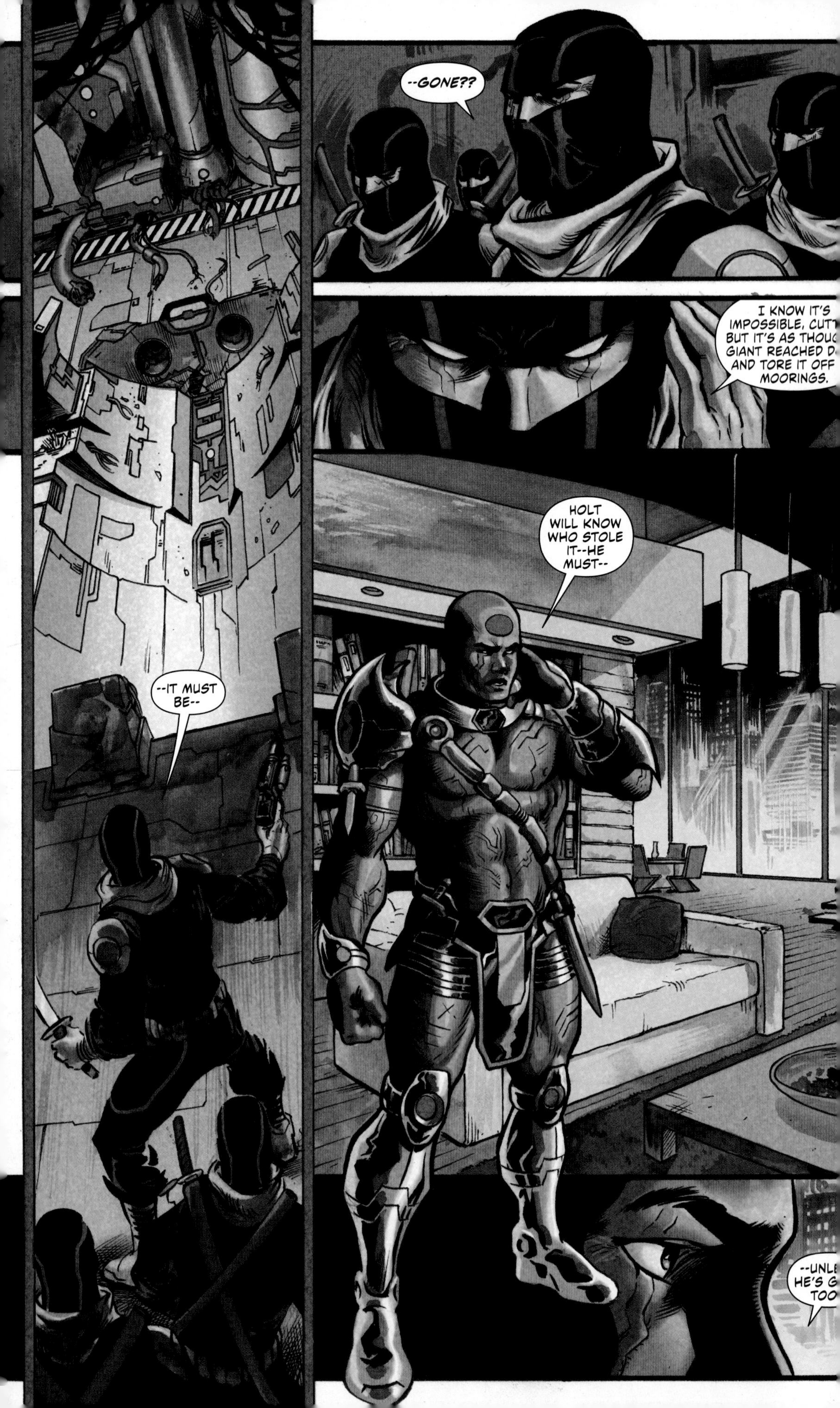
--GONE??
I KNOW IT'S IMPOSSIBLE, CUTT BUT IT'S AS THOUG GIANT REACHED D AND TORE IT OFF MOORINGS.
--IT MUST BE--
HOLT WILL KNOW WHO STOLE IT--HE MUST--
--UNLE HE'S G TOO

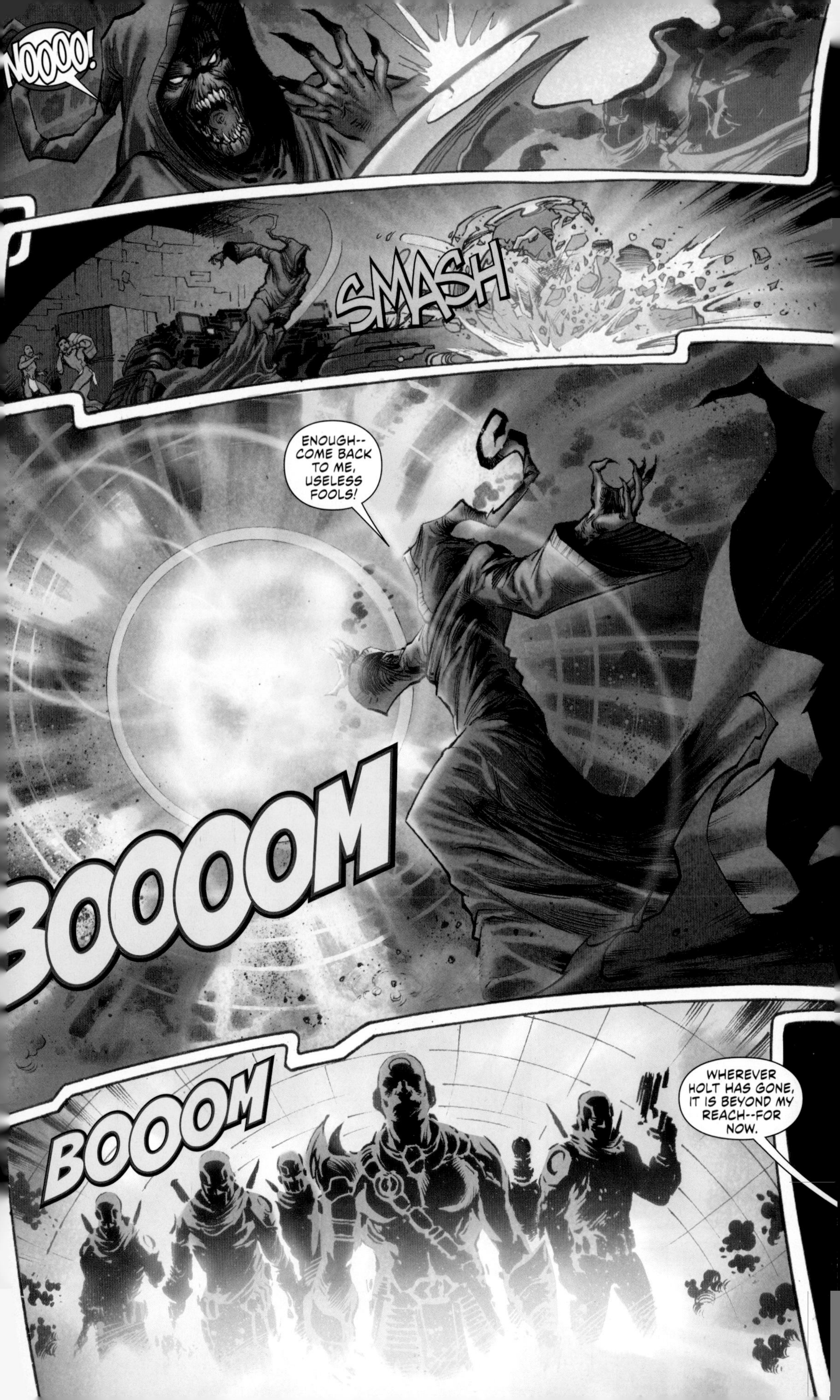
NOOOO!
SMASH
ENOUGH--COME BACK TO ME, USELESS FOOLS!
BOOOOM
BOOOM
WHEREVER HOLT HAS GONE, IT IS BEYOND MY REACH--FOR NOW.

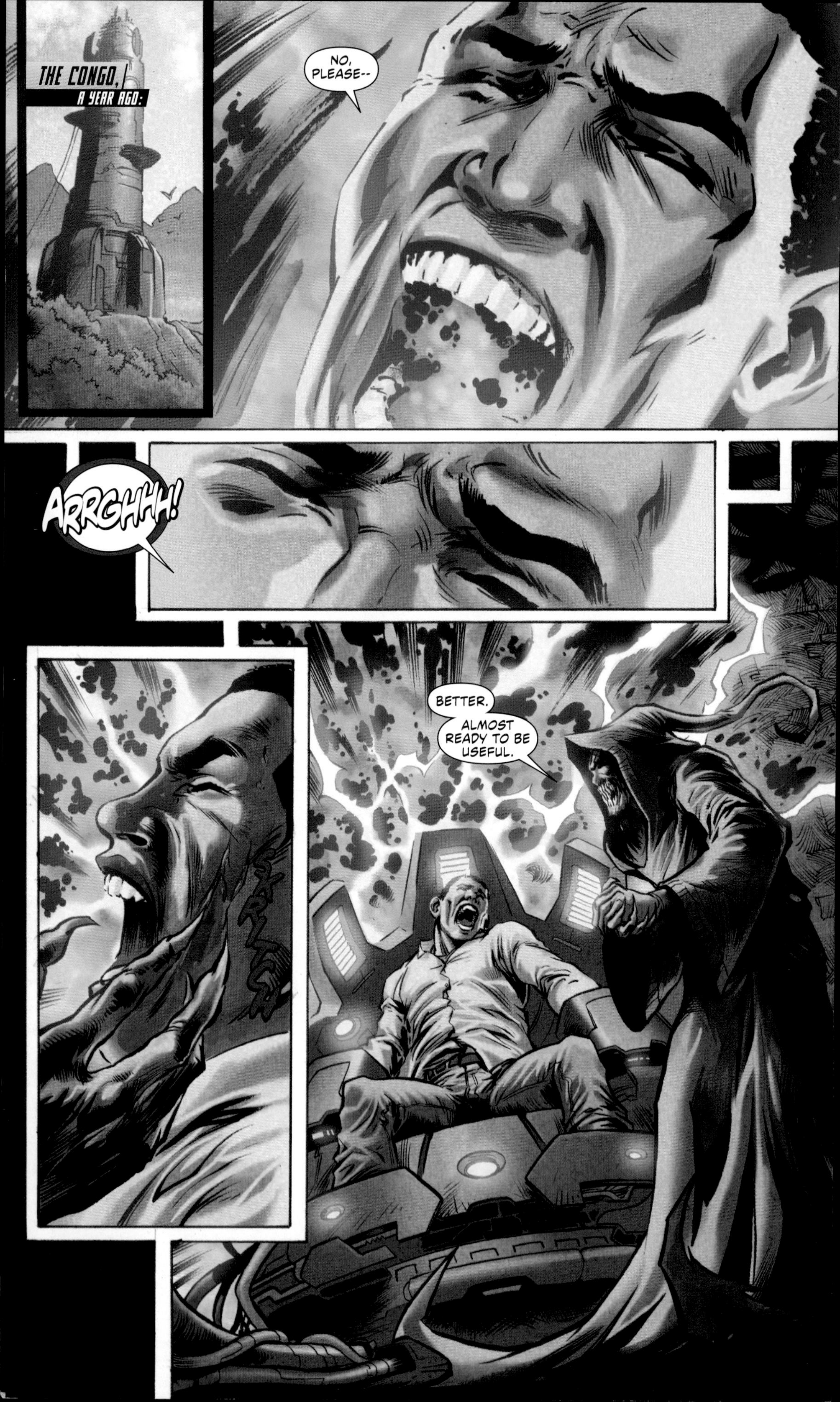

THE CONGO, A YEAR AGO:
NO, PLEASE--
ARRGHHH!
BETTER.
ALMOST READY TO BE USEFUL.

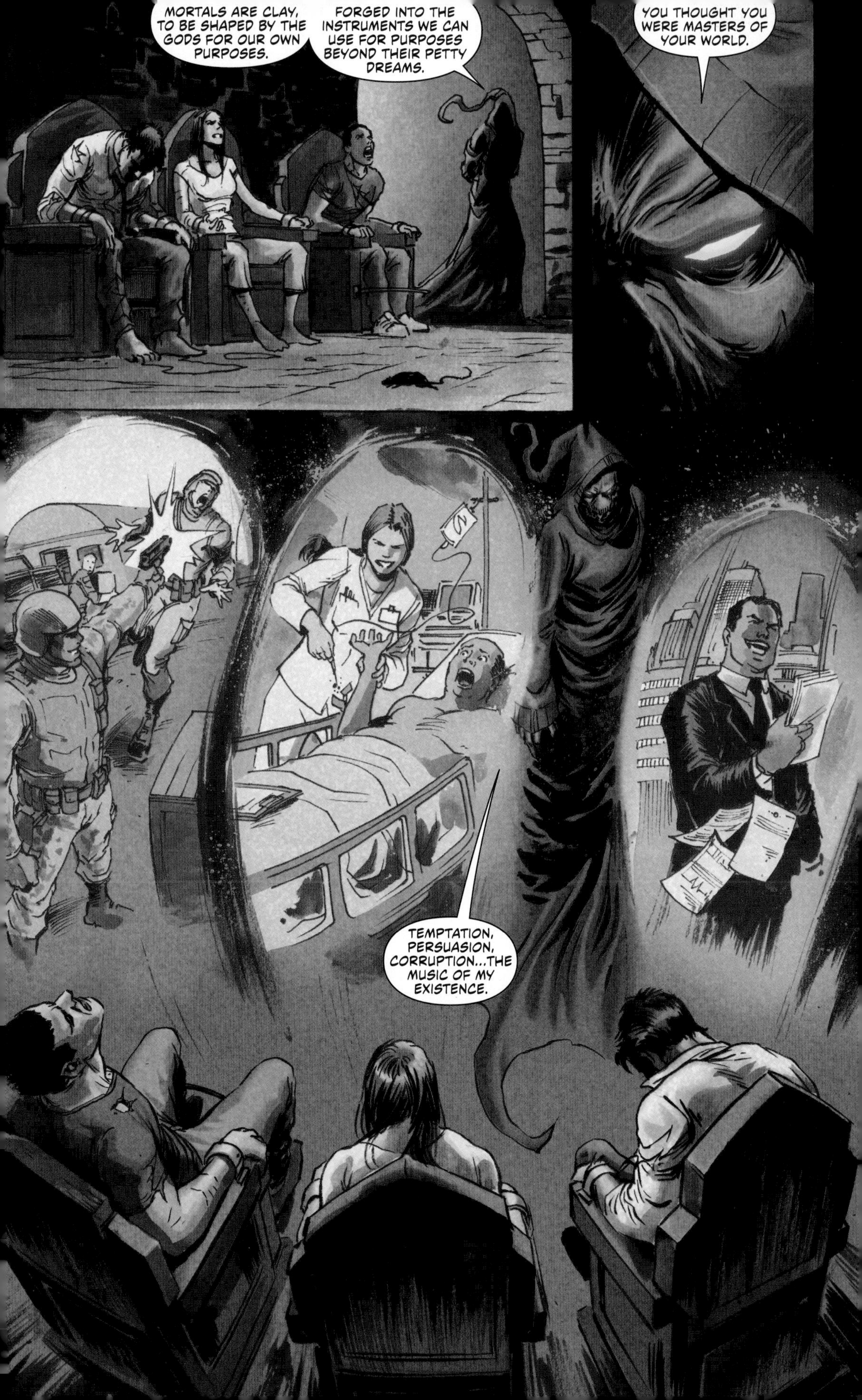
MORTALS ARE CLAY, TO BE SHAPED BY THE GODS FOR OUR OWN PURPOSES.
FORGED INTO THE INSTRUMENTS WE CAN USE FOR PURPOSES BEYOND THEIR PETTY DREAMS.
YOU THOUGHT YOU WERE MASTERS OF YOUR WORLD.
TEMPTATION, PERSUASION, CORRUPTION...THE MUSIC OF MY EXISTENCE.

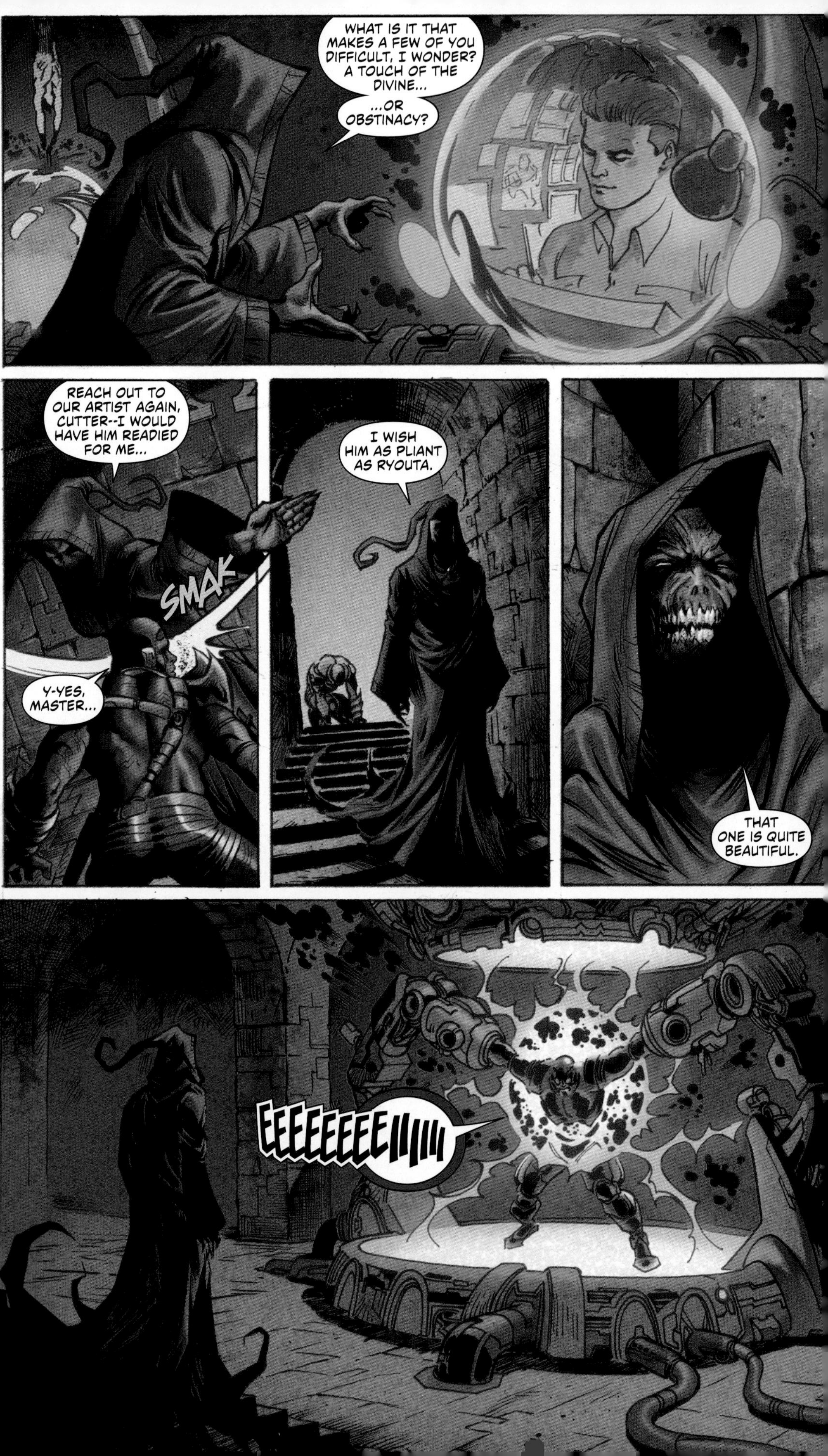
WHAT IS IT THAT MAKES A FEW OF YOU DIFFICULT, I WONDER? A TOUCH OF THE DIVINE...
...OR OBSTINACY?
REACH OUT TO OUR ARTIST AGAIN, CUTTER--I WOULD HAVE HIM READIED FOR ME...
SMAK
Y-YES, MASTER...
I WISH HIM AS PLIANT AS RYOUTA.
THAT ONE IS QUITE BEAUTIFUL.
EEEEEEEEIIIIII

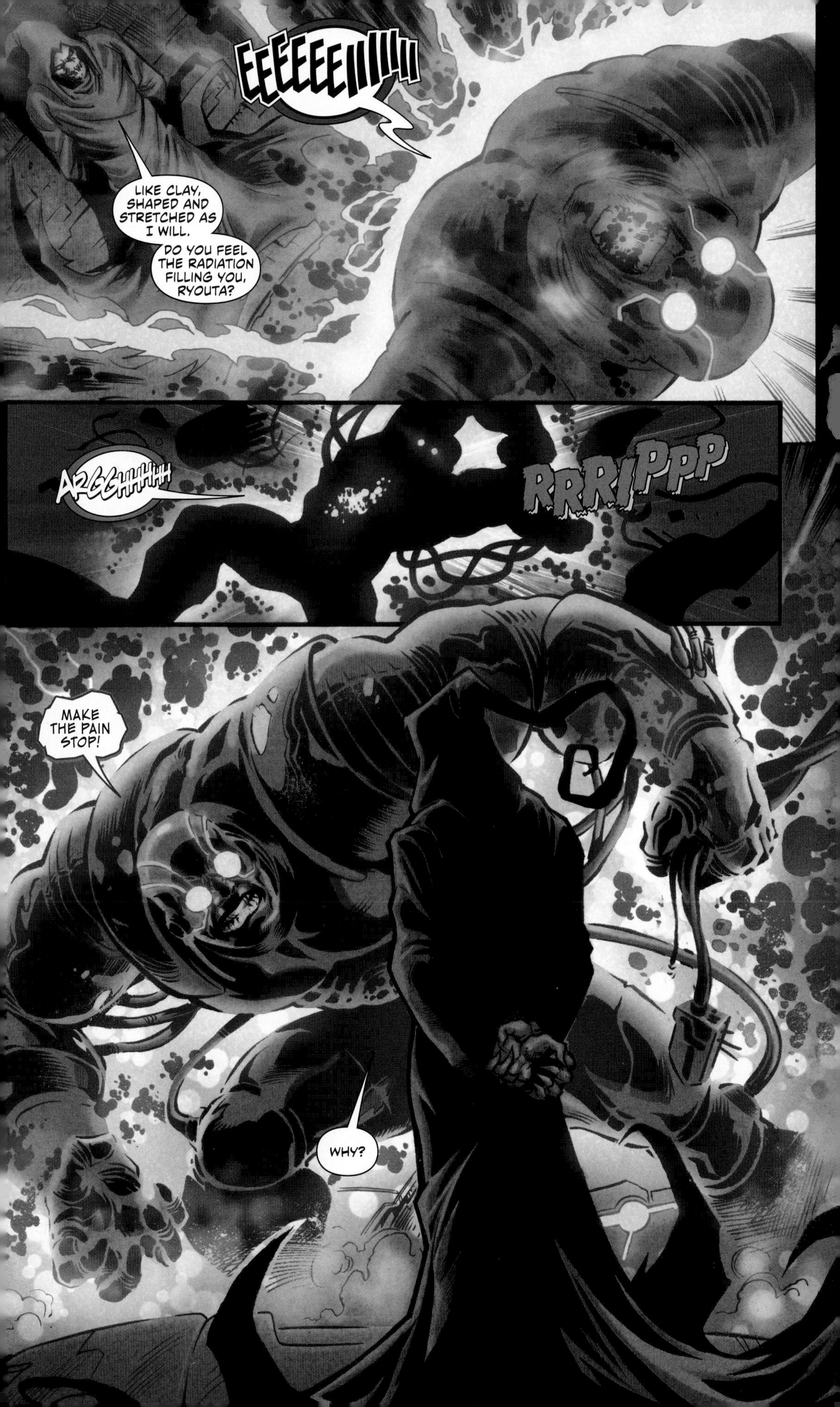
EEEEEEIIIIIII
LIKE CLAY, SHAPED AND STRETCHED AS I WILL.
DO YOU FEEL THE RADIATION FILLING YOU, RYOUTA?
ARGGHHHHH
RRRIPPP
MAKE THE PAIN STOP!
WHY?

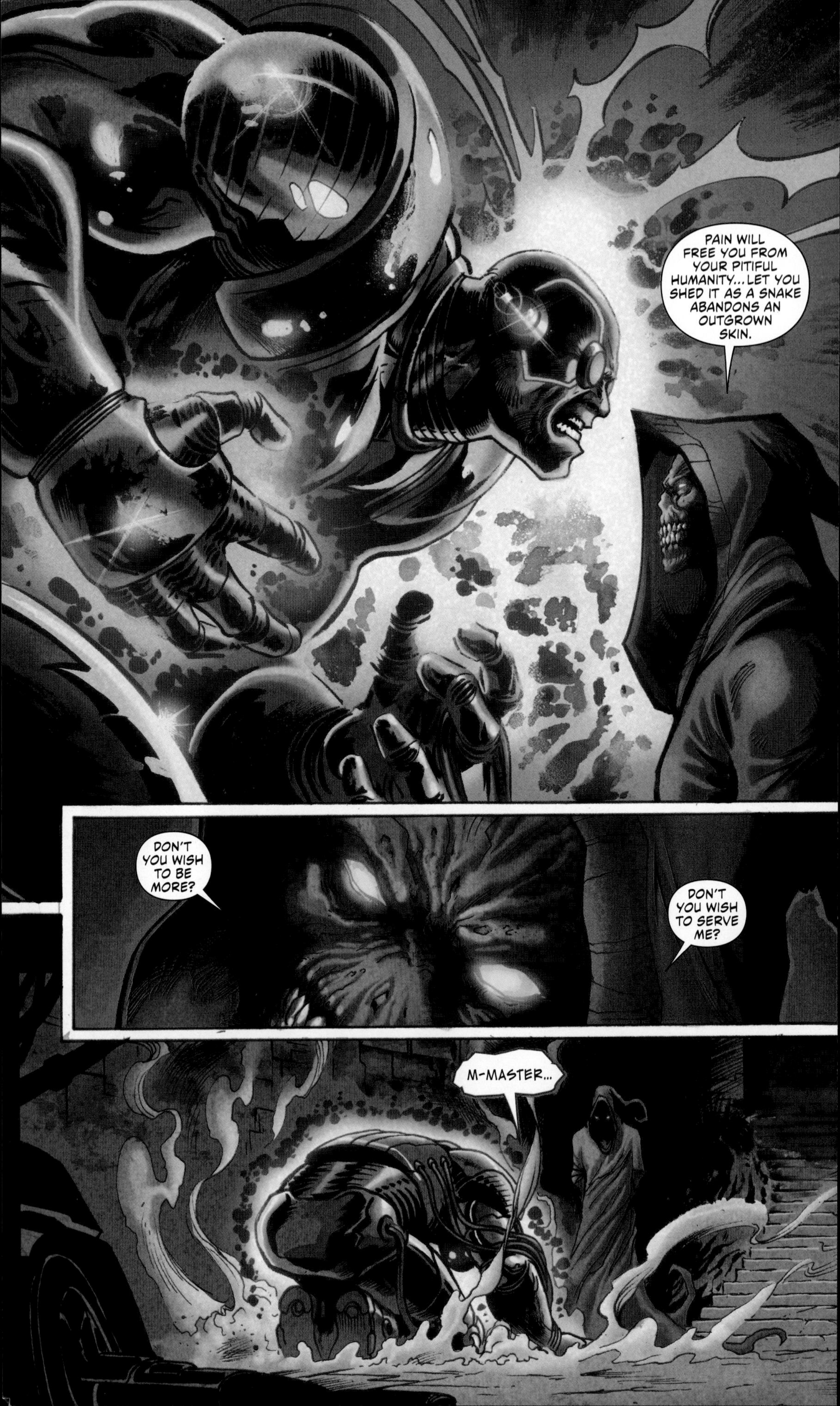
PAIN WILL FREE YOU FROM YOUR PITIFUL HUMANITY...LET YOU SHED IT AS A SNAKE ABANDONS AN OUTGROWN SKIN.
DON'T YOU WISH TO BE MORE?
DON'T YOU WISH TO SERVE ME?
M-MASTER...

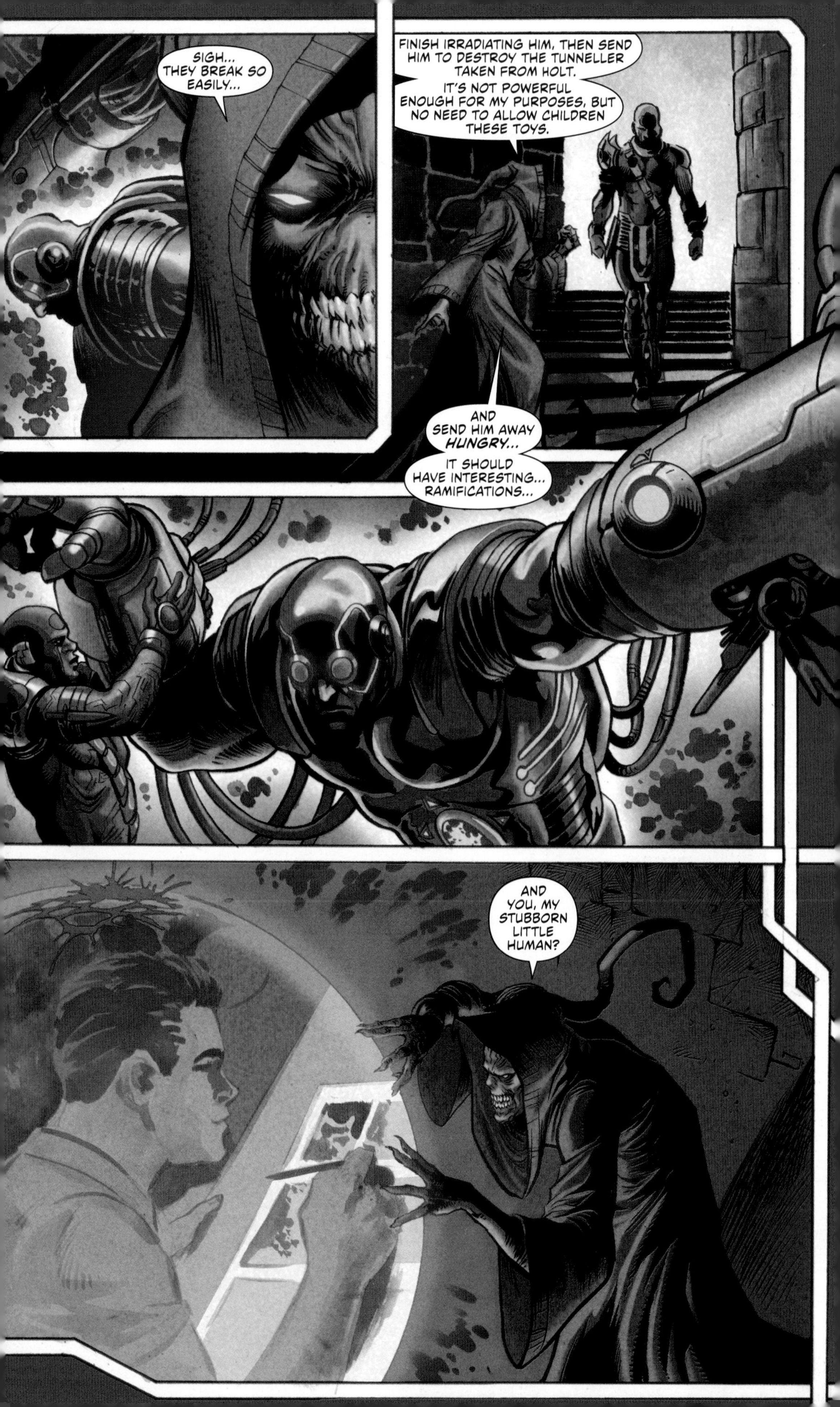
SIGH... THEY BREAK SO EASILY...
FINISH IRRADIATING HIM, THEN SEND HIM TO DESTROY THE TUNNELLER TAKEN FROM HOLT.
IT'S NOT POWERFUL ENOUGH FOR MY PURPOSES, BUT NO NEED TO ALLOW CHILDREN THESE TOYS.
AND SEND HIM AWAY *HUNGRY*...
IT SHOULD HAVE INTERESTING... RAMIFICATIONS...
AND YOU, MY STUBBORN LITTLE HUMAN?

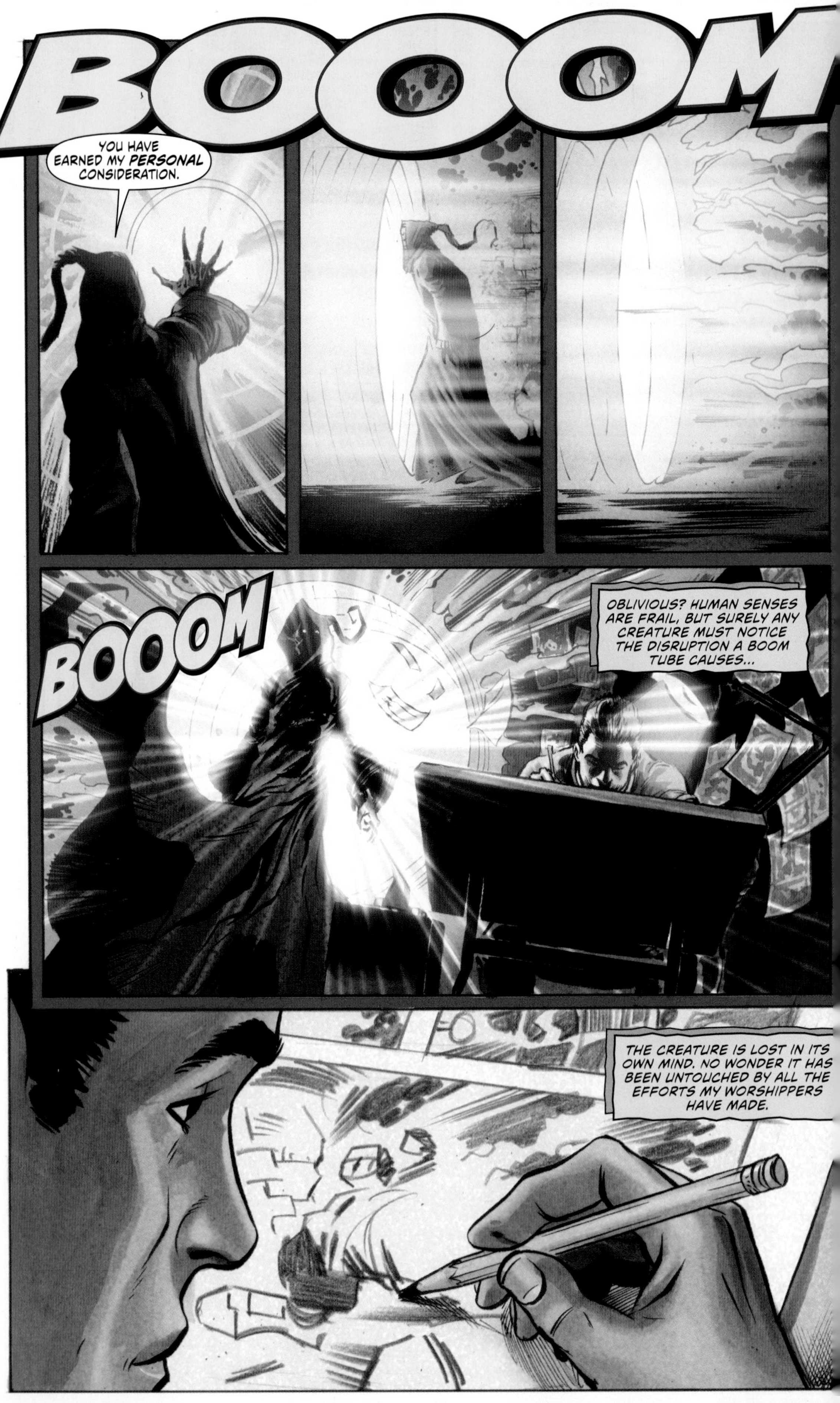
BOOOM
YOU HAVE EARNED MY PERSONAL CONSIDERATION.
BOOOM
OBLIVIOUS? HUMAN SENSES ARE FRAIL, BUT SURELY ANY CREATURE MUST NOTICE THE DISRUPTION A BOOM TUBE CAUSES...
THE CREATURE IS LOST IN ITS OWN MIND. NO WONDER IT HAS BEEN UNTOUCHED BY ALL THE EFFORTS MY WORSHIPPERS HAVE MADE.

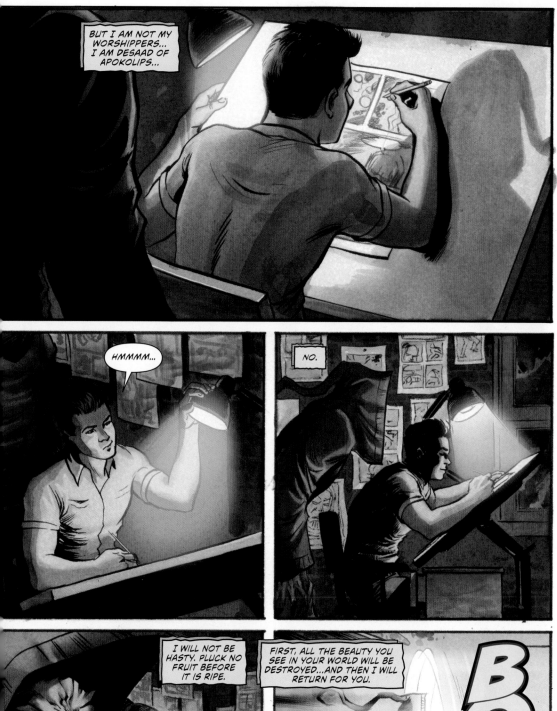

BUT I AM NOT MY WORSHIPPERS... I AM DESAAD OF APOKOLIPS...

HMMMM...

NO.

I WILL NOT BE HASTY. PLUCK NO FRUIT BEFORE IT IS RIPE.

FIRST, ALL THE BEAUTY YOU SEE IN YOUR WORLD WILL BE DESTROYED...AND THEN I WILL RETURN FOR YOU.

BOOOM

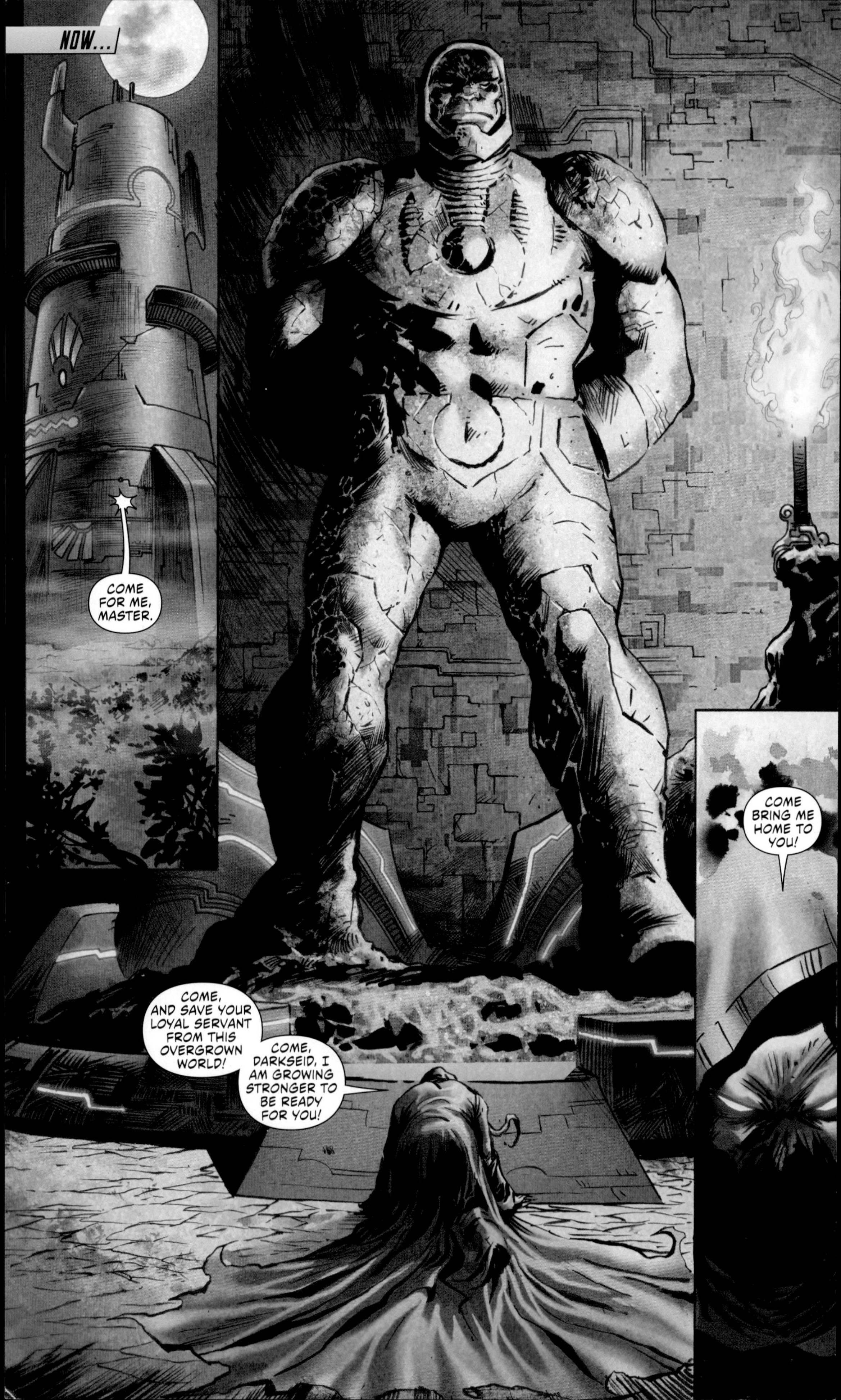
NOW...
COME FOR ME, MASTER.
COME BRING ME HOME TO YOU!
COME, AND SAVE YOUR LOYAL SERVANT FROM THIS OVERGROWN WORLD!
COME, DARKSEID, I AM GROWING STRONGER TO BE READY FOR YOU!

DC COMICS™

"Welcoming to new fans looking to get into superhero comics for the first time and old fans who gave up on the funny-books long ago."
—SCRIPPS HOWARD NEWS SERVICE

START AT THE BEGINNING!

JUSTICE LEAGUE VOLUME 1: ORIGIN

AQUAMAN VOLUME 1: THE TRENCH

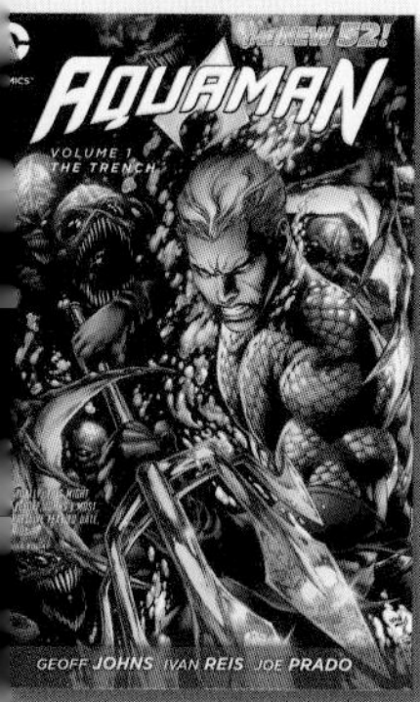
AQUAMAN
VOLUME 1
THE TRENCH
GEOFF JOHNS IVAN REIS JOE PRADO

THE SAVAGE HAWKMAN VOLUME 1: DARKNESS RISING

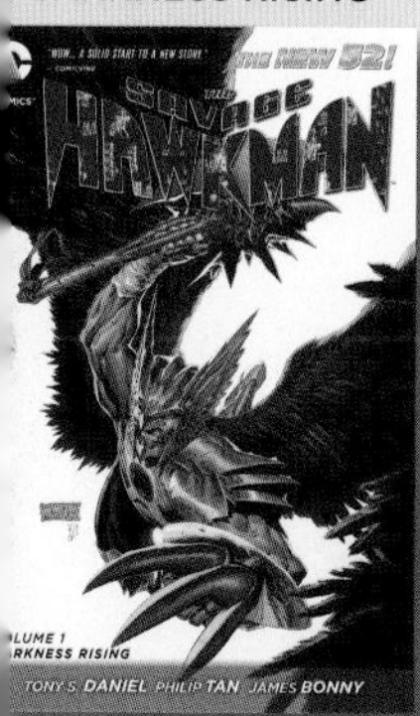
THE NEW 52!
SAVAGE HAWKMAN
TONY S. DANIEL PHILIP TAN JAMES BONNY

GREEN ARROW VOLUME 1: THE MIDAS TOUCH

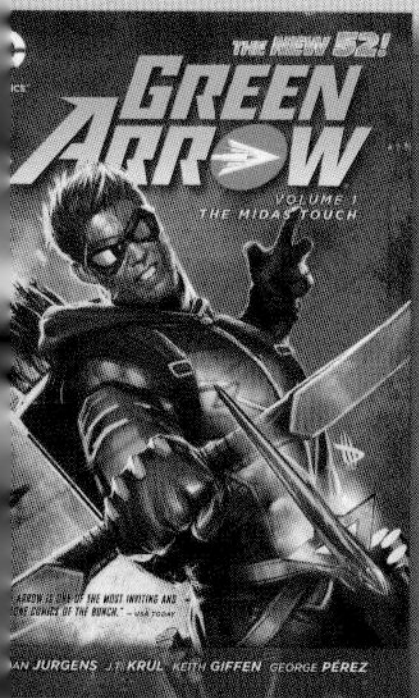
THE NEW 52!
GREEN ARROW
VOLUME 1
THE MIDAS TOUCH

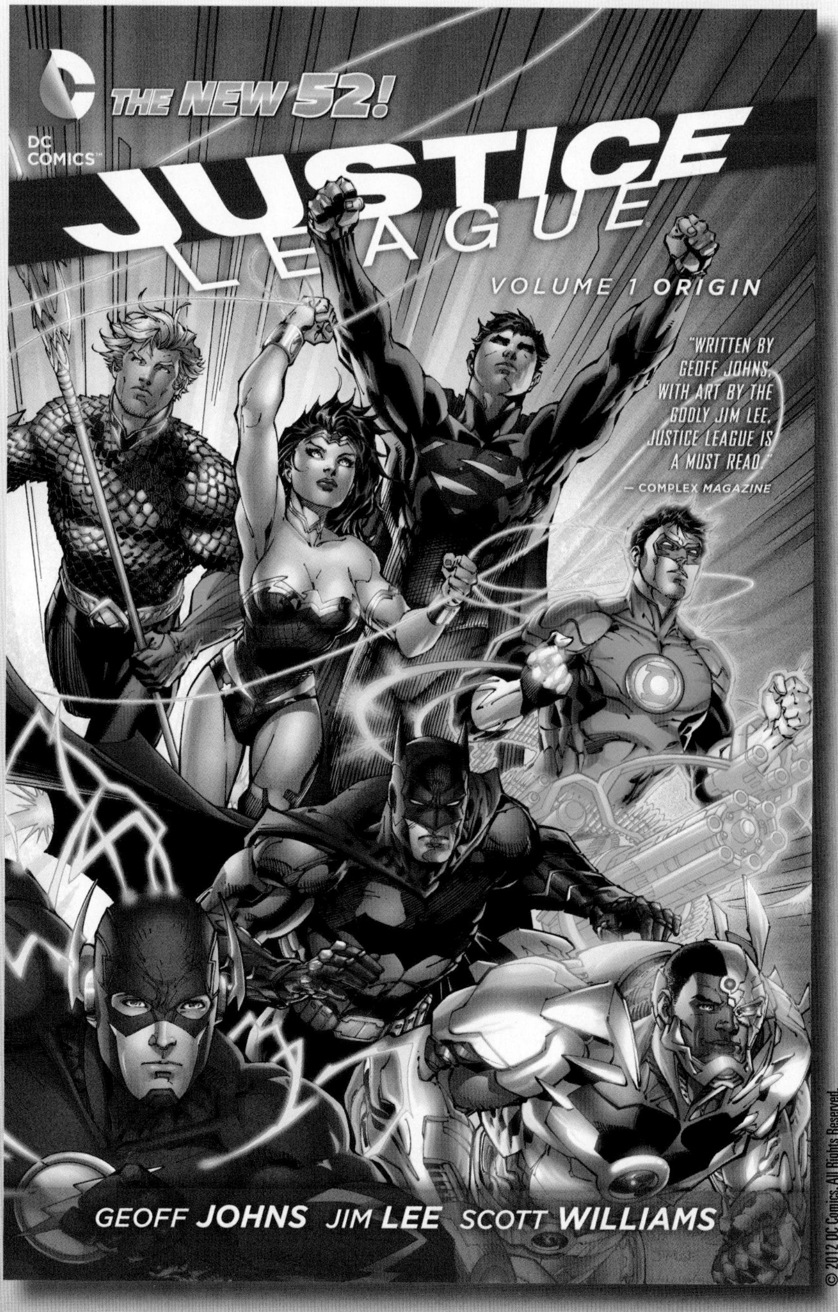
THE NEW 52!
DC COMICS™
JUSTICE LEAGUE
VOLUME 1 ORIGIN
"WRITTEN BY GEOFF JOHNS, WITH ART BY THE GODLY JIM LEE, JUSTICE LEAGUE IS A MUST READ."
— COMPLEX MAGAZINE
GEOFF JOHNS JIM LEE SCOTT WILLIAMS

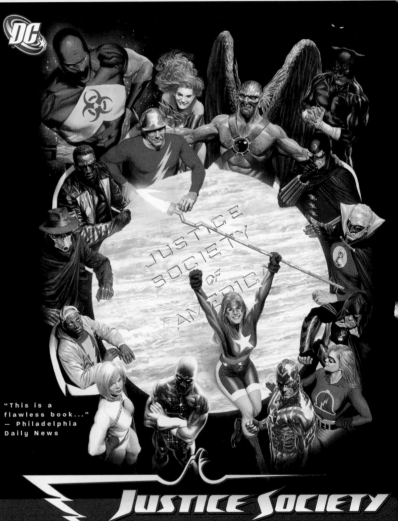